TRAILS 1860

N
W — E
S

NION

UNORGANIZED

MISSOURI RIVER

MINNESOTA
1858

T. PIERRE

KA

NEBRASKA CITY

ORY

1854

RT LARAMIE

PLATTE R. PLATTE R.

ATTE R.

TRAIL

OMAHA ∙ ∙ COUNCIL BLUFFS

IOWA
1846

MISSISSIPPI RIVER

∙ ST. JOSEPH

FORT LEAVENWORTH

KANSAS
TERRITORY 1854

∙ INDEPENDENCE

∙ ST. LOUIS

KANSAS CITY

KANSAS R.

BRANCH

RRON

TOFF

COUNCIL GROVE

MISSOURI
1821

TA FE TRAIL

UNORGANIZED

ARKANSAS

CANADIAN RIVER

ARKANSAS R.

1836

RED RIVER

LOUISIANA

TEXAS
1845

1812

GRANDE

0   100   200   300   400
MILES

BOOKS BY DAVID DARY

The Buffalo Book

True Tales of the Old-Time Plains

Cowboy Culture

True Tales of Old-Time Kansas

Entrepreneurs of the Old West

Entrepreneurs
of the Old West

ENTREPRENEURS
OF THE OLD WEST

DAVID DARY

Pen-and-ink drawings by Al M. Napoletano

ALFRED A. KNOPF · NEW YORK · 1986

THIS IS A BORZOI BOOK
PUBLISHED BY ALFRED A. KNOPF, INC.

Library of Congress Cataloging-in-Publication Data

Dary, David.   Entrepreneurs of the old West.

Bibliography: p.
Includes index.
1. Businessmen—West (U.S.)—History.   2. Entrepreneur—History.
I. Title.
HC102.5.A2D37   1986   338'.04'0978   85-45590
ISBN 0-394-52405-5

Manufactured in the United States of America

FIRST AMERICAN EDITION

To

Mary Blackman Parsons

who shares the Kansas roots

Eastward I go only by force;
but westward I go free.

—Henry David Thoreau,
"Walking" (1862)

CONTENTS

FOREWORD

UNTOLD numbers of books have been written about the settlement of the American West, but few of them deal extensively with the entrepreneurial aspect of pioneer life. The handful of works that do are generally limited in scope either geographically or in the period of time covered. This book pieces together a larger story, one that spans the length and breadth of the nineteenth-century American West. It is the story of what I have come to call the *silent army*.

It was not a disciplined army in the military sense, with all marching to a single beat and subordinating their personal interests and concerns to an overriding collective purpose. Rather, this was an army composed of highly mobile individuals, each seeking opportunity and profit in the American West. It comprised people with such qualities as imagination, optimism, self-reliance, initiative, ingenuity, individualism, and resourcefulness, qualities we still prize. On the other hand, because there were few societal restraints and because profit was involved, many of these early entrepreneurs were also greedy, unscrupulous, ruthless, devious, and even downright dishonest.

Their story began when Americans first moved west across the Appalachians. Some members of the silent army established trade between the Spanish Southwest and Missouri early in the nineteenth century. Others made their way up the Missouri River and into the Rockies and the country beyond—in many instances, ahead of the official explorers. Steamers took still others around Cape Horn to find their opportunities in Nevada or California or elsewhere along the Pacific Coast. Later, still more moved onto the Great Plains to till the virgin soil, build towns, and change the Great American Desert into what some people called the "Garden of America." Trade developed as these pioneers continued westward, and in time trade became the civilizer of the West.

Members of the silent army included traders and mountain men, and following in their footsteps came wagon freighters, ranchers, homesteaders, merchants, town builders, railroad men, and other entrepreneurs. Their activities in the West often went unreported in the emerging public press in the East. Communications with the East, and even between many areas in the West, were slow and often unreliable. Isolation was commonplace, and news was often weeks or months in arriving from the East until the advent of mail service and the telegraph in the middle of the nineteenth century.

By then the experiences of the silent army had generally become commonplace and seemingly insignificant, and in consequence still went unreported. But some sensed the historic significance of what they were doing and kept diaries, wrote letters, or otherwise recorded their recollections. For those who left no personal records, their stories must be pieced together from scattered reminiscences of others, official documents, and contemporary newspaper accounts.

Most members of the silent army chose to conduct their business in private. They learned early that minding one's business was usually the best insurance for success as they moved about the West with little or no fanfare. Some sought to maintain the status quo in the areas where they settled because nature enabled them to make a profit there, but others sought to control their environment and change the shape of the land for their benefit.

The bigness of the West—the vast distances that had to be overcome— was a major obstacle for the silent army. Hurdling that obstacle required greater eastern influence, especially of capitalism with its developing corporations. It was capitalism that built the railroads, greatly reducing the West's transportation problem. At the same time the bigness of the West fostered the expansion of eastern businesses as new markets developed. Easterners put cash and credit on wheels and rolled onto Western prairies and plains and across the mountains. Soon the West began to change, to pattern itself after the East.

This, then, is the story of men and women who sought to take advantage of opportunities in the American West that would enable them to better themselves and their condition, economic and otherwise. It is the story of their struggles, hardships, and final prevailing—the workaday human experience of the nineteenth-century American West as the far side of the Mississippi River was being explored and settled. Members of the silent army represent vanished days, but their legacy is today part of the national character. They laid the foundation for the American dream, the belief that anyone could find success, happiness, and wealth in America. But in so doing they impregnated the nation's outlook with the notion that wealth and material possessions are essential for happiness.

I AM INDEBTED to many people for helping to provide material for this work. But I owe a special debt of gratitude to Joseph Snell, Portia Allbert, and Nancy Sherbert, Kansas State Historical Society, Topeka; Mr. and Mrs. James Nottage, Los Angeles, California; Tim Cochrane, James Laird, and Bill Barton, Wyoming Historical Department, Cheyenne; Emmett D. Chisum, Western Heritage Historical Center, University of Wyoming, Laramie; Catherine T. Engel, Colorado Historical Society, Denver; Kathryn D. Otto, South Dakota Historical Resource Center, Pierre; the late Lee G. DeLay, Anne P. Diffendal, and Andrea I. Paul, Nebraska State Historical Society, Lincoln; Steven Hallberg, Oregon Historical Society, Portland; Lenore M. Kosso, Special Collections, University of Nevada Library, Reno; James A. Hamilton, Museum of New Mexico, Santa Fe; Beverly D. Bishop, Missouri Historical Society, St. Louis; Guy Louis Rocha, Nevada Historical Society, Reno; Don Dedera, *Arizona Highways*, Phoenix; Don Kelly, U.S. Geological Survey, Reston, Virginia; Tom DuRant, National Park Service, Springfield, Virginia; Alford J. Banta and Audrey Barnhardt, Scottsbluff National Monument, Nebraska; Ken Long, Union Pacific Railroad Museum, Omaha; Lawrence Dinnean, Bancroft Library, University of California, Berkeley; William Wurtz, California Historical Society, Los Angeles; Cynthia Reed Miller, Henry Ford Museum, Dearborn, Michigan; Roger White, Smithsonian Institution, Washington, D.C., Joan M. Metzger, Arizona Historical Society, Tucson; Gary Mason, Lawrence, Kansas; David Allred, Austin, Texas; and Jeff Dykes, College Park, Maryland.

And I especially want to thank Ann Close for her helpful advice, suggestions, and guidance.

DAVID DARY

Along the Kaw
Lawrence, Kansas

Entrepreneurs
of the Old West

I

TO WHERE THERE WAS
LITTLE WATER

*The philosopher and lover of man have much harm to say of trade; but
the historian will see that trade was the principle of liberty; that trade
planted America and destroyed Feudalism; that it makes peace and
keeps peace . . .*

—RALPH WALDO EMERSON[1]

SINCE the dawn of civilization rivers have held a special fascination for
man. Early man found he could quench his thirst with what rivers carried
and catch food from beneath the surface. As civilization progressed, man
began to understand that water is essential for most plant and animal life.
Even today, although civilized man usually gets his drinking water from a
tap, people are still attracted to rivers almost instinctively, as if their bodies
acknowledge the importance of the fluid. A wide and flowing stream conveys
the assurance of continued life. Certainly it is relaxing on a hot summer's
day to sit under a large shade tree on a river's bank, catch a cool breeze,
and watch the stream meander by. A lazily moving river can be almost
hypnotic and cause the worries and cares of civilized life to vanish, at least
for a while. Rivers also may inspire travel and adventure. A wide flowing
stream often seems to say: Come join me on my journey to a larger stream
or even an ocean. One may react to such a river much the way Mark Twain's
Huckleberry Finn reacted to the Mississippi. For centuries rivers also have
been viewed in a more practical sense. If one is wide and deep, it can
provide an easy means of transportation, especially if you float with the
current.

About two centuries ago, when the American frontier began at the crest
of the Appalachian Mountains, westward-bound pioneers found the Ohio
River to be the easiest and fastest route west through the wilderness. The

3

river flows nearly a thousand miles from its origin in Pennsylvania through the rolling country of Ohio, across Indiana, and along the southern edge of Illinois to where it runs into the Mississippi at Cairo. From east to west along its route, pioneers gradually stopped and built their cabins and settlements. By 1784 nearly fifty thousand Americans were living along the Ohio River and its tributaries. The land was productive. People consumed their own products, swapped with their neighbors, and traded on a limited basis with itinerant peddlers. Gold and silver money was scarce, and barter became the chief form of trade. Since the pioneers produced a surplus of wheat, corn, pelts, whiskey, and other goods, they sought distant markets. The best were along the Atlantic Coast, but transporting the goods was difficult and at times impossible because of poor roads and few bridges. It was much easier to build a barge or flatboat, load it with the goods, and float down the Ohio to the Mississippi and on south to New Orleans, where the cargo could be sold for gold coins, mostly Spanish dollars, or loaded aboard American sailing ships and carried to Atlantic ports.

FLATBOAT

Flatboats were cheap and easy to construct. Many were made of sawed lumber, which a settler could use to build his cabin home after he reached his destination along the Ohio River. Once established, and having produced a surplus of goods, the settler might build another flatboat or trade for one worth about thirty-five dollars at one of several boatyards on the upper Ohio. Most flatboats were thirty to forty feet in length and about twelve feet wide. A framework fastened together with wooden pins served as the bottom of the boat. To this was attached a flooring that was well caulked to prevent leaking. Thin planks, about breast high, were used for the sides, and many flatboats had some kind of covering to keep the rain out. Such a covering was commonplace on a Kentucky flat or "broadhorn," as such boats were called. The nickname developed because invariably someone on board carried a tin horn that would be blown to announce a flatboat's arrival or make known its whereabouts in a fog. Most flatboats had a long oar on either side that was used in steering the vessel to and from the bank or to direct it away from obstructions in the river channel.[2]

But flatboats were downstream vessels. There was no way for them to move upstream against the current. Therefore the owners sometimes burned their flatboats at their downstream destination if they could not be sold for the lumber they contained. During the early 1780s much commerce was carried by flatboats down the Ohio and Mississippi rivers to New Orleans without Spanish objection—the Spanish then owned New Orleans and the vast territory west of the Mississippi. In 1784, however, the Spanish revoked the right of free navigation on the Mississippi and imposed exorbitant tolls and duties on all boats descending the Mississippi from the United States. The Spanish did so apparently in hopes that western settlers would withdraw from the union of states and swear allegiance to the Spanish crown. But American frontiersmen along the Ohio objected to being deprived of what they believed to be their natural right to conduct trade at the most feasible outlet. Pelts, liquor, and ginseng were almost the only products of the frontier that would pay the cost of transportation over the rugged trails and roads to Philadelphia. The pelts the settlers hunted were rabbits, coyotes, muskrat, weasel, bear, and some deer skins, and they distilled their corn and rye and fruit into liquor and brandy. Ginseng, an herb with a long fleshy root, was used as a medicine. American ginseng, superior to the Chinese and Korean varieties, grew wild in many areas east of the Mississippi River until the great demand used up the supply. The profits derived from the sale of ginseng, liquor, and pelts were sufficient only to purchase necessities such as salt, gunpowder, and iron tools, using a variety of foreign coins received as payment. But at New Orleans the Americans could sell other goods for a profit, and the cost of getting there was much less. The Spanish dollar, adopted as the basic monetary unit in the United States under the Articles of Confederation, was plentiful in New Orleans.

The closing of the Mississippi by the Spanish became an explosive issue, and it did not cool until Spain signed a treaty with the United States in 1795 which allowed Americans free navigation of the Mississippi. The treaty gave Americans the privilege of unloading their boats at New Orleans and storing the cargo on shore free of duty until it was sold or picked up by American ships. Even though the United States had started minting its own gold and silver dollars less than three years earlier, the value of silver was beginning to decline by 1795. Gold U.S. dollars were being hoarded, but the gold Spanish dollar was still plentiful in New Orleans. Soon many flatboats and keelboats loaded with tobacco, pork, corn, wheat, whiskey, and brandy again moved down the Ohio and Mississippi to New Orleans.[3]

While the flatboat had existed on the Ohio from the earliest days of white settlement, the keelboat was something new. Tarascon, Berthoud and Company of Pittsburgh introduced the use of keelboats on the Ohio in 1792, three years before the Spanish signed the treaty to reopen the Mississippi to American navigation.[4] Unlike the flatboat, the keelboat could move upstream, but the travel was very slow. Varying from fifty to seventy-five feet in length and from twelve to twenty feet wide, the typical keelboat was pointed at both bow and stern. On either side were running boards extending from end to end. The space between them was enclosed and roofed over with shingles or boards. Each keelboat also had a mast and sail. Most of them could carry twenty to forty tons of freight. The crew usually consisted of six to ten men plus a captain who also served as steersman. Sweating men, lined up on the running boards, pushed the boat upstream by lifting

KEELBOAT

and setting their long poles to the cry of the steersman. Where currents were swift the boat was edged in next to the bank so that the men might pull on the branches of willows or other low-hanging trees to propel the boat. If the water was too deep for this "bushwhacking," as it was called, boatmen would swim ashore with a towline and pull the keelboat through the deep water. The towline or rope, often more than a thousand feet long, was fastened to the high end of the mast. Once the boat reached shallower water the men would swim or wade back to the keelboat and resume their toil with the poles.[5]

American flatboats and keelboats became a common sight on the Mississippi below the Ohio River. Most flatboat owners, after disposing of their goods and boats in New Orleans, would sail through the Gulf of Mexico and around Florida to Philadelphia or Baltimore, buy manufactured goods, and go west over the mountains by wagon or horseback to their homes. A round-trip journey took several months. Some boat owners chose to return home by going overland from New Orleans, especially if they had traded their goods for sugar and molasses. Most of these men followed a route across Lake Pontchartrain and northwest to Natchez on the Mississippi, where they turned northeast to Nashville over what became known as the Natchez Trace. Because bandits often robbed these boatmen in the low country north of New Orleans, it was not unusual for the boat owners to travel in large groups for protection.[6]

When Spain, under a secret treaty in 1800, gave back the Louisiana Territory to France, it stipulated that the transfer occur only after Napoleon fulfilled certain promises. In the meantime, the Spanish, still in control, permitted American commerce to continue. But in the fall of 1802 the Spanish intendant, or administrator, in New Orleans suddenly withdrew the duty-free rights of Americans once again. Frontiersmen along the Ohio River and its tributaries soon became enraged, and American troops were sent to Kentucky to prevent an armed expedition of Americans from leaving for New Orleans. The Spanish government quickly disavowed the action of its administrator, and in April 1803 the Mississippi was once again open for free American commerce. The likelihood of the problem ever reoccurring vanished in October 1803, when the United States purchased the Louisiana Territory, including the Mississippi River, from France.

With the swift movement of a quill, the size of the United States doubled. The new territory encompassed the present states of Arkansas, Oklahoma, Kansas, Missouri, Nebraska, South Dakota, Montana, and parts of Mississippi, Alabama, Louisiana, Texas, New Mexico, Colorado, Wyoming, and North Dakota. Only a small portion of this vast territory had been explored by the Spanish and French. Aside from New Orleans only a few white settlements had been established in the territory, and most were along the Mississippi River. One of these was located about a hundred and fifty miles above where the Ohio River flows into the Mississippi. Pierre Laclède Liguest, a French trader, had established in 1764 the settlement on the west bank of the Mississippi just south of where the Missouri River flows into the larger stream. He named it St. Louis in honor of the French king Louis IX. By the time the United States acquired the vast territory west of the Mississippi, St. Louis had a population of about a thousand people, and the Missouri River was becoming an extension of the Ohio River as the major westward route for national expansion.

Even before 1803 some Americans had settled along the Missouri. Perhaps the first to do so was Daniel Boone, who was offered about a thousand acres of land in 1798 if he would settle in what became Missouri. Boone accepted the offer from the Spanish government, then in control of the territory, and in 1799, at the age of sixty-five, moved with his family by dugout canoe from western Virginia to Missouri. The Boones settled near some salt springs that became known as Boone's Lick, located on the Missouri River in present-day Howard County. The settlement was so named because wild animals came to lick the natural salt deposit. Boone's two sons—Nathan and Daniel—soon began producing salt by boiling the saline spring water in kettles. They periodically took loads of salt down the Missouri and sold it in St. Louis. Daniel Boone's sons were among the first Americans to use the Missouri River for commerce.[7]

Other Americans settled along the Missouri, especially after the United States formally took possession of the Louisiana Territory on March 9, 1804. Meriwether Lewis, who had been President Jefferson's private secretary, witnessed the ceremonies at St. Louis on that day. A little more than a month later Lewis and William Clark headed up the Missouri River with a fifty-five-foot keelboat, two small log canoes, and a party of more than forty men. It was the first exploration of the new territory sponsored by the United States. Two years later, even before Lewis and Clark had returned, Zebulon Pike, a military officer, was sent west to explore the southern plains. Pike journeyed by boat up the Missouri to the mouth of the Osage River. With a company of twenty-one men, Pike followed the Osage and other smaller streams as far west as he could. After moving overland to the Rocky Mountains and turning south, Pike and his party were arrested by Spaniards and escorted to Santa Fe and on down to Chihuahua, where they were soon released. Pike and his men returned to Missouri.

The population of Missouri doubled between 1804 and 1810, and by 1817 perhaps sixty thousand people called Missouri home. The settlement of Franklin was established in 1817 about a hundred and fifty miles west of the Mississippi on the north bank of the Missouri. Two years later, on the south bank opposite Franklin, but on higher ground, the town of Boonville was founded. In that year, 1819, the first steamboat, a dozen years after Robert Fulton had proved it practical, arrived on the Missouri. It was called the *Independence*, and it traveled up the Missouri from St. Louis. The boat, constructed at Pittsburgh especially for use on the shallow Missouri, took thirteen days to make the journey from St. Louis to Franklin, arriving on June 5, 1819. The return trip downstream required only three days.[8]

A little more than two months later, another steamboat, choking and sputtering, arrived at Franklin. It was the *Western Engineer*, also built in Pittsburgh for use on the Missouri. The vessel was seventy-five feet in length, thirteen feet wide, and drew nineteen inches of water. Aboard was Major Stephen H. Long, who had convinced President James Monroe that the upper Missouri should be explored with a steamboat. To mystify and impress Indians along the river, the bow of the *Western Engineer* was shaped like the neck and head of a strange aquatic monster from whose open mouth rolled clouds of smoke. The steam engine and other equipment were hidden

THE *Western Engineer*

from view by a superstructure, as was the paddle wheel at the stern, which violently agitated the water like the tail of the make-believe monster.[9]

Long's Yellowstone Expedition, as it is called, was soon marred by difficulties. When it reached the site of present-day Council Bluffs, Iowa, the expedition set up camp for the winter. Long, however, returned east to Washington before ice prevented travel on the Missouri. Because his expedition was already becoming more costly than planned, Long asked Congress for additional funds. The lawmakers turned down his request. When he returned to the West in the spring of 1820, Long carried new orders. He was to abandon his exploration of the Missouri and take a small party of men west across the plains to the Rocky Mountains. There he was to explore the region where the Arkansas, Platte, and Red rivers begin.

Major Long learned firsthand, as had earlier explorers, that the nation's major water route across the center of the land ended at what is now the western boundary of Missouri. A traveler going up the Missouri follows a generally westward course from St. Louis to the great bend in the river, located at present-day Kansas City. There the traveler must turn and follow a north-northwesterly course upstream. Although the river does turn west for a short distance near the Kansas and Nebraska border and again along the northeastern border of Nebraska, the route follows a generally northwesterly course until it turns straight west near the western border of North Dakota. Americans, accustomed to using water transportation to cross the central portion of the nation, found only smaller streams like the Kansas and Platte rivers. Flowing east from the vast region that by 1820 was being called the Great American Desert, these smaller streams were and are too shallow for reliable riverboat navigation.

THE IDEA that much of the Louisiana Purchase was nothing more than a vast desert was rooted in the beliefs of President Thomas Jefferson, who viewed the territory as nothing more than a wide strip of country that would protect the western frontier of the United States. It is doubtful that Jefferson ever thought of the region as a place to be populated, even at some future date. The desert concept became firmly established following Zebulon M. Pike's 1806–8 expedition across the plains. After he returned to the East, Pike concluded:

These vast plains of the western hemisphere may become in time as celebrated as the sandy deserts of Africa; for I saw in my route, in various places, tracts of many leagues where the wind had thrown up the sand, in all the fanciful forms of the ocean's rolling wave, and on which not a speck of vegetable matter existed. But from these immense prairies may arise great advantage to the United States, viz: the restriction of our population to some certain limits, and thereby a continuation of the Union. Our citizens being so prone to rambling and extending themselves on the frontiers will, through necessity, be constrained to limit their extent on the west to the borders of the Missouri and Mississippi, while they leave the prairies incapable of cultivation to the wandering and uncivilized aborigines of the country.[10]

Pike's report, published in 1810, and Edwin James's report of Major Long's later expedition, published in 1823, firmly established the vast new territory of the United States west of the great bend in the Missouri as a desert. The authors of school books, map makers, and others saw to it that this notion was conveyed to many Americans. In the eyes of official U.S. explorers the land *was* a desert. Certainly the country was different from the woodlands of the East, where Americans like Pike, Long, and James had been accustomed to thick vegetation, more than adequate water, and countless trees that provided a plentiful supply of wood to construct homes, barns, and fences and to build large towns. Certainly none of these resources were plentiful west of the great bend in the Missouri. But the early American explorers, rooted in eastern ways and a different natural environment, did not see the new western territory for what it really was, nor did they begin to imagine its potential. There also is no question that the broad and open country, so unlike the eastern woodlands, made them feel uncomfortable. Edwin James, among others, made reference to this in his account of Major Long's expedition, which had followed a different route than Pike's party. James wrote:

These vast plains, in which the eye finds no object to rest upon, are at first seen with surprise and pleasure; but their uniformity at length becomes tiresome. For a few days the weather had been fine, with cool breezes, and broken flying clouds. The shadows of these coursing rapidly over the plain, seemed to put the whole in motion; and we appeared to ourselves as if riding on the unquiet billows of the ocean. The surface is uniformly of the description, not inaptly called *rolling*, and will certainly bear a comparison to the waves of an agitated sea. The distant shores and promontories of woodland, with here and there an insular grove of trees, rendered the illusion more complete. The great extent of the country contemplated at a single view, and the unvaried sameness of the surface, made our prospect seem tedious. We pursued our course during the greater part of the day along the same wide plain, and at evening the woody point in which we had encamped on the preceding night was yet discernible.[11]

What James and other men associated with the official American expeditions directed and financed by the government failed to recognize was that life in the new western territory, with its plains, deserts, and scarce water, was not impossible but that it required, as Walter Prescott Webb wrote in 1931, "adjustments and modifications, of giving up old things that would no longer function for the new things that would, of giving up an old way of life for a new way in order that there might be *a* way."[12]

ZEBULON PIKE and Stephen Long were not the first men to cross the vast country west of the great bend in the Missouri. Indians had done so for centuries, and they had adapted to the land. Indians were also the first traders in the region. The Plains Indians and the Pueblo Indians had a system of trade among themselves long before the Spanish arrived. The Plains Indians traded buffalo hides and robes and other articles made from the shaggies for cotton blankets and maize. Human beings—slaves—were also traded. As the Spanish pushed north into New Spain, they tapped the trading system that had been established by the Indians. After the Spanish horse was acquired by Indians in New Spain, the animal became a trade item and spread northward from New Mexico onto the Great Plains and into the Great Basin of Utah. Some horses also changed hands through stealing. Eventually the horse was acquired by Indians on the northern plains and elsewhere, and changed their way of life forever by making them vastly more mobile. In time the French began to cross the plains from the east, some going to Santa Fe, the provincial capital and trading center of Spanish New Mexico, founded very early in the seventeenth century on the banks of the Santa Fe River, a small tributary of the Rio Grande.

Perhaps the earliest white traders to reach Santa Fe from the east were Pierre and Paul Mallet in 1739. Like the Indians and the Spaniards, the Mallets adapted to the land they crossed en route to Santa Fe. As practical businessmen of their day, they seem to have recognized the need to adjust to conditions as they found them. With six other Frenchmen, they traveled

up the Missouri to what is now eastern Nebraska. Only then did they realize
that they had traveled too far north and that the Missouri River did not cross
the center of the continent. Leaving the river and moving overland, the party
followed a southwesterly course. On June 20, 1739, they lost seven packhorses carrying trade goods during a river crossing on the south fork of what
may have been the Solomon River in present-day Kansas. The party arrived
empty-handed at Santa Fe in late July. The Mallets sought permission to
open trade between Missouri and Santa Fe, but Spanish officials ruled against
it because all commerce with its New World holdings was controlled by the
home government in Spain, which wanted to maintain its monopoly over the
raw goods produced there and feared the effects of trade with outsiders. In
fact, any contact with outsiders was discouraged, as it had been since 1560,
when Philip II decreed that no foreigner might enter a Spanish colony without
first obtaining a royal license or passport.[13]

Other French traders, perhaps inspired by the Mallets' journey, also
headed for Santa Fe during the 1740s. Some of them apparently succeeded
in bribing Spanish border guards to look the other way and successfully
traded guns for mules. But other traders were arrested. A few Frenchmen
chose to make their homes in Santa Fe, including Joseph Michel Ravallo
and Pierre Satren, both carpenters by trade, and Louis Febre, a tailor. These
men probably found peace in the sleepy settlement of fewer than four thousand souls with its rambling adobe structures. One outsider who did not stay
was John Rowzee Peyton, a Virginian who made his way to Santa Fe after
having been shipwrecked near the mouth of the Rio Grande in the Gulf of
Mexico. Peyton was arrested by the Spanish and held prisoner at Santa Fe
in 1773. A year later he escaped and made his way overland to St. Louis.
There he probably told of his adventures, and his stories inspired others.[14]

Of all the traders who arrived in Santa Fe during the eighteenth century,
a Frenchman named Pedro Vial is perhaps the most important in this history.
He was in the employ of the Spanish and found a trade route from San
Antonio in present-day Texas to Santa Fe in 1786. In 1792 he was instructed
by the Spanish governor in Santa Fe to find a route to St. Louis. Vial, whose
accomplishments seem as noteworthy as those of Zebulon Pike and Stephen
Long, left Santa Fe in May 1792 with two young Spaniards and some pack-
horses loaded with supplies. Although Vial and his companions were taken
prisoner by a hunting party of Kansa Indians near what is now Great Bend,
Kansas, they succeeded in escaping and reached St. Louis by early October.
The following spring they set out for Santa Fe and arrived there about mid-
November.[15]

What made Santa Fe so attractive to traders, aside from its physical setting and quiet way of life, was its isolation in far northern New Spain, where it was difficult for the Spanish government to supply the silks, hardware items, calicoes, velvets, domestic cottons, dry goods, and iron the inhabitants wanted. Santa Fe had to be supplied by wagon trains that carried goods over El Camino Real—"The King's Highway"—from Mexico City, a distance of sixteen hundred miles, or twice the distance to Missouri. Travel over the unimproved road was slow. An average of only one wagon arrived in Santa Fe each year, and the quantity of goods was not sufficient for the needs of the people. Many items, moreover, were too expensive. Thus there was a waiting market for less expensive goods arriving from Missouri. For the traders there was the appeal of the Spanish specie, both gold and silver, which was more valuable in St. Louis than in Santa Fe. Beaver pelts and other furs, sometimes traded for goods, seem to have been of secondary importance to the early traders because of their bulk, but pelts were traded if no specie could be obtained.The pelts brought a good profit to the traders in Missouri.

As the nineteenth century began, efforts continued in Missouri to open regular trade with northern New Spain. William Morrison, a wealthy merchant at Kaskaskia, Illinois, on the Mississippi, sent Batiste La Lande, a French Creole, to Santa Fe with trading goods in the spring of 1804. La Lande went with instructions to sell the goods, evaluate the trading potential, and return to Missouri, but when he reached Santa Fe, he stayed. The Spanish gave him land, perhaps to discourage his return to Missouri, where he might inspire others to head for the Spanish settlement. Less than a year later, in June 1805, another American, James Purcell, a native of Bardstown, Kentucky, arrived in Santa Fe. He also decided to remain.

By the time the United States acquired the Louisiana Territory in 1803, stories of men crossing the plains to Santa Fe and back were common knowledge among the frontiersmen in Missouri country. One man who had heard these stories was a Spaniard named Manuel Lisa, who teamed up with a trader of Portuguese descent named Jacques Philippe Clamorgan. They came up with a scheme designed to circumvent the Spanish order against outsiders trading in Santa Fe and northern New Spain. They planned first to establish friendly relations with the Pawnee Indians on the plains east of Santa Fe. Once this was done they would bring trading goods to a Pawnee camp reasonably close to Santa Fe, take a few samples of their goods into Santa Fe, and induce as many Spaniards as possible to return with them to where the actual trading would be conducted. Lisa and Clamorgan figured that the Indians would protect their goods from Spanish soldiers who might try to confiscate the merchandise.

Clamorgan, then in his seventies, obtained an American license to trade with the Pawnees. He and Manuel Lisa next formed a company and purchased the necessary goods. But things did not go as planned. James Wilkinson, at the time acting governor of the Louisiana Territory in St. Louis and a man who hoped to establish trade with Santa Fe for his own profit, learned of the plan. He sent word to Zebulon Pike, who had just left on his expedition across the southern plains, to "take all prudent and lawful means to blow it up."[16] Manuel Lisa, to avoid trouble with Wilkinson and the government, publicly disavowed his intentions to establish trade with Santa Fe. Privately, Lisa kept his financial interest in the venture, and Clamorgan and four other men, including a black slave, left St. Louis in early August 1807 with four pack mules loaded with trading goods. They reached Santa Fe on December 12. The Spanish directed him to Chihuahua, where he was allowed to sell his goods. The following year he returned to St. Louis by way of Texas. Clamorgan became the first man to make a trading journey to Santa Fe and return to Missouri with his profits.[17]

In retrospect, Clamorgan's accomplishment appears to have surpassed those of Pedro Vial, Stephen Long, and Zebulon Pike, especially if one considers his age. But it was Pike and not Clamorgan who gained national attention and a prominent place in the history books. Pike had conducted an *official* expedition that was well publicized. Clamorgan's was neither. After Pike returned east in 1810 his report was published by the government, and it contained the first account in English of a possible route to Santa Fe. Pike's bleak description of the southern plains, however, seems to have overshadowed his observations on trading possibilities, at least in the eyes of many Americans. In Washington, government officials did pay attention to Pike's observations, since they were interested in establishing trade with New Spain. But before they could follow up on his report, America went to war against Great Britain, and these officials found themselves with more pressing business to conduct.

In Missouri the war seemed a long way away for Manuel Lisa, who by 1812 was even more determined to establish regular trade with Santa Fe. Lisa, already involved in the fur trade on the upper Missouri, may have read that portion of Pike's report describing the economic situation in Santa Fe. Pike reported that the country produced sheep, tobacco, dressed deer, some furs, buffalo robes, salt, and "wrought copper vessels of a superior quality." Pike noted that everything else needed by the New Mexicans in their daily lives was brought to Santa Fe and northern New Spain from Mexico City and other points to the south. Such goods were expensive by Missouri standards. For instance, Pike wrote that a hundred pounds of flour sold for two dollars, a mule-load of salt cost five dollars, and a yard of superfine cloth cost twenty-five dollars in Santa Fe. Since the same goods cost far less in Missouri, it was only natural that the news encouraged Lisa and other Missouri traders.[18]

Lisa decided to send another man, Charles Sanguinet, to Santa Fe. Although many details are lacking, it is known that Sanguinet lost the goods he was carrying in an Indian attack. Finally Lisa gave up his dream of developing trade with Santa Fe and turned his full attention toward the fur trade of the upper Missouri and the Rocky Mountains. Lisa would go on to establish the Missouri Fur Company and would lay the foundation for the occupation that would earn the label of "mountain man."

About the time Manuel Lisa learned of the failure of Charles Sanguinet's expedition, other Missourians were preparing to leave for Santa Fe. Like those who had gone before them, they also hoped for great financial success. Perhaps encouraged by reports of a pending revolution by the people of New Spain, Robert McKnight, Samuel Chambers, James Baird, and at least seven other men set out for Santa Fe from Missouri. They reached Santa Fe safely but were jailed and their trade goods confiscated by the Spanish. The revolution against Spanish rule had failed. Other men also tried to reach Santa Fe during the next few years, but the land or politics or Indians or a combination of the three served as barriers. In 1819, when the United States and Spain agreed on the Arkansas River as the international boundary between their two countries, regular trade between Missouri and Santa Fe was still only a trader's dream.

The barriers still existed in 1821, the year Missouri became a state and Mexico won her independence from Spain. The news of the start of the Mexican Revolution probably reached Missouri by late spring or early summer. It received much attention. On June 25, 1821, the *Missouri Intelligencer,* published at Franklin, ran an advertisement inserted by William Becknell, an experienced plainsman and veteran of the War of 1812. Becknell sought seventy men willing to join together and invest in an expedition whose purpose was to trade for horses and mules and trap fur-bearing animals. By early August only seventeen men had applied, but they met, organized a company, and elected Becknell captain of the expedition. Some of the men may have put up gold or silver as their part of the investment, and some may have provided trading goods. By September 1, 1821, the day the

A PACK TRAIN TO SANTA FE, 1820.
Drawing by Frederic Remington.

expedition crossed the Missouri River at Arrow Rock and headed west, there were perhaps twenty or more men in the party.

Most written accounts suggest that the expedition intended to trade with Indians on the southern plains, but Becknell probably had his sights set on Santa Fe from the beginning. He knew, as Zebulon Pike had reported, that Don Facundo Melgares, the governor of New Mexico, was a fair man who was also friendly toward Americans. Since Becknell was aware that the people of New Spain were declaring their independence from Spain, the timing of his journey was no coincidence. But Becknell appears to have been a very cautious man. From the beginning he was vague on the expedition's destination, perhaps fearing that if he announced it as Santa Fe, word could reach there before the party left Missouri. If so, and if the revolution failed, Spanish soldiers might be waiting for him. Becknell seems to have played it safe from the outset, although most of the men in the party probably had a good idea where they were going. Unfortunately for historians, Becknell's own account does not provide much help. It is terse and contains little detail.[19]

On Tuesday morning, November 13, 1821, about six weeks after leaving Arrow Rock, Missouri, Becknell and his party met a group of Spanish soldiers in what is now eastern New Mexico. The Spaniards were very friendly, but spoke no English, and no one in Becknell's party spoke Spanish. The two groups camped together for the night, and the following morning the soldiers took the Americans to a village on the Pecos River. Its inhabitants, Becknell recalled, "gave us grateful evidence of civility and welcome." He met a Frenchman in the village who could speak Spanish. Becknell possessed enough French to communicate with the man, so he was hired as an interpreter. It was probably from him that Becknell learned of the triumph of the Mexican Revolution, although he may have guessed as much from the warm reception he and his men received. Soon after arriving in Santa Fe, Becknell met with Governor Melgares, who expressed his desire that Americans should come to Santa Fe. "If any wished to emigrate, it would give him pleasure to afford them every facility," the governor told his visitor.[20]

Becknell's party turned a handsome profit with their trading goods. When they gathered to plan their return trip to Missouri, all but one announced that they wanted to stay in Santa Fe. The village, the people, and the life in Santa Fe delighted them. A man named M'Laughlin and Becknell were the only two members of the party to leave for Missouri, and they were joined on the trip by two other traders who had arrived in Santa Fe after Becknell and his group. The four men left for Missouri in mid-December and arrived in Franklin early in 1825, about forty-eight days later. Tradition has it that when they unloaded their pack animals on the main street of Franklin, rawhide packages of silver dollars were dumped on the sidewalk. One of the traders, perhaps Becknell himself, cut the thongs on a bag and its silver coins spilled out, clinking on the stone sidewalk and rolling into the gutter. One Franklin resident who had invested sixty dollars in Becknell's expedition received nine hundred dollars as her share of the profits. The dream of profit from the new trading route had been realized, and the dream of regular trade between Missouri and Santa Fe would become a reality.

The dream, of course, stemmed from man's age-old desire for wealth. Europeans, from its discovery (while seeking new trade routes), viewed America as a land of mysteries, wonders, and enchantments. Ponce de León searched for the fountain of youth, and Coronado tried to locate the seven cities of gold. Others sought "reefs of pearls, springs gushing forth wine of unexcelled bouquet and fruits that would make the pomegranates of Eden taste like dry husks in comparison."[21]

But as explorer after explorer returned with no tangible evidence of these treasures, most such beliefs gradually died out. New wealth-producing trade routes were a fact, however, and men like the Mallets, Morrison, Clamorgan, Lisa, and Becknell continued to dream about and to look for new ones. Whatever other desires they may have had, these men were seeking

"SILVER COINS SPILLED OUT"

to make a profit. They were laying the foundation for the free enterprise system in the American West. In so doing they adapted to the land as they found it and sought to adjust as well to the conflicting cultures they encountered. They were something like an advance party for the silent army, a vanguard of the great regiments of traders, merchants, wagon freighters, fort sutlers, frontier storekeepers, and others who would sweep across the plains, prairies, and mountains of the American West during the nineteenth century.

II

OVER THE ROAD
TO SANTA FE

*The Santa Fe Trail was a good deal more than a local route for trade;
it provided access to a huge portion of the West and helped to shape
the development of a quarter of a continent.*

—JACK RITTENHOUSE[1]

FOR Jacob Fowler, a seasoned plainsman in his late fifties, the sight was
unbelievable. Fowler reined in his horse, dismounted, and stared at the
signs in the dusty earth. Other men in the party also dismounted, inspected
the signs, and shook their heads in amazement. None of them had ever seen
such a sight on the plains. It was June 28, 1822, as Fowler wrote in his
diary, and he and the other men were perhaps fifty miles west of the Missouri
border in what is now Franklin County, Kansas. They were returning to
Missouri. The signs were the tracks of wagons clearly visible on the ground.
Wagons were unheard of west of Missouri. Fowler noted in his diary that he
and the others followed the tracks for about two days before losing them,
but whether or not Fowler and the others recognized the significance of the
tracks is unknown. They were the tracks of the *first* wagons to cross the
plains, and they had been made by wagons used in William Becknell's
second expedition to Santa Fe.[2]

Becknell, after returning to Missouri from his first successful trading
venture in Santa Fe, spent much of the winter of 1822 preparing to take
a larger trading party back to Santa Fe. He formed a company of twenty-
one men, and they purchased three thousand dollars' worth of trade goods.
The merchandise was loaded onto three farm wagons, and in mid-May
1822 the party left Franklin, Missouri, bound for Santa Fe. On May 22
they crossed the Missouri River on the ferry located at Arrow Rock, and
by early June they had entered what is now Kansas. The party traversed the

WAGON TRACKS ON THE PLAINS

rolling prairie, which soon gave way to the plains as they followed a course south of west.

A year earlier, Becknell and his first expedition had followed the Arkansas River to just east of where La Junta, Colorado, stands today. There they forded the river and headed southwest, crossing over the 7,834-foot-high Raton Pass leading their packhorses laden with trade goods. Becknell, remembering the difficulties experienced in getting the packhorses over the pass, chose on this second journey to seek a more level route to Santa Fe to reduce the risk of losing the party's three wagons. At a point probably in present-day Rice County, Kansas, Becknell again crossed the Arkansas River. It cost the party no small effort and trouble to bring the wagons safely across. Exhausted, they made camp on the river's south bank.

At about midnight their horses were frightened by some buffalo. The country abounded with the shaggies. Twenty horses ran off in different directions with Becknell and a few others giving chase. Two of the men, searching together, ran into a party of Osage Indians the following morning. The two were stripped of their clothing, whipped, and robbed of their horses, guns, and other belongings before the Indians turned them loose. Naked and embarrassed, they made their way on foot back to their camp on the river. Another man, searching alone for the horses, was meantime taken prisoner by another group of Osages, who escorted him to their camp. The Indians apparently planned to rob him; but Auguste P. Chouteau, a trader from Missouri, was conducting business in the camp, and he persuaded the Indians to free their prisoner, who made his way to safety.

It was six days before William Becknell and his party resumed their journey. Although they were more watchful than ever for Indians, they saw none as they followed the Arkansas River west along its south bank past the river's great bend to near where Dodge City, Kansas, stands today. There the party turned southwest, crossing the sand hills and entering what became known as the Cimarron Desert. It is not a true desert but a sixty-mile piece of arid land with little vegetation, much alkaline dust, and little water. Becknell and his men, however, probably viewed the region as a desert, especially after their water supply was exhausted. Just as they began to think they would not survive, the party came upon a stray buffalo that had drunk deep in the Cimarron River farther to the southwest. The groggy buffalo was killed and cut open, and men drank the water in the buffalo's stomach. They were thus able to reach the Cimarron River itself, where they quenched their thirst and filled their water containers. After resting and regaining their strength, the party continued southwest across what is now the Oklahoma and Texas panhandles until they reached the Canadian River in modern northeastern New Mexico. The country was rockier near the Canadian River, but they made good time with their wagons as they neared the site of today's Watrous, New Mexico. There Becknell found familiar ground. He had traveled over the same country a year earlier after crossing Raton Pass to the north, and he had no difficulty in leading his party to San Miguel, where the men divided into small groups to conduct their trading in and around Santa Fe.

The expedition soon turned a reported profit of 2,000 percent on an investment of three thousand dollars in trade goods, which probably included broadcloth, muslin, drills, prints, some taffeta, calico, linen, velveteen, and perhaps other textiles. In addition, Becknell's party probably sold clothing, buttons, buckles, handkerchiefs, razors, razor strops, writing paper, thread, needles, thimbles, knitting pins, scissors, pots, pans, coffee mills, knives, shovels, hoes, axes, and other tools. They may even have taken a few cases of sherry and claret to Santa Fe. A great quantity of smaller items could be carried in the expedition's three wagons, and even the wagons were sold. Becknell's wagon had cost him about a hundred and fifty dollars in Missouri. He sold it for seven hundred and fifty dollars before leaving Santa Fe. The owners of the other two wagons did the same.

Later, after returning to Missouri, Becknell reported that the New Mexicans wanted "goods of excellent quality and unfaded colors." He found that the people of Santa Fe suspected the traders of bringing goods that were "the remains of old stock, and sometimes damaged." But if one brings good trading merchandise, he observed, the New Mexicans, with plenty of "money and mules" to spend, would not hesitate to pay the price demanded if the articles "suit their purpose, or their fancy."[3]

The story of Becknell's second journey to Santa Fe contains many of the ingredients emphasized by writers of western novels and those who have produced traditional films about the American West. Such works tend to stress the pioneers' hardships, determination, adventure (romantic by today's standards), and freedom from restraints. While these elements are an important part of their accomplishment (and make for good entertainment), they often have overshadowed the simple fact that traders were in search of profit and in their role as businessmen brought capitalism—investment of capital in businesses—to the West. To some degree Becknell has been the victim of this misguided emphasis. He does have a secure place in history books as the man who opened regular trade between Missouri and Santa Fe, who took the first wagons from Missouri westward across the plains, and who pioneered the use of the shorter Cimarron or dry route to Santa Fe. But these adventuresome firsts have overshadowed another first, one that is perhaps not as exciting but probably had a more lasting effect: Becknell was the man who organized the first stock company of traders to cross the western plains.

Becknell's contribution is documented in the columns of the *Missouri Intelligencer* of June 25, 1821, about two months before he set out with his first expedition across the plains. It seems to be further evidence that Becknell had set his sights on New Mexico, and Santa Fe in particular, from the beginning. It is unlikely that such an organization would have been necessary if his party had simply gone westward for, as Becknell publicly stated, "the purpose of trading for Horses and Mules, and catching Wild Animals of every description." The fact that mules were found only in Spanish New Mexico leaves little doubt that the expedition was Santa Fe–bound. Becknell's "article for the government of a company of men" became the model for other groups who followed in the Santa Fe trade, and it was used, in part, by those who later made an industry out of such trade. Even emigrant wagon trains that crossed the plains years afterward would employ a similar organization. Becknell's article, organizing the first joint-stock company of traders to cross the plains, is well thought out. It reads, in part:

> Every man will fit himself for the trip, with a horse, a good rifle, and as much ammunition as the company may think necessary for a tour of 3 months trip, & sufficient cloathing to keep him warm and comfortable.

Every man will furnish his equal part of the fitting out of our trade, and receive an equal part of the product. If the company consists of 30 or more men, 10 dollars a man will answer to purchase the quantity of merchandize required to trade on.

No man shall receive more than another for his services, unless he furnishes more, and is pointedly agreed on by the company before we start. If any young man wishes to go on the trip, and is not in a situation to equip himself, if he chooses to go for any person that may think proper to employ and equip him with every necessary required by this article, the employer shall receive an equal dividend of the benefits arising from our trade. There will be no division until we return to the north side of the Missouri river, where all persons concerned shall have timely notice to attend and receive their share of the profits. It will be necessary that every man shall be bound in a penalty of fifty dollars, to be recoverable in any court in this state [Missouri became a state in 1821], and the money appropriated to the use of the company, if he signs and does not perform the trip, unless some unavoidable accident occurs; in such a case immediate notice must be given to any officer belonging to the company, and it shall be the duty of the officer to discharge such a man on his giving satisfactory proof that it is not in his power to comply with this article, and the officers shall fill the vacancy as soon as possible.

It is requisite that every 8 men shall have a pack horse, an ax, and a tent to secure them from the inclemency of bad weather.

I think it necessary for the good order and regulation of the company that every man shall be bound by an oath to submit to such orders and rules as the company when assembled shall think proper to enforce.[4]

All but one of Becknell's rules apparently were followed by members of his first expedition. The lone exception dealt with when the profits were to be divided among the members. Because most of the members decided to remain in Santa Fe, the profits probably were divided there and not in Missouri.

In 1824, after having made two trips to Santa Fe and back, Becknell decided to engage in trapping in the mountains of New Mexico because the prices of trade goods in New Mexico were falling due to an increase in the quantity of goods being brought from Missouri and because an export duty of 3 percent was imposed on all specie taken to the United States from Mexico. Becknell, however, did not find trapping to his liking. He apparently had little success and eventually went back to Missouri, never to return to

New Mexico. In 1835 he sold his farm in Missouri and moved to what was then the Mexican province of Texas. He and his family settled on Sulphur Fork Prairie, a few miles west of modern Clarksville in northeastern Texas. There Becknell prospered, not as a trader of goods, but as a farmer, cattle broker, and stock raiser. He also served as a Texas Ranger and as a representative in the Congress of the Republic of Texas. Becknell, the father of the Santa Fe trade, lived out his life in northeastern Texas and died on April 25, 1856, at the age of sixty-eight.[5]

DURING the first three years of the Santa Fe trade, Becknell and others who traversed the plains experienced many hardships. The actual task of trading goods in Santa Fe was easy work compared to getting there. Knowing when to set out on their journey was as important as deciding what goods to take. For instance, an 1822 expedition headed by James Baird left Missouri for Santa Fe in August, much too late to cross the plains safely before early-winter storms struck. In September, after reaching the Arkansas River in present-day Ford County, Kansas, Baird's party was caught in an early blizzard and spent three months waiting for temperatures to moderate. During that time they lost all of their animals to the cold. In early spring they dug two deep pits in a slope on the north side of the river above their winter camp. There they cached their trading goods and set out on foot for Taos, about three hundred and fifty miles to the southwest. Once in Taos, a walk of about twenty days or more, they obtained mules and started back to where they had hidden their trade goods near what is now Dodge City, Kansas. As they neared the spot a party of sixty Indians attacked and robbed the traders of their mules and belongings. Again the traders had to walk back to Taos.[6]

During the early years of the Santa Fe trade the Indians along the road to Santa Fe frequently harassed traders. In early June 1823, while camped on the bank of the Little Arkansas River in present-day Rice County, Kansas, the expedition headed by Stephen Cooper had all but six of its horses stampeded by Indians. Cooper and five other men rode back to Missouri to obtain more horses while the remaining members guarded the expedition's goods. After the party resumed its journey and turned southwest following the Cimarron route toward Santa Fe, the traders ran out of water. To survive, they killed a buffalo and drank the animal's blood.

Why these men took such gambles with their lives and put their bodies through such physical torment is a question that is still debated. Certainly some of them were enticed by a spirit of adventure, the urge to go where few other Americans had gone; but the promise of wealth at the end of the trail seems to have played a more significant role. It was, very likely, the dream of bettering themselves that above all gave these men the stamina, patience, and endurance needed to cross the plains and to confront unfriendly Indians. The desire for financial reward seems to have been the common denominator regardless of other motives. This desire would impel thousands of other men to venture westward before the end of the nineteenth century, and it persists today.

As the traders adapted to the environment of the plains, they also adapted to overland travel through often hostile Indian country. By the spring of 1824, traders realized that one way they might avoid problems with the Indians along the road to Santa Fe was to cross the plains in large numbers. That year the traders gathered at Franklin, Missouri, and organized into one large expedition, the only major caravan bound for Santa Fe that year. There were eighty-three men in the party, and Alexander Le Grand, Maryland-born and educated in law, was elected captain. The caravan left Franklin in mid-May with two carts, two road wagons, a small cannon, and twenty Dearborn wagons. The road wagons had a bed about twelve feet in length, three and a half feet in width, and two and a half feet in depth. Each such wagon could carry about a thousand pounds. The Dearborns were smaller, drawn by two or four mules or horses, with a front seat for the driver, and each was equipped with bows and a cloth cover. A Dearborn wagon could carry about five hundred pounds. Assuming that all of the wagons were fully loaded, the expedition carried about thirteen thousand pounds. Most of this probably was trade goods. One account suggests that the goods were valued at $30,000.[7] Several prominent Missourians went on this journey, including Augustus Storrs, Meredith M. Marmaduke (later governor), and Thomas L. "Pegleg" Smith, who had been farming near Boone's Lick before turning to trading. Unlike most of the others, Smith was an independent trader with his own pack animals and trade goods. He probably joined the expedition for company and the security of numbers.

The caravan reached the Arkansas River on June 28, 1824, and then followed the Cimarron or dry route to Santa Fe, arriving in late July. A journal kept by Marmaduke, the principal source of information about the expedition, reflects something of the flavor of traveling across the unsettled plains in 1824. Some of the more vivid excerpts include:

June 6th — Travelled over a road exceedingly bad and mountainous. Saw a great many prairie dogs, and shot at one. Heretofore with considerable difficulty we have been able to procure wood for cooking purposes; this evening we have been obliged to use buffalo dung.

June 8th — Travelled 14 miles, and encamped on one of the branches of the Little Arkansas; killed 3 buffaloe and 1 antelope. An alarm was this evening given by our hunters that several hundred Indians were approaching; a party went out to reconnoitre, and found them to be buffaloe.

June 10th — Passed the Sand Hills—saw this day at least ten thousand buffaloe, the prairies were literally covered with them for many miles. Killed 9 buffaloe today—we this evening arrived at the G. Arkansas river, and encamped on it; this river is at this place about 200 yards wide, but quite shallow, as our hunters forded it, and killed several buffaloe on the south side. At this place there is not the smallest appearance of any kind of tree or shrubbery of any kind; the whole country being entirely prairie. . . .

June 29th — Travelled 30 miles; left our encampment at 4 o'clock, a.m., and travelled without making any halt until about 4 o'clock, p.m., without a drop of water for our horses or mules, by which time many of them were nearly exhausted, as well as a number of the men; a dog which had travelled with us during our journey, this day fell down and expired, such was the extreme heat and suffering. Fortunately for us all at about 4 o'clock a small ravine was discovered and pursued for a few miles, and after digging in the sand at the bottom of it, water was procured in sufficient quantity to satisfy both man and horse, but not till after five or six wells were sunk; and such was the extreme suffering of the animals that it was with the utmost difficulty they could be kept out of the holes until buckets could be filled for them. I never in my life experienced a time when such general alarm and consternation pervaded every person on account of the want of water.

July 8th — Travelled about 23 miles over a very sandy barren prairie, without water. Saw many green grapes, wild currants, etc. . . .

July 17th — Crossed Red river, the water of which is a very deep red color, resembling thin, weak blood. . . .

July 28th — Arrived at Santa Fe about dusk. This is a quite populous place, but is built entirely of mud houses; some parts of the city are

tolerably regularly built, others very irregularly. The inhabitants appear
to be friendly, and some of them are very wealthy; but by far the greater
part are the most miserable, wretched, poor creatures that I have ever
seen; yet they appear to be quite happy and contented in their miserable
priest-ridden situation.

August 1st — Remained in town and endeavoring to sell goods, which
we find difficult to do to advantage owing to the scarcity of money and
the quality of the goods.[8]

When it became obvious that buyers in and around Santa Fe could not
absorb all of the goods brought from Missouri, some of the traders headed
south into Chihuahua in northern Mexico. There they sold about three thousand dollars' worth of goods, with everybody apparently making a profit.
When the expedition returned to Missouri, it was reported that the men
brought back furs valued at $10,000 and $180,000 in specie transported in
leather bags. The silver dollars "were dumped in quantities of about five
thousand into or upon a green or fresh beef-hide, and done up by having a
rawhide rope interlaced around the edge of the hide and drawn up tightly.
Then a fire was built near it so as to shrink the hide solidly to its contents
to prevent friction of the coin."[9] One nineteenth-century writer wrote that
this process made the bags "hard and their contents as immovable as if the
metal had been melted and poured into a mould."[10]

IF CAPTAIN ALEXANDER LE GRAND was asked by his friends upon his return
to Missouri to describe the road to Santa Fe, and in all likelihood he was,
Le Grand probably smiled and replied, "What road?" There really was no
road or anything that resembled a trail running continuously between Missouri and the Spanish settlements to the east and northeast of Santa Fe.
There was only unsettled country for nearly nine hundred miles. The traders
simply crossed the country that lay before them, sometimes relying on distant
landmarks as points of reference and using the sun and stars to get their
bearings. In some areas the traders followed trails made by buffalo. Such
trails were usually the easiest to follow since the buffalo took the line of
least resistance going to and from water. Whenever possible, the traders
traveled parallel to creeks and rivers. Water was essential for man and beast.
Trees, which grew mostly along the streams, provided timber for fuel. Where

there was no timber, the traders used dried buffalo dung for their evening campfires. Buffalo chips produce a hot fire and little smoke.

The first person to suggest publicly that a road be laid out between Missouri and Santa Fe appears to have been William Becknell. After he returned to Missouri from his second successful expedition to Santa Fe, the *Missouri Intelligencer* at Franklin quoted Becknell as saying: "An excellent road may be made from Fort Osage to Santa Fe. Few places would require much labor to make them passable."[11] Becknell, of course, was not speaking of a graded and improved road covered with gravel similar to what one sees today in many rural areas of America. Such roads did not exist in Missouri in the early 1820s. In fact, aside from two or three roads covering only short distances in southeastern Missouri, the only major road in the state was from the town of St. Charles in eastern Missouri west to Franklin. It was nothing more than a wide path with log-canoe ferries located on the deeper streams which intersected its course. This wilderness trail was known as Boone's Lick Road. Becknell probably envisioned a similar road between Missouri and Santa Fe, one that would be marked at intervals and improved at stream crossings or in places where the lay of the land made wagon travel extremely difficult.

Becknell may have been the one who planted the idea of such a road in the mind of Thomas Hart Benton, one of Missouri's first United States senators. Benton, however, had believed for some years that Missouri's strategic location as gateway to the West offered a means to help strengthen the state's economy. In 1823, when Becknell suggested that such a road be laid out, Missouri was trying to recover from deep financial trouble. Farming was the state's chief occupation, and it was very expensive to ship produce out of Missouri. There was a lack of hard money, the state's only bank having gone out of business in 1822, and counterfeit paper money flooded the state. People were restless. Many had turned to a barter economy. The only encouraging sign was the Mexican silver and gold specie being brought in by Santa Fe traders.

Realizing that such trade could help boost his state's economy and perhaps provide an outlet for the restless, Benton sought to develop the trail to Santa Fe. Using the experiences of Augustus Storrs, who had gone to Santa Fe with Captain Le Grand in 1824, Benton succeeded in focusing national attention on Missouri and the trading potential of Santa Fe, and in 1825 he persuaded Congress to authorize ten thousand dollars to survey and mark the road. Congress, however, stipulated that the survey commissioners had to obtain by treaty the consent of Indians living in the country through which the trail would pass, and that the Indians must agree not to molest citizens of the United States using the trail, which in a sense was an extension of the National Road started by Congress at Cumberland, Maryland, in 1811, to extend westward to St. Louis.

In mid-July 1825 the United States commissioners and the survey crew started from Fort Osage on the Missouri River east of modern Kansas City. They did not begin at Franklin because by then there were other settlements to the west. The survey caravan consisted of forty men, fifty-seven horses and mules, and seven baggage wagons. When they reached a crossing on the Neosho River a hundred and sixty miles southwest of the big bend in the Missouri River, the commissioners and chief representatives of the powerful Osage nations met to sign a treaty. The meeting took place near the crossing in the Neosho River valley, under a venerable monster of an oak tree that became known as the Council Oak. The government paid the Osage five hundred dollars in money and merchandise valued at three hundred dollars to obtain permission for the Santa Fe road to cross land claimed by the Indians. It was a small price to pay.[12]

By early September the trail had been surveyed to the upper Arkansas River, then the international boundary between the United States and Mexico. The Mexican government, apparently fearful of the military potential of such a road, delayed giving their permission for the survey to continue across Mexican territory until early in 1826. Even then the survey crew could not mark the trail in Mexican territory. The survey party continued to Taos, the closest Mexican port of entry, and not to Santa Fe, but a branch trail to Santa Fe was later laid out.

In retrospect, the actual survey was pretty much wasted effort. Most of the traders followed the trails they were familiar with, including the shortest route via the Cimarron. Even the survey crew's marking of the trail was of little significance. The earth mounds erected as markers were soon eroded by rain, snow, and wind, and the physical evidence of the survey crew's work was little visible to traders within a few years. The survey even became a political issue, with supporters of Andrew Jackson accusing the surveyors of having gone out in blue-painted wagons loaded with good things to eat and drink and of having squandered the money. The men who made the survey were supporters of President John Quincy Adams.[13] But the survey did succeed in bringing attention to the Santa Fe trade. The trail became an international road and attracted traders from the United States and Mexico.

The treaty signed with the Osage Indians was one of the first steps toward an Indian policy in the American West.

DURING the early years of the Santa Fe trade anyone could buy merchandise, load it on a wagon, and go to Santa Fe and sell it. Some men borrowed money to buy trade goods; others persuaded friends to provide the necessary backing. Many of the traders were young men in their twenties or early thirties. William Becknell was about thirty-three years old when he made his first successful trading journey to Santa Fe in 1821. A few men in their forties and older also made the trip during the beginning years of the trade, but for the most part it was a young man's game. The men who engaged in trading came from various occupations, including the professions, but most seem to have been Missouri farmers, perhaps seeking a quick means of earning money to pay off their mortgaged farms or to buy land to farm.

Until the middle 1820s most of these men purchased their trade goods with gold or silver at stores in Franklin, a town of perhaps two thousand people built around a public square. A two-story log jail was located on the west side of the square, and a brick market house on the southwest corner. Nearby was an inn called the Square and Compass, a popular establishment. The buildings that faced the square included a few two-story frame structures, but most were one-story and made of logs.[14] One building on the square housed the federal land office, which had been established in 1818. A trader could buy goods from any one of thirteen general stores in Franklin plus an assortment of other businesses, including several taverns. The general stores, among them one operated by James Harrison and Company, another owned by the St. Louis firm of Sanquinet and Bright, and a store owned by the Lammes, handled a great variety of wares—dry goods, hardware, building materials, household furnishings, groceries, and whiskey. Occasionally a trader might travel to St. Louis to purchase goods. The St. Louis firm of Smith and Knox, among a few others, advertised in the Franklin newspaper promoting goods expressly for the Santa Fe trade. The firm proclaimed its prices to be as reasonable as those found elsewhere, and in St. Louis and Franklin the cost of trade goods was pretty much the same, about 20 to 30 percent above eastern wholesale prices. Still, the traders could earn 40 to 100 percent above those prices in Santa Fe and elsewhere in northern Mexico.[15]

By the early 1830s many Missouri merchants had entered the trade.

The increase in the number of traders created a glut of American goods in Santa Fe. Prices dropped, so much so that individual traders with only one wagonload of merchandise found it difficult to break even. Only traders with several wagons and hired help could make a profit. Even then these traders had to know what goods would sell in New Mexico. In an effort to increase profits, Missouri traders soon began to eliminate the middlemen and buy direct from eastern wholesalers. Many would travel to the East and purchase trade goods with gold or silver specie. In some instances the more established merchants were given credit. Mexican traders—the first apparently came up the road to Missouri in 1825—brought gold and silver specie and soon joined the Missourians in purchasing goods direct from wholesalers. Some Missouri retailers who lost business because of the change entered the Santa Fe trade themselves to make up their losses. One merchant who did so was James Aull, a native of Delaware, who had moved to Missouri with his brother in 1825. Aull established general stores at Richmond, Independence, and Lexington, and he later operated a store at Liberty, Missouri, in partnership with his brother. Each January, James Aull traveled to Philadelphia to buy goods from wholesale houses, especially Siter, Price and Company, his eastern representative. By March or early April, Aull would be back in Missouri awaiting the arrival of the goods he had purchased. Most of his items were shipped by steamer to New Orleans and then by steamboat to St. Louis and up the Missouri River. Aull would often meet the riverboats carrying his goods and supervise the delivery of merchandise to his warehouse. During the weeks that followed he would devote much time to overseeing preparations for the annual spring caravan that, after 1831, left Independence, Missouri, for Santa Fe during May.[16]

The influence of businessmen in the Santa Fe trade is reflected in a table compiled by Josiah Gregg, who was active in the trade between 1831 and 1840. Gregg, who was born in 1806 and raised on a Missouri farm, gathered material and took careful notes on the trade and traders, even for the beginning period. Gregg wrote *Commerce of the Prairies* (1844), a book that remains a classic on the early Santa Fe trade. His table, reproduced on pages 34–35, shows the amount of merchandise, number of wagons and men, number of proprietors or businessmen involved in the trade, and other information on an annual basis from 1822 to 1843.

When traders like James Aull began dealing directly with eastern wholesale houses, much of their business was conducted on credit. The eastern firms generally extended credit for from six to twelve months before charging interest, but even twelve months was often not long enough to sell goods in

Santa Fe or points south and obtain profits. There were times when traders in Missouri delayed going East early in a new year to purchase more goods because they did not have the cash needed to pay the previous year's bills. In 1831, James Aull advised his creditors that he had received only $1,200 from the $10,000 worth of goods he had sent to Santa Fe the previous spring. Aull and other traders also had to bear the expense of transporting their purchases from the East to Missouri and from there to Santa Fe and Chihuahua. From the East Coast to Missouri, transportation could cost from 10 to 25 percent of the price of the merchandise, but when several traders combined their consignments into one shipment, as was often done, transportation costs could be reduced. The cost of taking trade goods from Missouri to Santa Fe was not as great. It was about ten to twelve dollars to transport each hundred pounds of merchandise over the road to Santa Fe, and an additional six to eight dollars per hundredweight to take goods from Santa Fe to Chihuahua.[17] Gregg's table indicates the approximate dollar amount of goods taken to Chihuahua from 1824 to 1843.

Still another expense for the traders was the duty paid on goods brought into New Mexico. Beginning in 1824, when the traders arrived in Santa Fe, they were required to go to the custom house, where Mexican officials placed a value on the merchandise without regard to the invoice prices. The value set by officials might be 10 percent or 100 percent or even 130 percent above the actual cost paid by the traders in the States. The tax paid by the trader was then computed on the arbitrary value set on the goods by the officials. During the early days of the trade the government also demanded an entry tax of ten dollars per wagon. Later the tax was five hundred dollars per wagon with no import duty on goods. The tax was set by the governor of New Mexico and was often changed, sometimes from year to year. At one point during the first two decades of the trade, it was the practice for the official to receive a third of the duty for his personal use and the government the remainder.[18] Such corruption seems to have been a way of life among Mexican officials, and sometimes a trader could bribe them to accept a lower tax. Josiah Gregg observed in 1844 that perhaps only half of the tax revenue collected from traders ever reached the government treasury in Mexico City.[19]

Aside from adjusting to the whims of tax collectors, American traders also learned to cope with the land, the elements, and the lack of water along much of the road to Santa Fe. They adapted to conditions as they found them. Indians, however, remained another matter. While the United States treaty of 1825 with the Osage Indians—another, similar treaty was signed with the Kansa Indians—eliminated most problems between the traders and

Gregg's Table

Years	Amount of Merchandise	Wagons	Men	Proprietors
1822	$ 15,000		70	60
1823	12,000		50	30
1824	35,000	26	100	80
1825	65,000	37	130	90
1826	90,000	60	100	70
1827	85,000	55	90	50
1828	150,000	100	200	80
1829	60,000	30	50	20
1830	120,000	70	140	60
1831	250,000	130	320	80
1832	140,000	70	150	40
1833	180,000	105	185	60
1834	150,000	80	160	50
1835	140,000	75	140	40
1836	130,000	70	135	35
1837	150,000	80	160	35
1838	90,000	50	100	20
1839	250,000	130	250	40
1840	50,000	30	60	5
1841	150,000	60	100	12
1842	160,000	70	120	15
1843	450,000	230	350	30

* Gregg was in error, in that he apparently did not know that William Becknell's second expedition to Santa Fe in 1822 took three Missouri farm wagons.

In his notes to this table Gregg acknowledges that his figures may not be "perfectly accurate." He also notes that at first "almost every individual of each caravan was a proprietor," while in later years the capital was "held by comparatively few hands." Gregg's figure relating to

Taken to Chihuahua	Remarks
	Pack-animals only used.*
	Pack-animals only used.
$ 3,000	Pack-animals and wagons.
5,000	Pack-animals and wagons.
7,000	Wagons only henceforth.
8,000	
20,000	3 men killed, being the first.
5,000	1st U.S. Escort—1 trader killed.
20,000	First oxen used by traders.
80,000	Two men killed.
50,000	
80,000	Party defeated on Canadian; 2 men killed, 3 perished.
70,000	2nd U.S. Escort.
70,000	
60,000	
80,000	
40,000	
100,000	Arkansas Expedition.
10,000	Chihuahua Expedition.
80,000	Texas Santa Fe Expedition.
90,000	
300,000	3rd U.S. Escort—Ports closed.

the amount of merchandise transported to Santa Fe each year was recorded "at its probable cost in Eastern cities of the United States." He added in his notes: "Besides freights and insurance to Independence, there has been an annual investment, averaging nearly twenty-five per cent upon the cost of the stocks, in wagons, teams, provisions, hire of hands, &c., for transportation across the Prairies."

ARRIVAL OF THE CARAVAN AT SANTA FE.
From Josiah Gregg's 1844 classic, *Commerce of the Prairies.*

Indians along the eastern portion of the road, Comanches and Pawnees and occasionally Kiowas, Cheyennes, and Arapahoes caused trouble to the west. Some details of such encounters appear in Josiah Gregg's *Commerce of the Prairies*, and information may also be gleaned from dusty copies of old Missouri newspapers and a few early New Mexican newspapers after 1835, as well as scattered and often sketchy narratives and diaries left by those who traveled the road.

Until 1828 the Indians along the western portion of the road seem only to have robbed and harassed traders without doing them bodily harm. In that year, however, things changed. Late in the summer of 1828 twenty traders, including a twenty-one-year-old Missourian named Milton Bryan, started back to Missouri from Santa Fe after a successful trading expedition. With them they carried several thousand dollars in Mexican specie, their profits. A few days east of Santa Fe they encountered a large band of Comanche Indians. Two traders were killed. The remaining eighteen, after a running battle of three or four days, abandoned their corraled wagons under cover of darkness and set out on foot for Missouri, about five hundred miles away. Fearing they might encounter more Indians along the Santa Fe road to the east, the traders headed north. They carried what specie they could, having left much of it in their wagons. Soon the weight of the silver became too great. When they reached the Arkansas River in present-day Kearny County, Kansas, the traders buried a substantial part of the money on an island in the river. Eventually, half-naked and footsore, some of them suffering from starvation and exhaustion, they made it back to Missouri.

Milton Bryan regained his strength, and the following spring he and a companion from the expedition of a year earlier joined another trading caravan. They were determined to recover the buried specie. The caravan was commanded by Captain Charles Bent, who would later control much of the trade on the southern plains from what became known as Bent's Fort in what is now eastern Colorado. Bent's caravan, unlike previous trading expeditions, had a military escort. In response to traders' demands for protection from the Indians, President Andrew Jackson, who took office in early March 1829, directed that four companies of soldiers under the command of Brevet Major Bennet Riley escort the caravan as far west as the Arkansas River, then part of the boundary between Mexico and the United States.

MILTON BRYAN,
not many years after he traveled
the Santa Fe Trail as a trader.

Brevet Major Riley had two hundred soldiers of the Sixth Infantry under his command. On July 10, 1829, the traders' caravan with its foot-soldier escort (the U.S. Army then had no mounted units) reached the Arkansas River, near the island where Bryan and the others had buried their silver the previous year. The soldiers established a camp on the U.S. side of the river. The following morning Bryan and his companion went out with a squad of soldiers to recover the silver. They found that the river had washed the earth away, exposing the silver to the view of anyone who might have passed that way. But fortunately for the traders, no one had. Bryan and his companion placed the silver in sacks and left it with Brevet Major Riley for safekeeping. Saying their goodbyes, Bryan and his companion rejoined Captain Bent's caravan and headed for Santa Fe. Just on the other side of the Arkansas River the traders' caravan ran into some Indians. One man was killed. The others fired their cannon at the Indians as the soldiers crossed the river and joined the battle. The Indians, perhaps two thousand of them according to Bryan, fled. The soldiers accompanied the traders for a few days and then returned to their camp on the Arkansas River. The traders reached Santa Fe without difficulty, successfully sold their goods, and started back to Missouri. At the Arkansas River, Bryan picked up the money entrusted to the Army's care and, with the military escort and trading caravan, returned to Missouri.[20]

Captain Bent's trading caravan of 1829 was the first to include a military escort. It also was the first to use oxen as draft animals on the road to Santa Fe. Riley chose to use oxen to pull the U.S. Army vehicles—twenty heavily laden wagons and four carts—because he believed the oxen could survive by eating the grass along the road. As their supplies were used up and the load reduced, unneeded oxen could be used as a source of beef for the soldiers. The experiment worked well. In fact, when the military escort reached the Arkansas River, Riley loaned Captain Bent a yoke of oxen. Bent, who wanted to test them as draft animals, used them to help pull one of his wagons to Santa Fe. When Bent returned the oxen to Riley on the return trip, Bent reported that they performed well, except that their feet became tender from so much walking.[21]

Exactly what type of wagons were used by Bent's caravan of 1829 is unknown. They may have been Missouri farm or road wagons or both, and they probably were pulled by mules and perhaps a few horses. Mules were uncommon in Missouri before about 1823, when Stephen Cooper's expedition to Santa Fe returned home with four hundred of them. Missourians soon learned firsthand that mules were better than horses for pulling freight wagons

A CORRALLED WAGON TRAIN PREPARING TO HIT THE TRAIL.
Drawing by Thomas Willing.

A CONESTOGA WAGON BEING PULLED BY SIX HORSES.
Photographed in Pennsylvania in the late nineteenth century.

across the plains. A horse could not maintain its strength during the long journeys to Santa Fe by eating only the shortgrasses found along the western half of the road. Grain was usually not available since few traders wanted to use precious space in their freight wagons to carry forage for their animals. Mules, however, could maintain their strength on the shortgrasses, and mules also could withstand the heat, cold, and conditions of the plains better than horses. In addition, most mules had a longer working life. Certainly a major consideration for the change to mule power was that horses attracted Indians. Indians did not find mules as desirable. [22]

Gradually, as plains travel became more sophisticated, traders turned to using mules and oxen to pull their wagons, and they sought larger wagons in which to carry more merchandise. It was then that many traders turned to the Conestoga, the all-purpose wagon that had moved much freight east of the Mississippi beginning in the eighteenth century. The Conestoga originated in the Pennsylvania Dutch section of southeastern Pennsylvania sometime between 1720 and 1750. [23] The wagon was heavily built with a bed that was higher at both ends than in the middle, and it was topped with a dull-white cloth cover that rested on several hoops stapled to the sideboards. The curve of the canopy was even more pronounced than the curve in the bed. Not only could the Conestoga carry a larger load than the smaller farm or road wagon, but its shape was such that the contents would not spill out the ends when it was going up- or downhill. By the late 1830s the Conestoga had become the most common freighting wagon on the road to Santa Fe. By then the boatlike outline of the wagon when viewed from a distance had given the Conestoga the nickname "prairie schooner." Some people also referred to it as a "Pitt schooner" since most of the Conestogas were then manufactured in Pittsburgh and shipped west by steamboat to Missouri.

When the governor of New Mexico eliminated the import duty on goods in 1839 and simply taxed each wagon arriving from the States regardless of size, the traders sought larger wagons: the fewer wagons, the less tax. A St. Louis wagonmaker named Joseph Murphy, a tall, serious-minded Irishman, met their needs by producing a vehicle even larger than the Conestoga. The Murphy wagon, as it became known, had rear wheels that were seven feet high. The rim of the wheels was eight inches wide. The wagon's body was six feet in height, and it was fifty feet from the back of the wagon to the end of the tongue in front. One wagon could hold two to three tons of freight. By the early 1840s the Murphy wagon was perhaps the most popular freighting vehicle on the road to Santa Fe, not only because of its size but because of the craftsmanship of Joseph Murphy. He used only the finest, carefully seasoned woods in his wagons. All holes were bored with a hot iron, not an auger. This prevented cracking or rotting around the bolt. The holes were drilled one size smaller than the bolt to ensure a tight fit. A Murphy wagon sold for about one hundred and thirty dollars in the early 1840s.[24]

During the first two decades of the Santa Fe trade, Missourians were provided with a source of silver and mules, while New Mexicans were able to obtain inexpensive goods manufactured in the States. At the same time the road to Santa Fe also facilitated the growth of the fur trade in the southern Rocky Mountains and areas beyond. The high plateau country of New Mexico with its many mountain streams supported countless beaver and other fur-bearing animals. Europeans had sought furs from the New World since the early seventeenth century. By the early nineteenth century the demand for furs exceeded what Americans could supply, but when trade with Santa Fe and northern Mexico was established, the road to Missouri offered a means of transporting pelts to the States. The market was waiting. Also, the use of wagons on the Santa Fe road demonstrated that they could traverse the plains and prairies. Only Indians blocked such travel in some regions. As the Santa Fe trade grew, so did the fur trade, although it was not limited to the northern regions of Mexico. Like the Rocky Mountains themselves, the fur trade spread the length of America.

III

ALONG THE UPPER MISSOURI AND BEYOND[1]

For forty years after the purchase of Louisiana the people of the United States were at a loss to know what to do with their new possession. . . . The single attraction that it offered in a commercial way was its wealth of furs . . .

—HIRAM MARTIN CHITTENDEN[2]

ONE of Lewis and Clark's missions on their journey to the Pacific was to claim for the United States the fur resources held by the Indians on the plains and by the British in the northern Rockies. When the explorers returned to St. Louis in 1806, they reported that the region along the upper Missouri was indeed rich in furs. This news excited the established traders at St. Louis, who were already engaged in the fur trade along the lower Missouri. While these men, most of them French, pondered how best to develop the upper Missouri, the Spaniard Manuel Lisa came up with a plan and put it into action. Lisa, about thirty-one years old, formed a partnership with Pierre Menard and William Morrison, merchants at Kaskaskia, Illinois. In the spring of 1807, Lisa led an expedition of forty-two men up the Missouri and built a trading post named Fort Raymond at the mouth of the Bighorn River in what is now Montana. This was the beginning of the American fur trade in the West.

The practice of using trading posts to procure pelts from the Indians was the system then used by the United States government in the East. It had been set up by Congress in 1795 to supply Indians with goods, making them dependent upon the white man, and then to control them by withholding goods until amicable relations favorable to settlers were established. In this manner the government hoped to dominate the western frontier. The President was given the power to establish trading posts and appoint white Indian agents to sell goods to the Indians. But since the Indians had little specie, the agents accepted furs in trade for the goods. The agents had to be bonded, and they were prohibited from receiving guns or other weapons, cooking utensils, or articles of clothing except for skins or furs from the Indians. But the agents could trade such items to the Indians. In fact, the goods offered by most agents included guns, rifles, lead, powder, muskrat spears, muskrat and beaver traps, powder horns, silks, sewing thread, calico and other types of cloth, blankets, strouds, shirts, pantaloons, waistcoats, jewelry including brass finger rings, looking-glasses, kitchen utensils including kettles, pots, tin cups, jugs, crockery, forks, spoons, and candle molds. Groceries, such as salt, sugar, flour, currants, tea, raisins, and coffee, were also commonly traded along with tobacco and pipes. And wampum—small beads made of shells—were also popular. The Indians used them as money and as ornaments.

Although the factory system, as it was called, was the first attempt by the federal government to enter business in competition with private industry, the system was not intended to make a profit for the government or the Indian agent. The agents could not engage in private trading with the Indians. The money earned was to offset the cost of operating the trading posts and maintaining soldiers on the frontier. The furs collected at the trading posts were sold at public auctions in New Orleans, St. Louis, Savannah, Washington, Philadelphia, and New York City.

Trading with Indians was first limited to government agents, but Congress passed a law in 1799 providing for the issuing of licenses to private traders; the licenses were granted by the Superintendent of Indian Trade, or by any other person authorized by the President, for a period not to exceed two years. (The same law required a license to purchase a horse from an Indian or any white man in Indian country.) Before receiving a license, a trader had to post a thousand-dollar bond as surety for his faithful observance of all government regulations controlling commerce with the Indians. Manuel Lisa posted such a bond to obtain his license before starting up the Missouri River in the spring of 1807.[3]

The fur trade was significantly different from the Santa Fe trade. Fur traders dealt in one commodity—pelts—with beaver pelts the most prized. They were used in Europe and elsewhere to make hats. While some Santa Fe traders dealt in pelts, especially beaver, most concentrated on general merchandise. They bought and sold goods and carried on their business between two principal areas, Missouri and New Mexico. The fur traders, however, were suppliers, and they roamed the length and width of the

American West seeking beaver wherever they could find them. The hardships of the trade were much greater than those of the Santa Fe expeditions, and the journeys to and from beaver country, in addition to the uncertainties associated with finding and trapping the animals and selling the pelts, required a considerable investment, certainly more than that of the average Santa Fe trader. As a result, the fur trade in the American West was controlled by fewer men than was the Santa Fe trade, and the successful fur traders appear to have been greater gamblers than most of their Santa Fe counterparts. Manuel Lisa was such a man.

Lisa, a sharp competitor and hard worker, gambled in taking an expedition to the upper Missouri. After building Fort Raymond in 1807, he sent his men out to establish good relations with the Indians and to encourage them to trade at his post. The men had good success with all the Indians they met except the Blackfeet, who had been hostile toward Americans ever since two of their people had been killed a few years earlier by members of Lewis and Clark's expedition. Lisa and his men were able to trade goods for some beaver pelts with the friendly Indians, but too much merchandise was bartered away for friendship and pelts to make the trade profitable. Then, too, the Indians were reluctant to kill as many beaver as the traders wanted. It being late in the fall, Lisa decided to winter his party at Fort Raymond, and while there directed some of his men to go out themselves to kill beaver in the vicinity of the post. The sluggish streams and wooded banks nearby abounded with the large aquatic rodent. A beaver, with its thick brown fur, webbed hind feet, paddlelike hairless tail, and sharp front teeth, might weigh as much as sixty pounds. Lisa's men killed many.

During the early 1800s many white men killed beaver much the way the Indians had done for years, by snaring them and then clubbing them to death. Others chose to shoot the animal. It was not until 1823 that a steel trap was invented in New York City by Sewall Newhouse, son of a blacksmith. A steel trap was more reliable than a snare, and it increased the number of beaver that could be taken by one man. It weighed about five pounds and was attached to a chain about five feet long that had a swivel and ring at one end. Joseph L. Meeks, a Virginian who came West and became a trapper in 1829, recalled that the swivel and ring "played round what is called the float, a dry stick of wood, about six feet long. The trapper wades out into the stream, and drives it into the mud, so fast that the beaver cannot draw it out; at the same time tying the other end by a [rawhide] thong to the bank. A small stick or twig, dipped in musk or castor, serves as bait, and is placed

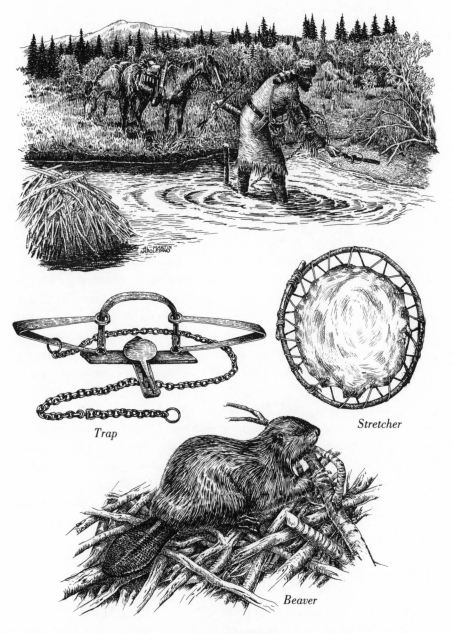

Trap

Stretcher

Beaver

TRAPPING BEAVER

so as to hang directly above the trap, which is now set. The trapper then throws water plentifully over the adjacent bank to conceal any footprints or scent by which the beaver would be alarmed, and going to some distance wades out of the stream."[4]

The trap was usually set in three or four inches of water. The stick or twig, dipped in musk or castor, was directly above the trap. When a beaver was attracted to the spot by the bait, it was caught. Frightened, the beaver would dive into deeper water with the trap attached, but would soon find itself held by the chain, which it could not gnaw in two. It would struggle, finally sink to the bottom, and drown. If, as sometimes happened, a beaver pulled the chain from the float or stick, the trapper often had to search for the animal, and the search might require him to wade into deep water, which was particularly uncomfortable during cold weather.

More often than not, the trapper skinned the beaver near where it was trapped. He would clean, dress, cure, and mark the skin; then he often obtained a fresh supply of bait, or "medicine," from the perineal glands of the beaver. The "medicine"—castoreum, a creamy, bitter, orange-brown substance—was obtained by removing the perineal glands from the base of the beaver's tail and then smoking or drying them in the sun. The glands were next mixed with alcohol, cinnamon, nutmeg, and cloves in a bladderlike bag. The mixture was finally sealed in an airtight wooden box until needed. Castoreum supposedly can attract beaver from as far as a mile away, and it probably was the "medicine" used most by Lisa and his men on snares to attract beaver.[5]

By the spring of 1808, Manuel Lisa and his men had killed enough beaver to earn a profit. The experience convinced Lisa that it was better for traders to kill beaver themselves than to rely solely upon the Indians. Thus it was on Lisa's first expedition to the upper Missouri that the concept of the "mountain man" of the American West was born, although it was years before the label was used. Meantime, the fur trade would undergo many changes. Methods and techniques used by fur traders in the East would be cast aside in the West as traders learned to adapt to the country, and they would find that success often was determined, not by how many pelts were taken, but by the economic conditions in the East and Europe and the demand for beaver pelts.

When Lisa and his party returned to St. Louis in the fall of 1808, their success in acquiring pelts impressed the French traders and others, and many men soon sought to join Lisa in his venture. When some of them offered to invest in his enterprise, Lisa was receptive because the expedition had been costly. He knew more capital would be needed, more than he had, and soon he and nine other men formed the St. Louis Missouri Fur Company. The words "St. Louis" were later dropped from the name. The partners were Lisa, Pierre Menard, Benjamin Wilkinson, Pierre Chouteau, Auguste P. Chouteau, Jr., Sylvestre Labbadie, Reuben Lewis, Andrew Henry, William

Clark (of Lewis and Clark fame), and William Morrison. It was the first of several fur companies to operate from St. Louis.

The St. Louis Missouri Fur Company sent its first expeditions up the Missouri in the spring of 1809. Andrew Henry, who had been engaged in lead mining near St. Louis, was the field captain. Pierre Menard, a sensitive French Canadian seemingly resigned to suffering the hardships of wilderness life in order to make a living, was manager. The expedition spent the winter of 1809–10 at Fort Raymond, and when the snows began to melt in the spring, pushed farther up the Missouri and began to build another trading post at Three Forks in the heart of rich beaver country. But it was also Blackfeet country, and the Indians soon began attacking the traders. The men managed to beat off the Indians and to complete the construction of the trading post, but Pierre Menard became discouraged by the hardships and the Indian troubles. He took a few men and what pelts had been gathered and set out for St. Louis, leaving Henry completely in charge.

Henry worked out a plan whereby half of the remaining men stayed on guard at the trading post. The other half went out after furs, and half of those acted as guards while the rest killed beaver. The plan worked well against the Indians, but it was not an efficient way to obtain pelts. One day, after it appeared that the Blackfeet had withdrawn from the area, a small group of trappers became careless and failed to station a guard. A party of Blackfeet attacked and killed three of the trappers, no more than two miles or so from the post.

The loss of three men convinced Henry that he should leave Blackfeet territory. He sent several men down the Missouri to St. Louis with what pelts had been accumulated. With the remaining men, Henry headed up the Madison River in search of beaver in more peaceful surroundings. Crossing the Continental Divide, Henry and his trappers discovered the north fork of the Snake River (now called Henry's Fork) and built a trading post consisting of a few log cabins and a dugout near present-day St. Anthony, Idaho. There Henry and his men spent a miserable winter. While they did find beaver, there was little edible wild game for food. They apparently did eat beaver meat, but only as a last resort. Although the dark red meat, fine in texture, is good, it must be soaked for about twelve hours in salt water to draw excess blood. The preparation is not difficult, but Henry and his men apparently did not enjoy beaver, and the animal may not have been as plentiful in the heavy snow and bitter cold as accounts suggest. It is known that they killed their horses for meat.

Their trading post, called Fort Henry, was the first American habitation west of the Rocky Mountains. When spring arrived, Henry divided his party into three groups. He sent one group south out of the mountains toward the Spanish settlements of the Southwest. Another group was sent east toward the Teton Mountains in what is now northwestern Wyoming. Both groups were to search for beaver. It appears that Henry offered commissions to his men for the beaver they trapped, thereby introducing a new business method to the western fur trade. Henry took the third group back to the Three Forks area and then started down the Missouri River, meeting Manuel Lisa coming upstream with supplies for the expedition. It was a welcome meeting. Henry delivered forty packs of beaver pelts to Lisa, caught up on the news from the outside world, and continued downstream to St. Louis. Once there, Henry retired from active involvement in the Missouri Fur Company and returned to the less hazardous business of lead mining, apparently with a partner named William Ashley.

WHILE LISA, HENRY, and the Missouri Fur Company were trying to develop the fur trade along the upper Missouri, John Jacob Astor, a native of Waldorf, Germany, was trying to develop the same trade in the Pacific Northwest. At the age of sixteen Astor had left his native Germany and gone to London with his brother. There they established a business making and selling musical instruments. John Jacob Astor, however, had a burning ambition to achieve success. At the age of twenty-one he came to New York and soon sold his stock of musical instruments and invested his capital in furs. Within a few years Astor became a wealthy man, controlling much of the fur trade east of the Mississippi. He then sought to expand his fur empire into what is now Oregon and Washington, and in 1810 formed the Pacific Fur Company as a subsidiary of the American Fur Company, which began in 1808. From New York, he sent a ship around South America to the Northwest coast carrying firearms, powder, tools, Indian trade goods, provisions, and clothing. He also sent an expedition overland from Montreal, then the stronghold of the North West Company, a large Canadian fur outfit. Astor's expedition followed waterways to St. Louis and then traveled up the Missouri River and over the Rockies to the mouth of the Columbia River. There Astor's men established a trading post called Astoria. British influence in the region was so great, however, that Astor was soon forced to sell his post, equipment, and furs to the British to avoid armed conflict at the start of the War of 1812 between the United States and England.

The war brought a complete halt to the American fur trade in the Pacific

ASTORIA TRADING POST

Northwest, along the upper Missouri, and in much of the nation east of the Mississippi. The uncertainties of the war caused a decline of fur prices in the East. Fortunately for the United States, the earlier efforts of Lisa, Henry, and other American traders to gain the support of the Indians living along the upper Missouri helped to weaken British influence in the region. When the war ended in 1815, the United States signed a treaty with Britain fixing the international boundary line along the 49th parallel from west of Lake of the Woods in present-day Minnesota to the Continental Divide. The British also agreed to share control of the territory called Oregon, located to the north and west of the Louisiana Purchase.

By 1819 the fur prospects on the upper Missouri and along the Columbia River again looked promising for American traders. The government's Yellowstone Expedition, headed by Major Stephen H. Long, was moving west with plans to break the remaining British trade among the Indians, although it never reached the upper Missouri. All seemed to augur well until a financial panic depressed the nation's business, including the fur trade, and tragedy struck the Missouri Fur Company when Manuel Lisa died in August 1820.[6]

One of Lisa's partners, Joshua Pilcher, took over the company and set about to run it much as Lisa had done. Pilcher, a native of Virginia then thirty years old, was an energetic man of fine character. But in 1820, because of the nation's economic troubles, he and the Missouri Fur Company could not raise sufficient capital to send another expedition up the Missouri. The West, as we have seen to some extent with the Santa Fe trade, was still dependent on the East for large influxes of capital. And when the growing pains of the young nation's economy produced such a disruption as the depression of 1819, its repercussions were felt in the West.

To understand the cause of the depression, it is necessary to review at least briefly the nation's political and economic history. The Federalists had controlled the national government between 1789 and 1801. One of the main architects of the Federalist economic program was Alexander Hamilton, Secretary of the Treasury, who favored a strong national government. The Federalists passed a tariff law in 1789 to raise revenue and protect American industry, of which there was little by modern standards. They also established a monetary policy that included chartering the First United States Bank in 1791. It received a twenty-year charter and was a joint venture involving both private enterprise and the federal government. The government's share of its ten million dollars in capital was only two million. The actual control and management of the bank was in private hands, a board of directors elected by the stockholders. The bank served as a federal depository and was also authorized to accept deposits from other government agencies and from private individuals. It could make loans to the federal government, to states, or to any citizen, and it issued banknotes which circulated as paper money.

Hamilton believed the nation should have great manufacturing establishments, unlike Thomas Jefferson, who believed that the United States should always remain predominantly agricultural. In 1801 the Democratic-Republicans (usually called simply Republicans) came to power under Jefferson's leadership. Although they seemed to favor a narrow interpretation of the Constitution, within a few years Jefferson and his Republican successors were exercising federal powers even greater than those advocated by the Federalists. For instance, the Louisiana Territory was purchased in 1803—a transaction of dubious constitutionality—and, beginning in 1807, laws were passed to protect American commerce and neutrality on the high seas during the time England and France were at war. In 1811, Congress failed to renew the charter of the First United States Bank, perhaps because it had been too successful; state banks viewed it as unfair competition and feared the federally supported central bank. After its dissolution, the number of state banks increased.

When the United States entered the War of 1812, the federal government, without a national bank to borrow from, had to issue five million dollars in notes to help pay for the war. It was the first paper money issued by the federal government, and it was well received by Americans because the value of many state banknotes was dropping. State banks found it difficult to redeem U.S. notes in specie. Gold and silver were scarce, owing partly to the payment for imports from Europe and partly to the capture of Washington, D.C., by the British in 1814. Hoarding of gold and silver by the end of the war was commonplace, and federal notes outstanding amounted to about eighteen million dollars. The following year Congress established the Second United States Bank, giving it a twenty-year charter and approving an organization similar to that of the First United States Bank. By then, however, the damage to the nation's economy had been done. The large quantities of notes issued by state banks, their liberal credit policies that resulted in a wave of land buying and speculation, and the dumping of British goods upon the American market immediately after the war all combined to cause the panic of 1819.[7]

Isaac Lippincott, in his book *Economic Development of the United States* (1927), wrote that the men who ran the state banks "had no adequate conception of sound banking principles and no way to learn except by experience." He added:

Along with pioneers in other lines they made mistakes. To many of these bankers money, no doubt, meant capital, and they were under the impression that they were increasing the capital of the community when they enlarged their circulation. They did not distinguish between loans for commercial and investment purposes; consequently, accommodations were granted not only to merchants, but to purchasers of land, and to founders of shops and factories. Thus the resources of these banks were often involved in investments which could not readily be converted into cash. Moreover, the banks of the times were large buyers of Government loans, and such securities were sometimes a source of embarrassment because they could not at all times be converted promptly into money. Loans were extended freely to all kinds of enterprises, usually in the form of notes.[8]

Joshua Pilcher thus was not able to obtain the capital he needed from an eastern firm until early 1821. That spring he sent a Missouri Fur Company expedition up the Missouri. In that same year, John Jacob Astor succeeded in persuading Congress to abolish the government's "factory system," leaving the fur trade solely in the hands of private companies. This move attracted new attention to the fur trade, and several other fur companies were organized, although, with the exception of Astor's American Fur, most of them were small. When Astor's company created a new department and extended its operations west of the Mississippi and onto the Missouri River in 1822, it was the beginning of the end for the Missouri Fur Company. Competition and financial and Indian problems along the upper Missouri plagued the firm, and it went out of business three years later.

EARLY IN 1822, William Ashley inserted an advertisement in the *Missouri Gazette and Public Advertiser* at St. Louis. It read:

TO ENTERPRISING YOUNG MEN.

The subscriber wishes to engage one hundred young men to ascend the Missouri river to its source, there to be employed for one, two, or three years. For particulars enquire of Major Henry, near the lead mines in the county of Washington, who will ascend with, and command, the party; or of the subscriber near St. Louis.[9]

Ashley was about forty years old when he and Andrew Henry, who was perhaps in his late forties, sought to hire young men to trap beaver for profit. For some unknown reason Henry had decided to return to the fur trade. He and Ashley had similar backgrounds. They were born in the East—Ashley in Virginia and Henry in Pennsylvania—and both men came West in search of wealth and became partners in lead mining near St. Louis. But there most of the similarities end. Ashley was flamboyant and interested in politics and social life. In 1820 he was elected the first lieutenant governor of the state of Missouri and was a general in the state militia by 1822. In contrast, Henry had only a passing interest in politics. He enjoyed reading and playing the violin. Both men seem to have been confident that they would succeed in spite of competition, but confidence alone was not enough to be successful in the fur trade. Business knowledge and experience were essential, and together Ashley and Henry had both. They also needed men and money. The newspaper advertisement brought the men, and Ashley raised perhaps $30,000 from the St. Louis mercantile firm of Tracy and Wahrendorff to launch their entry into the fur trade.

When their first expedition left St. Louis in the spring of 1822, Henry was in command of the "enterprising young men," including Jedediah Smith and James Bridger, names that have become legendary in the American West. Ashley's role was to provision Henry and his men, but the supplies were lost in the Missouri River while Ashley was transporting them upstream, and Ashley had to return to St. Louis to purchase more goods on credit. The delay took many weeks. When Ashley was ready to leave St. Louis, it was too late in the year to start up the Missouri, and his journey was postponed until the following spring after the ice melted and the river was again navigable.

Henry and his party wintered near the mouth of the Yellowstone River. In the spring of 1823, as Ashley started up the Missouri with supplies, Henry and a few men went to scout the Three Forks area. His worst fears were realized when Blackfeet Indians attacked and killed four trappers. Meantime, to the southeast, Ashley's supply party was attacked by Arikara Indians along the Missouri River. Henry and some of his men soon learned of the attack and went to Ashley's aid, as did other fur traders and soldiers of the U.S. Sixth Infantry stationed at Fort Atkinson near modern Council Bluffs, Iowa. When the Indians retreated, Ashley and Henry made plans to salvage what had been thus far an unprofitable expedition. They decided to concentrate on the Rocky Mountains instead of the Indian-plagued upper Missouri. While Ashley returned to St. Louis, Jedediah Smith took one party of men and moved overland toward the Rockies to search for beaver. Henry took the remaining men and started for Fort Henry to retrieve the rest of his expedition.

Both parties trapped many beaver during the winter of 1823–24 and into the following summer. Back in Missouri, Ashley, unaware of their successes, was defeated as a candidate for governor. Henry probably did not learn of this until the fall of 1824, when he took the accumulated pelts down the Missouri to St. Louis. He also learned there that the fur market had become depressed. The pelts he carried were worth only about $10,000, much less than anticipated, and certainly not enough to pay off the expedition's accumulated debts. For Ashley, the future probably looked very bleak. For Henry, then about fifty, it was the end of his fur-trading days. He retired and lived out the rest of his life in Washington County, Missouri, with his wife and five children. He died there on January 10, 1832.[10]

IT IS DIFFICULT to imagine the vast distances that had to be traversed by the early fur traders unless one tries to duplicate their travels. It is more than two thousand five hundred miles from Three Forks in present-day Montana, where the Missouri River begins, to where the river flows into the Mississippi above St. Louis. The Platte River, draining into the Missouri near modern Omaha, Nebraska, serves as the dividing line between the upper and lower

Missouri. Traders moving up and down the river frequently referred to the Platte as something like a road marker, and newcomers going up the river for the first time received an initiation similar to that of modern travelers crossing the equator for the first time. The bed of the Missouri is composed of an unstable sandy sediment that is always whirling and boiling in the current. This gives the river a muddy appearance that long ago suggested the nickname "Big Muddy."

Modern travelers can go from St. Louis to Three Forks by plane in a matter of hours, but early in the nineteenth century, before the arrival of steamboats, it took months to cover the same distance moving upstream. There were no motels or eating establishments awaiting the traders each night. These men ate, worked, and slept out of doors and often lived off the land until they reached their destinations. Even then these conditions often continued until the men built their trading post or fort, as it was often called. The structure not only served as their shelter and living quarters but provided protection from unfriendly Indians. Most posts were constructed next to streams, which provided drinking water and a means of transportation, and traders sought to locate their forts in areas where wild game was plentiful. In late fall and winter the traders often had to endure each other in the confines of log huts for days and weeks as the snow piled up outside, the temperatures dropped to below zero, and their food supply dwindled. Life was not easy.

In retrospect, the lives of the fur traders and their men seem glamorous, perhaps even romantic, because we admire their stamina and regard them as free of what we consider the restraints of modern life. It is doubtful, however, that Lisa, Ashley, Henry, or other leaders of the early fur trade ever viewed their lives as romantic or glamorous. They were practical men who seem to have been seeking the best of two worlds—the freedom and riches of the West which would enable them to partake of the fruits of the civilized world of the East. They may have enjoyed the scenery and times of fellowship around a roaring fire, but survival probably was uppermost in their minds. Next came profit, a corollary of survival, and profit likely motivated not only the traders but the "enterprising young men" hired by Ashley and Henry. In 1823, for instance, Ashley had to offer instant pay as an incentive to entice a sufficient number of young men to go West. His second series of newspaper advertisements offered a two-hundred-dollar salary *in advance* to any man willing to spend a year in the mountains.

There were, however, reasons other than money for men to come West. Some may have signed up with Ashley and Henry to escape from something or someone, or they may have been in search of something intangible that they hoped to find in the West. More often than not they may have been searching for peace of mind. Certainly not all of the young men who came West found what they were looking for. Many became disillusioned and returned East at the first opportunity, but between 1820 and the late 1830s most of those who did remain in the West beyond the frontier settlements became mountain men, and William Ashley was responsible for creating this legendary profession.

A TRAPPER AND HIS PONY. DRAWING BY FREDERIC REMINGTON.

After Ashley lost the race for governor of Missouri and Andrew Henry retired for good from the fur trade, Ashley put all of his efforts into the trade in hopes that beaver pelts might pay off his debts. He completely abandoned the upper Missouri with its Indian problems and concentrated on the Rocky Mountains. He came up with a plan to cut his investment and overhead by abolishing the trading post system entirely. He also eliminated salaries to all employees except clerks, got trappers to agree to perform any work that was required on the journey to the mountains in exchange for food and

HUNTING ON A BEAVER STREAM, 1840. DRAWING BY FREDERIC REMINGTON.

transportation, and established a commission payment system. Once the men reached the Rockies, they were on their own, free to go where they wanted and to trap where they found beaver. The trappers remained in the mountains, and they agreed to purchase their supplies from Ashley on credit, to turn over half of their accumulated pelts to him and to sell him the remaining pelts at the current market price. Under Ashley's plan the trappers had a high incentive to trap beaver. For Ashley, his costs were far less than before and his profits potentially much greater.

A similar commission system had been used by Donald McKenzie of the North West Company in the Canadian Rockies beginning about 1818. The system remained in use until about 1821, when the North West Company was acquired by Hudson's Bay Company. Ashley probably learned of it through Canadian trappers or perhaps from Andrew Henry, who occasionally had contact with such trappers. Ashley, however, modified the system to his own needs and designated an annual meeting place somewhere in beaver country where the trappers would bring their pelts and obtain supplies to be used for another year of trapping. This annual meeting became known as the "rendezvous."

The first rendezvous was held at Henry's Fork near present-day Burnt-fork, Wyoming, in June 1825. About a hundred and twenty men attended, including twenty-nine deserters from the Hudson's Bay Company, men who may have been eager to participate in Ashley's operation. Ashley received his free pelts and then gave the trappers credit on their remaining pelts at an average of $5.00 for each pelt, or $3.00 per pound. The trappers, in turn, used their credit to obtain supplies from Ashley at "mountain prices" (much higher than in St. Louis)—coffee and sugar, $1.50 per pound; tobacco, $3.00 per pound; fishhooks, $1.50 per dozen; powder, $2.00 per pound; flints, $1.00 per dozen; scissors, $2.00 each; knives, $2.50 each; blue cloth, $5.00 per yard; scarlet cloth, $6.00 per yard; lead, $1.00 per pound; buttons, $1.50 per dozen; and three-point North West blankets, $9.00 each. The trappers could also obtain assortments of trinkets, including beads and ribbons, to use as trade goods with the Indians, plus horseshoes, salt, axes, and hoes.[11]

To reach the rendezvous Ashley went overland, thereby avoiding travel on the Missouri River through hostile Indian country, and he found routes across the plains and prairies of present-day Kansas and Nebraska and through the Rockies. Many of these routes would later be followed by other traders and by emigrants bound for Oregon, California, or the promised land of the Mormons. Ashley's first supply train followed a route in present-day Nebraska along the Platte River to its south fork, up the south fork, up the fork to Cache la Poudre, up that stream to where the north fork of the Platte River begins in what is now northern Colorado. From there the train followed the north fork northward into present-day Wyoming and then west to Pacific Creek and down the Big Sandy to the Green River. Ashley's first supply train consisted of twenty-five men, fifty packhorses, and *a wagon and a team.* Although the wagon was abandoned in heavy snow, probably in what is now far western Nebraska, it was the first wagon to travel over a portion of what would later be called the Oregon Trail and the California Road. It is doubtful that Ashley realized the significance of this attempt to use wheeled vehicles to cross the northern plains and the Rocky Mountains.

When Ashley and his men left the first rendezvous to return to St. Louis, they carried with them about a hundred packs of beaver pelts. A pack weighed about fifty-two pounds and usually contained about thirty-two pelts. The trappers usually placed the choicest furs in the middle of the pack—a choice pelt was called a "plus"—and used lesser pelts to protect the better ones. The packs were carefully prepared and wrapped with the fur side facing inward. Each was then securely tied with rawhide. The hundred packs transported to St. Louis by Ashley were valued at about $48,000, a small fortune in 1825. Although Ashley did have expenses, his financial condition improved considerably.

From all indications the first rendezvous was a mild affair compared with those that followed. Certainly there was celebration, with eating, the telling of stories and playing of games, trading and merriment, but it does not appear to have been a wild and drunken gathering like some subsequent ones. In fact, William Ashley apparently forgot to bring any whiskey to the first rendezvous, and none of the trappers seems to have invited any Indians. Although whiskey was available at the second rendezvous, in 1826, it also seems to have been a rather sober affair in comparison with those of later years. One trapper who attended the 1826 rendezvous was Daniel T. Potts, who wrote in a letter that the trappers "celebrated the 4th of July by firing three rounds of small arms, and partook of a most excellent dinner, after which a number of political toasts were drunk."[12]

By the end of the second rendezvous, Ashley had acquired a hundred and twenty-three packs of beaver pelts valued at $60,000. He then sold his interests to Jedediah Smith, William Sublette, and David Jackson, all three of whom had been recruited for the fur trade by Ashley a few years earlier. Jackson, whose home was in Ste. Genevieve County, Missouri, was the oldest of the three men. Married and the father of four grown children, Jackson was perhaps in his late thirties. Sublette, a native of Kentucky, had moved to St. Charles, Missouri, in 1817 and worked with his father in land speculation, business, and politics. Young Sublette served as a constable for a time, but after his father and mother died, he joined Ashley in 1823 and later accompanied Jedediah Smith's party to the Rocky Mountains after Ashley's battle with the Arikara Indians on the Missouri. The third partner, Jedediah Smith, was a native of Chenango County, New York, and he joined Ashley to make money. Smith was strongly religious, something uncommon among most mountain men and fur traders.

These three men in partnership agreed to pay Ashley $16,000 for his company, with the debt to be paid either in beaver pelts delivered to Ashley in the Rockies during the rendezvous of 1827 or by Ashley transporting the pelts to St. Louis, selling them, and deducting $1.12½ per pelt as his payment. They also contracted with Ashley to provide them with supplies worth not less than $7,000 nor more than $15,000 at the 1827 rendezvous. There is no question that Ashley decided to sell out to divest himself of the high-risk phase of the trade—trapping—and instead move into the more secure and profitable function of supplying goods to the mountain men and marketing their pelts.

When Ashley returned to St. Louis after following a route along the Sweetwater, Platte, and Missouri rivers, he was interviewed by a newspaperman named Charles Keemle, who asked about his overland journey. Keemle later wrote that Ashley's route "lay through a level and open country, better for carriages than any turnpike road in the United States. Wagons and carriages could go with ease as far as General Ashley went, crossing the Rocky Mountains at the sources of the north fork of the Platte; and descending the valley of the Buenaventura [Bear River] towards the Pacific Ocean."[13]

Such newspaper accounts probably convinced many readers that wheeled vehicular travel across the northern plains and prairies and into the Rocky Mountains could be accomplished with the same ease with which wagons were traversing the southern plains over the Santa Fe Trail. But there was little reason for most people to travel across the plains of present-day Kansas and Nebraska in the late 1820s. The region west of the Missouri was still unsettled, and it was still a wilderness in the eyes of most Americans.

The fur company of Smith, Jackson, and Sublette had much success during its first year. Jackson assumed the role of field manager, keeping many trappers busy in the mountains. Sublette took a small party of men and headed north to search for new sources of beaver, and Jedediah Smith took a party of fifteen men and headed south, also in search of beaver. Before Smith returned, he would open an overland route through the Sierra Nevada mountains to California and explore much of the region in between. At the rendezvous of 1828 Ashley received more than seven thousand pounds of beaver pelts, more than a hundred otter skins, and other mountain goods, thereby canceling much of what Smith, Jackson, and Sublette owed him. Ashley extended another $9,000 credit to the partners for the following year's supplies. It appears that the company also contracted to use Ashley's services as a banker and agent.

Sublette, Jackson, and Smith continued to operate what had been Ashley's company through 1829 and into the summer of 1830, when Sublette undertook the task of going East to get supplies for the summer rendezvous. His supply train included ten wagons drawn by five mules each, two Dearborn carriages drawn by one mule each, and twelve head of cattle and one milch cow. Aside from the wagon that Ashley took across part of present-day Nebraska in 1824 and a small cannon mounted on two wheels taken West by Ashley's men through South Pass in 1827, Sublette's wagons were the first to make the long journey over the Rockies.

It appears that many months before the 1830 rendezvous, Smith, Jackson, and Sublette—like Ashley—had decided to retire from the mountains. They, too, had experienced the financial uncertainties of the fur trade. They realized that the number of beaver was declining from overtrapping, and that the American Fur Company was moving into the Rockies from the upper

Missouri. Astor's company would establish three trading posts—Fort Clark, at the Mandan-Hidatsa villages; Fort Cass, in Crow country; and Fort Piegan (later Fort McKenzie) in Blackfeet country, where a treaty with the Piegan band of Blackfeet was being secured by Kenneth McKenzie, who was now associated with Astor's American Fur Company. McKenzie was also building another new trading post, called Fort Union, on the Missouri River near the mouth of the Yellowstone.

McKenzie, a native of Scotland, had come to America in 1816, when he was about twenty. He became an American citizen at St. Louis and soon became a partner in the Columbia Fur Company, a small group composed mostly of Canadians. The company received a license from the U.S. government to trade on the upper Missouri and soon expanded its operations on the Yellowstone and into the Pacific Northwest. McKenzie, shrewd and aggressive, came to dominate the company, and Astor's American Fur Company was unable to crush the new rival. Astor finally bought out Columbia in the summer of 1827 and put McKenzie to work developing the upper Missouri. Meantime, in St. Louis, Astor convinced another rival, Bernard Pratte and Company, to join forces. Pratte had been a partner with Manuel Lisa years earlier. Together the American Fur Company and Pratte's firm sought to outbid all other traders in the buying of beaver pelts. Three years later, in 1830, Astor's American Fur Company decided to build a steamboat to supply its upper Missouri posts and to transport furs and pelts to St. Louis.

These developments combined to convince Smith, Sublette, and Jackson to leave the Rockies. At the rendezvous of 1830 they sold their interests to five of their most experienced trappers—Henry Fraeb, Milton G. Sublette (William's younger brother), James Bridger, Thomas Fitzpatrick, and Jean Baptiste Gervais. These men formed what became known as the Rocky Mountain Fur Company. As for Smith, Sublette, and Jackson, they left the mountains and soon invested some of their profits in the Santa Fe trade. Jedediah Smith was killed by Comanche Indians in what is now far southwestern Kansas on their first wagon-train journey from Missouri to Santa Fe. Jackson left the partnership in Santa Fe and headed for California in hopes of trading for mules, and Sublette began supplying goods to the Rocky Mountain Fur Company.

William Sublette, like Ashley, recognized that there was less financial risk in the supply end of the business. The Rocky Mountain Fur Company, in the meantime, had experienced many problems. While the five partners knew the mountains and the trapping of beaver, they lacked good business sense. No supplies reached them during the rendezvous of 1831, and they found it difficult to dispose of their pelts. They were forced to make an arrangement with William Sublette in order to obtain supplies at the rendezvous of 1832, and that agreement put William Sublette in charge of the Rocky Mountain Fur Company's finances.

The troubled Rocky Mountain Fur Company and Astor's American Fur Company were then the two major American fur companies in the American West. To the north and the west was the Hudson's Bay Company, dominating the trade in Canada and much of the region called Oregon. The British company's policy was to trap the southern and eastern fringe of Oregon country, including portions of present-day California, Utah, Nevada, Idaho, and Montana, areas not then part of the United States. By doing so they hoped to create a "fur desert" that would discourage American traders and trappers from pushing into Oregon.[14]

Sublette delivered supplies to the Rocky Mountain Fur Company at the 1832 rendezvous held at Pierre's Hole, located on the western side of the Teton Range near what is now the Idaho-Wyoming state line. That rendezvous was wilder than those of earlier years, for as many as a thousand traders, trappers, and Indians (who also trapped beaver from time to time) attended. Joseph L. Meek, a Virginian who supposedly became a mountain man to escape a forceful stepmother, attended the 1832 affair. He was a trapper with the Rocky Mountain Fur Company. Meek later recalled that when the traders arrived with their trade goods, including whiskey, "the birds began to sing." Meek remembered:

The fast young men of the mountains outvied each other in all manner of mad pranks. In the beginning of their spree many feats of horsemanship and personal strength were exhibited . . . but horse-racing, fine riding, wrestling, and all the manlier sports, soon degenerated into the baser exhibitions of a "crazy drunk" condition. The vessel in which the trapper received and carried about his supply of alcohol was one of the small camp kettles. "Passing around" this clumsey goblet very freely, it was not long before a goodly number were in the condition just named, and ready for any mad freak whatever. It is reported by several of the mountain men that on the occasion of one of these "frolics," one of their number seized a kettle of alcohol, and poured it over the head of a tall, lank, redheaded fellow, repeating as he did so the baptismal ceremony. No sooner had he concluded than another man with a lighted stick, touched him with the blaze, when in an instant he was enveloped in flames. Luckily some of the company had sense enough to perceive his danger, and began beating him with pack-saddles to put out the blaze. But between the burning and the beating, the unhappy wretch nearly lost his life, and never recovered from the effects of his baptism by fire. Beaver being plenty in camp, business was correspondingly lively, there being a great demand for goods. When this demand was supplied, as it was in the course of about three weeks, the different brigades were set in motion.[15]

The first brigades, or parties, to leave the 1832 rendezvous were those of Milton Sublette, Henry Fraeb, Nathaniel Wyeth, and a few independent trappers. They moved southeast of the main camp some eight miles and camped for the night. The next morning they saw a large line of horsemen approaching from a mountain canyon. Wyeth, using his field glass, saw they were Gros Ventre (Blackfeet) Indians. There were perhaps two hundred of them, dressed in their war paint. As the Indians neared the traders' camp, an Indian chief rode out ahead of the main body. He was unarmed, holding a peace pipe above his head. The traders and trappers, many of them suspecting a ruse, remained on guard in camp, but Antonine Godin, an Iroquois half-breed trapper with Milton Sublette, and a Flathead Indian rode out to see what the chief wanted. As they neared, the chief raised his hand in a token of friendship. In a flash, Godin, whose father had been killed by Blackfeet, shot and killed the chief. Godin seized the chief's scarlet blanket as a trophy and with the Flathead Indian raced back to the traders' camp. A battle began and both sides dug in for the siege. Milton Sublette sent a courier to the main rendezvous camp for help. At first the fighting was at long range and there were few casualties on either side, but as more traders, trappers, and friendly Indians arrived from the main rendezvous camp, the Gros Ventres sent their women and children into the mountains. The warriors dug in behind their breastworks, and the battle became more fierce. Alexander Sinclair was killed and William Sublette was wounded in the shoulder. Five other trappers also died. Both sides held their positions as darkness fell over the valley, but during the night the Gros Ventres fled, taking their wounded with them. When the traders and trappers overran the Indians' fortifications the following morning, they found ten dead Indians and more than thirty dead and wounded horses. The battle of Pierre's Hole was over.[16]

Alexander Sinclair, killed in the battle, and Nathaniel J. Wyeth, who also fought in the battle of Pierre's Hole, had come West in the early 1830s as traders with independent fur companies. Four such companies entered the fur trade around that time, each hoping to profit from beaver. Sinclair and Robert Bean had formed a company in western Arkansas and headed into the Rockies in 1830. They trapped beaver from New Mexico northward into the Green River country. When Bean's leadership failed in a battle with some Pawnee Indians, Sinclair took command, but the company was disbanded after he was killed in the battle at Pierre's Hole. Wyeth, a former Boston iceman, had gained financial backing from some New England businessmen and came West in search of beaver and wealth in 1832. His company even sent a ship loaded with trade goods and supplies around South America and up the West Coast to Oregon. A third independent company was formed at St. Louis by John Gantt and Jefferson Blackwell. They came West in 1831 and began trapping in present-day Wyoming, but the company soon went bankrupt, with many trappers joining the Rocky Mountain Fur Company at the rendezvous of 1832. The largest independent company was headed by B. L. E. Bonneville, who took leave from the Army in 1831, raised the necessary capital in New York City, and assembled an expedition of more than a hundred men. They headed west following the Platte and Sweetwater rivers and then crossed South Pass to reach the Green River country. There Bonneville established a trading post called Fort Bonneville near present-day Daniel, Wyoming.

These small independent fur companies and most of the larger ones experienced financial problems during the early 1830s. It was not uncommon for partnerships to collapse a few months after they were formed, with the interested parties either returning East or forming new partnershps with other traders or trappers. Some trappers also moved from one company to another because of new friendships or better opportunities. Business relationships were very fluid and rivalries between companies became commonplace during the 1830s. About 1831, William Sublette, for example, entered into a partnership with Robert Campbell, an Irishman who had joined Ashley's company in 1825. In addition to supplying goods to the Rocky Mountain Fur Company, Sublette and Campbell decided to compete against Astor's American Fur Company on the upper Missouri. This was quite an undertaking even though the Blackfeet Indians had since become friendly to the fur traders. Sublette and Campbell built a trading post called Fort William near the junction of the Missouri and Yellowstone rivers, but soon after sold their rights to trap on the upper Missouri to Astor's company. With its vast financial resources, the American Fur Company continued to escape the monetary difficulties encountered by most of the other fur companies. In 1833, however, Astor sold his fur-trade holdings west of the Mississippi to Pratte, Chouteau and

Company of St. Louis. Astor, while visiting Europe a few months earlier, had sensed the coming decline of the beaver market. Beaver hats were going out of style. When he returned to New York, he decided to sell out while he could still make a profit.

News of Astor's decision attracted much attention in the West, but for William Sublette other news from the East was of more pressing interest in 1833. Sublette learned that Thomas Fitzpatrick and Milton Sublette, his younger brother, had contracted with Nathaniel J. Wyeth to provide their Rocky Mountain Fur Company with supplies at the 1834 rendezvous. It was an attempt to break William Sublette's control over the company's finances. Wyeth started west from Independence, Missouri, with a supply train bound for the rendezvous on the Green River, but William Sublette and his supply train got there first. Sublette demanded that the company pay its debt to him. When the five partners could not pay, the Rocky Mountain Fur Company was dissolved, with William Sublette taking the beaver pelts that had been accumulated. Wyeth, unable to collect on the goods he brought to the rendezvous, soon built a trading post called Fort Hall in present-day Idaho to dispose of the merchandise to mountain men in the region.

When the Rocky Mountain Fur Company was dissolved during the rendezvous of 1834, Thomas Fitzpatrick, Milton Sublette, and James Bridger formed a new partnership, but their company soon merged with another and became Fontenelle, Fitzpatrick and Company. It also experienced financial difficulties, and at the rendezvous of 1836 was sold to Pratte, Chouteau and Company, Astor's successor. Two years later, by the time the rendezvous of 1838 was held, Pierre Chouteau, Jr., had gained control of Pratte, Chouteau and Company. It became known as Pierre Chouteau, Jr., and Company, but old-timers still referred to it as the American Fur Company. The company then controlled the fur trade on all of the Missouri River and in the Rocky Mountains, but the beaver were nearly gone and the demand had diminished. The last rendezvous was held in 1840. Its location and the locations of earlier rendezvous are as follows:

1840   On the Green River near present-day Daniel, Wyoming.
1839   Same as 1840
1838   On the Wind River near present-day Riverton, Wyoming.
1837   Same as 1840 and 1839.
1836   Same as 1840, 1839, and 1837.

1835   Same as 1840, 1839, 1837, and 1836.

1834   On Ham's Fork on the Green River near present-day Granger, Wyoming.

1833   Same as 1840, 1839, 1837, 1836, and 1835.

1832   Pierre's Hole in the vicinity of present-day Felt and Tetonia, Idaho.

1831   Willow Valley (Cache Valley) near present-day Cove, Utah; a second rendezvous (smaller in size) on the Green River near present-day Daniel, Wyoming.

1830   Same as 1838.

1829   One rendezvous in July on Popo Agie Creek near present-day Lander, Wyoming; a second rendezvous in August at Pierre's Hole in the vicinity of present-day Felt and Tetonia, Idaho.

1828   South end of Bear Lake near present-day Laketown, Utah.

1827   Same as in 1828.

1826   Willow Valley (Cache Valley) near present-day Cove, Utah.

1825   Henry's Fork near present-day Burntfork, Wyoming.

RENDEZVOUS

The last rendezvous, in 1840, was depressing for the mountain men. Robert Newell, an Ohio native who became a trapper in 1829, was in attendance and is supposed to have said to Joseph L. Meek: "Come. We are done with this life in the mountains—done with wading in beaver dams, and freezing or starving alternately—done with Indian trading and Indian fighting. The fur trade is dead in the Rocky Mountains, and it is no place for us now, if ever it was. We are young yet, and have life before us. We cannot waste it here; we cannot or will not return to the States. Let us go down to the Wallamet [Willamette Valley] and take farms . . . What do you say, Meek? Shall we turn American settlers?"[17]

Newell and Meek did settle in Oregon, as did a few others. Details are known of the lives of nearly three hundred of the perhaps six hundred white men who at one time or another followed the vocation of the mountain man between 1825 and 1840. Of those known, at least seventy turned to farming and ranching, another twenty-four became businessmen, twenty-four entered careers tied to the government, while perhaps fifty others moved into a variety of occupations, including teacher, miner, carpenter, Indian agent, interpreter, surveyor, post trader, and guide. Sixty-six known mountain men retired in the mountains and eventually died there. Of two hundred and thirty-three mountain men whose life spans are known, the average age at death was sixty-four years, but many lived into their eighties. One mountain man named Jacques "Old Pino" Fournaise lived to be a hundred and twenty-four years old. Born in Canada in 1747, Fournaise joined some trappers in St. Louis about 1815 and eventually made his way to the Rockies, where he spent much of the next thirty years. Late in 1845, nearing the age of a hundred, he retired and settled in what is now Kansas City, Missouri, where he died on July 15, 1871, while working in his garden. The cause of death was sunstroke.[18]

The era of the fur trader with his mountain men, beaver pelts, and the annual rendezvous was colorful. It was exciting, and today, as we look back, the exploits of the mountain men seem almost romantic, but this legendary figure would not have existed had it not been for the fur trader and a demand in the civilized world for beaver pelts. The mountain man was dependent upon the fur trader, who in turn was dependent upon businessmen in the East and in Europe. Unfortunately the exploits of the mountain men have overshadowed the fur traders and the dozen or more companies—large and small—that operated in the West at one time or another between 1807 and 1840. The legend of the independence of the mountain men has also obscured the fact that the fur trade in the American West was monopolistic, with companies seeking to dominate all the trade in one region or another. Certainly John Jacob Astor's American Fur Company stands out above the rest in this regard and reflects the emergence of capitalism in the American West. Astor's profits from the fur trade along with extensive real estate and business investments in New York City, plus profits made from the War of 1812, made Astor the wealthiest man of his time. Still, a few other fur traders gained wealth, some by taking advantage of other opportunities that existed in the fur trade east of the Rocky Mountains.

IV

TRADERS AND INDIANS

The assumption has always existed that the mountain men were locked into a single exciting job, and that when it ended they were left broken and disoriented. The fact is that the hunting-gathering existence can take many forms. It is . . . an efficient and flexible form of survival. At the same time the trader, whether on the frontier or in the city, is also flexible.

—HOWARD R. LAMAR[1]

EVEN before the demand for beaver pelts began to decline in the early 1830s, some western traders were dealing in buffalo robes. These traders sold a few thousand robes annually during the 1820s for about two dollars each. The robes were used in the East for floor coverings, carriage and sleigh blankets, and a few were made into coats and wraps by manufacturers in Boston, New York, and Montreal. By the late 1830s the popularity of buffalo robes had grown as the supply and demand for beaver pelts dropped. In the year 1839, western traders sold more than 90,000 robes at six dollars each.[2]

Unfortunately the mountain man was not the supplier of buffalo robes. If he had been, his occupation might have survived longer. Mountain men did find scattered bands of buffalo in some areas of the Rocky Mountains, and there are accounts telling how mountain men killed buffalo for meat and for their robes, but most shaggies, as they came to be called, were found east of the Rockies, on the plains. It was there that buffalo roamed in countless numbers, and it was there that the traders acquired the robes from Indians, who killed and skinned the buffalo and tanned the robes, as they had done for years. The traders supplying the increased eastern demand for robes during the 1830s were those who built trading posts and established good relations with the Indians. On the northern plains it was John Jacob

Astor's American Fur Company that captured this business even before the rendezvous system and the beaver trade in the Rockies came to an end.

The American Fur Company dominated the trade in buffalo robes from three principal and nearly two dozen smaller posts along the upper Missouri. The three major posts were Fort Cass on the Yellowstone and Forts Union and McKenzie on the Missouri River. Fort Cass, the first American Fur Company trading post in Crow Indian country, was established in 1832 about three miles below the mouth of the Bighorn River on the east bank of the Yellowstone. It was about a hundred and thirty feet square, made of sapling cottonwood pickets with two bastions at the extreme corners. Fort McKenzie was also constructed in the spring of 1832 about six miles above the mouth of the Marias River on the Missouri. It stood a hundred and twenty yards back from the river and was a hundred and forty feet square with an exceptionally strong gate provided with double doors. Fort Union was located on the bank of the Missouri about five miles above the mouth of the Yellowstone River.

Kenneth McKenzie, who was then associated with Astor, ordered the construction of Fort Union in 1828, and the site was not chosen by accident. McKenzie, in directing his men to find a good location, wrote that they should keep in mind "a union at some convenient point" where the company

A BUFFALO WITH THE PACK. DRAWING BY FREDERIC REMINGTON.

HUNTING BUFFALO

could control the trade of both the rivers and the mountains. The post's name—Fort Union—appears to have come from the wording of McKenzie's orders.[3] It was to this new trading post that an old trapper named Jacob Berger brought a band of Blackfeet Indians in 1831. With Berger's help, McKenzie succeeded in arranging peace with this hitherto hostile people. This opened trade along the upper Missouri, something other traders, beginning with Manuel Lisa, had failed to accomplish. Fort Union became the headquarters for the American Fur Company on the upper Missouri and the firm's most important post.

At this point Astor's American Fur Company, at McKenzie's suggestion,

TRADING POST ON THE PLAINS

decided to experiment with steamboat transportation. McKenzie believed a
steamboat could be used to supply the company's posts on the upper Missouri
and to transport pelts and robes downstream to St. Louis. A small steamboat
called the *Yellowstone* was built at Louisville and delivered to the American
Fur Company in early April 1831. The boat left St. Louis about two weeks
later loaded with supplies and bound for Fort Tecumseh, an American Fur
Company post located at present-day Pierre, South Dakota. The steamboat
returned to St. Louis by mid-July with a full cargo of buffalo robes, furs, and
ten thousand pounds of smoked buffalo tongues packed in salt. Convinced
that steamboats could save both time and money, company officials judged

TRADING SKINS

the experiment a success. The following year the *Yellowstone* made a trip farther up the Missouri to Fort Union and then returned safely to St. Louis.[4]

While most of the advantages of using a steamboat were anticipated by
the traders, one was not: The *Yellowstone* made an unexpected impression
on the Indians. In fact, the *Missouri Republican* noted: "Many of the Indians
who had been in the habit of trading with the Hudson Bay Company, declared
that the company could no longer compete with the Americans, and concluded thereafter to bring all of their skins [buffalo robes and other pelts]
to the latter; and said that the British might turn out their dogs and burn
their sledges, as they would no longer be useful while the *Fire Boat* walked
on the waters."[5]

No other post on the upper Missouri could compare with Fort Union.
The impressive structure was two hundred forty by two hundred twenty feet,
the shorter side facing the Missouri River. A fence of square hewn pickets

about a foot thick and twenty feet high surrounded the post. Bastions or fortifications were located at the southwest and northeast corners. Each bastion was a two-story building constructed of stone, twenty-four by twenty-five feet and thirty feet high, with pyramidal roofs. At the entrance to the post was a large and very secure gate. Opposite the gate, on the far side of the compound, was a well-built two-story house where Kenneth McKenzie resided when at the post. It had glass windows, a fireplace, and other modern conveniences of circa 1830. Around the compound were the barracks for the employees, stone houses, workshops, stables, a cut-stone powder magazine that could hold fifty thousand pounds of gunpowder, and a reception room where Indians came to trade. In the center of the compound was a tall flagpole around which the half-breeds who worked for the company would pitch their tents. Aside from the stone buildings, all other structures were built of cottonwood lumber cut from trees found near the post. Everything was unusually elaborate, and the post—like most others—was self-sufficient. There were cattle and hogs to supply the larder, and corn and vegetables were raised in a garden during the summer months. The company employed a large number of blacksmiths, carpenters, coopers, shoemakers, and other craftsmen. By the mid-1830s the company, then under the ownership of Pierre Chouteau, Jr., maintained twenty-three small posts in the region. Fort Cass, however, was abandoned in 1835, and aside from Fort McKenzie, used as late as 1843, most of the remaining posts owned by the American Fur Company under Chouteau were nothing more than log huts, quickly built and often left unmanned.[6]

While the demand for buffalo robes rose during the late 1830s, the market did not increase substantially until about 1842, when the American Fur Company under Chouteau's leadership undertook a campaign to make Americans buffalo-robe-conscious. It included advertising, the placement of articles in magazines, and inducing merchants to carry buffalo robes in their shops. The company succeeded in making buffalo robes, meat, pemmican, and tongues a curiosity from St. Louis east. The buffalo, really a bison, came to symbolize the American West, that vast unsettled region that seemed so mysterious to most Easterners. Buffalo robes became trophies of the West, conversation pieces, especially when they were used as rugs or made into coats, wraps, and blankets. Yet during cold winters in the northeastern United States they provided much warmth for the users. Buffalo tongues, while also symbolic of the West, were delicacies and were enjoyed by many patrons of the finer restaurants in New York City, Boston, and Washington, D.C. The tongues, like the robes, were acquired from the

Indians, smoked, and then packed in salt and transported down the Missouri to St. Louis, where they were marketed. There are numerous accounts of Indians killing buffalo for their tongues alone, especially during the summer months, when the buffalo's "robe" is poor. When artist George Catlin traveled up the Missouri and stopped at Fort Tecumseh (the post was renamed Fort Pierre for Pierre Chouteau, Jr., when a new structure was built near the old post soon after Catlin's arrival in 1832), he learned that only a few days earlier perhaps six hundred Sioux Indians had gone buffalo hunting and returned with 1,400 buffalo tongues, for which the traders gave them a few gallons of whiskey.[7]

Chouteau also succeeded in increasing the buffalo-robe market in England, but he failed to get German furriers to use buffalo robes for military coats and covers. German furriers continued to use sheepskin because it was less costly.

Though buffalo tongues could be obtained at any time of the year, good buffalo robes could not. The buffalo carried a good coat only between November and March, the winter months when Nature gives the animal a full and thick covering as protection from snow and bitter-cold temperatures, and then only buffalo cows and young bulls provided really good robes. The hair on the hindquarters of buffalo bulls more than three years of age is only as long as that of a horse. The cow's robe and that of young bulls is uniformly the same thickness in the winter. After a buffalo was killed for its robe, Indians expended much time and labor in preparing and dressing the hide properly. Indian women did most of the work, and an Indian family could

SMOKING TONGUES

produce only a limited number of robes each year. John B. Sanford of the American Fur Company wrote: "It is seldom that a lodge trades more than twenty skins a year."[8]

To prepare a buffalo robe, most tribes on the northern plains fastened the edges of a raw or green hide to pole frames, using rawhide thongs, much like an old-fashioned quilting frame made of four stout poles tied together at right angles. On the southern plains it was not uncommon for Cheyenne women to stake the edges of a skin to the earth with the robe's hair resting on thick grass. Regardless of how the robe was stretched out, all of the tribes generally scraped the hide clean of the last pieces of flesh. They then sprinkled the hide with water and smeared it with buffalo brains and grease. After the hide dried in the sun, the Indian women would rub it with a sinew cord until it was soft and pliable. This often took several days. The final quality of any robe was determined by how good the hide was to begin with and how much effort went into working it.[9]

Perhaps a fourth of the robes taken by Indians were traded. The remainder were used by the Indians themselves. In trade, a skin brought three or four pounds of sugar, or two gallons of shelled corn, or two pounds of coffee. On the upper Missouri each robe cost the trader less than a dollar, but transportation charges to St. Louis were high, and an average robe sold for little more than its total costs to the American Fur Company. The key to making a profit was to buy and sell in volume.

BUFFALO SKINS

Thousands of buffalo robes were traded at Fort Union during the early 1830s, when Kenneth McKenzie ruled the post and the upper Missouri like a king. At first, McKenzie does not appear to have been alarmed when William Sublette and Robert Campbell organized a company to compete against him and the American Fur Company in 1832, but after Sublette and Campbell began to capture some of the trade by offering the Indians whiskey in trade for robes, McKenzie became concerned. Using whiskey in the Indian trade was a violation of federal law, but Sublette and Campbell ignored the law and smuggled it up the Missouri. To meet the competition, McKenzie purchased a still and had it shipped by steamboat to Fort Union, where he made whiskey from corn raised by the Mandan Indians. From what is known, American Fur Company officials in the East approved of the still. Soon after it was placed in operation, Nathaniel Wyeth visited Fort Union and may have sampled the product. When he returned downstream and told authorities at Fort Leavenworth of the still's existence, they told other officials in Washington, and lawmakers there soon threatened to eject Astor's American Fur Company from the upper Missouri. Astor's powerful lobby, however, saw to it that the company did not lose its trading license. Instead, McKenzie was sacrificed by the company and forced to retire from the fur trade in 1834. He traveled to Europe and then settled in St. Louis. Later he became a wholesale grocer and an importer of fine wines and liquors, amassing a fortune before his death in St. Louis in 1861.

The same year McKenzie retired from the fur trade, Astor sold his American Fur Company operation on the Missouri to Pratte, Chouteau and Company of St. Louis. To make peace on the upper Missouri, the new owners bought out Sublette and Campbell's competing company and reestablished their monopoly in the Indian trade along the upper Missouri. They maintained the monopoly until 1841, when John A. N. Ebbetts, a native of New York and inexperienced in the fur trade, received backing in St. Louis from capitalists who disliked the American Fur Company. Ebbetts and twenty-nine men received a trading license and traveled up the Missouri. Using whiskey in trade, Ebbetts and his men had good success, but Ebbetts lacked sufficient capital to charter steamboats to carry robes and furs down the Missouri to St. Louis. Instead he either purchased or built mackinaw boats upstream and floated his robes and furs down the river. The mackinaw, or *mackinaw bateau*, was scow-shaped, about forty feet long and ten feet wide. It was controlled by a steersman and four oarsmen. The oarsmen usually sat in the bow or in groups fore and aft. The cargo of robes and furs was tightly packed, covered by a lodge skin fastened over a wooden frame. The cargo was carried in the center of the mackinaw, a boat designed to draw only fifteen to twenty inches of water, even when loaded with ten tons of robes, furs, and supplies.

Ebbetts not only succeeded in competing against the American Fur Company, then controlled by Pierre Chouteau, Jr., but obtained more capital in the East and began using steamboats and constructing trading posts on the upper Missouri. One was Fort Mortimer, located near the mouth of the Yellowstone River. Another was Fort George, situated about twenty miles below Fort Pierre. By then Chouteau and the American Fur Company were fighting back. They undersold Ebbetts, who learned firsthand the cutthroat character of the fur trade. Ebbetts's apparent inexperience helped Chouteau's American Fur Company, and after three years of losing business, the Union Fur Company (Ebbetts's firm) sold out in 1845 to American Fur.[10] Other traders also sought to compete against the American Fur Company, but in each instance American Fur won out and dominated the Indian trade on the northern plains and along the upper Missouri.

A MONOPOLY of Indian trade on the southern plains seems to have been the goal of Charles Bent and Ceran St. Vrain. Charles Bent, whose father had been a prominent St. Louis judge, worked for Joshua Pilcher and the Missouri Fur Company before that firm went out of business. It was then that Bent, in his twenties, entered the Santa Fe trade. He was soon joined by a younger brother, William. Ceran St. Vrain, born in Missouri, had been a clerk for Bernard Pratte and Company in St. Louis before entering the Santa Fe trade about 1824, a few years before the Bents. By 1830 Charles Bent and Ceran St. Vrain had joined forces in an effort to make a larger profit in Santa Fe. By then Missouri merchandise was plentiful in Santa Fe, but money was scarce. Traders arriving from Missouri were forced to sell their goods for what they could get and then return home. Bent and St. Brain concluded that if they had an office in Santa Fe where they could store their merchandise until demand increased in the fall, they could make a better profit. Under this plan Charles Bent made the buying trips to Missouri while St. Vrain remained in Santa Fe to sell the goods. The plan worked well, and soon they opened a store on the south side of the main plaza opposite the Palace of the Governors and another store in Taos about seventy miles to the north. Their business prospered, first as the firm of Bent and St. Vrain and later, after William Bent entered the partnership, as Bent, St. Vrain and Company. The company then expanded its operations onto the southern plains, a move that would make it the largest and strongest merchandising and fur-trading firm in the Southwest during the mid-nineteenth century.

Charles Bent's younger brother, William, played a significant role in helping the firm capture some of the Indian trade. About 1830, he was operating a trading camp somewhere between present-day Canon City and Pueblo, Colorado. A party of Cheyenne warriors stopped at the camp one day and inspected the trade goods, and then most of them left. But two Cheyennes lingered and were still in the camp when Bent saw a party of Comanches approaching. The Cheyennes and Comanches were enemies, and William Bent quickly hid the two Cheyennes before the Comanches arrived. the Comanches, however, saw the Cheyenne moccasin prints in the earth and demanded to know where their enemies were. Bent lied and said all of the Cheyennes had left his camp. The Comanches departed, apparently to find the Cheyennes. Because William Bent had thus saved the lives of two Cheyenne warriors, a close relationship was established between the Bents and the Cheyennes.[11] (It became even closer in the late 1830s after William Bent married Owl Woman, daughter of a Cheyenne medicine man named Gray Thunder.)

By 1831 William Bent had convinced his brother Charles and Ceran St. Vrain that there was much money to be made in the Indian trade along the Arkansas River, then the international boundary between the United States and Mexico. The river, a major waterway through the southern plains, begins in central Colorado and flows south for about sixty miles along the Sawatch Mountains before turning toward the east near present-day Salida, Colorado. From there the river, over many centuries, has cut a deep trench through the front range of the Rockies. That trench is called the Royal Gorge. As the stream comes out of the gorge, it enters the plains near modern Pueblo, Colorado, and flows in an eastwardly direction across southeastern Colorado and more than half of Kansas before turning south into present-day Oklahoma. From there it flows southeast through Oklahoma and Arkansas until it empties into the Mississippi. Although the river was too shallow for steamboats, the Bents and St. Vrain decided to build a trading post on the U.S. side of the river in a large grove of tall cottonwood trees known as the Big Timbers, about twenty-five miles east of where the Purgatory River flows into the Arkansas. The site was west of present-day Lamar, Colorado. William Bent had the task of supervising the post's construction.

As the firm's Indian trade began to grow, it attracted the attention of John Gantt and Jefferson Blackwell, who built a trading post called Fort Cass, also on the Arkansas River but closer to the Rockies. It was located on the site of modern Pueblo, Colorado, about ninety miles west of the post built by William Bent. To meet the competition, the Bents and St. Vrain moved toward the Rockies themselves and built a new post, called Fort William, about three miles east of Fort Cass. In an apparent effort to show up the rather crude trading post constructed by the Bents and St. Vrain, Gantt and Blackwell hired some Mexicans in the spring of 1833 to build a larger and more impressive post of adobe about six miles below the mouth of Fountain Creek on the Arkansas River east of Fort Cass.

Competition between the two groups became intense as each sought to control the Indian trade. So as not to be outdone, the Bents and St. Vrain made what might be considered a bold move. They moved their business east on the Arkansas River to a spot that may have been suggested by an old Cheyenne Indian. Near the location of present-day La Junta, Colorado, they began construction of a large castlelike trading post of adobe on the north bank of the Arkansas. William Bent brought crews of men from New Mexico to make the adobe using raw wool as a binder, and these men built Fort William, as the post was officially known. However, smallpox swept through the Mexican workers and delayed construction. Soon after the epidemic subsided, the Bents and St. Vrain sent a wagon train out of Santa Fe toward Missouri, but because the train carried supplies for Fort William, the wagons followed a different route. The caravan went from Santa Fe to Taos and then over Raton Pass to the Arkansas River and then east to Fort William. Their journey opened to wagons what became known as the mountain branch of the Santa Fe Trail. Although longer than the Cimarron route, it was better watered, and therefore safer. The eleven wagons in the caravan appear to have been the first to traverse Raton Pass. After dropping off supplies at Fort William and then loading whatever pelts and robes had been taken in trade with the Indians, the wagon train continued east to Missouri.

Bent's Fort, as most people came to call Fort William, probably was completed early in 1835. It was indeed impressive and put to shame Gantt and Blackwell's trading post many miles to the west. Bent's Fort was not quite as large as Fort Union on the upper Missouri, but its location on the open plains gave it a massive appearance. The post probably was about a hundred eighty by a hundred thirty-five feet in size, but unlike Fort Union's large picket fence, the walls of Bent's Fort were constructed of thick adobe blocks. There were two bastions, one located at the southeast corner, the other at the northwest corner of the structure. Inside each bastion at the second-floor level hung sabers, heavy lances with long, sharp blades, pistols, and flintlock muskets. These were to be used should attackers attempt to

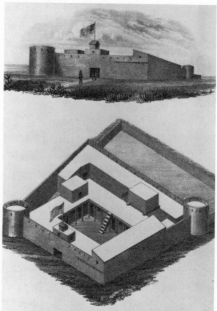

LEFT: WILLIAM BENT, WHO HELPED HIS OLDER BROTHER CHARLES
capture the Indian trade on the southern plains in the 1830s. RIGHT: Bent's Fort,
constructed during the early 1830s near present-day La Junta, Colorado.

take the fort by using ladders on the outside walls. Over the main gate on
the east side was a watchtower room, on top of which was a belfry and a
flagpole that flew the American flag. The watchtower was a single room
containing a chair and a bed. Windows were on all four sides, and on a
pivot in the center was a long telescope. If the man on duty in the watchtower
noticed anything unusual outside, he would give the alarm and signal the
herder outside the post to bring in the horses. The horses were never turned
loose to graze unguarded. The belfry above the watchtower contained a large
bell, which was used to sound alarms and to signal the hours of meals.
Inside the post's adobe walls at ground level were the stores, warehouses,
and living quarters. They ranged around the walls and opened into a large
patio. On the west side of the post, opposite the main entrance, was another
gate; this opened into a corral that was actually outside the main walls of
the post. The corral, however, had adobe walls of its own that were eight
feet high. The corral gate leading to the outside was constructed of metal
plate.

On the west side of the post's second level a large room served as a billiard room, the table having been transported from Missouri with the other necessary game supplies. A bar was built along one end of the room. About two hundred yards southwest of the post near the Arkansas River stood an icehouse, also built of adobe. In the winter when the river was frozen the building was filled with large squares of ice chopped from the stream. When summer arrived, fresh meat was kept cool in the icehouse, which also provided an ample supply of ice for cold drinks.[12]

By 1835, the year Bent's Fort was completed, the Bents and St. Vrain were attracting much of the Indian trade in the region. It appears that they had anticipated the declining beaver market and sought to adjust to the growing demand for buffalo robes. Gantt and Blackwell, however, had sought both the Indian and the mountain trade. When the Bents and St. Vrain captured the Indian trade and the mountain trade began to collapse, their business failed. Gantt and Blackwell had been forced out of business by the end of 1835. For a time it appeared that the Bents and St. Vrain had no competition in the region, but by 1837 three new trading posts had been built on the South Platte River about a ten-day journey northwest of Bent's Fort. The posts were Fort Lupton (sometimes called Fort Lancaster), built by Lancaster P. Lupton, a soldier turned trader; Fort Vasquez, built by Louis Vasquez and Andrew Sublette; and Fort Jackson, built by Peter A. Sarpy and Henry Fraeb, agents of Pratte, Chouteau and Company of St. Louis. The Bents and St. Vrain met the new competition by building a fourth trading post on the South Platte called Fort Lookout, later called Fort St. Vrain, and in 1838 they bought out Fort Jackson, the major competition on the South Platte, from Pratte, Chouteau and Company.

When William Bent arrived to take over Fort Jackson on October 3, 1838, he and his men took inventory. The record of that inventory gives us some idea of what was found in a small western trading post in the late 1830s. The inventory:

Livestock: one yoke of oxen, one heifer, six horses, six mules, and one mare lame with the foot evil.

Housekeeping items: a dozen pans, four sheet-iron kettles, eleven iron spoons, six table forks, six pewter plates, one coffeepot, and one pair of damaged candle snuffers.

Tools: a grindstone, blacksmith tongs, carpentry and farming implements.

Trade goods: blue and scarlet chiefs' coats, gilt coat buttons, ornamental brass tacks, pans, knives, lead, powder, cloth, blankets, a bale of tobacco, great heaps of beads, 380 pair of earbobs, 350 clay pipes, awls, combs, and 300 sewing needles, 200 trout fishhooks, a dozen fox tails.[13]

Since Fort Jackson was only ten miles south of Fort Lookout, William Bent did not want other traders to occupy the structure. After removing everything that was inside, he had the post destroyed.

THE BENTS and St. Vrain accumulated much wealth as traders. Just how much is not known, but Captain Lemuel Ford, who visited Bent's Fort in 1835, offered an insight into how they became wealthy: Ford noted that they would buy a buffalo robe for about twenty-five cents' worth of trade goods and later sell the robe in St.Louis for five or six dollars—in short, they bought low and sold high. There also is no question that much of their wealth came from buffalo robes. On June 12, 1840, the *Daily Missouri Republican* reported that the Bents and St. Vrain "had bought upwards of 15,000 buffalo skins" during the season just past. If they sold those robes for six dollars each, they earned $90,000. On May 19, 1842, the same newspaper reported that the annual caravan of the Bents and St. Vrain had arrived in Missouri "bringing 283 packs of robes, 30 packs of beaver, 12 sacks of [buffalo] tongues, and 1 pack of deer skins."

In addition to their Indian trade from Bent's Fort, the firm also had income from trading in Santa Fe, Taos, Chihuahua, and to the north on the South Platte. In 1843 their annual caravan east consisted of fourteen loaded wagons plus a drove of cattle raised near Bent's Fort. The cattle were being driven to Charles Bent's farm in Missouri. Ceran St. Vrain caught up with that caravan near Walnut Creek in present-day Kansas with five additional wagons loaded with robes. St. Vrain had tried to transport the robes by boat down the Arkansas, an experiment that did not work because the river was not deep enough. St. Vrain had had to send for wagons from Bent's Fort to transport the robes overland.

St. Vrain's attempt to use water transportation may, in part, have been a diversion to break up the routine of annual caravan travel to Missouri. By the early 1840s life at Bent's Fort and the general routine of trading had become fairly predictable. This was especially true of the annual trip east.

The caravan bound for Missouri usually left Bent's Fort in late April or early May. Details of the caravan's operation were gathered late in the last century by George Bird Grinnell, editor, author, and authority on the American Indian. Grinnell talked to many men who had participated in the caravan or had personal knowledge of how it functioned. He wrote that the caravan usually started east about the time the Cheyennes and other Indian tribes on the southern plains set out on their summer buffalo hunts. Grinnell observed that William Bent or one of the other partners always served as wagon master on the five-hundred-and-thirty-mile journey to Westport, Missouri, now Kansas City. The heavy wagons, each drawn by six yoke of oxen (sometimes by oxen and mules), were stacked high with bales of buffalo robes. A few of the teamsters were Delaware or Shawnee Indians, but the rest were white. Kept close to the wagons were herds of horses and mules being taken to Missouri to be sold. Many of these animals had been traded from the Indians.

Grinnell wrote that travel was slow, between twelve and fifteen miles a day, and that the caravan often was held in camp by streams swollen by spring rains. The traders had regular campsites along the route, which was the Santa Fe Trail. Once the wagon train arrived at a campsite the wagons were corraled, the oxen freed from the yokes and driven off to the best grass available. Night herders watched the animals until morning. The horses and mules were usually taken in another direction to graze and were held by men hired to guard them each night. During the day these night herders and guards slept in the moving wagons. Within the corral of wagons, fires were built and the mess cooks prepared a simple meal of bread, baked earlier in the day, and coffee. Before dawn the herds were driven into the corral of wagons, the oxen yoked up, blankets rolled and tied and thrown into the wagons. Before the sun appeared on the eastern horizon, the train was in motion.

The caravan usually halted for noon—this was called "nooning"—about ten or eleven o'clock in the morning. The time often depended upon the weather and how far the wagon master wanted to take the train that day. If the day was hot and the next good campsite was only ten or twelve miles away, the noon halt might last until the middle of the afternoon. Again the wagons were corraled and the animals turned out. The men had a light meal, which was called "breakfast," and then rested in the shade of the wagons or trees, if any were to be found at the campsite. Sometimes the men carried out chores and repaired their gear. Just before the breaking of camp in the afternoon, the principal meal of the day was served. This was called "dinner," and it included cooked meat and fresh-baked pan or skillet bread. Grinnell wrote that enough bread was made to supply the men in the evening and early the following day. The meat was brought into camp by two hunters. Each morning they set out ahead of the wagon train to hunt for game. They often killed a buffalo or an antelope, skinned and butchered the animal where it fell, and then carried the meat on a packhorse to where the caravan planned to stop at noon. When they found no game, as was sometimes the case, everyone had to eat dried meat, of which the train carried a good supply.

At each meal, according to Grinnell, the men were organized into messes. The Bents, sometimes more than one, or St. Vrain, members of the traders' families, and any guests traveling with the train messed together. The teamsters and Mexicans also ate together, but the Delawares and Shawnees, by preference, formed a separate mess of their own. Each man had his own quart cup and tin plate and carried his own hunting knife in a sheath. No one had forks or spoons. Each man marked his cup and plate, usually by scratching his initials or mark on them. The men of each mess chose a cook from among their own number, and after each meal every man washed his own cup and plate. The food, though simple, was wholesome and abundant. Meat was the staple, but they also had bread and plenty of coffee, and occasionally boiled dried apples and rice. Usually there was brown sugar, though sometimes they had to depend on the old-fashioned "long sweetening"; that is, according to Grinnell, "New Orleans molasses, which was brought out to the fort in hogsheads for trade with the Indians."

The wagon master was the caravan's "absolute governing head," wrote Grinnell. He fixed the length of the march, the time for starting and for halting. If a difficult stream was to be crossed, he rode ahead of the train to examine the ground, and then directed the crossing of the teams, not leaving the spot until the last wagon was safely to the other side. Besides looking after a multitude of details, such as shoeing the oxen, greasing the wagons, which was done every two or three days, and inspecting the animals, yokes, and harness, the wagon master issued rations to the men. He was "the fountain of all authority," according to Grinnell. If one of the teamsters became sick or was disabled, the wagon master himself often drove the lead team.

On reaching Westport, Missouri, the bales of robes were unloaded on the levee along the Missouri River, and the train then pulled out into the country and went into camp. This was necessary, according to Grinnell, because grass and water were scarce in the settlement. The usual camping

WESTPORT LANDING, NOW PART OF KANSAS CITY, MISSOURI.
In the distance, left of center, is the settlement of Westport. The view is west-southwest, with the Missouri River on the right.

KANSAS CITY, MISSOURI, ABOUT 1852.
The steamboat is moving downstream toward St. Louis. Lithograph from *United States Illustrated*.

ground for wagon trains waiting over at Westport was about six miles southwest of the settlement in what is now Johnson County, Kansas. About two
miles south of Westport, on the Santa Fe Trail, was a saloon and dance hall
called the Last Chance, where the teamsters belonging to the passing trains
and to the trains that were waiting in camp for loads did their drinking and
dancing. Grinnell noted that this "typical frontier amusement resort was
outside the town limits [actually across the western border of Missouri in
what was then considered Indian territory] and the local officials had no
authority either to close or to regulate the place."

While the wagon train waited in camp and the teamsters enjoyed the
offerings of Westport, the trader in charge, normally William Bent, went
down to St. Louis by steamboat with the buffalo robes. He usually sold them
to Robert Campbell, the same man who had been a partner earlier with
William Sublette in the Rockies and on the upper Missouri. Campbell was
a lifelong friend of William Bent and his brothers. After selling the robes,
Bent laid in the stock of trade goods and supplies required for Bent's Fort
and their other posts. Much of this stock was purchased from Robert Campbell. The bales, bags, and cases were then loaded aboard a steamboat and
Bent returned to Westport. There his wagon train was brought to the levee,
the wagons were loaded with the goods, and the train pulled out. A brief
halt was usually made at the Last Chance saloon, and then the wagons moved
out on their long return journey to Bent's Fort.[14]

The round trip between Bent's Fort and Missouri took about five months,
sometimes longer. When the wagons returned to the post, the oxen were
turned out into the post herd that grazed nearby. The wagons were parked
along the corral wall, and the yokes and chains for each bull were carried
into the fort and piled up in a shady place. The keys for the bows were tied
to the yokes and the chains lay close by. The traders made certain the oxbows
were secure because the Indians coveted the seasoned hickory wood out of
which they were made. If an Indian did acquire an oxbow, wrote George
Grinnell, he would steam and straighten it and from the wood make a strong
bow.

Between April and late September or early October, while the annual
caravan had gone east, few people remained at Bent's Fort. These were slack
trading months at the post. There were the clerks, a trader or two, and a
few laborers and herders. Indians frequently visited the post during the
summer as they traversed the southern plains in search of buffalo. They
usually stopped for arms, ammunition, and trade goods. Occasionally, especially in later years, other travelers would stop for a day or two. The

trading post closed early during the summer months, and it was not uncommon for the trader in charge to refuse to admit anyone after dark. Most Indians did not have the freedom to roam the post at will, but during the daylight hours the Cheyennes had free access. They understood they were not to touch anything. This reflected the special relationship between the Cheyennes and the Bents and St. Vrain.

During the winter months Bent's Fort had a large population. All of the employees were there except those traders, teamsters, and laborers who were away visiting and trading in Indian camps. The traders were busy acquiring buffalo robes. For the men at the post, there was very little to do. Many spent their time playing games or hunting on the plains nearby. During the late 1830s, when the Bents and St. Vrain probably had trappers seeking beaver in the mountains, it was not uncommon for these mountain men to come to the fort, often with their Indian wives and children. They would purchase supplies and outfit themselves for their spring trapping. All visitors were welcome at the fort, and they could stay as long as they wished.

There were other amusements for people at Bent's Fort. In addition to the games and hunting, dances were often held during the winter months, with "the moccasined trappers, merry-faced, laughing Indian women in the rough and hearty dances of the frontier," according to Grinnell. He noted that on holidays "such as Christmas and the Fourth of July, balls were often held at the fort, in which the travelers present, the trappers, employees, Indians, Indian women and Mexican women all took part. Before each Fourth of July, a party of men were sent into the Rockies to gather wild mint for mint juleps. For mixing the drinks ice was brought from the ice house where it had been stored since winter."[15]

BY THE EARLY 1840s the Bents and St. Vrain pretty much had a monopoly on the Indian trade from the South Platte southward into what is now the Texas panhandle. It was a vast empire. After Charles Bent arranged a peace treaty with the Comanche and Kiowa Indians in 1840, the three established a trading post on the north bank of the Canadian River about two hundred miles southeast of Bent's Fort on the Arkansas. The first post was built of logs, but about 1846 a new one of adobe was constructed. It was much smaller than Bent's Fort on the Arkansas and not as elaborate, but it served its purpose. Adobe Fort, as it was called, was about eighty feet square with walls that were nine feet high. This post remained in use until about 1849, and during its years of operation perhaps six thousand Comanche and more than a thousand Kiowa Indians traded there. But by 1849 it could not be operated because of Indian troubles. The West was changing. The empire of the Bents and St. Vrain was collapsing, and there had been tragedy. George Bent, a younger brother of Charles and William, died of what is described only as the "fever" at Bent's Fort in the fall of 1847. He was thirty-three years old. Another younger brother, Robert, was killed at the age of twenty-five by Comanche Indians while accompanying a wagon train along the Arkansas River in 1841. Charles Bent, the oldest of the brothers, was killed at Taos early in 1847 during an Indian revolt. By 1849, only William Bent, then about forty, and Ceran St. Vrain, forty-seven, survived, and the changes in the Southwest and on the southern plains had severely affected their trading empire.

While the Bents and St. Vrain probably sensed the coming changes on the southern plains, they were not in a position to affect them. The changes were vast and began in earnest in 1846, a year that is often referred to as a "year of decision" in the history of the United States. After more than two decades of neglect, the vast region of the West took on new importance. The government and the people were pulled together by a desire to expand the boundaries of the nation westward to the Pacific. The United States declared war on the Republic of Mexico in May 1846, because of a boundary dispute and Mexico's failure to pay American claims. At the same time the government wished to acquire the northern Mexican provinces. The Mexican War that followed, the resulting annexation of Texas, the acquisition of Oregon, and the purchase of California and the Southwest from a defeated Mexico reflected the sweeping nationalism of the 1840s that is often labeled as "manifest destiny."

This catchall phrase meant different things to different people. For some it meant that U.S. citizens had a natural right to occupy all of the land between the Atlantic and the Pacific. Many Americans believed it was predestination and simply an extension of the freedoms enjoyed in a nation that was only seventy years old. Others accepted their government's actions as testimony that God had granted the United States title to the vast region west and southwest of the Louisiana Purchase. There were those who believed that God intended the vast expanse of plains and prairies to be used by farmers instead of nomadic Indians who followed the buffalo. Still others believed it was land from which to make a profit, and nothing more. Some even viewed the expansionism in a more altruistic sense, believing that the land was needed to improve the lives of others, something Frederick Merk described as the true foundation of American national character, but which other historians have rejected as too theoretical.[16]

Regardless, western traders, including the mountain men, were greatly responsible for the new attention given the West. Their unheralded explorations and trading activities, especially during the 1830s, had by the 1840s finally spurred the imaginations of many Easterners. The individualism of the traders came to be admired in the East. When successful traders came East on business, it probably appeared that any man who went West and worked hard could become wealthy. Of course, this was not always the case, but as the United States expanded its borders after 1846, the West gained even more appeal. It was this individualism, as historian Frederick Jackson Turner wrote, that promoted democracy from the beginning. Turner argued that American intellect owes its striking characteristics to the frontier experience. Those characteristics, he wrote, included "coarseness and strength combined with acuteness and inquisitiveness; that practical, inventive, turn of mind, quick to find expedients; that masterful grasp of material things, lacking in the artistic but powerful to effect great ends; that restless, nervous energy."[17]

These were the characteristics of the successful western traders, including the Bents and St. Vrain. For William Bent and Ceran St. Vrain, however, these characteristics were not strong enough to maintain the status quo. The American military presence in the Southwest engendered hostility among many Indians, who renewed their attacks against white men. William Bent found it impossible to carry on trade at his Adobe Fort along the Canadian River, and trade at Bent's Fort slowed. Learning that the military was thinking seriously of establishing a network of forts to use as bases for subduing the Indians, William Bent offered to sell Bent's Fort for a reported $15,000. When the government in Washington offered him only $12,000, he became angry. According to tradition, he was so infuriated that he set Bent's Fort afire and abandoned the post on August 21, 1848. By then he had already moved his home to Big Timbers, many miles to the east, and the firm's business seems to have been centered at Fort St. Vrain (formerly Fort Lookout) on the South Platte River. Whether or not William Bent and Ceran St. Vrain welcomed the changes is unknown, but in all likelihood they did welcome the coming of the American social and economic system of the East, for this would have meant new opportunities to make a profit.

V

WHEN THE EMIGRANTS STARTED WEST

The lure of the West did not affect all easterners in the same way.
Perhaps many desired to take advantages of frontier opportunity, but
few were able to do so; every individual's migration depended on three
ingredients: proximity, skill in pioneering techniques, and capital.

—RAY ALLEN BILLINGTON[1]

PERHAPS it was only natural that missionaries followed American traders into the West. Taking the gospel to the uninformed was a pattern first established in the Western Hemisphere by the Spaniards as they conquered New Spain. Franciscan padres sought to impose the discipline of Christianity and mission life on Indians in an effort to control potential opposition. The Franciscans failed in what is now Texas, but enjoyed moderate success in California until the Mexican Revolution. To the east, Jesuits next tried to establish missions among the Potawatomi Indians in present-day Iowa and the Miamis, Kickapoos, and Potawatomis in what is now Kansas. They failed except among the Kansas Potawatomis.

Until the early 1830s Protestant missionaries paid little attention to the American West, but during the summer of 1831 three Nez Perces and one Flathead Indian came east to St. Louis from their homes west of the Continental Divide beyond the Bitterroot Mountains. They came, they said, to get someone to come and preach the white man's religion to their people. They had learned of the religion from Canadian voyageurs who were Roman Catholic. In St. Louis the Indians became celebrities, although two of them died, apparently after sampling too much of the white man's way of life. The two surviving Indians, disillusioned with the white world, decided to return West. At a banquet held before they left St. Louis, according to tradition, one of the Nez Perces said:

My people sent me to get the "White Man's Book of Heaven." You took me to where you allow your women to dance as we do not ours, and the book was not there. You took me to where they worship the Great Spirit with candles and the book was not there. You showed me images of the good spirits and the picture of the good land beyond, but the book was not among them to tell us the way. I am going back the long and sad trail to my people in the dark land. You make my feet heavy with gifts and my moccasins will grow old carrying them, yet the book is not among them. When I tell my poor blind people, after one more snow, in the big council, that I did not bring the book, no word will be spoken by our old men or by our young braves. One by one they will rise up and go out in silence. My people will die in the darkness, and they will go a long path to other hunting grounds. No white man will go with them, and no White Man's Book to make the way plain. I have no more words.[2]

While there is doubt that the Nez Perce actually spoke these words, the remarks were reported in the East and published in *The Christian Advocate and Journal* of March 1, 1833. The Methodist publication also published an editorial asking: "Who will respond to go beyond the Rocky Mountains and carry the Book of Heaven?" The Nez Perce's purported remarks made a profound impression on most readers, and in 1834 the Methodist Church responded by sending the Reverend Janson Lee, his nephew Daniel Lee, and four assistants to spread the gospel among the Indians on the western side of the Rockies. The missionaries traveled west with Nathaniel J. Wyeth's expedition, which was bound for the annual fur-trade rendezvous of 1834 on the Green River. From there the missionaries traveled to Oregon country and the Willamette Valley with a Hudson's Bay Company trading party. The Reverend Lee later settled on the site of modern-day Salem, Oregon.

Presbyterian missionaries Dr. Marcus Whitman and Samuel Parker followed in 1836, and a year later Henry Harmon Spalding and William H. Gray headed for Oregon, as did others, including Pierre Jean De Smet in 1840. De Smet, a Jesuit missionary, traveled west with a fur-trade supply train, commanded by Andrew Drips, bound for the last rendezvous in the Rockies. The caravan, however, was unlike most of the earlier supply trains heading for the annual rendezvous. Perhaps a fourth of the travelers were not connected with the fur trade. In addition to De Smet, there were five other missionaries—Congregationalists—and the Walker family, the first declared emigrants for Oregon to undertake the long journey westward. In all, there were perhaps sixty people in the caravan along with thirty heavily laden two-wheeled carts, each drawn by two mules in tandem, sixty pack mules carrying trading goods, and four wagons loaded with household goods and belongings. Two of the wagons carried the belongings of the missionaries while the other two carried those of Joel P. Walker, his wife, Mary, their four children, and Mrs. Walker's sister, Martha Young. Joel Walker, on his way to Oregon, was a brother of mountain man Joseph R. Walker, who may have urged Joel to settle in the West.

Joseph R. Walker was not with the caravan, but mountain men James Bridger and Henry Fraeb and several of their trappers traveled with it. They were returning to the West after conducting business in Missouri. The presence of the emigrants probably did not surprise Bridger and Fraeb, who had witnessed the decline in beaver and had seen the arrival of missionaries. Undoubtedly Bridger and Fraeb realized that the West was changing, but instead of adjusting their lives to the changes, both men returned to trapping and trading after the last rendezvous in 1840. Fraeb went as far west as Los Angeles, then nothing but a sleepy village on the Pacific Ocean. There he sold 417 pounds of beaver for $1,147 to Abel Stearns, a merchant. By July 1841, Fraeb was back on the Green River in present-day Wyoming, where Bridger had been trapping and building a small trading post called Fort Bridger. The post was located between the mouths of the Big Sandy and Black's Fork on the Green River. Soon after Fraeb returned, however, he was killed by Indians while hunting buffalo, and Bridger's plans to complete his fort were delayed. In the spring of 1842, he moved into the Black's Fork area and built another trading post overlooking the stream, but for some reason he soon abandoned it.

By the fall of 1842 Bridger was back in Missouri obtaining blacksmithing and other supplies. At that time he teamed up with Louis Vasquez, an old friend, who had earlier operated a trading post with Andrew Sublette on the South Platte River. Bridger, with Vasquez and the supplies, returned to Black's Fork in the summer of 1843 and constructed a third Fort Bridger in a beautiful valley below the snowcapped Uinta Mountains. It was situated at a spot where Black's Fork, fed by cool mountain water from melting snows, divides into several small streams. Each of the several branches was lined with cottonwoods, some willows, and other trees kept alive by the moisture from the streams. This trading post was the first to be built west of the Mississippi expressly for the convenience of emigrants traveling west.

Jim Bridger knew the West. He was only eighteen when he joined

MOUNTAIN MAN JIM BRIDGER,
who built the first trading post west of the Mississippi expressly for the
convenience of emigrants traveling west.

William H. Ashley's other "enterprising young men" in 1822 and ascended
the Missouri River. About two years later he was one of the first white men
to see the Great Salt Lake, and by 1840 he had crisscrossed much of the
West. Bridger knew that as emigrants headed west for the country called
Oregon, they would cross South Pass on the Continental Divide and then
travel west-southwest through dry, barren, and sandy country until they
reached the valley of the Green River. It was the best route over the Rockies,
and he knew that the lush grass, cool mountain water, and trees would be
a welcome and inviting sight. It was there that Fort Bridger was built. He
probably concluded that most emigrants would stop to rest, and with a trading

post in such a setting, the place would be even more enticing. The site of Fort Bridger on Black's Fork was what Grenville Dodge later called "an oasis in the desert." The selection of the site "does great credit to the good judgement of its founder," wrote Dodge in 1905.[3]

Beginning in 1843, Fort Bridger became a stopping point for emigrants bound for Oregon, where retired Hudson's Bay Company employees and former members of Astor's Pacific Fur Company had settled in the rich Willamette Valley. Some mountain men also settled there after the last fur-trade rendezvous in 1840. By then Easterners' fears concerning the dangers of the West—Indians, starvation in the "desert," and the myth that the Rocky Mountains were a barrier to overland travel—were being alleviated by accounts of life and travel in the West. These accounts were reported in newspapers and circulated by word of mouth. Stories also likened the rich Willamette Valley to the humid forested region east of the Mississippi. The name "Oregon" came to suggest a land of promise. In the early 1840s there was a gradual increase in the number of Americans crossing the West to Oregon country, and by 1843 there were perhaps a hundred Americans and British and perhaps sixty French Canadians living south of the Columbia River in Oregon. They formed a provisional government in the summer of 1843 at the same time that nine hundred or so emigrants from Missouri and Illinois were pushing westward across the plains toward Oregon. Another twelve hundred came in 1844. They all followed the route used by traders and missionaries, a route that became known as the Oregon Trail.

It began at Independence, Missouri, just east of present-day Kansas City, crossed a portion of what is now northeastern Kansas, and then turned north into modern Nebraska until it reached the south bank of the Platte River near present-day Kearney, Nebraska. There the trail followed a northwesterly direction along the Platte and then along the South Platte. At one point or another in the vicinity of present-day Ogallala, Nebraska, the emigrants would leave the South Platte and follow the south bank of the North Platte into what is today Wyoming until they reached a point near modern Casper. There the trail turned west and southwest before crossing the Continental Divide at South Pass and the barren country northeast of Fort Bridger. From Bridger's post the trail followed a northwesterly course to Fort Hall, a trading post built in 1834 by Nathaniel J. Wyeth on the east bank of the Snake River, between the mouths of the Portneuf and Bannock rivers, fifteen miles northwest of present-day Pocatello, Idaho. From there the trail followed the Snake River to American Falls, where the Snake River drops about fifty feet in several waterfalls. Crossing the Snake near the falls, the emigrants traveled northwest to the Boise River and the site of modern Boise, Idaho, and on across the eastern border of modern Oregon. The trail continued northwest to where Pendleton, Oregon, stands today and then west to what is now Portland. The western end of the Oregon Trail is now marked by a granite monument in the southwest corner of Kelly Field in Oregon City, Oregon. At that point emigrants would have traveled slightly more than 1,932 miles from Independence. Of course, not all emigrants bound for Oregon went all of the way across the territory. Many settled to the east.[4]

When emigrants reached Fort Bridger they had traveled more than half the distance to the end of the trail. Jim Bridger's trading post was 1,026 miles from Independence. For most emigrants it took about seventy days to cover that distance, averaging about fifteen miles a day. Exactly when Bridger and Vasquez opened their trading post and who their first customers were are unknown. It appears that the supplies they brought out from Missouri in the summer of 1843 were not sufficient for their needs. On December 10, 1843, while visiting Fort Union on the Missouri River, Bridger dictated— he could neither read nor write—to E. S. Denig a letter to be sent to Pierre Chouteau, Jr., in St. Louis. In part, the letter read:

> I have established a small store with a Black Smith Shop, and a supply of iron in the road of the Emigrants, on Black's Fork, Green River, which promises fairly. They [the emigrants] in coming out are generally well supplied with money, but by the time they get there, are in want of all kinds of supplies. Horses, Provisions, Smith work, &c, bring ready cash for them; and should I receive the goods hereby ordered, will do a considerable business in that way with them! The same establishment trading with the Indians in the neighborhood, who have mostly a good number of Beaver among them.[5]

While the text of Bridger's letter has survived, his list of supplies ordered from Chouteau and Company has not. The list probably included powder, lead, flour, beans, salt pork, coffee, tobacco, cornmeal, cloth and/or ready-made clothes, needles and thread, tar, rope, logging and trace chains, bells and tacks, brass rings, frying pans, wire, and soap. Regardless of what Bridger ordered from Chouteau, he received nothing. Bridger was already heavily in debt to Chouteau and Company. No additional credit was issued. Scattered accounts left by emigrants who stopped at Fort Bridger between 1843 and 1846 suggest that they found only a few basic essentials such as grass, water, fuel, fresh meat, and smithwork available at the post.[6]

When Joel Palmer, an emigrant, stopped at Fort Bridger on his way west in the summer of 1845, he recorded in his journal that the post was "built of poles and daubed with mud; it is a shabby concern. Here are about twenty-five lodges of Indians, or rather white trappers' lodges occupied by their Indian wives. They have a good supply of robes, dressed deer, elk and antelope skins, coats, pants, moccasins, and other Indian fixens, which they trade low for flour, pork, powder, lead, blankets, butcherknives, spirits, hats, ready made clothes, coffee, sugar, &c. They ask for a horse from twenty-five to fifty dollars, in trade. . . . They have a herd of cattle, twenty-five or thirty goats and some sheep. They generally abandon this fort during the winter months."[7]

Between 1843 and 1846 Bridger and Vasquez apparently did little to improve the physical condition of their trading post. Nearly all accounts from this period left by emigrants are uncomplimentary about Fort Bridger, but then Bridger and Vasquez did not remain at the post during the winter months. In addition, during the spring, summer, and early fall, Bridger was often away from the post trapping or serving as a guide and left the running of the post to Vasquez. The two traders began to pay more attention to their post after 1844. In that year some emigrants began to follow what was first called the Greenwood Cutoff and later the Sublette Cutoff to the north of Fort Bridger. The cutoff took emigrants over a long stretch of barren country to the Green River south of modern La Barge, Wyoming. It saved them perhaps sixty or seventy miles as they headed toward Fort Hall, but there was no water and little forage for their animals. The route to Fort Bridger provided water and grass.

How many emigrants used the cutoff and missed Fort Bridger is not known, but the alternate route apparently caused Bridger and Vasquez much concern until 1846, when, the Mexican War having been won, many emigrants began to trek to California. The best-promoted route was via Fort Bridger. Credit for this goes to Lansford W. Hastings, a young attorney from Ohio. In 1842 he had traveled overland to Oregon. Dissatisfed with the country, he moved south and fell in love with California, then under Mexican rule. Other Americans had done the same, but Hastings soon was determined to see California become part of the United States. He realized that before that could happen more American settlers were needed, and returning East in 1844, he wrote *The Emigrants' Guide to Oregon and California,* published at Cincinnati in 1845. The small 152-page book contained narratives of his trip to Oregon and then to California, a discussion of the different routes to the Pacific Coast, plus recommended trail conduct, equipment and supplies needed for the journey, and methods of travel. Hastings also sought a new route that would reduce the distance from Missouri to California by as much as two hundred and fifty miles. While he believed that such a route existed from Fort Bridger to the Great Salt Lake and then westward to the Humboldt River and California, it is doubtful that Hastings ever traveled the route before he began promoting it. Nevertheless, the attention given California by Hastings and others ensured the movement of emigrants via Fort Bridger.[8]

Fort Bridger was operated by Bridger and Vasquez from 1843 to 1853. Additional log cabins were constructed in 1848, some for Vasquez, who brought his family from Missouri to live at the post. By then Bridger was a widower. His first wife had died in 1846, but in 1848 he married a Ute Indian woman, and she joined him at the trading post, where both families spent the winter of 1848–49. The winter was severe, with deep snow and very cold temperatures, but the families managed to survive by eating cattle that had frozen to death.

With Mormon migration to the Salt Lake Valley and the California gold rush, thousands of people stopped at Fort Bridger. To keep them coming, Bridger and Vasquez decided to establish a branch post at the last crossing of the Sweetwater River about a hundred and fifty miles east of Fort Bridger. It was in operation by early June 1849. Its purpose seems to have been to intercept emigrants and under the guise of trading convince them to follow the trail to Fort Bridger and then the Mormon Trail to Salt Lake City and on west to California, if that was their destination. Vasquez operated this branch trading post.

One emigrant who met Vasquez at this post was William G. Johnston. He arrived on or about June 10, 1849, and later described Vasquez in his diary as "a fine, portly looking gentleman of medium height, about fifty years of age," who impressed him as being of medium intelligence and shrewdness. The goods on sale, Johnston noted, "consisted of buffalo robes, deer skins, and buckskin goods in process of making, besides horses and mules. . . . Our mess traded some bacon and a lot of beads, trinkets, etc., and a mule for a horse."[9]

Johnston added that his party had planned to bypass Fort Bridger, but Vasquez insisted that the better route was by way of the post and the Great Salt Lake. Vasquez took a pencil and paper and sketched the two routes. He proved persuasive, and Johnston's party went by way of Fort Bridger, arriving there on June 17, 1849. Johnston's diary provides one of the better descriptions of Fort Bridger and the life of its owners:

There are several log buildings, surrounded by a high picket fence, and having a heavy, wooden entrance gate. . . . I visited several of the apartments of the Fort, among others, the rooms occupied by families of the proprietors, through which we were conducted by Mrs. Vasquez, who entertained us in an agreeable and hospitable manner, notably by inviting us to "sit on chairs"! Opening upon a court were the rooms occupied by the Bridger family. Mr. Bridger, with a taste differing from that of his partner (who has a wife from the States), made his selection from among the ladies of the wilderness, a stolid, fleshy, round-headed woman, not oppressed with lines of beauty. Her hair was intensely black and straight, and so cut that it hung in a thick mass upon her broad shoulders. In a corner of Mrs. Bridger's room was a churn filled with buttermilk, and dipping from it with a ladle . . . [she] filled and refilled our cups, which we drank until completely satisfied.

In the course of the conversation, Mrs. Bridger mentioned the loss of a skillet lid; and her inability, thus far, to replace it. . . . Our own skillet had been fractured and thrown away . . . but for some reason we had treasured the skillet lid . . . and before one could say "Jack Robinson," it was transferred to Mrs. Bridger's kitchen. Fifty skillet lids would not have been worth the smile which greeted us. . . . As we turned to leave . . . we were given a roll of freshly churned butter, of a rich golden yellow, and glistening as it were, with drops of dew.

In a store room of the Fort was a considerable stock of buffalo robes, one of which I purchased for the sum of $5. It was an exceptionally large, fine robe, with long, silky hair, and its equal I have rarely seen . . . Other store rooms were nearly bare of goods. In one was a keg of whiskey, a jar of tobacco, and a box of clay pipes, but little else. . . . Some long, red stone pipes of St. Peter's Rock, from the upper Mississippi . . . that sold at $5; Mr. Bridger informed us there is a ready sale for them.[10]

After the Mormons colonized the Salt Lake Valley a hundred miles southwest of Fort Bridger, conflicts developed between Bridger and Mormon authorities concerning Bridger's practice of selling liquor to the Indians of the region. Late in the summer of 1853 a Mormon posse went to the post to arrest Bridger for illegal liquor traffic. Bridger, however, left before the Mormons arrived. He appears to have gone East, leaving Vasquez and some of his mountain trapper friends to run the post. Bridger did not return until the spring of 1855, and a few weeks later he sold Fort Bridger to Lewis Robinson, a Mormon, for $4,000.[11]

Some of the emigrants who were bound for Oregon in the early 1840s had undoubtedly suffered in the East from the national depression that began in 1837. It was caused by a number of factors. President Andrew Jackson, who regarded banks as the pawn of an eastern, anti-democratic ruling class, vetoed a bill that would have renewed the charter of the Second United States Bank. Jackson then ordered all federal deposits in the bank placed in state banks. The President's action reflected his belief and that of most Americans involved in agriculture that credit was bad for farmers and for honest men generally, and therefore, since banks thrive on providing credit, they should not be tolerated. State banks, of course, cheered the action, but they soon became rather loose in granting loans. As the national deficit increased, President Jackson in 1836 ordered the U.S. Land Office to accept only specie in payment for federal lands. Since many of the state bank loans went to land speculators, it was hoped that the order would reduce both the loans and the issue of state bank notes. But the banks were overextended, and often they had no reserves. Many failed. This, combined with a growing federal deficit and a general shortage of currency in the East, resulted in the depression of 1837, which lasted until 1843.

For the emigrants heading for Oregon after 1843, to California after 1845, and to the Great Salt Lake region, money was more plentiful, since economic conditions in the East had improved. Some emigrants undoubtedly hoarded a little money before heading West, but traders already in the West were waiting to capture as much of it as possible. Between Missouri and Fort Bridger there were few trading posts until about 1846, and the smart emigrants who left Missouri in groups usually carried one or two months' supply of foodstuffs. Most did not begin to run low on staples until they reached what is now central Nebraska or beyond. If they did run out of flour or coffee or something else and could not obtain more from other emigrants in their train, they did without until they reached what is now southeastern Wyoming and the area where Fort Laramie and a few other trading posts existed.

One of the lesser-known posts was called Fort Platte, or sometimes Richard's Fort. It consisted of twelve buildings, including a blacksmith shop, surrounded by a large adobe wall. Lancaster P. Lupton started to build the post in 1839 for the fur trade, but he never finished it. Lupton sold it to Sybille, Adams and Company, who in turn sold it to Bernard Pratte and John Cabanne in 1843. Pratte and Cabanne operated it until about 1845, providing emigrants with a place to rest and blacksmithing service, although they never carried much in the way of groceries or other supplies. Their principal trade was in whiskey that sold for four dollars a pint.

About a mile to the southwest was the better-known post Fort Laramie, first called Fort John when it was built by the American Fur Company in 1841 above the mouth of the Laramie River. Fort John was more impressive than Fort Platte, having high adobe walls, bastions at the south and north corners, and a blockhouse over the main gate. The post, which outlived all others in the area, provided emigrants with blacksmithing and wagon repairs plus supplies, including groceries. When Pratte and Cabanne sold Fort Platte to the American Fur Company in 1845, it was abandoned and left to the elements to eliminate competition. About five miles southeast of Fort Laramie, Joseph Bissonette constructed a post called Fort Bernard in the summer of 1845. Fort Bernard, however, was short-lived. While the trader in charge was in Taos during the winter of 1846–47, the post burned to the ground.

Following the discovery of gold in California, the number of emigrants heading West greatly increased, and more and more trading posts were established. One such post between Fort Laramie and Missouri was built by Joseph E. Robidoux late in 1848 or early 1849 in what is now Scotts Bluff County in western Nebraska. Robidoux, who also traded with the Indians in the area, lived in an Indian lodge during the summer months. Nearby he constructed a small log building with a blacksmith's forge in one end and a combination grogshop and small grocery in the other end. He acquired most of his grocery stock in trade with emigrants, although at the start of each season he brought supplies from St. Joseph, Missouri. He also rented his blacksmith shop and tools to emigrants for seventy-five cents an hour. His trading post was about nine miles west of present-day Gering, Nebraska.[12]

West of Fort Bridger on the trail to Oregon, the next major trading post was Fort Hall. In 1837 the post was sold to the Hudson's Bay Company, which remodeled it in 1838. When emigrants reached Fort Hall, the English traders sold or traded them goods and services. Joel Palmer, on his journey to Oregon in 1845, stopped at Fort Hall. He wrote in his journal:

The garrison was supplied with flour, which had been procured from the settlements in Oregon, and brought here on pack horses. They sold it to the emigrants for twenty dollars per cwt. [hundredweight], taking cattle in exchange; and as many of the emigrants were nearly out of flour, and had a few lame cattle, a brisk trade was carried on between them and the inhabitants of the fort. In the exchange of cattle for flour, an allowance was made of from five to twelve dollars per head. They also had horses which they readily exchanged for cattle or sold for cash. The price demanded for horses was from fifteen to twenty-five dollars. They could not be prevailed upon to receive anything in exchange for their goods or provisions, excepting cattle or money.[13]

Some of the cattle would be fattened and later resold for a handsome profit or driven to Oregon and sold to settlers, but others provided milk and dairy products or meat for the English traders at Fort Hall. The money accepted— gold or silver coins—was usually stored and used to purchase fresh supplies in Oregon. The traders frowned on trading for clothing, household goods, or other items of uncertain value, opting instead for cattle or money of definite value.

Farther to the northwest, on the western border of present-day Idaho, was Fort Boise, another Hudson's Bay Company trading post. Like Fort Hall, it had been established in 1834. When John C. Frémont stopped at the post in early October 1843, he recorded that only "slight attempts at cultivation" had been made by the people at Fort Boise. A few vegetables were available, but salmon and dairy products were plentiful. The trading post, he noted, had its own dairy, "which was abundantly supplied."[14]

The last major trading post on the trail west was Fort Walla Walla, also operated by the Hudson's Bay Company. The site of the post is now under the waters of Lake Wallula behind McNary Dam, but during the 1840s emigrants could stop and obtain food and trade their footsore stock for other animals to be picked up in the Willamette Valley to the west. Some emigrants were transported down the Columbia River in boats belonging to the Hudson's Bay Company. Other emigrants, unable to pay for water transportation, continued overland following the Columbia. A few did stop at Fort Walla Walla long enough to construct their own boats for the last leg of their journey to the Willamette Valley or elsewhere along the Columbia in Oregon country.

There is no question that most traders at the posts run by the fur companies took advantage of the emigrants. Their high prices were not new. Long before the emigrants moved West, the fur companies had marked up their prices to keep the trappers and hunters dependent upon them. Mountain man Osborne Russell estimated the usual markup in the mountains as 2,000 percent on St. Louis prices.[15] As a result, many emigrants viewed the company traders as "their natural enemies," according to Francis Parkman, who spent considerable time at Fort Laramie in June 1846. In a letter to his mother, Parkman wrote that the emigrants "were plundered and cheated without mercy. In one bargain, concluded in my presence, I calculated the profits that accrued to the fort and found that at the lowest estimate they exceeded *eighteen hundred per cent.*"[16]

On June 16, 1846, Parkman wrote in his journal:

> Prices are most extortionate. Sugar, two dollars a cup—5-cent tobacco at $1.50—bullets at $.75 a pound, etc. American Fur Cmp'y. exceedingly disliked in this country—it suppresses all opposition, and keeping up these enormous prices, pays its men in necessaries on these terms.[17]

But many of the posts operated by independent traders appear to have charged lower prices than those owned by the American Fur Company or the Hudson's Bay Company. For instance, John Baptiste Richard and Joseph Bissonette, who operated Fort Bernard close to Fort Laramie, sold flour for 40 percent less and bacon for 30 percent less than did the Laramie traders, and still made a profit. But because of Laramie's reputation and size Fort Bernard apparently failed to attract much emigrant trade.[18]

The large fur-company posts encountered more competition during the middle 1840s, after the great migration to Oregon began. Traders from Taos and Bent's Ford moved north during the late spring and summer months to capture some of the emigrant trade. These traders, working east of the Rockies, traveled back and forth along the Oregon Trail selling or trading mules, flour, and other supplies to emigrants they met. Edwin Bryant, who went to California in 1846, recorded that these traders without posts were extremely generous men—except when trading. They were then "as keen as the shrewdest Yankee that ever peddled clocks or wooden nutmegs." Bryant, whose experiences were published in 1848, noted that "whenever they see their advantage" they extorted money from the emigrants.[19]

EXTORTION OF MONEY from emigrants was not limited to traders along the Oregon and California roads. Given the chance, traders and merchants in the jumping-off points along the Missouri River also took advantage. Independence, Missouri, was the first outfitting point during the early 1840s. Already the eastern terminus of the Santa Fe Trail, Independence also became the starting point for fur-trading expeditions, for journeys by missionaries into the West, and for the Oregon-bound emigrants. Not many miles west of Independence near present-day Gardner, Kansas, there was a

Y in the trail. The left fork led to Santa Fe; the right fork was the road to Oregon. Nearly all of the emigrants heading to Oregon in the early 1840s started from Independence, and most of them were farmers looking for richer soil to till. In most instances they carried with them their earthly possessions, including at least one wagon, several draft animals, food, and other supplies for the long journey. Therefore most of these early emigrants did not need to buy much, and they had little economic impact on Independence, then a town of fewer than eight hundred people.

When the great migration to Oregon began in 1843, however, many emigrants arrived at Independence by steamboat with only their clothes and a few personal belongings. They came from various walks of life. Some had been clerks, some teachers, storekeepers, gamblers, gunsmiths, and some were from other lines of endeavor. These people found it necessary to buy wagons and animals to pull them, and all their supplies. This certainly was the case after gold was discovered in California. Many gold seekers left their families somewhere to the east and headed west, planning to strike it rich and then return home wealthy men. They often came totally unprepared for the journey from Missouri to Oregon country, and it was only natural that they purchase the goods they needed for their journey at the jumping-off point.

In 1849, Independence had a population of between 1,500 and 2,000

INDEPENDENCE, MISSOURI, AS IT APPEARED IN THE EARLY 1850S.
Engraving from *United States Illustrated*, 1854.

ST. JOSEPH, MISSOURI, IN THE LATE 1840S OR VERY EARLY 1850S.

people, and the traders and merchants undoubtedly smiled as more and more gold seekers and emigrants filled the streets and stores. Mule traders and even farmers from the vicinity of Independence took advantage of the emigrants' need for animals to ride or pull wagons or pack supplies. The inexperienced emigrant often bought broken-down or unbroken mules. Kimball Webster, a gold seeker from New England, probably paid forty to sixty dollars each for some unbroken mules, apparently having been told it was an easy task to break them. What happened next is recorded in Webster's own words:

> We tried our skill today [May 5, 1849] at breaking mules, but having heretofore had no experience or acquaintance with the long-eared animals, we found it a more difficult task than we had supposed it to be, and consequently did not make much progress. They were young mules which had never been halter-broken, and were almost as wild as the deer of the prairie. A wild, unbroken mule is the most desperate animal that I have ever seen. . . . We tried in vain [for three weeks] to break our mules by putting large packs of sand on their backs and leading them about, but it availed very little, as the second trial was as bad as the first; and they were nearly as wild and vicious when we started on our journey as they were when they were first packed. . . . It took as

many men to pack a mule as could stand around it, and we were obliged to choke many of them, before we could get the saddle on their backs. They would kick, bite and strike with their fore feet, making it very dangerous to go about them.[20]

By 1849 the town of St. Joseph, Missouri, had not only joined Independence as a jumping-off point but had even surpassed it in numbers of emigrants and gold seekers. St. Joe, as the town was and is called, was founded in 1803 by Joseph Robidoux, son of the St. Louis fur trader. It is located upstream from Independence about fifty-five miles as a bird flies. Robidoux built a log cabin and stocked it with Indian trade goods and traded with the Indians in the area. When the region became government land in 1836 (Platte Purchase), Robidoux laid out a townsite, named the east-west streets after members of his family, and prepared to sell town lots to settlers. He sold some, but by 1843 the town he named after himself had only two hundred residents. That year, however, a few emigrants used St. Joseph and Robidoux's ferry across the Missouri River as their starting place. The town grew and by 1845 it claimed twelve stores, three hotels, a church, and a weekly newspaper. The following year it became the county seat, and by then St. Joseph was outfitting more emigrants bound for Oregon than was Independence. The merchants and traders of St. Joseph were pleased.

Early in the spring of 1847 the weekly St. Joseph *Gazette* published advice for Oregon-bound emigrants and told them what they needed for their journey. The newspaper advised them to take new wagons "made of thoroughly seasoned timber and well ironed and not too heavy; with light beds, strong bows, and large double sheets." In addition, the emigrants should have one yoke of good oxen and an extra yoke in case the first should break. Also, it would be a good idea to bring along two milch cows, "as milk is a great luxury on the road." Emigrants also were urged to take a few beef cattle. As for staples, the editor listed the following:

> 200 pounds of flour and crackers
>
> 100 pounds of bacon
>
> 12 pounds of coffee
>
> 1 to 5 pounds of tea
>
> 12 pounds of sugar
>
> 10 to 50 pounds of rice

½ to 2 bushels of beans

½ to 2 bushels of dried fruit

1 to 5 pounds of saleratus (baking soda)

5 to 50 pounds of soap

plus some cheese, dried pumpkins, onions and cornmeal

The newspaper advised against taking furniture: the emigrants should carry with them only a sheet-iron cooking stove and a *few* cooking utensils, plus enough clothing and medicine for one year. All of these items, of course, could be purchased from merchants and traders in St. Joseph. The newspaper pointed out that flour was fifty cents cheaper in St. Joseph than in Independence, and reported all other prices as similarly reasonable and much lower than in other towns.[21]

One of St. Joseph's early retail houses was opened by John Corby of St. Louis. In 1845 his general merchandise outlet had a stock valued at

A CROSSING SOMEWHERE ON THE MISSOURI RIVER,
perhaps near St. Joseph, Missouri. The photograph may have been taken from
a ferry crossing the river, possibly by Albert Bierstadt.

$300, but by 1849 it was valued at more than $4,000. Corby also entered the pork-packing business in St. Joe in 1848, and during his first year of business slaughtered and pickled fifteen hundred hogs. Corby supplied the military at Fort Leavenworth and many emigrants using St. Joseph as a jumping-off point. He also had government contracts to supply Fort Leavenworth with five hundred steers annually in 1845, 1847, 1848, and 1854. This trade in cattle induced some Oregon-bound emigrants with farm backgrounds to settle in the vicinity of St. Joseph and raise stock.[22]

Many of the emigrants who remained around St. Joseph had also been attracted by the success of a Virginian named Isaac Miller, who first settled about two miles from Joseph Rodiboux's trading post in 1838. Miller, in the southern tradition, had brought slaves with him to the West, and he controlled, by squatter's rights, more than five hundred acres of land from 1839 to 1848, when President James Polk granted him the land for services

OMAHA, NEBRASKA TERRITORY,
a few years after the town captured the emigrant trade from Council Bluffs located across the Missouri River (top) in Iowa.

rendered to the Army post at Fort Leavenworth. Miller's farm, with holding pens for cattle, sheep, and horses, was impressive. When Joel Palmer headed for Oregon in 1845, he traveled through Independence and not St. Joseph, but in his classic overland guide, *Journal of Travels over the Rocky Mountains, to the Mouth of the Columbia River* (1847), he advised emigrants from Ohio, Indiana, Illinois, northern Missouri, Michigan, and Iowa to start from St. Joseph. Palmer wrote: "I think St. Joseph the best point; as by taking that route the crossing of several streams (which at the early season we travel are sometimes very high) is avoided. Outfits may be had at this point, as readily as at any other along the river. Work cattle can be bought in its vicinity [at Isaac Miller's farm] for from twenty-five to thirty dollars per yoke, cows, horses, &c., equally cheap."[23]

When gold seekers bound for California joined the emigrants in 1849, business boomed even more. Through newspaper advertising St. Joseph managed to capture much of the outfitting business for forty-niners, although some went to Independence and still others went to a place called Kanesville, then the third major outfitting town along the Missouri. (What was then Kanesville became Council Bluffs, Iowa, opposite present-day Omaha, Nebraska. The name Council Bluffs came from an Indian council held in the area by Lewis and Clark in 1804.) A group of Mormons led by Brigham Young crossed Iowa and made winter camp near modern Omaha in 1846. The following year many of them moved west toward what would be their promised land in Utah, but some remained behind and crossed to the east side of the river, where they built homes. Their settlement became known as Kanesville, named for a Pennsylvanian, Thomas M. Kane, a friend and sympathizer of the Mormons. By the summer of 1848 emigrants were stopping there to fit out for their jouney before crossing the Missouri. Kanesville had gained a population of five hundred people and a dozen stores by 1849, but it did not have its own ferry across the Missouri. Emigrants had to use one of four within twelve miles of the town. In the spring of 1852, however, a steam ferry was proposed at Kanesville and this attracted even more residents, although it was not installed until 1853.

Merchants, traders, and even farmers took advantage of the growing emigrant trade. One yoke of oxen sold for sixty-five to eighty dollars. Some Kanesville men purchased corn, hauled it sixty miles east along the major road leading to Kanesville, and sold it to unsuspecting emigrants for a dollar and a half per bushel. When the emigrants arrived in the town they learned that local farmers were selling corn in the streets for twenty-five cents a bushel.

Newspaper accounts from the early 1850s describe Kanesville as having five hotels, four groceries, sixteen general stores, two jewelers, two cabinet shops, five boot and shoe makers, two livery stables, eight wagon shops, two tinsmiths, one gunsmith, one cooper, three barbershops, four bakeries, one mill, five "practical physicians," nine lawyers, seven preachers, and a population of nearly fifteen hundred people. There were even two photographers offering to take daguerreotypes of emigrants just before they began their journey across the wilderness.[24]

Kanesville was no longer an all-Mormon town. Gentiles, as the Mormons called non-Mormons, had arrived and were competing for business. The Mormons already had been told by church fathers to move on to the Great Salt Lake Valley. They resisted the order until 1852, when most of them moved west, leaving Kanesville to the drinking and gambling gentiles. Frederick H. Piercy, an English artist, visited Kanesville in 1853 and later wrote:

I found Kanesville to be a very dirty, unhealthy place, and withal a very dear place to make an outfit for the plains, notwithstanding the assertions of holders of property and merchants there to the contrary. They assure emigrants that their wisest plan is to take their money there to purchase their outfit, but I hope few will believe them, for as there is not much competition they get prices the very reverse of their consciences.[25]

On December 10, 1852, a few months after most of the Mormons had left for Salt Lake, the name of the post office was changed to Council Bluffs, and early the following year the Iowa legislature approved the incorporation of the town as Council Bluffs City. But within two years Omaha was founded in Nebraska Territory on the west bank of the Missouri River across from Council Bluffs. Within a few more years Omaha had captured the emigrant trade from Council Bluffs, and that town's outfitting days had ended.

By the early 1850s, Independence, Missouri, had also lost its emigrant trade to other Missouri River towns, but this was caused in part by the shifting of the Santa Fe trade to neighboring Westport, Missouri, now part of Kansas City. Westport was then located a few miles west of Independence. Four miles north of Westport was the settlement's landing on the Missouri River. It was and is a large limestone ledge projecting into the river's deep water. Steamboats could always dock there even if the river level was low, and wagons carried freight delivered by boat up over the bluffs to Westport. There, caravans were organized to carry goods to Santa Fe. Geography favored

Westport even further. The Big Blue River, between Independence and Westport, was usually swollen in the early spring, and the high water often delayed wagon trains bound for Santa Fe for two or three weeks. There were no such delays at Westport. Thus as the Santa Fe trade shifted from Independence to Westport, so did the remaining emigrant trade.

One early Westport trader was William Miles Chick, who moved from Howard County, Missouri, to Westport in 1836 and established a trading house. Three years later George W. Ewing and Joseph Clymer opened another trading business in Westport. They came from Logansport, Indiana, where they had been merchants. Their first account book, now preserved in the collections of the Kansas City (Missouri) Public Library, shows that they traded goods with Indians as well as with the early residents of Westport. The merchandise listed includes knives, axes, pans, beads, spurs, bridles, coats, gloves, fur caps, powder, scarlet cloth, calico, shoes, salt, flour, and blankets. The same year they established their business at Westport, Thomas A. Smart also opened a similar type of trading house in the settlement. He carried a general assortment of groceries and Indian goods. Anthony Richters opened still another general merchandise store at Westport in 1840. One early observer described the business in Westport as the "truck and dicker trade" with neighboring Indians, employees of mountain fur traders, freighters and mackinaw-boat men on the Missouri River, and occasional soldiers from nearby Fort Leavenworth.[26] By the early 1850s, however, the town's commerce centered on the Santa Fe trade, the business of freighting, and occasional gold seekers bound for California, where members of the silent army were already well established.

VI

ALONG THE
PACIFIC SLOPE

California of the 1830s was a semiwilderness, a terra incognita, *to the people of the East. Whalers and occasional traders told incredible stories of the* Californios, *with their huge ranchos ranged by enormous herds of cattle valued only for their hides and tallow.*

—REUBEN L. UNDERHILL[1]

WHEN the British trading ship *John Begg* sailed into Monterey Bay in 1822, it was the first foreign vessel to be openly welcomed by Mexican authorities in California. Less than a year earlier Mexico had secured its independence from Spain, and under Spanish rule foreign trading vessels were no more welcome in California than overland traders had been in New Mexico. At first the new Mexican government continued the Spanish policy, but the governor in Monterey soon decided that trade was needed. He established an import tax and opened the ports of Monterey and San Diego. Aboard the *John Begg* were Hugh McCulloch and William E. P. Hartnell, British traders. McCulloch, Hartnell and Company became the first commercial firm established in Mexican California, and they obtained a contract to buy cattle hides from the missions at the bargain price of a dollar each.

The same year that McCulloch and Hartnell arrived, the American ship *Sachem* also sailed into Monterey carrying William A. Gale, an agent for Bryant, Sturgis and Company of Boston. Gale also entered into agreements to purchase hides, which would in time enable New England to establish its great shoe and leather industry of the nineteenth century.[2]

As these British and American traders acquired hides from missions and a few private ranchos, the Californios demanded that the new government in Mexico City restore to the public domain the land held by the Franciscan

CATTLE BEING DRIVEN PAST THE MISSION OF SAN GABRIEL.
Etching by Frederich Solomon Wyttenbach.

padres, who years earlier under royal decree had established twenty-one missions along El Camino Real from San Diego to Sonoma and had been provided with much land surrounding each mission. The Mexican government moved slowly, but the padres soon realized that the era of their wealthy missions with Indians as slaves was nearing its end. Some of them began to slaughter the mission cattle for their hides and tallow to produce as much revenue as possible. The end for the mission system came for good when the Secularization Act of 1833 was passed by the Mexican government. It not only gave the mission Indians their freedom but in 1836 enabled the government to distribute grants of land to politically active Californios. Huge private ranchos developed, establishing the owners as near-feudal lords. Many Indians freed from the missions went to work on the ranchos, whose owners became the ruling class in California.

As the mission system decayed and the rancho system grew, more New England trading vessels discovered California, where they found a waiting market for the goods they carried. Many of the ships owned by Bryant, Sturgis and Company brought not only trading goods but more Americans to settle in California. Richard Dana, who first sailed around Cape Horn to California in 1834, worked as a sailor on a ship owned by Bryant, Sturgis and Company. Dana later wrote the classic *Two Years Before the Mast* (1840), in which he noted that traders brought spirits of all kinds, teas, coffee, sugar, spices, raisins, molasses, hardware, crockery, tinware, cutlery, cloth of all kinds, boots and shoes, calicoes, cotton, crepes, silks, scarves, necklaces, jewelry, and combs. According to Dana, they even brought furniture, Chinese fireworks, and English-built wheels with iron tires for small carts.

But Dana, who later returned to New England to become a lawyer, described Californios as "idle, thriftless people" compared with the New England Yankees. He could not understand why they would buy at high prices bad wine made in Boston when California abounded in grapes. "Their hides, too, which they valued at two dollars in money, they barter for something which costs seventy-five cents in Boston; and buy shoes (as like as not made of their own hides; which have been carried twice around Cape Horn) at three and four dollars, and 'chickenskin boots' at fifteen dollars a pair. Things sell, on an average, at an advance of nearly three hundred per cent upon the Boston prices," wrote Dana.[3]

The hide-and-tallow trade was centered at Monterey, the civil, military, and social capital of Mexican California. Monterey was also the location of the one custom house in the province, where the captain of each sailing ship had to obtain a trading license and pay a duty on his cargo. With a license and duty paid, the captain could sail up and down the coast trading and distributing his cargo. Such trading sometimes lasted two or three years. It was not uncommon, however, for a ship to sail out to sea from Monterey after obtaining a license and paying duty on its cargo, and there take on additional trading goods from unlicensed traders. In this manner the licensed ship did not have to pay duty on some goods. Still other ship's captains bribed customs officials or simply smuggled trading goods ashore under cover of darkness.

Several of the early American traders married into the best Mexican families in California, the Protestant traders converting to the Roman Catholic faith before their marriages, since the Roman Catholic Church ordained that no Protestant could marry a Catholic woman without first becoming a convert. Abels Stearns, a native of Massachusetts, who arrived at Monterey in 1829, married the beautiful daughter of Juan Bandini, and Stearns became one of the largest landholders in California. After Stearns's death, his widow married Robert S. Baker, another American. There were also Daniel Hill, another native of Massachusetts, who married into the Ortega family, and Robert Ridley, who was employed by the Hudson's Bay Company until it pulled out of California in 1843. Ridley married the daughter of Apolinario Miranda. Thomas M. Robbins, who operated a store in Santa Barbara, married the daughter of Carlos Carrillo. And there were others, including Alpheus B. Thompson, a native of Maine, who arrived in California in 1825, settled in

THE ARRIVAL OF U.S. SHIPS IN MONTEREY, CALIFORNIA,
the early center of the hide and tallow trade, 1842.

ANOTHER VIEW OF MONTEREY, CIRCA 1840.

Santa Barbara, and married into the Carrillo family as well. Thompson
became a prominent trader and ranchero. In time many of these men controlled the hide-and-tallow trade, and after it began declining they developed
the lands they had acquired by marriage. Historian Howard Lamar noted
that such intermarriage in California and elsewhere in the early American

West was, "as in medieval Europe, a form of diplomacy, a trade alliance, or a swapping of hostages, and that all of these were normal processes."[4]

One trader who did not marry a Mexican woman was Thomas Oliver Larkin, a native of Massachusetts. He arrived in California in 1832 and soon entered the mercantile business. Settling in Monterey, Larkin married a young American widow whom he had met a year earlier aboard the ship that had carried him to California. She was one of the first women in California not of Spanish or Indian blood. Thomas Larkin's papers, now preserved in the Bancroft Library of the University of California at Berkeley, provide many insights into the life and business practices of early American traders in California. For instance, Larkin's business transactions were nearly all trades. Apparently very little gold or silver changed hands. Long-term credits

RICHARD HENRY DANA, WHO SAILED AROUND CAPE HORN TO CALIFORNIA
in 1834 and later wrote the classic *Two Years Before the Mast* (1840) detailing
the early hide and tallow trade in California.

LEFT: ABEL STEARNS, WHO CAME TO CALIFORNIA IN 1829.
By 1860 he was one of the largest landowners ever known in the state.
RIGHT: William Heath Davis, an early California businessman.
He first arrived in California as a cabin boy aboard a sailing vessel in 1831. He
returned in 1833 and again in 1838, when he remained.

were customary, and the open accounts of the California ranching families who dealt with Larkin often ran for many years. During the 1830s and early 1840s, the word of the Californio was his bond. No security was better. Larkin's business grew, but life was not easy. Larkin and other American and English residents craved fresh vegetables, the products of flour, and butter, milk, and cheese. But these items, not being part of the native or Spanish diet, were scarce in California. Larkin began importing cheese, vegetables, and flour from the Sandwich Islands (now Hawaii) for his own dinner table and the larders of his friends. Later, Larkin added these items to the stock of his store in Monterey to satisfy the increasing number of foreigners arriving in California.

Larkin's store boasted the only iron safe in the region, and it became a popular receptacle for important papers and jewelry. Californios and Mexican officials kept their valuables in Larkin's safe, and this service helped to increase his political influence. In time Larkin entered banking. Since checks were not in use in California, and hard cash was scarce, Larkin's bank was unlike banks of today. Cattle hides served as "California greenbacks," and their value was established by the hide merchants from Boston.

Larkin's bank, apparently located in his store, became something of a clear-inghouse for traders' notes and drafts. Larkin handled the paperwork on them and collected, usually in hides, adding a substantial charge for his services. When he had accumulated a large quantity of hides, he sent them to Boston via the Sandwich Islands, then the trade center for the Pacific Coast. With his trading and banking profits, Larkin hired agents in Val-paraiso, Mazatlán, Honolulu, and Canton, China, and began importing hides and tobacco from Mexico and fine china, silk, and other goods from China. Larkin also became United States consul in California in 1844. About a year later Secretary of State James Buchanan appointed Larkin as a confidential agent with instructions to work for a peaceful secession of California from Mexico. But it took the Mexican War for that change to occur.[5]

Another early merchant at Monterey was Nathan Spear. He was also involved in the import business but not to the extent that Larkin was. Spear primarily sold merchandise to farmers and stock raisers in the region around present-day San Francisco. The merchandise was delivered to customers on two small schooners he owned. Spear was an uncle of William Heath Davis, another pioneer California businessman, who first arrived there as a cabin boy aboard a sailing vessel in 1831. Davis returned in 1833 and again in 1838, when he remained to become a permanent resident. Davis, unlike Spear, recorded his recollections of Mexican California, which were pub-lished in *Seventy-five Years in California* (1889). Of the trade in hides, Davis wrote:

Merchants trusted the rancheros largely for the goods they sold them, and the indebtedness was paid after cattle were killed. The ranchero, being more or less in debt at all times, would promise a merchant to supply him with a certain quantity of hides and tallow at a stipulated time; but shortly before the specified date the ranchero would be called upon by another merchant to whom he was likewise indebted for goods, and who was also anxious to secure hides and tallow, on account of what was owing to him, and also to make up a cargo for shipment. By persistent efforts and persuasion he would so work upon the ranchero—who was good-natured and obliging, and desirous of accommodating all his friends, as far as he was able—as to secure for himself a large part of the hides and tallow which had been promised to the first one, and carry them off triumphantly, somewhat to the chagrin and discomfiture of the merchant who had the first contract, who, coming shortly after-ward, would find that his competitor had got ahead of him. The ranchero would then make the best of it, explaining that he could not resist the importunities of the other, and had been obliged to let the hides and tallow go to the first arrival. To make good his original promise, he would collect everything about the place that could be made available, even frequently ordering more cattle to be slaughtered, the hides taken off, and some tallow melted out forthwith.

When this happened, hides were often taken in a green state, and staked out and dried by the merchants . . . I have also seen them hung up thickly on ropes stretched over the decks of vessels, the same way the clothes of the crew of a man-of-war are hung in the rigging to dry. The tallow in a very soft state was sometimes taken on the vessel— before it had cooled and hardened, after having been put into the bags.[6]

Trade in hides and tallow continued until the Mexican War began in 1846. American vessels were then not welcome in Mexican California. Such trade might have returned to its earlier level following the war had gold not been discovered near Coloma, at a sawmill owned by John Augustus Sutter, nine days before Mexico and the United States signed the treaty of Guadalupe Hidalgo on February 2, 1848, ending the war. Mexico ceded California and New Mexico (including much of modern Arizona) to the United States and agreed on the Rio Grande in Texas as the international boundary. There was

SAN FRANCISCO BAY, 1837.

THE RAISING OF THE AMERICAN FLAG AT YERBA BUENA,
now San Francisco, in 1846.

some trading in hides and tallow early in 1848, but when the gold seekers
began arriving in present-day San Francisco, rancheros began driving their
cattle from southern California north to the goldfields, where they found a
waiting market for beef among hungry miners.

California ranchers began earning more money from the sale of their
cattle on the hoof than most had ever imagined possible. And most of them
hurriedly spent their money, buying "saddles trimmed with solid silver,
spurs of gold, bridles with silver chains," and anything else that caught their
fancy. And their wives purchased expensive rugs, four-poster bedsteads with
lace curtains, and other luxuries. Many of the California ranchers became
so eager to make money that they failed to keep their breeding stock, selling
their bulls along with their cows and steers. The normal increase of the cattle
herds in southern California began to fall off, from about fifteen thousand
head annually to less than half that figure by 1855. And by the summer of
1856 the cattle industry that existed in California was a fraction of what it
had been in the early 1840s.

In addition, as word spread eastward telling of the discovery of gold,
ranchers in Texas and Missouri and elsewhere had begun driving herds of
cattle westward to California, glutting the market. Prices dropped to sixteen
to eighteen dollars a head, with young stock bringing only seven to eight
dollars. Before the summer of 1856 ended, a severe drought struck parts of
California, forcing many ranchers to sell their remaining cattle at even lower

prices. The markets were completely saturated with cattle as 1857 began, much to the dismay of the owners of herds who had driven cattle overland to California from points east during the summer of 1856.[7]

When word of the discovery of gold first spread throughout California early in 1848, many Californios rushed to the goldfields. Some settlements, including San Jose, about forty miles southeast of San Francisco, became almost deserted. Josiah Belden had opened a general store in San Jose only a short time before. When most of his customers took off for the goldfields, Belden decided to join them and see what was going on. He got an old gentleman he called Brenham—probably Isaac Branham—to look after his store. What happened next is told in Belden's own words:

I went up to the mining region about where Placerville is now, stayed there a few days, took observations, and started to return to San Jose. In the meantime, while I was away, a considerable number of the Spanish population, who had been in the mines from San Jose, and most of whom had succeeded in getting quite a quantity of gold, returned to that place, and with their newly acquired wealth had gone into the store to buy goods of Brenham, and were very eager to get goods for their gold, seeming to have a kind of apprehension that the gold would lose its value, and were anxious to realize something from it as soon as possible. They commenced trading at such a rate that I found on my return the man I had left in charge had sold out nearly my whole stock of goods. I had been gone some two or three weeks. From that time on I had frequently to renew my stock of goods from San Francisco, and the Spanish people coming in from the mines were anxious to trade. Money was rather a new thing to them, and having come easy and quickly, they were just as ready to spend it, and having a fancy for all kinds of dry goods, fancy goods, dress goods, they spent it quite freely.

Belden then recalled how he conducted his business:

I understood the language by that time, and I succeeded in gaining their confidence to such an extent that when they came from the mines with a bag of gold dust, they would bring it into the store, and tell me to weigh it and see how much there was of it. I would weigh out the dust which might be worth anywhere from fifty to five or six hundred dollars, as the case might be. After weighing it, and telling the value of it, they would tell me to take it and put it away. I would put it into

MINERS WORKING A STREAM IN CALIFORNIA DURING THE GOLD RUSH.
Drawing by William Henry Jackson.

MARSHALL FINDS GOLD. A SCENE IN CALIFORNIA
following the discovery of gold in the middle nineteenth century.
Drawing by William Henry Jackson.

a box where I kept the gold I had on hand, and make a memorandum of the amount, and they would commence calling for goods, one kind and another, whatever they wanted, and would make purchases of various articles for some time, I keeping a memorandum of what they took, and after they had selected a considerable quantity, they would ask me to count up and see how much the goods amounted to, and how much there was left of the gold dust unspent. So, after adding up the amount of their purchases, I would report the balance left to them, and they would commence calling for more goods, and go on buying, until after awhile they would ask me to count up again, and see how much they had left then, and so I would figure it up, and if there was still a balance left they would call for something more, and so on until the whole amount of gold was exhausted, when they would take the bundle of goods and go off satisfied. I had an old pair of scales I had rigged up for the occasion, and had correct weights, and I had got their confidence in regard to my dealings with them, and in regard to my weighing out the gold, and I was always careful to allow them for the exact amount of gold, and to give them a fair amount of goods for their money, of course, charging a good profit, as goods were then high. I carried on business there through the years '48 and '49, and then finally sold out my whole business to another party and retired from it . . .[8]

William Heath Davis, who had set up a business in San Francisco, had similar experiences. In fact, he apparently purchased the first gold from the fields in the San Francisco area. Two miners brought in more than a hundred dollars' worth of gold. Davis had to summon a local jeweler to attest that the dust was really gold. He then paid sixteen dollars an ounce, half of the total in coin and half in goods. Within days all of the merchants in San Francisco were accepting gold. Davis recalled:

All merchants transacted an immense business, and there was no trouble in selling goods if we had them to sell. The receipts of gold from the mines was so great, and the means of weighing it so limited, that we had trouble from the scarcity of scales. [Benjamin R.] Buckelew, being the only maker of scales, was kept at work from morning till night manufacturing to fill orders.

Gold and silver coin became very scarce in the market. The duties on goods from foreign ports had to be paid in coin, and the merchants were unable to comply with the customs laws. An arrangement was

made with the collector of the port to receive gold dust on deposit from
them at $10 per ounce, for duties, redeemable at the end of sixty days
with coin. Most of the gold pledged for duties was sold at auction by
the government, at the expiration of the time, for about $10 per ounce,
and less in some instances. The action of the government was a great
hardship to the merchants, as they incurred a loss of $6 for each ounce
thus sold, and particularly when it was known at the Treasury department in Washington that the true value of the gold was from $18 to
$20 per ounce, assayed and made into coin at the mint in Philadelphia.[9]

The foreign goods on which duties had to be paid came from Honolulu, ports
in South America and Mexico, and elsewhere in the Pacific. Davis recalled
that as soon as word of the California gold discovery spread across the Pacific,
sailing ships loaded with goods were dispatched to San Francisco. The owners

ALTHOUGH THIS PHOTOGRAPH OF THE SAN FRANCISCO PIERS
was taken about 1900 by William Henry Jackson, the scene probably was
similar half a century earlier when square-riggers like these
arrived carrying gold-seekers to California.

of the stock and the captains of the ships hoped for their share of gold in exchange for goods, and many of them succeeded.

The population of California grew very rapidly following the discovery of gold. There were about ten thousand people in all of California in 1846, but by August 1849 the population was at least fifty thousand. Although California became U.S. territory in 1846, the U.S. military remained in control; Congress had failed to make any provisions for a civilian government. Because of this and its rapid growth, California never passed through a formal territorial stage in its political development. A constitutional convention was held in Monterey in the fall of 1849, and delegates drew up a constitution prohibiting slavery. They did so not for humanitarian reasons but rather because most of the gold miners—Southerners and Northerners alike—feared that slaves would be brought into California and used to compete against the white miners in the goldfield diggings. When the proposed constitution reached Washington and Congress, there was a long and bitter debate, but on September 9, 1850, California was admitted to the Union as a free state in the Compromise of 1850, an agreement that left open the slavery status of New Mexico and Utah.

By then San Francisco had become the center of all business and financial operations in California and for much of the region west of the Rocky Mountains. It was only natural that transportation developed rapidly between the mining towns and the ports, especially San Francisco and San Jose, where the capital was situated until 1854. Since the value of gold depended on its being transported out of California, many express companies were formed to carry it from the goldfields to San Francisco, from where much of the gold was shipped to the East Coast by sailing vessels. Some of these express companies used stagecoaches to carry not only gold but passengers. Adams and Company of Boston, a nine-year veteran of the express business in the East, moved quickly into California and established a San Francisco office in 1849. The company soon gained a large share of the express and banking business. Its growth and success caused Henry Wells, William G. Fargo, and Johnston Livingston—men with express experience in the East—to promote a new express firm for California, which became Wells, Fargo and Company. It was founded in March 1852 in New York City with Edwin B. Morgan, a wealthy New York financier, as president. Before 1852 ended, the new company had established a network of express lines in California by buying out several smaller express businesses that had been competing against Adams and Company with some difficulty. The first shipment of gold dust and nuggets by Wells, Fargo to New York City totaled $21,000, compared with a shipment of $600,000 in gold at the same time by Adams and Company. A California banking firm, Page, Beacon and Company, a subsidiary of the bank of Page and Beacon of St. Louis, shipped $682,000. Competition soon became fierce for the forwarding and banking business of California.

The nation was on the verge of another financial depression by 1854. Business expansion had been carried on by many eastern firms in a reckless manner. Early in 1855, following the collapse of the St. Louis bank of Page and Beacon and in turn their California banking house, all California express companies and banks suspended operations. Mobs of depositors stormed the offices of Adams and Company, but the doors remained closed and the firm went into receivership. Perhaps two hundred other San Francisco businesses also closed their doors as a serious depression struck. But Wells, Fargo and Company, which made a practice of keeping a large cash balance on hand for emergencies, proved to be solvent and quickly reopened. Although former employees of Adams and Company reorganized as the Pacific Express Company, the firm did not last. By the end of 1855, Wells, Fargo operated fifty-five offices throughout the mining districts, and the number increased to a hundred and forty-seven by 1860. The firm not only made money by buying gold dust for fifteen or sixteen dollars an ounce in the mining camps and then selling it for eighteen dollars an ounce, but conducted general banking as well. It received money on deposit, made collections, extended credit, issued bills of exchange, and handled the execution, recording, and delivery of important business documents. By the start of the Civil War in 1861, Wells, Fargo and Company had a monopoly on the express business in California.

Samuel Bowles, editor of the Springfield, Massachusetts, *Republican* visited California during the summer of 1864. Concerning Wells, Fargo, Bowles wrote:

It is the omnipresent, universal business agent of all the region from the Rocky Mountains to the Pacific Ocean. Its offices are in every town, far and near; a billiard saloon, a restaurant, and a Wells & Fargo office are the first three elements of a Pacific or Coast mining town; its messengers are on every steamboat, and rail-car and stage, in all these States. It is the Ready Companion of civilization, the Universal Friend and Agent of the miner, his errand man, his banker, his post-office. It is much more than an ordinary express company; it does a general and universal banking business, and a great one in amount; it brings to market all the bullion and gold from the mining regions—its statistics are the only reliable knowledge of the production; and it divides with the government the carrying of letters to and fro.[10]

The combination of gold and the United States acquisition of California caused a boom along the Pacific Coast that surpassed anything that had occurred in the American West since the purchase of Louisiana Territory. And unlike most other areas west of the Mississippi, life in California became urban. Even the people living away from the coastal settlements were closely linked to the population centers there, and not only because many goods and supplies arrived by ships. As the settlements rapidly evolved into towns and then into cities, ranches, mines, and farms grew in number. Trade expanded by necessity, and businessmen increased their supply of investment capital by bringing in raw materials from outlying regions, making products, and then selling them not only in the cities but back to the areas where the raw materials came from. The products included hardware, coal oil, powder, lumber, grain and flour, dried fruits, and the Levi Strauss goods produced in the San Francisco area. It was the availability of investment capital by the late 1850s and the desire to expand the markets for their products to the East that eventually spurred the development of railroads in California even before the iron horse had pushed westward across the Missouri River.

The 1860 census of California, the first reliable census in the Far West, gave California more than 379,000 residents. The census figures leave no doubt that California was more urban than the rest of the nation, and the occupational patterns made it appear to be more like many of the older states in the East than the newer states along the Mississippi. This same pattern also developed later in Washington and Oregon, but it was in California that a special breed of businessman evolved. Samuel Bowles, the New England editor, observed this new type on his visit to California in 1864 and wrote:

People, who know they are smart in the East, and come out here thinking to find it easy wool-gathering, are generally apt to go home shorn. Wall Street can teach Montgomery Street nothing in the way of "bulling" and "bearing," and the "corners" made here require both quick and long breath to turn without faltering. Men of mediocre quality are no better off here than in older cities and States. Ten or fifteen years of stern chase after fortune, among the mines and mountains and against the new nature of this original country, has developed men here with a tougher and more various experience in all the temporalities of life, and a wider resource for fighting all sorts of "tigers," than you can easily find among the present generation in the eastern States. Nearly all the men of means here to-day have held long and various struggles with fortune, failing once, twice or thrice and making wide wreck, but buckling on the armor again and again, and trying the contest over and over. . . . In consequence partly of all this training, and partly of the great interests and the wide regions to be dealt with, the men I find at the head of the great enterprises of this Coast have great business power—a wide practical reach, a boldness, a sagacity, a vim, that I do not believe can be matched anywhere in the world. London and New York and Boston can furnish men of more philosophies and theories, men who have studied business as a science as well as practiced it as a trade—but here are the men of acuter intuitions and more daring natures; who cannot tell you why they do so and so, but who will do it with a force that commands success.[11]

One man of the type described by Bowles was John Parrott, who came to California from Mexico after the start of the Mexican War. In 1829 Parrott, a native of Tennessee, went to Mexico, where he worked for his brother, W. S. Parrott, a merchant. Six years later John Parrott went into business for himself in Mazatlán on the western coast of Mexico. To the east of Mazatlán in the Sierra Madre were some of the richest silver mines in Mexico, and from the west came trading ships. Parrott's mercantile business prospered, and in 1837 he became U.S. consul, a post he held in Mazatlán for twelve years. In 1841 his firm—Parrott and Company—was buying hides and trading with passing vessels and with natives. Parrott even imported tobacco, much to the satisfaction of the Mexicans. Then came the Mexican War. Most of Parrott's property and assets were confiscated at the beginning of the war, but he was able to flee the country with about $300,000 in minted Mexican money. He reached California in 1849 and invested the money in real estate and a quicksilver mine and began to construct buildings in San Francisco. From all indications Parrott also established a private bank and a mercantile business soon after he arrived. He was able to weather the economic depression of 1855 because, like Wells, Fargo and Company, he had maintained sufficient cash for emergencies. Parrott had erected the building that was first rented to Adams and Company and Page, Beacon and Company. After the economic crash it was rented by Wells, Fargo.

Before the depression subsided, however, Parrott and other San Francisco businessmen faced another problem. The bad times had helped an unsavory group of men to gain control of the city government by 1856. Earlier in the decade a vigilance committee had successfully rid the city of common street criminals, but when the municipal government became corrupt, street crime again increased and a second vigilance committee was formed. Parrott supported this new committee; he and other businessmen saw a need for an honest and stable city government as a precondition for attracting New York City investors. Conditions were so bad that Parrott became very discouraged, and in a letter to a St. Louis businessman for whom he handled business in San Francisco, he wrote:

If I could find a purchaser at 50¢ on the Dollar for all my property in California, I would take it and abandon the country forever. I at times am so much disgusted at the turn things have taken in the State, to say nothing about the thieves and corruption and insecurity of life and property, that I deeply regret ever having invested my all in it. I am the only one [sic] of the Old School that can say he has gained anything, and there is no telling how soon I may be robbed or assassinated for what I have. There is really no pleasure in living in a country like this and there is less hope of ever getting the villains out of the country.[12]

John Parrott did not sell out and leave California. The second vigilance committee accomplished its mission, and Parrott remained and continued to acquire property, including more than seventeen thousand acres of land near present-day Chico, California, at a cost of less than five dollars an acre. He raised sheep on much of the land, selling the wool they produced to clothing manufacturers and mutton to San Francisco cafés. John Parrott's interests extended eastward into Nevada and even Colorado, where the mining town of Parrott City once stood west of modern Durango, Colorado. When John Parrott died at the age of seventy-three in 1884, his estate included nearly eight million dollars in U.S. bonds and even a larger amount of California real estate.[13]

It was men like Parrott who laid the foundations in California for a diversified economy that grew more rapidly than the economy of areas to the east in the Rockies and on the plains and prairies. The economic growth of early California was based on an agricultural-mining economy. The discovery of gold caused California to be populated almost overnight, but other minerals were soon discovered. Quicksilver and some coal were mined very early, and oil was discovered in the early 1860s. In 1864 borax made its appearance, and a year later sulphur. Chromite was first mined commercially in 1869, and lead and silver production was underway by the middle 1870s. The influx of gold seekers brought a demand for foodstuffs, especially vegetables, to supplement a diet of mainly salted meat. Agriculture grew rapidly, establishing the foundation for an industry that still exists. It includes the citrus industry, begun in 1879, when the first railroad car of oranges was shipped to eastern markets. Although grapes were introduced into California by the Franciscan fathers in Spanish colonial times, it was Agoston Haraszthy, a Hungarian, who grew new European varieties for the first time in San Diego in 1849. Eight years later he established a vineyard near Sonoma, north of San Francisco, giving birth to still another industry that flourishes today.

VII

MILITARY POSTS
AND FREIGHTERS

*Oxen that rattle the yoke and chain, or halt in the leafy shade! What
is that you express in your eyes? It seems to me more than all the print
I have read in my life.*

—WALT WHITMAN[1]

THERE were ten frontier military posts in the American West just before
the Mexican War began in May 1846. All of them were located along
a rough line from Fort Snelling in Minnesota south to Fort Jessup in Lousiana.
Half of these posts could be supplied directly by steamboat. The others were
ninety miles or less from steamboat landings, and these posts were easily
reached overland by government contractors with wagons. Getting supplies
to American soldiers was not difficult. But when the Mexican War began,
a new problem developed. Colonel Stephen W. Kearny was ordered to take
an army from Fort Leavenworth and march about eight hundred miles to
Santa Fe. Fort Leavenworth, located on the Missouri River in what is today
northeastern Kansas, was the Army's main supply depot for all the West. It
was one of the frontier posts that was supplied directly by steamboat from
St. Louis and points east.

When reports were received in Missouri telling of a shortage of grain
in New Mexico, Kearny insisted that adequate provisions be sent along with
his army. But neither the Army nor commercial freighters had sufficient
wagons and manpower to do the job. The military decided to do its own
freighting. Quartermaster agents began buying wagons in Pittsburgh, St.
Louis, and anywhere else they could find them for sale; orders were given
to dismantle the wagons and ship them by steamboat to Fort Leavenworth.
Meantime, other agents crisscrossed Missouri buying oxen and mules to pull
the wagons. Still other agents bought thousands of pounds of bacon at five

TROOPS GOING TO MEXICO, 1847. DRAWING BY FREDERIC REMINGTON.

cents per pound plus large quantities of other foodstuffs from merchants in St. Louis. These provisions were also loaded aboard steamboats and sent usptream to Fort Leavenworth, where the Army began hiring teamsters at twenty-five to thirty dollars a month to drive the wagons. This was better pay than the soldiers with Kearny's army were receiving.

Unfortunately, the provisions arrived at Fort Leavenworth before most of the wagons. Kearny and his army could not wait—there was a war to win. He had all available wagons loaded with supplies and sent them with the first military units to leave for Santa Fe. As more wagons arrived by steamboat, they were assembled, loaded with provisions, and sent on to New Mexico in small groups. The wagons, however, were carelessly loaded. Some of them carried nothing but food; others carried tents or cooking utensils or miscellaneous supplies. The Army's inexperience in freighting stores across the plains was evident. Many of the teamsters hired to drive the wagons were new to the job, and few knew how to care for the oxen and mules. To make matters worse, when wagons reached Bent's Fort on the Arkansas River, many of the teamsters refused to continue the journey to Santa Fe, pointing out that they were contracted to drive only as far as Bent's Fort. Confusion reigned. Kearny and his army of about seventeen hundred men had either feast or famine, depending upon what supplies had been loaded in their freight wagons. The first soldiers to reach Santa Fe actually ran out of food about a day before they arrived. Fortunately Kearny's hungry men found no resistance and occupied Santa Fe without bloodshed and located food.[2]

The teamsters who freighted supplies to the soldiers in New Mexico also encountered many hardships. Many of them died during the winter storms of 1846 and 1847. Others perished in Indian raids on the unguarded wagon trains in 1847. The military did give the teamsters rifles and ammunition for self-protection but sent no soldiers to escort the trains. During the summer of 1847, for instance, an estimated forty-seven Americans, most of them teamsters, were killed, 330 wagons destroyed, and 6,500 head of cattle stolen by Indians along the Santa Fe Trail. While some of these raids were on private freighters and traders, most of the losses were to Army supply caravans. The teamsters, however, were not always harmed by the Indians. In one raid during the fall of 1847, a band of Indians overran a wagon train on the Santa Fe Trail and the teamsters fled. The Indians did not give chase, and from a distance the teamsters watched as some of the Indians engaged in "snowball" fights, throwing handfuls of flour at each other until they appeared to be white men. After the Indians had had their fun, they carried away arms and clothing from the wagons and stole fifty mules.[3]

The U.S. Army learned from its mistakes as it supplied troops in New

FORT LEAVENWORTH IN 1838. THE FORT WAS ESTABLISHED IN 1827
to protect travelers traversing the Santa Fe Trail. Drawing by George Gray.

Mexico during the war, but the experience was costly. The oxen and mules as well as the wagons were used for only five or six months of the year. Caring for the animals and maintaining and storing the wagons during the winter months was expensive. When the Mexican War ended, Captain Langdon C. Easton, quartermaster at Fort Leavenworth, totaled his department's expenses. The department had purchased 459 horses, 3,658 mules, 14,004 oxen, 1,556 wagons, and 516 pack saddles. Easton calculated that it cost the Army nearly fifteen cents to transport each pound of supplies from Fort Leavenworth to Santa Fe during the war. Here are his figures:

5 yoke of oxen	at $50.00 each	$250.00
1 wagon		$170.00
2 wagon covers	at $7.50 each	$ 15.00
5 oxbows	at $2.50 each	$ 12.50
4 ox chains	at $2.50 each	$ 10.00
1 teamster for 5 months	at $25.00 each	$125.00
extra yoke, chains, axletrees, coupling poles, etc., etc.		$ 10.00
Total expense of one wagon that will transport 4,000 pounds		$592.50
The Army's cost to transport one pound from Fort Levenworth to Santa Fe		14¾¢ [4]

During the Mexican War the Army constructed Fort Mann on the Santa Fe Trail west of modern Dodge City, Kansas, and established posts in New Mexico. To the north the Army built Fort Kearny on the Platte River in present-day Nebraska, and garrisoned U.S. troops at Fort Laramie and Fort Hall, which were originally trading posts, to protect emigrants moving over the Oregon Trail to Oregon and gold seekers bound for California. The soldiers at these forts had to be supplied, but in view of the great expense incurred in provisioning troops during the Mexican War, the Army concluded that it would be more economical to have private freighters do the work. In 1848, the Army opened its freighting in the West to private citizens with competitive bidding. And this marked the true beginning of the freighting industry in the American West.

Freighting, of course, had existed in the West for many years on a small and as-needed basis. Traders and merchants bound for Santa Fe owned their own wagons or contracted for the delivery of their goods with men who did. The same was true of traders who operated posts along the Oregon Trail or merchants in Utah. But commercial freighting as an industry did not develop in the West until the need arose. The new military posts, including many built after the Mexican War, provided the impetus needed for commercial freighting on a large scale. There was no other way to supply the soldiers at the forts.

The first man known to receive contracts to carry supplies to western military posts was James Brown of Pettis County, Missouri. On May 17, 1848, he signed a contract at Fort Leavenworth to haul 200,000 pounds of government stores to Santa Fe. The following day he signed another contract with Captain Langdon C. Easton, the Fort Leavenworth quartermaster, to carry "such government stores as may be delivered to Brown by Easton." The Army also agreed to sell Brown up to a hundred and twenty freight wagons plus ox yokes and chains at the price the government had paid for them. This undoubtedly helped Brown, who did not own a sufficient number of wagons to do the job. Obviously the Army was getting out of the freighting business, and the contracts Brown signed marked the beginning of extensive contract freighting for the Army on the plains.[5]

James Brown's background is sketchy. His experiences on the plains

OXEN ON THE PRAIRIE

before 1848, if any, are not known. Early newspaper accounts often refer to him as "Judge" Brown, suggesting that he had been a judge in Missouri. It is known that in 1849 he formed a partnership with William H. Russell, a Vermont native who had worked for the Aull mercantile firm in Missouri, and in April of that year they received a contract to transport government stores from Fort Leavenworth to Santa Fe. While Russell remained in Missouri, Brown took the trains to Santa Fe, where he appears to have sold the wagons and oxen. They were worth more there than in Missouri. Brown and a trader named Moses Goldstein of Independence, Missouri, and another man, who is not identified, then set out on horseback to return to Missouri. East of Rabbit Ear Creek in New Mexico, the three men were captured by a party of about forty Arapahoes and Apaches. The Indians robbed the men, debated killing them (perhaps to scare them), but then gave them some mules and allowed them to continue on their journey. Brown carried $84,000 in government receipts, which he hid from the Indians, but Goldstein lost about $600 to them. Three days after they were released, Brown and the others met three men bound for California. The gold seekers provided Brown, Goldstein, and the unidentified man with blankets and provisions.[6]

When Brown arrived in Independence, he was given a contract to freight merchandise to Santa Fe for the firm of Goldstein, Thompson and Flournoy. He bought twenty wagons and enough oxen to pull them and left Independence on October 1, 1849. The journey was uneventful until the train reached a point about forty miles south of the Arkansas River in what is now southwestern Kansas on November 17. A sudden early-winter storm struck the region. Heavy snow stranded the wagons and many oxen died. The traders found themsleves about thirty miles from the nearest source of firewood, but fortunately they had a few horses, and they managed to bring a supply of wood to the stranded wagons, where fires were built. The teamsters went into winter camp while Brown, taking one horse, set out for Missouri to purchase new oxen and to get help. Because of the winter weather, it was five months before a relief train from Independence reached the stranded wagons. Goldstein and the men guarding the wagons had survived in good order. With fresh oxen the wagon train resumed its journey and reached Santa Fe safely several weeks later.[7]

From all indications James Brown prospered as a commercial freighter. All of his freighting was carried out on the Santa Fe Trail until early March 1850. It was then that he and John S. Jones, another Missouri freighter, obtained a contract to transport government stores from Fort Leavenworth to the Army garrison in the vicinity of Fort Hall in present-day Idaho. As the wagon train was being organized in Missouri, Jones advertised in newspapers that the train would take eighty men through to California if each man would agree to drive a team from Fort Leavenworth to Fort Hall. Jones also offered to furnish each of the eighty men with one month's provisions after they arrived at the goldfields in California. U.S. troops, however, were removed from near Fort Hall in the spring of 1850 before the train left Fort Leavenworth, and Jones canceled plans to take working passengers west. When the caravan with Army stores did move west, it went only as far as Fort Laramie, where the supplies were unloaded.

The story of James Brown is one that reflects enterprise and imagination. He appears to have been a man who was always seeking to better his position. In the fall of 1850, he formed another partnership with William H. Russell and with John S. Jones, with whom Brown had freighted the previous summer. Their firm, Brown, Russell and Company, received a contract to transport at least 600,000 pounds of government supplies from Fort Leavenworth to Santa Fe. In September 1850 they sent five wagon trains, each carrying about 150,000 pounds in thirty wagons, to Santa Fe. It was a major undertaking that promised to net the freighters about $86,000.

All went well with the trains until late November, when a severe snowstorm stalled the first two or three trains within forty-five miles of Santa Fe. Many oxen died. Taking wagons to Santa Fe so late in the season was chancy, but the Army needed the stores. James Brown, who was in charge of the first train, went ahead to Santa Fe to seek help, but there he became ill with erysipelas, an infectious skin disease, and typhoid fever. He died in early December. Charles O. Jones, a brother of John S. Jones, was at the head of the second train, and he took charge of all the wagons. Under pressure from the Quartermaster Department to deliver the Army stores, Jones force-marched the trains to Santa Fe during December, but he had had to obtain many oxen in Santa Fe and hire additional men to do so. When William Russell learned what had happened, he presented the government with a claim for losses totaling $39,800. The government eventually paid the claim in installments. Meantime, the firm that had been known as Brown, Russell and Company was reorganized and became Jones and Russell.[8]

From the beginning of private contract freighting on the plains for the Army, the government insisted upon surety bonds for the freighters. In this way the government stores were protected. Between 1848 and 1851 these bonds ranged anywhere from a few thousand dollars to more than $200,000, depending upon the value of the supplies being freighted. Wealthy merchants in St. Louis, Independence, Westport, and elsewhere in Missouri usually posted these surety bonds and in doing so became investors. These frontier capitalists more than likely shared in the freighter's profit once the contract was fulfilled, or they were paid for making the bonds.

The business of freighting for the Army grew steadily between 1848 and 1852. But fewer than a dozen men seem to have captured government contracts. Aside from James Brown and William H. Russell, there was David Waldo. He was no stranger to the plains, having accompanied Charles Bent to Santa Fe in 1829. Other freighters with government contracts included Benjamin Holladay, a native of Kentucky, who later used his profits from freighting to enter the overland stage business; Joseph Clymer, who owned the trading house in Westport; and the firm of Perry and Young of Weston, Missouri. Young, whose first name is not known, may have been Joseph W. Young of Salt Lake City. Perry was Charles A. Perry, who owned a pork slaughterhouse in Weston. He later tried steamboat freighting on the Kansas River between Westport and new settlements along the river in present-day Kansas, but without much success. The river was very shallow.

The freighting rates paid by the government, the names of the freighters, and where they transported Army stores from Fort Leavenworth from 1848 to 1852 are shown opposite.[9]

By the early 1850s the United States had several thousand men garrisoned at more than seventy military forts in the West, including a dozen new posts established in Texas during 1848 and 1849 to control hostile Indians. Many of the new forts had been established in territory acquired at the end of the Mexican War, including what would become all or portions of California, New Mexico, Arizona, Nevada, Utah, Colorado, and Wyoming. The increase in the number of military posts explains why the cost of transporting supplies in the West and Southwest rose from about $120,000 in 1844 to $2,000,000 by 1850, an increase of about 1,500 percent. Some of this expense was for transporting stores by ship around Cape Horn to military posts on the West Coast, but about a fourth of the money was used to pay commercial freighters for taking supplies from Fort Leavenworth to New Mexico. Quartermaster General Thomas Jesup thought the cost of provisioning soldiers in New Mexico could be reduced if the supplies were shipped to San Antonio, Texas, and then freighted overland to Santa Fe, a distance of about six hundred miles. Orders were issued and stores were carried by ship through the Gulf of Mexico to Fort Lavaca on Matagorda Bay. From there the goods were taken by wagons to San Antonio, a hundred and twenty-five miles away, and then over the old military road across Texas into New Mexico to Santa Fe. There were no problems on the journey, but when

Year	Freighter	lbs. carried	From Ft. Leavenworth	Rate per 100 lbs.
1848	James Brown	200,000 +	to Santa Fe	$11.75
1849	David Waldo	?	to Ft. Laramie	$ 8.91
	Brown & Russell	?	to Santa Fe	$ 9.88
	John Dougherty	?	to Ft. Kearny	$ 6.00 + 5% to bacon weight
1850	David Waldo	?	to Ft. Kearny	$ 7.75
	Joseph Clymer	?	to Ft. Laramie	$ 7.74
	Brown & Jones	?	to Ft. Hall in modern Idaho*	$14.15
	David Waldo	125,000 +	to El Paso del Norte	$13.47
	Brown, Russell & Jones	600,000	to Santa Fe	$14.33⅓
	David Waldo	150,000 +	to Santa Fe	$14.33⅓
1851†	Jones & Russell	?	to Santa Fe	$ 8.59
	Jones & Russell	?	to Las Vegas, Moro, Rayado, N.M.	$ 7.78½
	Benjamin Holladay	211,593	to Ft. Kearny and Ft. Laramie	$ 3.80 to Kearny and $6.80 to Laramie
	Joseph Clymer	?	to El Paso, Dona Ana, and Don Fernando de Taos	$12.84, $12.50, and $8.83, respectively
	Perry & Young	?	to Ft. Mackay (Ft. Atkinson)	$ 4.23
	Jones & Russell	12,000 (corn)	to Ft. Kearny	$ 2.07 per bushel of corn
	David Waldo	12,000 (corn)	to Ft. Laramie	$ 3.94 per bushel of corn

* The Army garrison near Fort Hall was withdrawn in the spring of 1850. The Army stores were taken to Fort Laramie.
† Two-year contracts were given to all freighters in 1851.

Jesup's people figured the cost, it was greater than the cost of freighting supplies from Fort Leavenworth. The Texas route cost twenty-two dollars per hundred pounds; from Fort Leavenworth to Santa Fe the cost was thirteen to fourteen dollars per hundred pounds. Jesup decided to continue supplying posts in New Mexico from Fort Leavenworth.[10]

Because the Army freighting contracts issued at Fort Leavenworth in 1851 were for two years, no contracts were let in 1852, but on September 15, 1853, Alexander Majors, James B. Yager, and the firm of Russell, Waddell & Co. each signed a contract to transport stores from Fort Leavenworth to Fort Union, New Mexico, at the rate of sixteen dollars per hundred pounds. Exactly how many pounds of goods were taken to Fort Union is not known, but one of the three contractors—Alexander Majors—was paid $28,000 for his services. The following year, Majors apparently used some of his profit to expand his freighting operations. In his autobiography, he wrote:

> I added to my transportation, making 100 wagons and teams for that year, divided into four trains. Everything moved along . . . in a most prosperous way, without loss of life among my men, but I lost a great many of my work-cattle on account of the Texas fever. The loss was not so great, however, as to impede my traveling.[11]

What Majors and others called Texas fever was a splenetic fever caused by ticks carried by Texas longhorn cattle. Although the longhorns sometimes got sick from the disease, few of them died; for northern cattle, however, including many draft oxen used by freighters, it was usually fatal. During the warm months between April and November, when most freighters traversed the Santa Fe Trail, their oxen could come down with Texas fever if they came into contact with Texas cattle, or even grazed in an area where the longhorns had grazed or simply passed through, because they picked up the ticks that carried the fever. Fortunately for the freighters, the tick could not survive freezing weather, and the movement of the longhorns north from Texas during the early 1850s was limited to areas in western and southern Missouri and eastern Kansas.[12]

By 1854 the rates for transporting Army stores from Fort Leavenworth to posts in the West and Southwest were falling. One reason was that more freighters were vying for the government contracts. Since contracts were awarded to the lowest bidder, the firms sought to underbid each other whenever possible. In many instances this meant less profit for the freighter, although he could still make some. In turn, the Army saved money. For

YOKING A WILD BULL. DRAWING BY WILLIAM HENRY JACKSON.

GRUB PILE! THE DAILY SCENE WHEN FREIGHTERS STOPPED
along the trail to rest and eat. Drawing by William Henry Jackson.

instance, in 1854 the rate was $3.80 per hundred pounds to transport stores from Fort Leavenworth to Fort Kearny. Four years earlier it had been $7.75 per hundred pounds. The rate for hauling stores from Fort Leavenworth to Santa Fe also dropped, from $11.75 per hundred pounds in 1848 to $8.59 in 1851.

Another reason was that by 1854 experienced freighters had learned more efficient methods of handling oxen and mules and men. They often increased their profits even at the lower rates. Alexander Majors got good use of his men and animals by camping along the trail each Saturday afternoon until Monday morning to allow them sufficient rest. Majors even held worship services for his teamsters on Sunday. He sought to hire only the best men he could find, and every employee had to sign a pledge. It read:

> While I am in the employ of A. Majors, I agree not to use profane language, not to get drunk, not to gamble, not to treat animals cruelly, and not to do anything else that is incompatible with the conduct of a gentleman. And I agree, if I violate any of the above conditions, to accept my discharge without any pay for my services.[13]

Freighting for the government remained a highly speculative business during the early 1850s. When a freighter was awarded a contract he usually had to gather on short notice the required number of wagons, oxen, mules, and teamsters, plus the necessary supplies. Most freighters sold their oxen and often most of their wagons each fall after they returned to Missouri because there was no certainty the government would give them a contract the following year. But freighting was not as much of a gamble as the selling of food and other provisions to the Army. Merchants bid for these contracts as well, and they were let nine months before delivery. For most this was a gamble since they had to guess the cost of food items nine months in the future. If prices went down in the meantime, fine—the merchants made a greater profit. But if prices of items included in the contracts went up, the merchants lost. As a result, the quality of provisions delivered to the Army at Fort Leavenworth was not always the best. Decay and spoilage often occurred while the supplies were being transported to other military posts. For instance, at El Paso between October 1, 1849, and July 31, 1851, the military condemned the following:

> Three barrels and 68 pounds of pork; 58,561 pounds of bacon; 7,088½ hams; 36 barrels and 172 pounds of flour; 394 pounds of hard bread;

3 bushels and 7 quarters of beans; 517 pounds of rice; 96 pounds of coffee; 183 pounds of sugar; 12 pounds of candles; 4 quarts of salt; and 114 gallons of pickles.[14]

Not all of these items had been transported to the post at El Paso from Fort Leavenworth, but after a trip of several hundred miles under a hot summer sun, there was undoubtedly going to be decay and spoilage. The freighter's contract held him responsible for shrinkage but not for leakage. Inspectors for the Quartermaster Department recommended better packaging of provisions to reduce losses. One recommendation was to pack bacon and hard bread in barrels. This was done, but later George McCall, inspector general of the War Department, reported that round barrels left much unused space in the wagons. He recommended square boxes for both bacon and bread, noting that barrels weighed half as much as the contents. This, he reported, was costly. McCall even suggested that the Army send bakers to the posts in the West and Southwest to bake fresh bread for the soldiers, thereby eliminating the need of freighting hard bread. His suggestions were ignored.[15]

The year 1854 brought news of a change in the Army's policy of awarding freighting contracts on a consignment basis. Quartermaster General Thomas Jesup announced that beginning in 1855 the Army would let one two-year contract for the freighting of all Army stores to all posts in the West and Southwest served by Fort Leavenworth. The news caused much excitement among freighters who had been involved in government freighting. They realized that whoever received the contract would no longer be gambling. There was, however, a problem. No single freighting firm in western Missouri was financially able to handle such a contract alone. During the weeks following the Army's announcement, William H. Russell and William B. Waddell of Lexington and Alexander Majors of Westport decided to pool their resources and go after the contract. When the paper shuffling and legal work was finished, the firm of Russell, Majors and Waddell was formed in early 1855, and on March 27, 1855, they signed a two-year contract with the Army, the largest single contract let by the Quartermaster Department at Fort Leavenworth up to that time.[16]

While their firm was being organized, another change was occurring in the vast territory to the west and northwest of Missouri. What had been called Indian Territory became the territories of Nebraska and Kansas. They were organized with the passage of the Kansas-Nebraska Act by Congress and signed into law by President Franklin Pierce on May 30, 1854. The measure noted that when the people of Kansas Territory joined the Union

WILLIAM H. RUSSELL
of the firm of Russell, Majors and Waddell.

ALEXANDER MAJORS.   WILLIAM B. WADDELL.

as a state they might do so "with or without slavery, as their constitution may prescribe at the time of their admission." This, of course, made the settlement of Kansas Territory a political issue—free state or proslavery. On the day President Pierce created Kansas Territory with the sweep of his pen, there were fewer than fifteen hundred white people in the new territory. Nearly seven hundred of these were soldiers and military men stationed at Fort Leavenworth. An equal number were civilians living at a few missions and trading posts, including those located along the eastern slopes of the Rocky Mountains. Kansas Territory stretched from the western border of Missouri to the summit of the Rockies, including much of what is now eastern Colorado.

The first settlers to move into Kansas Territory came from western Missouri, and they moved across the Missouri River from Weston in the fall of 1854 to establish a town just south of Fort Leavenworth. The town was named after General Henry Leavenworth, who founded Fort Leavenworth in 1827. Lewis N. Rees built the first general store, a frame building twenty by forty feet, with a warehouse about the same size. He became the first postmaster and operated the town's post office in his store. Within weeks Leavenworth was booming. In six months there were a hundred buildings and a population of three hundred. The town even had a weekly newspaper.[17]

About a month after receiving the two-year contract for all freighting of Army stores from Fort Leavenworth, Russell, Majors and Waddell decided to move their headquarters to the new town just south of the post. They invested perhaps $400,000 in building offices, warehouses, a blacksmith and wagon shop, a store to outfit employees, and a packing plant to produce meat for teamsters on the trails. The firm hired 1,700 men, including twenty-five wagon masters and a like number of assistants, forty to fifty stock tenders, and twenty to thirty cooks. They bought 7,500 oxen, and in May 1885 began loading the first of five hundred wagons that would make twenty trains. The firm went into debt, but the partners were prepared to handle the government contract.[18]

In his memoirs Alexander Majors recalled the events of 1855:

> We carried all the Government freight that had to be sent from Fort Leavenworth to the different posts . . . The cholera prevailed among our men that year. Not more than two or three died, however, but quite a delay and additional expense were caused on account of this dire disease among our teamsters, with a train load of freight for Fort Riley. This was in June, and the train was almost deserted. Another train was

entirely deserted, the sick men being taken to some of the farmers in the neighborhood, the well ones leaving for their homes, our oxen scattering and going toward almost every point of the compass. It was not long, however, until we got straightened again, and the train started for its destination.[19]

Fort Riley, mentioned by Majors, was established in 1853 near where the Republican and Smoky Hill rivers meet to form the Kansas River, about a hundred and ten miles west of present-day Kansas City. The post was named for Major General Bennett Riley, a distinguished military man who served as the last territorial governor of California. While permanent buildings were being constructed at the new post in 1855, cholera struck the workmen, soldiers, and their dependents. It also struck some of the teamsters who were delivering stores to the new post.[20]

When their two-year contract ran out, Russell, Majors and Waddell signed a one-year agreement with the quartermaster at Fort Leavenworth, Captain Thomas L. Brent, on February 25, 1857. Under the new terms, the firm agreed to transport from fifty thousand to five million pounds of Army supplies from Fort Leavenworth and Fort Riley in Kansas Territory, from Fort Union, New Mexico, and from the town of Kansas (Kansas City, Missouri) to any military post or depot in the territories of Kansas and New Mexico, the post at El Paso, Texas, the Gadsden Purchase (southern Arizona), Fort Laramie, and Oregon south of the fortieth parallel. It was a good contract, giving the firm a monopoly on the freighting of all military supplies west of the Missouri River. By the time the last trains left the eastern departure points, the firm's clerks counted only a hundred and fifty oxen and thirty-three unused wagons on their available lists. To the southwest toward Santa Fe and to the northwest on the Oregon Trail, the firm had 645 wagons, 7,740 oxen, and 700 teamsters delivering the Army stores to various posts. There were forty-eight trains carrying a combined total of 3,870,797 pounds of military supplies.[21]

Russell, Majors and Waddell had invested more than half a million dollars to meet their 1857 contract. They had planned carefully, and from all indications they would have made a handsome profit by the end of the year. But that spring in Washington, D.C., President James Buchanan decided to take firm action against the Mormons in Utah, who appeared to be resisting federal authority. Buchanan appointed Alfred Cumming as territorial governor to succeed Brigham Young, and ordered an army to accompany Cumming to Utah to make certain the federal government was in control.

A GOVERNMENT TRAIN, PROBABLY BELONGING TO RUSSELL, MAJORS AND WADDELL, is seen moving west across present-day Nebraska in the late 1850s carrying supplies to U.S. troops in Utah.

A VIEW OF RUSSELL, MAJORS AND WADDELL'S GOVERNMENT SUPPLY HOUSE in Nebraska City in 1859. Drawing from *Leslie's Magazine*, January 8, 1859.

In mid-June, on orders from Washington, the quartermaster at Fort Leavenworth notified the freighting firm that under its contract it must transport two and a half million pounds of supplies to Salt Lake City for what was being called the Army of Utah, a force of twenty-five hundred soldiers, including two batteries of artillery, then being organized to march from Fort Leavenworth to Utah.

The order took the freighters by surprise since their contract with the Army included no reference to military posts in Utah. The terms of the contract called for the Army to give the freighters sixty days' notice for each shipment, and the Army wanted the stores moved sooner. Also, the terms called for the freighters to transport no more than five million pounds of stores in 1857. The new order meant they would be freighting far more than that amount. Russell, Majors and Waddell did not have sufficient wagons, equipment, oxen, and teamsters to fulfill the order. What they had was already in use. The freighters estimated that it would cost them at least twenty dollars per hundred pounds to move the required stores to Utah. This was much higher than their contract called for, and they expressed their concerns to Captain Brent, but he told them the order had to be followed. He assured them that Congress would pay them just and fair compensation for the work. Not wanting to lose their monopoly on government freighting, Russell, Majors and Waddell decided they had no other choice than to go into debt and fulfill the Army's request.

As an army of twenty-five hundred U.S. troops was gathering at Fort Leavenworth, Russell, Majors and Waddell sent their representatives to buy oxen, wagons, and provisions and to hire teamsters. Word had spread about the Army of Utah, and the buyers found the price of oxen inflated by more than 25 percent. They had to pay a premium for each of the 3,432 head purchased. The same was true for 350 wagons, which cost nearly two hundred dollars each. Because it was late in the season and teamsters might not be able to return to their homes until the spring of 1858, the firm had to offer higher wages than usual to hire a sufficient number of men. Russell, Majors and Waddell spent $241,789 to outfit the fourteen wagon trains used to carry the stores for the Army. The firm had also agreed to furnish two thousand head of beef cattle for the troops. Twelve hundred of these animals would be the oxen used to pull the freight wagons to Utah. The remaining eight hundred cattle would be driven overland, and just before the first trains left Fort Leavenworth, herders started these cattle on the trail toward Utah.

All went well for the cattle herders until they reached a point about thirty miles west of Fort Kearny. Cheyenne Indians attacked, killed one herder and wounded another, and then drove the cattle away. Meantime, as the army moved westward, Brigham Young learned of President Buchanan's actions and of the approaching army. Young called the militia to arms. The details of what happened next have been told many times in history books. Brigham Young was determined to fight, but he soon decided to avoid bloodshed by cutting off the supplies of the advancing U.S. troops. Mormons burned trading posts, including Fort Bridger, as well as the forage in front of the advancing troops, and destroyed most of the wagons in three of the fourteen wagon trains sent by Russell, Majors and Waddell. The Mormons, however, did not injure the teamsters. In fact, they permitted them to remove their personal belongings from the wagons before setting them afire.

U.S. troops did not occupy Utah in 1857. Some of them wintered about thirty miles from Fort Bridger at Camp Winfield, a hurriedly established post along Ham's Fork on the Green River. Many more wintered at Camp Scott, another hastily constructed post, about two miles from burned-out Fort Bridger. The soldiers spent the winter in tents, dugouts, crude huts, and lean-tos, as did many of the teamsters who had delivered supplies. The teamsters were still on the company's payroll. As the Army of Utah waited for spring, politicians in Washington began to question Buchanan's actions. He was already under pressure to solve an economic panic spreading across the nation and to put an end to the bloody trouble in Kansas Territory, where free-staters were engaged in a struggle with proslavery forces (backed by Buchanan). Influential friends of the Mormons took advantage of the situation and resolved the Mormon dispute with the federal government by the spring of 1858, gaining a pardon for alleged Mormon offenses. The pardon was accepted by Brigham Young on June 12, 1858. Two weeks later U.S. troops passed through Salt Lake City to establish Camp Floyd about forty miles away. The bloodless Mormon War was over.[22]

Well before the Mormon War was settled, two of Russell, Majors and Waddell's men arrived in Leavenworth with receipted bills for the freighting of supplies to the West. The accountants soon realized the firm had suffered great financial loss. Its expenses had been much greater than the revenue derived from the government. In his autobiography, Alexander Majors wrote that the loss amounted to the firm's "previous two years' profit."[23] But even before the firm had totaled all of its 1857 losses, it signed two more contracts with the Quartermaster Department. Both contracts were to run through 1859—one for transporting military stores to posts along the Oregon Trail and in Utah, and the other to posts along the Santa Fe Trail and in New Mexico. The agreements called for the firm to freight a greater maximum weight—ten million pounds.

Because of the partnership's financial problems, Russell turned to credit to raise the necessary capital with which to purchase wagons and oxen and hire teamsters. He persuaded Secretary of War John B. Floyd to endorse the firm's issuance of drafts, or "acceptances," as they were called. He wanted to give banks and individuals these drafts in exchange for capital.

Floyd wrote to banks and individuals explaining that the firm had government contracts and that the drafts would be paid by the company after it had been paid by the government. The plan worked, and soon Russell, Majors and Waddell had sufficient funds to meet the terms of the contract.

Those terms, however, suggested that the freighting firm establish a new depot and loading point on the west bank of the Missouri River north of the fortieth parallel. From all indications Alexander Majors asked that the government contract call for a new depot somewhere in Nebraska Territory. Fort Leavenworth had become crowded. Fodder for animals had become scarce in the area around the post, and Majors did not like the trail conditions between Leavenworth and the Blue River in north-central Kansas Territory. There were many streams to cross and few bridges. The route was nearly always muddy in the spring. Conditions were better north of the fortieth parallel in Nebraska Territory, and because there the Missouri River was farther west, a new depot would actually be closer to Fort Kearny and other posts.[24]

In February 1858, Alexander Majors and Lieutenant Beekman Du Barry, an Army quartermaster, went up the Missouri from Leavenworth, examined several possible sites along the river, and made their selection. They chose Nebraska City, a town with about twenty-five stores and five hotels, located a hundred and seventy miles north of Fort Leavenworth. But Majors made two demands on the people of Nebraska City: that a levee be completed by the opening of spring navigation on the Missouri River and that the town's saloons be closed. The townspeople of Nebraska City held a public meeting, welcomed the firm, and then passed resolutions meeting the demands. The levee was finished and a large warehouse was soon built. The city council appointed a wharf master to take charge of the freight once it began arriving by steamboat. The company acquired a hundred acres on the edge of town and constructed boardinghouses, carpenter and blacksmith shops, and even a church for use by the firm's employees. Majors also acquired six hundred acres of prairie west of Nebraska City and had it planted in corn to provide feed for 16,000 yoke of oxen, which the firm advertised to buy. It wanted oxen from four to seven years old and would pay seventy-five dollars per yoke. The firm also advertised for fifteen hundred men of "good habits," offering each twenty-five dollars a month (in addition, every man would be given a Bible and a hymnbook), and for forty wagon masters "with recommendations."[25]

Nebraska City's location was ideal for a freighting depot. It was on high ground overlooking the Missouri River about fifteen miles south of where the Platte flows into the Missouri. U.S. troops were first located there in 1844, and two years later the Army built a blockhouse on the site at the start of the Mexican War. The post was called Fort Kearny, but within two years the name was transferred to a new post that had been constructed to the west along the Platte River on the Oregon Trail. The town was founded early in 1854 on the site of the old Fort Kearny. To the west was open prairie, as far as the eye could see, and a military road led across it to the site of the new Fort Kearny, about a hundred and seventy-five miles away. Over this road in 1858 traveled thirty-four wagon trains belonging to Russell, Majors and Waddell carrying government stores to Fort Kearny, Fort Laramie, and Utah. Nebraska City, within a few months, had become the freighting capital of the West. To the south in Kansas Territory, Leavenworth had faded as a transportation center, but in the far reaches of Kansas Territory events were occurring that would once again change the face of the West and provide profit seekers with new opportunities.

VIII

RUSH TO THE ROCKIES

The lust of gold succeeds the rage of conquest;
The lust of gold, unfeeling and remorseless!
The last corruption of degenerate man.

—SAMUEL JOHNSON[1]

W HEN the territories of Nebraska and Kansas were established by
Congress in 1854, both covered larger areas than their respective
states do today. Nebraska Territory was huge. It stretched from what is now
southwestern Montana east to the Missouri River and from the modern Canadian border south through present-day Montana plus portions of North and
South Dakota, Wyoming, Colorado, and all of modern Nebraska. Kansas
Territory ran from the Missouri River west to the Continental Divide, en-
compassing much of present-day Kansas plus the eastern half of modern
Colorado. The act creating these new territories allowed the residents at the
time of statehood to determine whether their states would be free or slave.
Some politicians in the East apparently believed that Kansas Territory would
be settled by Missourians and in turn become a slave state, while Nebraska
Territory would be settled by people from Iowa, Illinois, and other northern
states and therefore would be free. This would maintain some balance between the number of free and slave states in the Union.

But New England abolitionists and others opposed to slavery decided
to make Kansas a free state. They organized their forces and sent emigrants
to Kansas Territory. Missourians, most of them favoring slavery, also came to
Kansas. Some settled, but more came to vote in the first territorial elections
in 1855 and then returned home to Missouri. A proslavery territorial legislature was elected. Violence and corruption followed in eastern Kansas
Territory, where most of the population was then centered. The frontier town
of Lawrence, about forty miles west of Kansas City, Missouri, was sacked
by Missourians in May 1856, and open warfare followed in the area. Lawrence

was a stronghold of the free-state settlers. By 1858, however, the matter cooled as the free-staters gained the upper hand. And when Minnesota entered the Union as a free state, followed in 1859 by Oregon, the balance between slave and free states no longer existed. The importance of Kansas in national politics declined, but the discovery of gold in far western Kansas Territory focused new attention there.[2]

One of the first persons to carry the news of the discovery of gold to eastern Kansas Territory was a husky Delaware Indian named Fall Leaf. On a spring day in 1858 he rode his horse into Lawrence. He had gone west the previous summer as a guide with Colonel E. V. Sumner's expedition against the Arapahoe Indians. As the expedition was returning eastward the following spring, it met a group of Missourians who had found gold along the eastern slope of the Rockies. Fall Leaf had some gold for himself by the time he started for his home north of Lawrence on a Delaware Indian reservation. His arrival in Lawrence probably would have gone unrecorded had he not stopped to show his gold freely. Fall Leaf even offered to guide anyone to where it could be found in the Rockies.

Indians had found the precious metal in the mountain streams of present-day Colorado during the eighteenth century, if not earlier. But they kept the location secret. Some Mexicans found gold in the Rockies during the 1840s, but their discovery was accompanied by little fanfare. About 1850 a band of educated Cherokee Indians from Lumpkin County, Georgia, bound for California's goldfields, discovered gold in the Rockies as they paused to pan streams in what became far western Kansas Territory, now Colorado. One of the Cherokees, Lewis Ralston, found gold in a branch of Clear Creek near present-day Arvada, Colorado, but the strike soon played out. The Indians continued their journey to California, where they apparently spent many months searching for the precious metal. Later they returned to Georgia, where William Green Russell, a white man who had married a Cherokee woman, heard the stories of gold in the Rockies. In the spring of 1858 he and a party of gold seekers left Georgia to strike it rich in the Rocky Mountains.

About the time Russell and his party left Georgia, Fall Leaf carried the news of the discovery to eastern Kansas Territory. That region, like much of the nation, was beginning to feel the effects of the economic panic of 1857. Prices and wages had dropped sharply and some businesses had failed. The panic, produced by the rapid expansion of the nation westward and the speculation that followed, caused hard times. It was only natural that a dream of quick riches suddenly seemed more like reality. The gold fever struck many residents of Lawrence. Two gold parties were soon organized—

one at Lawrence and another at nearby Lecompton, the territorial capital. Fall Leaf, however, was unable to keep his promise of guiding the gold seekers. Tradition suggests that he got drunk, was injured in a fight that followed, and could not travel. Regardless, both gold parties left without Fall Leaf and journeyed to the vicinity of Pike's Peak in the Rockies. They searched without success for gold.

Meanwhile, about sixty-five miles to the north, William Russell and his party had arrived in the vicinity of present-day Denver, where they looked unsuccessfully for gold. Discouraged, many of the Cherokee Indians who had joined the party gave up and returned home, but Russell and twelve other men kept searching. At the mouth of Dry Creek, near modern Englewood, Colorado, they made a placer strike which yielded about ten dollars a day per man. When this news reached the gold seekers camped to the south near Pike's Peak, many of them hurried north to find Russell's party. By the time they arrived, however, the gold had played out. Discouraged, the Lawrence and Lecompton parties soon started east, and Russell's party split up to look for gold elsewhere in the Rockies.[3]

When stories of the discovery of gold first reached Leavenworth, located about thirty miles northeast of Lawrence, the editor of the Leavenworth *Weekly Journal* reported them as fact. The merchants of the town then set about to capture what they believed would be the trade from a large group of gold seekers anticipated from the East. The merchants knew their town could use the business since Russell, Majors and Waddell had moved their freighting headquarters north to Nebraska City only a few months earlier. They formed a committee to publicize Leavenworth as the best jumping-off point for the Kansas goldfields, and had a map drawn showing the route west from Leavenworth. Many copies of the map were printed and distributed, along with information and advice for prospectors. The merchants also produced a list of supplies that they said would be needed by four men during six months in the fields. The list reads:

Flour	800 lb.	One-gallon water keg	1
Bacon	600 lb.	Coffee mill	1
Coffee	100 lb.	Gun caps	2,000
Sugar	100 lb.	Picks	8
Salt	50 lb.	Shovels	4
Pepper	6 lb.	Axes	4
Soda	5 lb.	Gold pans	4

Dried fruit	2 lb.	Pit saw	1
Beans	2 lb.	Chisels	2
Soda crackers	1 box	Augers	2
Tea	6 lb	Frower [froe]	1
Rice	26 lb.	Drawing knife	1
Tobacco	27 lb.	Skillet	1
Powder	1 case	Coffee pot	1
Smoking tobacco	1 box	Tin plates	6
Pipe and stems	2 doz.	Tin cups	6
Lead	25 lb.	Frying pan	1
Rosin	10 oz.	Butcher knives	4
Whiskey	½ bbl.	Blankets	16 prs.
Matches	2 gross	Tent	1
Pickles	1 box	Oxen	2 yoke
Soap	25 lb.	Wagon	1
Sheets		Yokes	
Chains			

The total weight of these supplies, according to the merchants, was 2,641 pounds. No prices were listed, thereby enabling the merchants to adjust their prices to demand. They claimed, however, that the cost of outfitting in their "city" was 10 percent less than in Kansas City, Missouri, about twenty-five miles down the Missouri River from Leavenworth.[4]

The merchants of Atchison, Kansas Territory, another Missouri River town about twenty miles northwest of Leavenworth, began to organize their campaign for the gold-rush trade about the time Leavenworth started its push. Because the Missouri River bends westward at the point where Atchison is located, the town was a few miles closer to the Rockies than Leavenworth, Kansas City, and St. Joseph, Missouri. The merchants of Atchison used this as a selling point as well as the fact that the military road from Leavenworth to the Oregon Trail in Nebraska Territory passed to the west of Atchison. The merchants publicized this route, claiming it was a third shorter than any other, and more direct. They described it as running along "high, level divides" with ferries and bridges available where needed.[5]

While rumors of the discovery of gold apparently reached Kansas City about the time they were heard in other Missouri River towns, the editor of the *Journal of Commerce* ignored them. He did not tell his readers about the discovery until August 26, 1858, and then only after some respected traders of the American Fur Company reported that gold had indeed been found in the Rockies. The traders even brought samples. One of them said that men had uncovered more than six hundred dollars' worth of gold in one week using "nothing but their knives, tomahawks and frying pans."[6] Many other newspapers up and down the Missouri River copied the story from the Kansas City paper and the gold fever spread rapidly. Several parties of gold seekers had set out for the Rockies by early September 1858, but the merchants of Kansas City, already comfortable from their Santa Fe trade, seem to have reacted slowly. Only after promotional material from Leavenworth and Atchison began to flood Kansas City in the early fall did the merchants there begin to plan how they could capture some of the expected business. The editor of the *Journal of Commerce* cooperated and published three issues containing news from the goldfields and advice on routes to follow and on outfitting, and he took the position that the Santa Fe Trail route from Kansas City southwest to the Arkansas River and then west to the Rockies was the best route for gold seekers to follow. The editor noted that the route had been used for twenty-five years by wagon freighters, and that gold parties would find plenty of wood and water, U.S. mail stations and blacksmith shops, and an abundance of game. The newspaper pointed out that the Arkansas River route was free of "sand deserts" like those found on the route west from Leavenworth. The paper also reported that Kansas City had the largest stock of merchandise and groceries in the West.[7]

Exactly how many prospectors came West in 1858 is not known, but it is likely that the number was large. Most of those who headed for the Rockies came from towns near the Missouri River. By early in 1859, however, all of the larger towns along that river between Kansas City, Missouri, and Council Bluffs, Iowa, were trying to attract gold seekers from the East. Merchants in St. Joseph, Missouri, formed a committee and offered a prize of fifty dollars to the person "who shall write the best article on the advantages of St. Joseph as an outfitting and starting point for the Kansas mines."[8] Who won the essay contest is not known, but a review of the town's newspapers suggests that St. Joseph did not do as much propagandizing as most of the other Missouri River towns. Their growing community already had a good reputation as a jumping-off point for the West. Life in St. Joseph was becoming cosmopolitan. Residents were eagerly awaiting the completion of the Hannibal and St. Joseph Railroad, the first line to cross Missouri. The merchants apparently believed that once the railroad arrived it would deliver the prospectors to their doors without too much effort on their part.

When the railroad did arrive in the fall of 1859, it did make a difference. Gold seekers who could afford train travel used St. Joseph as a jumping-off point. The merchants also were able to receive new merchandise faster from the East. The St. Joseph *Gazette* published its own list of articles necessary for a complete outfit in the "mines." The list was similar to the one published earlier by the Leavenworth newspaper, but it included such luxuries as catsup, oysters, and sardines, suggesting an improved standard of living in St. Joseph, due in part to the arrival of the railroad. But not all gold seekers who arrived in St. Joseph could afford such things. Some of those bound for the Rockies came pushing wheelbarrows and handcarts containing their scanty supplies. These people purchased very little at St. Joseph, since money was scarce. But many of the gold seekers who came by rail did buy. During the summer of 1859 merchants raised their prices to take advantage of the increased demand for goods. So did farmers in and around St. Joseph, who sold butter for seventy-five cents per pound and mules for as much as a hundred fifty dollars each.[9]

Up the Missouri River at Nebraska City, many of the same conditions existed. But the town was already benefiting from the business provided by Russell, Majors and Waddell's freighting terminal, and the editor of the Nebraska City *News* was slow to publish stories of the discovery of gold. Not until September 4, 1858, did the newspaper tell of it, and even then it only quoted the late August article that had appeared in the *Journal of Commerce* at Kansas City. The editor apparently did not believe the story until F. H. Britain of Lawrence, Kansas Territory, visited Nebraska City. Britain had been to the Rockies with a gold party. His tales of finding gold seem to have been the evidence the Nebraska City editor had been waiting for, since from then on the paper began to report the discovery as fact, and merchants in Nebraska City soon claimed that their town was the best jumping-off point on the Missouri River because Nebraska City was even closer to the goldfields than Atchison due to the westward curve of the Missouri River. Some Nebraska City residents contracted the gold fever themselves and headed for the Rockies in the fall of 1858.

By early in the spring of 1859, the merchants of Nebraska City were outfitting many prospectors, but Leavenworth, St. Joseph, Kansas City, and even Atchison were doing a greater business. Still, there was enough activity to keep merchants in Nebraska City happy. One unidentified emigrant from

Michigan, who passed through Nebraska City in March 1859, reportedly
wrote:

> I am perfectly astonished at the business done in your town [Nebraska
> City]. There is three times the activity, "git up and howl," and business
> done in your three year old [town] of fifteen hundred inhabitants, than
> in my native town of over four thousand inhabitants.[10]

Whether this letter was written by an emigrant from Michigan or was the
work of merchants at Nebraska City seeking to attract more business is not
known.

Up the Missouri River from Nebraska City was the town of Council
Bluffs, Iowa. The first people bound for the goldfields passed through there
in late February 1859. One party used a "sheet-iron long tom," described
as a sleighlike conveyance. Horses or mules were probably used to pull it.
By early spring the westbound stages across Iowa and the Missouri River
steamboats delivered more gold seekers to Council Bluffs. By early April
hundreds of people were arriving en route to the Rockies. Six hundred wagons
carrying goldfield emigrants passed through Council Bluffs during May. Most
of them followed the Oregon Trail or Platte River route once they crossed
the Missouri River by ferry at Council Bluffs. But even before summer
arrived, rumors were reaching Council Bluffs and other jumping-off points
that there really was no gold in the Rockies. The first rumors were spread
by seekers who either were unsuccessful or became discouraged and sold
out before they reached the goldfields. The editor of the Council Bluffs
Weekly Bugle appears to have investigated the rumors. In his May 18, 1859,
issue, he wrote:

> We are fully persuaded that the return stampede has been caused by
> speculators beyond Fort Kearny, who have turned the Emigration back—
> bought out their out-fits for almost nothing and are making a big spec-
> ulation out of their frauds, falsehoods and lying.
>
> Speculators upon the road turn back the Emigration within two hundred
> miles of the mines—buy their flour for $2.50 per sack, and their bacon
> for two cents per pound, and send it forward to the Mines, where they
> get $15 per sack for the flour, and 70 cents per pound for the bacon;
> and a like profit on the balance of the outfit.

Such newspaper accounts appear to have restored the confidence of most
gold seekers coming from the East, much to the relief of merchants at the

jumping-off points. But at Council Bluffs the merchants soon had new competition.

Omaha, Nebraska, is across the Missouri River from Council Bluffs, Iowa. In 1859 it was the territorial capital of Nebraska. When news of the discovery of gold reached Omaha, many residents made plans to leave for the Rockies. Most of the town's merchants, however, remained, and they did more business in outfitting residents than emigrants during 1858. But by early 1859 the trade from gold seekers began to dominate Omaha's commerce. The following year Omaha not only had grown to the size of Council Bluffs—about four thousand people—but had surpassed Council Bluffs and become the principal outfitting town at that point on the Missouri River. [11]

THE IMMEDIATE BENEFACTORS of the Kansas gold rush were the merchants of the Missouri River towns between Kansas City and Council Bluffs and their suppliers in St. Louis, New Orleans, and points east. The steamboat companies also benefited since they carried increasing amounts of goods and gold seekers to the jumping-off points. But west of the Missouri River those looking for gold faced the problem of traversing the prairies and plains. It was the same problem encountered in turn by explorers, fur traders, mountain men, missionaries, and emigrants bound for California, Oregon, or Utah. Such overland travel was slow, much slower than via the steamboats or stage lines that had delivered many of them to the Missouri River. To reach Denver City, Kansas Territory, from the Missouri River, they either walked, rode horses or mules, or traveled in wagons or buggies. The mode of transportation usually depended upon what they could afford. The same problem had existed during the California gold rush. Many forty-niners went overland, but others sailed around the Horn to reach California, a journey that was much longer but often more pleasant, with less hardship than was endured on the overland journey. During the California gold rush no one succeeded in providing reliable passenger service overland. But the Kansas goldfields were only about seven hundred miles west of the Missouri River, and there were now settlements to the west of the river in the new territories of Kansas and Nebraska.

For two entrepreneurs who were experienced in overland travel, the distance did not seem a great obstacle. During the winter of 1858–59, William H. Russell and John S. Jones, a subcontractor for Russell, Majors and Waddell and co-owner of perhaps the second-largest overland freighting

ATCHISON, KANSAS TERRITORY, LOCATED ON THE MISSOURI RIVER, IN 1860.
Atchison was a jumping-off point for the Kansas gold fields.

A CONCORD COACH BUILT BY THE ABBOT-DOWNING COMPANY
of Concord, New Hampshire. The coach pictured here was used during the late
1860s on runs between Atchison, Kansas, and Denver, Colorado,
by Wells, Fargo and Company.

firm on the plains, made plans to establish the Leavenworth and Pike's Peak Express Company. The stage line would take passengers, freight, and mail between Denver City and Leavenworth. Russell and Jones sent an expedition west across Kansas Territory in March 1859 to survey and mark a new direct route to Denver City. Stage stations were established twenty-five miles apart, and six men were placed at each station. Four of the men were stage drivers; the other two were to operate the station. Meantime, the company ordered fifty Concord coaches built by the Abbot-Downing Company of Concord, New Hampshire, founded in 1813. The firm's Concord coaches were considered the best vehicles of the kind in the world by the late 1850s.

Each coach was well constructed, mostly hand-built. White ash was used for the body frame, pole, axle beds, perches, and the felloes, or wheel rims. The wood was dried and sun-warped so that it would not shrink in the arid West. The wooden wagon bed was supported by iron bands, or perpendiculars, abutting upon wooden rockers, which in turn rested on strong thoroughbraces that were three or four inches thick and about five inches wide. The leather thoroughbraces not only broke jolts better than steel springs as a coach rolled overland but could also be repaired in the field. Nearly all of the metal used in the construction of each coach was hand-forged from strong, light Norwegian iron. One early western traveler on a Concord wrote that the tires were of unusual thickness and had been polished like steel on the hard dry ground. The wheels were dished inward so that they would defy centrifugal force as a coach sped around corners.[12]

The Leavenworth and Pike's Peak Express Company paid about $250 for each of the fifty coaches purchased on credit. The total cost was about $12,500. Ten more coaches were ordered later. The company also bought 543 mules, costing $60,890, to pull the coaches. About a hundred stage drivers were hired for forty to seventy-five dollars a month plus board, stock tenders for forty to fifty dollars a month, and division agents for a hundred to a hundred twenty-five dollars a month. In addition, the company had to obtain more than a hundred freight wagons to carry supplies, plus animals with harness to pull the wagons. And its work force, about 175 employees, cost the company some two hundred dollars a day in wages alone.[13]

The new direct route to Denver City ran west from Leavenworth to Ozawkie, from Hickory Point to near Topeka, to St. Marys, Manhattan, Fort Riley, Junction City, and then west between the Republican and Solomon rivers, across the upper branches of the Republican River, over the branches of the Platte in sight of the Rockies, and then across unsettled plains to Cherry Creek near the new town of Denver City. The distance over this route was 687 miles. The Leavenworth and Pike's Peak sent men, supplies, coaches, mules, and forage west along the route. The first coaches arrived in Denver City in early May. The company's first eastbound stages from Denver City reached Leavenworth on May 21, 1859. The first westbound stages to leave Leavenworth departed four days later. The company ran their stages in pairs at the beginning, not so much to meet the great demand for transportation as to afford protection against marauding bands of Indians along the western third of the route. [14]

Albert D. Richardson, an eastern newspaper correspondent, was the only passenger aboard the first stages to leave Leavenworth on May 25, 1859, for Denver City. He later wrote:

> The little capital of the Granite State alone has the art of making a vehicle which like the one-hoss shay, "don't break down, but only wears out." It is covered with duck or canvas, the driver sitting in front, at a slight elevation above the passengers. Bearing no weight upon the roof, it is less top heavy than the old-fashioned stage-coach for mud-holes and mountain-slides, where to preserve the center of gravity becomes, with Falstaff's instinct, "a great matter." Like human travelers on life's highway, it goes best under a heavy load. Empty, it jolts and pitches like a ship in raging sea; filled with passengers and balanced by a proper distribution of baggage in the "boot" behind, and under the driver's feet before, its motion is easy and elastic. [15]

Richardson's stage ride probably became smoother after Horace Greeley, the editor and publisher of the New York *Tribune*, climbed aboard at Manhattan, Kansas Territory. Greeley, who had been touring the settlements of eastern Kansas Territory, had decided to move on to Denver City. As the coaches pushed west beyond the last settlements, Greeley took advantage of the stage stops to write letters to his New York City newspaper. At Pike Creek, Kansas Territory, on May 29, 1859, he wrote:

> I believe I have now descended the ladder of artificial life nearly to its lowest round. . . . The progress I have made during the last fortnight toward the primitive simplicity of human existence may be roughly noted thus:
> May 12th. — Chicago. — Chocolate and morning newspapers last seen on the breakfast-table.

23d. — Leavenworth. — Room-bells and baths make their final appearance.

24th. — Topeka. — Beef-steak and wash-bowls (other than tin) last visible. Barber ditto.

26th. — Manhattan. — Potatoes and eggs last recognized among the blessings that "brighten as they take their flight." Chairs ditto.

27th. — Junction City. — Last visitation of a boot-black, with dissolving views of a board bedroom. Beds bid us good-by.

28th. — Pike Creek. — Benches for seats at meals have disappeared giving place to bags and boxes. We (two passengers of a scribbling turn) write our letters in the express-wagon that has borne us by day, and must supply us lodgings for the night. Thunder and lightning from both south and west give strong promise of a shower before morning. Dubious looks at several holes in the canvas covering of the wagon. Our trust, under Providence, is in buoyant hearts and an India-rubber blanket.[16]

The stage carrying Greeley and Richardson arrived in Denver City on June 7, 1859. Denver City was nothing more than a collection of about a hundred and fifty tents and cabins. Most of the cabins were without roofs. There was one hotel, forty by two hundred feet, built of logs and covered with canvas. Richardson described Denver City as "a most forlorn and desolate-looking metropolis. If my memory is faithful, there were five women in the whole gold region; and the appearance of a bonnet in the street was the signal for the entire population to rush to the cabin doors and gaze upon its wearer as at any other natural curiosity."[17]

A little more than a month later Libeus Barney, a gold seeker from New England, also commented on women in a letter from Denver City to his hometown newspaper at Bennington, Vermont. On July 12, 1859, Barney wrote:

The present stationary population of Denver is about 300, with some 200 log houses, of which not more than six can boast of a floor. There are three frame houses in course of erection, and every third building is a groggery, dealing out whisky at from 10 to 20 cents a "nip," and warranted to kill at fifty yards. There are but a few *ladies* here yet there are many females of questionable morality about town, some in bloomer costume and some in gentlemen's attire throughout, while squaws are more than plenty. The latter seem to have no sense of shame, and live a dissolute, licentious and uncivilized life . . .[18]

THE DEMAND FOR GOODS in Denver City and other mining settlements of present-day Colorado resulted in the establishment of a rather loose trading system that soon gave way to a tighter economic structure. When the first flood of gold seekers arrived in the fall of 1858, the only sign of civilization on the site of present-day Denver was a crude trading post operated by John Smith, a former mountain man and Indian interpreter turned trader. He had established the post in 1857 to trade with Indians in the area. His trading goods were purchased from the firm of Gerry and Bordeaux at Fort Laramie, a hundred and seventy-five miles to the north. When gold was discovered in 1858, Smith's trading post was the only place in the vicinity of Cherry Creek where supplies could be obtained. Those supplies, however, appear to have been limited. Elbridge Gerry's account books, now preserved in the State Historical Society of Colorado, list the goods sold to Smith and probably available to prospectors in the fall of 1858, when the gold rush really began. The goods and the prices Smith paid for them were:

10½ pairs indigo blue blankets	$ 84.00
12 yards scarlet cloth	$ 13.20
49½ yards brown muslin	$ 7.27
88 yards blue drill	$ 11.00
2 rifles	$ 20.00
3 kegs powder	$ 21.00
1,000 percussion caps	$ 0.50
40 pounds tobacco	$ 8.80
200 bundles seed beads	$ 33.33
16 pounds brass wire	$ 6.40
2 dozen mirrors	$ 1.00
2 gross finger rings	$ 1.80
2 decks playing cards	$ 2.50
100 pounds flour	$ 4.50
25 pounds tea	$ 25.00
30 pounds cocee [?]	$ 3.90

3 yoke of cattle $240.00

1 wagon $100.00

1 auger .... $ 0.75

Smith joined the prospectors in founding the towns of St. Charles and Auraria, which were combined to create Denver City on November 22, 1858. Although Smith did some prospecting, he returned to trading and shared with an unidentified man the expense of building a double log cabin, the first permanent house on the site of present-day Denver. Smith, with his Indian wife and children, lived in Denver City until about 1860, when at the age of fifty he moved his family and trading post north of Denver to conduct trade with Elbridge Gerry and other traders among Indians along Big Thompson Creek.[19]

John Smith had a monopoly on trading in the goldfields until October 1858, when Charles H. Blake and Andrew J. Williams arrived on the scene with four wagonloads of merchandise and opened a store in a large tent. They soon constructed a double cabin similar to the one occupied by Smith. On Christmas Eve 1858, Richens Lacy Wootton, better known as "Uncle Dick" Wootton, arrived in Denver City from New Mexico with four wagons. Three of the wagons contained New Mexico flour and one wagon carried "Taos Lightning," a moonshine sometimes described as the "world's worst whiskey." It had been used by some of the Indian traders on the southern plains. Wootton unloaded the whiskey and invited everyone to help themselves. They did, and Christmas Eve 1858 became memorable for most of the residents of Denver City. Wootton sold the flour without difficulty and at his price.[20]

At about the same time a gold seeker wrote relatives in the East that prices in Denver City were "exorbitant and will be higher in the spring. Good clothing, provisions, medicines, building hardware, sheet iron, books, stationery, and such articles will sell readily."[21] Prices did go up in the spring before more goods arrived from the East, but they also went down. Supply and demand determined prices. Gold seeker Libeus Barney wrote on July 12, 1859:

Merchants are doing nothing, owing to the emigrants arriving with eight and ten months' supplies and selling out at ruinous discounts and returning. For instance, today one hundred wagons will arrive, and tomorrow twenty will depart, next day and day after *vice versa*, and so alternate from day to day. Such has been the history of the last four weeks.[22]

DENVER, KANSAS TERRITORY, ABOUT 1859.

THE OVERLAND COACH OFFICE, DENVER, COLORADO.
Drawing by Theodore R. Davis in the January 27, 1866, issue of *Harper's Weekly*. It shows the growth of Denver by the end of the Civil War.

Wagon trains loaded with supplies and merchandise began arriving at Denver City in early June. One of the first trains from Leavenworth was owned by Jones and Russell and consisted of twenty-five wagons pulled by six-mule teams. The train carried staples and other goods to be sold. In July 1859, the firm of Russell, Majors and Waddell sent a caravan to Denver. It then decided to take advantage of the new market and started a store in Denver City. Robert B. Bradford was hired to run it; he received a salary and a third of the store's profits. Bradford opened the store in a log building belonging to Russell and Jones, but soon constructed a two-story frame building, fifty by sixty feet, at what is the southeast corner of Blake and G streets in present-day Denver. Meantime, another partner in the big freighting firm established his own freight line to Denver and made plans to open his own store there. Starting separate business ventures and forming outside partnerships seem to have been commonplace for Russell, Majors and Waddell. [23]

There were many other entrepreneurs who sought to gain a piece of the profit, not from gold mining, but from the miners. A correspondent for the *Missouri Republican,* writing from Denver City on August 17, 1859, included in his story a list of the firms then doing business in Denver City and nearby Auraria, and where the merchants had come from. Combined, the two towns had nineteen firms dealing in groceries and provisions, four firms of land agents, three hotels, one barbershop, one bakery, one butcher, two tenpin alleys, one newspaper (*Rocky Mountain News*), two dealers in liquors, one blacksmith, one billiard saloon, two jewelers, one firm selling lumber, a company that made wood shingles, one variety store, two restaurants, and one lawyer, who was also listed as judge of the probate court. Fifteen of the businesses had been started by men from Missouri, thirteen by merchants from Leavenworth, eight by New Mexicans (most from Santa Fe), and four by men from Nebraska Territory. The balance of the firms were started by men who gave their homes as Iowa, Ohio, Wisconsin, Illinois, Pennsylvania, or New York City. Several of the firms were extensions of houses operating in Leavenworth, St. Louis, or Kansas City. [24]

The businesses relied on freighters for their merchandise and supplies. But plains freighting was dictated by the seasons of the year. While bad winter snowstorms often made travel impossible, it was the availability of natural grass and not the weather that restricted freighting between November and late March. Because there were few settlements between eastern Kansas Territory and the Rockies where sufficient forage could be obtained for oxen and mules, the freighters had to rely on grass to feed their animals. Carrying

THIS UNIDENTIFIED PHOTOGRAPH SHOWS AN APPARENT BULLWHACKER
during the late 1850s. Previously unpublished, it was reproduced from an
ambrotype recently discovered in Laramie, Wyoming.

grain for feed was possible but very expensive. Therefore freighters usually
waited until spring grass was high enough to serve as feed. This normally
occurred in late March or early April. During the late 1850s most freighters
traveled between the Missouri River and the Rockies only from early spring
to October. Two or three round trips annually were not unusual for ox trains,
three or four round trips for mule trains. The freighters could start mule
trains across the plains earlier than ox trains because mules were better
adapted to scanty forage than oxen. The same was true in the fall of the
year. About 1859, a few freighters wintered in the vicinity of Denver City.
They placed their oxen on the buffalo grass just east of the mountains. The
animals put on weight and gained strength. This meant that freighters could
leave the Missouri River towns later in the fall, knowing that they would
not have to return until spring.

The location of Denver City about midway between the Missouri River and Salt Lake City was an advantage to some freighters. Wagon trains carrying freight to Utah stopped in Denver City on their return trips east, sometimes bringing goods from Utah, including flour, vegetables, and other fresh produce. It was not unusual for the freighters then to take shipments east from Denver City to Leavenworth, Kansas City, or other Missouri River towns. During the late 1850s there was no tariff set by the government to control the charges made by freighters. Time, costs, distance, competition, and the volume and weight of a shipment determined what any freighter charged. Freighters learned early that it cost as much to move a light but bulky load as it did to move a heavy but compact load. This resulted in what was called a "differential." For example, the freighting rates per pound from Atchison, Kansas Territory, to Denver City during the late 1850s and very early 1860s were:

Flour	9¢	Crackers	17¢
Tobacco	12½¢	Whiskey	18¢
Sugar	13½¢	Glass	19½¢
Bacon	15¢	Trunks	25¢
Dry goods	15¢	Furniture	31¢

The rates on shipments of corn, hay, coffee, salt, and hardware were about the same as the rates for flour.[25]

Frank A. Root, who spent many years associated with overland travel, wrote in 1901 that there was an "enormous amount of traffic on the overland route in those days":

There were trains constantly outfitting and crossing the plains from Omaha, Nebraska City, St. Joseph, Atchison, Leavenworth and a few other points. This, it should be remembered, was before the railroads had passed west of the Missouri River, and everything had to be hauled by oxen, mules or horses. Twenty-one days was about the time required for a span of horses or mules to make the trip to Denver and keep the stock in good condition; and they walked all the way. For ox trains, the average time was five weeks, thus making the distance of from eighteen to twenty miles a day. To make the trip to Salt Lake it took horses and mules about six weeks; ox trains were on the road from sixty-five to seventy days.[26]

NEBRASKA CITY, NEBRASKA, PROBABLY DURING THE CIVIL WAR,
with freight wagons belonging to the Nebraska City firm of Hawke & Nuckolls,
one of the first firms to ship goods to the Kansas gold fields.

NEBRASKA CITY, ON THE MISSOURI RIVER,
with the freighters arriving and departing. Drawing by Alfred Matthews, 1865.

Many of the freight trains sent to Salt Lake City in 1860 were owned by Russell, Majors and Waddell, who had also signed another contract to carry government freight to Santa Fe and other points in the Southwest. Leavenworth had been abandoned in favor of Kansas City as a starting point for the trains taking military supplies over the Santa Fe Trail, while trains bound for Salt Lake City continued to outfit at Nebraska City. But by 1860, Russell, Majors and Waddell was in serious financial difficulty. The company had little capital and was heavily in debt. Majors and Waddell sought ways to save the company, but William H. Russell, instead of joining them, turned his attention to a new enterprise. Using the financial backing of Jones, Russell and Company and Miller, Russell and Company, two firms that were not in financial difficulty, Russell established the Pony Express to carry the mail from St. Joseph, Missouri, to Sacramento, California. He wanted not only to secure for himself a $600,000 mail contract held by the Overland Mail Company (organized in 1857 by John Butterfield, a New York native) but also to demonstrate that overland travel to California was practical during the winter months. Russell gave employees of Jones, Russell and Company only sixty-five days to prepare the Pony Express service. The company purchased horses and hired station keepers, stock tenders, and eighty riders.

A PONY EXPRESS RIDER CARRYING THE MAIL.

The stations, an average of ten miles apart, numbered one hundred and ninety. And on April 3, 1860, at 7:15 p.m., the first rider set out from St. Joseph. At about the same time another rider left San Francisco for St. Joseph, a distance of 1,966 miles.

The Pony Express was an efficient service, with riders carrying the mail between Sacramento and St. Joseph in thirteen days. Exactly how much the service cost Russell is not known, but between April 3, 1860, and October 24, 1861, three hundred and eight runs were made each way. The riders covered a total of 616,000 miles on horseback, carrying 34,753 pieces of mail. During this time the company grossed only $90,141, or about the cost of purchasing horses for the service. The Pony Express failed as a profitable enterprise, but it went out of business in October 1861 because the overland telegraph was completed.[27]

Even before the Pony Express ceased to exist, Russell tried to save the sagging empire of Russell, Majors and Waddell. In the East he obtained Indian Trust Fund Bonds, representing money set aside by the government for Indians, through a friend at the Interior Department. These he used as collateral for loans, and when lenders asked for more collateral, Russell went back to his friend and obtained $870,000 in additional bonds. When the misuse of these bonds was disclosed, President James Buchanan called a special meeting of his cabinet. The Secretary of the Interior was instructed to order the arrest of Russell and his friend in the Interior Department. Russell, Majors and Waddell went into bankruptcy. The company failed in 1862, but by then the Civil War had begun and the West was undergoing still more change.

IX

THE CIVIL WAR

Out of the Civil War slowly rose a new nation; a nation that differed nearly as much from its past, in spirit, intent, and ideas, as the country of Jefferson and Hamilton had differed from colonial America. The process was necessarily slow. The war had swiftly destroyed slavery and erased the old opposition of the states to federal supremacy, but otherwise the new order represented an evolution, not a revolution.

—ALLAN NEVINS[1]

WHEN the Civil War began early in 1861, an economic recession occurred in the North. Many banks failed and hundreds of commercial houses were forced to close their doors. There were actually more bank failures during the first year of the Civil War than during the panic of 1857, but the amount of money involved was not as large. The depression was caused by the uncertainties of the war and the lack of adequate banking reserves, but few banks in the West were affected. For the most part, people in the West did not suffer as severely as those in the East from the depression, which continued into 1862. To understand why, some political history is necessary.

Only about one-seventh of the 31.4 million people in the United States in 1861 lived west of the Mississippi. Only the first tier of states beyond the river, plus Texas, Oregon, and California, had been admitted to the Union. Except for pockets of settlement in the goldfields of Kansas Territory (now Colorado) and Mormon Utah, much of the remainder of the West had been bypassed by settlers heading for the Pacific Coast. Most Americans in the West supported the Union, and there were no major political changes there as a result of the Civil War. Congress approved a free-state constitution and statehood for Kansas early in 1861, and President Abraham Lincoln appointed pro-Union officials in the newly created territories of New Mexico,

Utah, Nevada, and Washington the same year. Lincoln did the same when Idaho Territory was organized in 1862, Arizona Territory in 1863, and Montana Territory in 1864. Lincoln's Administration pushed statehood for Nevada in 1864 and succeeded in organizing the entire West into viable political units, each with a government loyal to the Union. Late in the war it even succeeded in putting down an attempt by some Californians to form an independent Pacific Republic, which was also to include the Pacific Northwest. And to avoid dissension in the West, Lincoln did not press the draft there. Thus in many ways the West and Westerners benefited from the political changes brought about as a result of the war.[2]

Retaining the Union, and not slavery, apparently was the overriding issue in much of the West. Slavery was more of a dominant issue in parts of the East, certainly in the South and in Texas, Louisiana, Arkansas, and Missouri. Slavery was a particularly bitter issue along the border between Missouri and Kansas, where struggles over whether Kansas would be a free or slave state had spurred conflicts beginning in 1856. Most Kansans were for the Union, but in Missouri the residents were mixed, and the peace of many neighborhoods was often threatened. The area in and around Kansas City, Missouri, was particularly volatile. It was not a safe place to live, and many people left.

When Percival G. Lowe, a Denver merchant and wagon freighter, learned what was happening, he hurried to western Missouri from Denver ahead of his eastbound wagon train. Lowe's "best girl" lived on the line between Platte and Clay counties near Kansas City. As he later recalled:

I persuaded myself and the girl, and her parents too, that it was best to get her away from such surroundings, and I urged the consummation of what we hoped might be brought about in the near future, so that on the 4th of June, 1861, I married Miss Margaret E. Gartin, a daughter of Andrew Gartin, Esq., of Clay County, one of the leading men of upper Missouri, and one of the best families in the State. I fitted up a Dougherty ambulanche [sic], got a good campaign cook, and every convenience for the trip. The train [Lowe's wagon train from Denver] came in and I had plenty of loading at 10 cents a pound, which, when grass alone was required for forage, was equal to 12 cents in March, when corn must be fed. The trip to Denver was uneventful. I had prepared a nice home in Denver and we moved into our own house. Besides extraordinary expenses, this trip cleared me $3,000.[3]

Although state bank notes were in circulation in Missouri, Lowe undoubtedly demanded payment in hard currency—gold. Bank notes were not trusted. There were perhaps fifteen hundred state banks in operation in the United States by early 1862, and they were producing about seven thousand different kinds of bank notes. Many were fraudulent. Because banks were still not trusted in much of the West, freighters like Lowe usually demanded hard currency.

Another freighter and merchant who did not trust paper money was R. M. Rolfe, a native of New York. He came West in the 1850s and soon owned an interest in a profitable commercial house in St. Louis. In September 1860, however, he sold out, purchased a good stock of groceries, and shipped them by steamboat, at $2.25 per hundred pounds, up the Missouri River 714 miles to Nebraska City, Nebraska Territory. There he opened a general store. He made a great deal of money because all but two other grocery houses had been destroyed by a fire that had swept through much of Nebraska City a few months earlier. Rolfe did so well that by the early spring of 1862 he was able to purchase several wagons and teams with which to transport his own merchandise to Denver. Rolfe recalled that his small wagon train was "one of the first to pull out from Nebraska City that season. On the route, a few miles west of Fort Kearney [sic], we struck a vast herd of buffalo that was making for the Platte for water. They were in such numbers that we made camp, thinking it not best to drive through them. . . . We made Denver in twenty-eight days, from Nebraska City, which was quick time for cattle [oxen]."[4]

Rolfe sold his merchandise for more than $10,000 in "Cherry Creek gold dust." Because the tiny particles of gold could easily be lost, he placed the dust in two-pound oyster cans, soldered them shut, and rolled the cans in his blankets and strapped them securely at the back of the saddle on his mule. He rode back to Nebraska City without losing any of the precious dust. Rolfe experienced few difficulties during the Civil War. His business prospered as the demand for goods increased in Denver. Years later Rolfe wrote his recollections of the time when he worked as a merchant-freighter transporting his own goods across the plains and prairie to Denver. Rolfe wrote:

The freight wagons used were the Murphy and Espenshied, made in St. Louis, and the Studebaker, made at South Bend, Ind. These wagons were constructed for the plains transportation business; made of the best timber, wide-tracked, strong and tight, high double box and heavy tired, and covered with heavy canvas over the bows. More of the Murphy make were used than either the Studebaker or Espenshied, though many claimed the Studebaker the easiest running.

Seven thousand pounds was the load drawn by five yoke of good cattle [oxen]; six yoke if cattle were light. A good team consisted of one yoke of heavy, well-broken cattle for wheelers, a good second best came next; two pair in the swing could be made up from partly broken cattle, with a good pair of leaders. The Texas steer made, when broken, the best leaders, holding his head high, with his long horns and soft wild eyes, like thouse of a deer, quick on his feet, quarters light, and tapering limbs clean cut, could run like a horse and quite as fast when alarmed.

A full train consisted of twenty-six wagons; twenty-five freight and one mess. A wagonmaster and assistant were in charge. They generally used mules for their riding; then there were with every train three or four plain's ponies for herding and extra riding. Sixteen to eighteen miles a day was made in two drives, one from early morning to about 11 o'clock a.m., and the second from about 1 o'clock to 6 o'clock p.m. Sometimes the drive would vary in making water and grass.

In making camp at the order of the wagonmaster, the lead team would circle to the right, the team following to the left, advancing until they met; then the next two in the same order, bringing the fore wheel close up to the hind wheel of the wagon ahead, the balance of the train in the same order, making a semi-circular corral with thirteen wagons on each wing, nearly closed at front with an opening at the rear of about twenty feet. The cattle were then turned loose, with the yokes on the ground where they stood. A mounted header takes charge of the cattle, watering first and then to grass. The drivers, each one with a heavy pistol at his hip and gun . . . divided in mess of six to eight, two with sacks start out for [buffalo] chips [used to fuel their cooking fires], another for water, another digs the fire trench, all do their part until the meal of bread, bacon and coffee is ready to be served out, and each one provided with a tin plate, quart cup, knife, fork and spoon. If the camp is for the night, after supper preparations are made for an early breakfast; then would come time for a good smoke, song and story, then rolling up in their blankets to rest under the wagons until "Roll out! roll out!" is called out at daybreak by the night herder. After an early breakfast the cattle are driven in the corral and at the command,

"Yoke up!" every driver starts in among the cattle with yoke on his left shoulder, ox-bow in his right hand, and key in his mouth, looking for his off-wheeler; when found the yoke is fastened to him with one end resting on the ground until the near one, his mate, is found. When yoked together they are taken to the wagon and hitched in their place; then come the others in their order, only a short time being required until ready for the order from the wagonmaster—"Pull out!" Then the bull-wacker [sic] is in his glory, with his whip, the least of which is twenty feet in length, large and heavy tapering to a small point and tipped with buckskin popper, hung to a handle eighteen inches in length, filling both hands in its grasp but small at the end; four or five swings over and around the head the lash is shot straight out with the reports sounding like the fire of a picket line of soldiers. A steer was seldom struck with these whips unless a deadhead. When hit with full force blood would surely follow.

Rolfe observed that the rations given to men employed on a wagon train crossing the plains were based upon the government rations, but that the private freighters were a little more liberal. Government rations per man per day were one and a quarter pounds flour, three-quarters to one pound of bacon, one and a quarter ounces of coffee, two and a half ounces of sugar. But each man with Rolfe's wagon train received two pounds of flour, one and a half pounds of bacon, one and a quarter ounces of coffee, and two and a half ounces of sugar per day.[5]

Another Nebraska freighting firm—Crow, Porter and Barrett of Brownville—did not have Rolfe's success. Francis Withee, a Stella, Nebraska, pioneer, in a letter now in the files of the Nebraska State Historical Society, recalled that in 1862 the firm bought a drove of hogs, loaded their freight wagons with corn, and started to drive the hogs to Denver to supply the market with fresh pork. They took large iron kettles and an experienced butcher with them. The corn lasted to Plum Creek, about thirty-five miles from Fort Kearny, where the hogs were butchered. The fresh meat was then loaded in the wagons without being cut up or salted. The freighters hoped the normally cool fall weather would keep the pork from spoiling, but the weather was unusually warm, and the lean meat along the backbones soured. The company lost a great deal of money on the venture, but most of the other freighters in Nebraska and several other river towns, including Atchison and Leavenworth, prospered during the Civil War.

Freighters in Kansas City, however, suffered financially during the early part of the war. Nearly all of them, including Irwin, Jackman and Company and several large mercantile houses, moved to Leavenworth to avoid trouble in Kansas City from Confederate guerrillas. This was a heavy blow to Kansas City, since the Army had moved its supply depot from Fort Leavenworth to Kansas City in 1860 to improve the supplying of military forts along the Santa Fe Trail in the territories of Kansas and New Mexico and in Indian Territory. Even Kansas City's *Journal of Commerce* suspended publication from August 1861 to late March 1862 because of the frequent violence in the area. Fearing that Confederate guerrillas—many of them were nothing more than outlaws—might loot Kansas City's two banks, which were branches of St. Louis banks, Union officers marched two companies of soldiers to the banks and demanded all of their currency. He collected about $80,000 in gold and carried it in a wagon to the levee under guard. There the gold was placed on a ferryboat and taken the short distance to Wyandotte. Soldiers continued to guard the gold until it was transported to Fort Leavenworth. Later it was shipped down the Missouri River by steamboat and returned to the parent banks in St. Louis.[6]

Nearly all the steamboats on the Missouri were owned by Union men, but all the Missouri River pilots except two were in sympathy with the South. The Union had to go to the Illinois River for river pilots when it wanted to move troops up the Missouri in 1861. More serious trouble was caused by Confederate guerrilla bands composed mostly of Missourians. They soon infested the country along the Missouri, fired into boats, and did all they could to break up river commerce. At first the guerrillas succeeded in driving most of the traffic off the river between St. Louis and Kansas City, but gradually activity resumed as steamboat captains realized that most of the danger came from the south bank of the river. The captains avoided trouble by remaining as close to the north bank as possible. They learned to expect trouble where the river's channel ran close to the high wooded palisades or in other sheltered localities. Ambushes and attacks by guerrillas often occurred at these points. It was not unusual for a captain to anchor in midstream during the night. Many pilothouses were equipped with shields constructed of semi-cylindrical boiler iron. The shields were placed around the wheels and could be turned as necessary to protect the wheelsman. Union troops usually were sent along when steamboats carried much government freight, especially between St. Louis and Kansas City, but otherwise the captains and their crews had to defend themselves as best they could when attacked.[7]

The trouble in Missouri interrupted commerce at the eastern end of the

Santa Fe Trail at the start of the war, but it soon resumed, with Leavenworth serving as the eastern terminal for government and private freighters, including New Mexicans. The freighters simply avoided the Kansas City area. Leaving Fort Leavenworth for Santa Fe, they either traveled south and west from the fort and crossed the Kansas River at Lawrence, hitting the Santa Fe Trail several miles south of that town, or followed the military road west from Fort Leavenworth to Fort Riley and then joined the Santa Fe Trail many miles to the south. In returning east they took one of these same routes to Leavenworth. Not until late 1862 and early 1863 was peace restored in the Kansas City area. Freighters and businessmen who had moved away gradually began to return. Before then, however, a few freighters under government contract apparently had skirmishes with Confederate guerrillas in eastern Kansas west of Kansas City, but no accounts have been found describing attacks on private freighters carrying nonmilitary goods. Certainly there was fear among all freighters and most residents of eastern Kansas that guerrillas might attack at any time. These fears extended as far southwest along the Santa Fe Trail as Council Grove, about a hundred miles southwest of Kansas City, Missouri.

In many ways Council Grove was typical of the early white settlements that sprang up on the prairies and plains because the location provided shelter, water, and wood for fuel. At Council Grove, the stand of timber in the small valley intersected by the Neosho River not only served as protection during the winter months from the often vicious north wind that swept unchecked over the Great Plains from far to the north, but also provided the wood that was one of two necessities for life in the West. The river supplied the other—water. Indians had camped on the site long before the arrival of white men, and it became an important stopping point for travelers on the Santa Fe Trail even before 1825, when United States commissioners and chiefs of the Osage nations met there to sign the treaty giving the United States the right to mark the Santa Fe Trail through Osage land and the free use of the road forever. In compensation the Indians were given eight hundred dollars in money and merchandise. The grove of trees where the meeting was held became known as Council Grove. Permanent white settlers did not arrive there until 1847, when Albert G. Boone and James G. Hamilton of Westport, Missouri, opened a log trading post in the grove. Seth Hays was put in charge of the post and instructed to trade with the Kansa Indians who lived nearby. Hays was the first white man to settle in Council Grove.

A few months after Hays arrived, George F. Ruxton, a British traveler and sportsman, stopped and visited with him. Ruxton was heading east with a wagon train after traveling through the West and down into Mexico. Of his visit Ruxton wrote:

> On approaching Council Grove the scenery became very picturesque; the prairie lost its flat and monotonous character, and was broken into hills and valleys, with well-timbered knolls scattered here and there, intersected by clear and babbling streams, and covered with gaudy flowers, whose bright colors contrasted with the vivid green of the luxuriant grass. My eye, so long accustomed to the burned and withered vegetation of the mountains, reveled in this refreshing scenery, and never tired of gazing upon the novel view. Council Grove is one of the most beautiful spots in the western country. A clear, rapid stream runs through the valley, bordered by a broad belt of timber, which embraces all the varieties of forest-trees common to the West. Oak, beech, elm, maple, hickory, ash, walnut, &c., here presented themselves like old friends; squirrels jumped from branch to branch, the hum of the honey-bee sounded sweet and homelike, the well-known chatter of the blue jay and catbird resounded through the grove; and in the evening the whip-poor-will serenaded us with its familiar tongue, and the drumming of the ruffed grouse boomed through the grove. The delight of the teamsters on first hearing these well-known sounds knew no bounds whatever. They danced, and sang, and hurrahed, as, one after the other, some familiar note caught their ear. Poor fellows! they had been suffering a severe time of it, and many hardships and privations, and doubtless snuffed in the air the johnny-cakes and hominy of their Missouri homes.[8]

The peace and tranquillity of Council Grove as described by George Ruxton in 1847 were not present in the summer of 1861. Most of the town's few hundred residents favored the Union and opposed slavery, and they lived in fear of attacks by Confederate guerrillas riding out from Missouri. They were especially fearful of Bill Anderson, who had earned the nickname "Bloody Bill." Anderson was a Missouri guerrilla, but before the Civil War he had moved to Kansas Territory with his parents and settled to the southeast of Council Grove. The Anderson family was said to make their living by robbing settlers and wagon trains traveling the Santa Fe Trail.

According to tradition, Bill Anderson and his brother James and two other young men announced they were taking sides with the South soon after the war began. One of the young men—not an Anderson—stole a horse but was caught. He was taken before the justice of the peace, Arthur I. Baker, who operated a general store near Council Grove. Baker had the young man bound over for trial. The Andersons did not like this and decided to kill Baker. On July 3, 1862, Bill and James Anderson rushed into Baker's store firing their guns. Baker and his brother-in-law, George Segur, were wounded but managed to flee to the basement of the store. Baker found a gun and fired through the basement door, wounding Bill Anderson. The Anderson brothers then set fire to the store and fled. Baker perished as the building was destroyed by flames; George Segur escaped through a basement window but died from his wounds the following day. Until "Bloody Bill" Anderson was killed in Missouri by Union soldiers in October 1864, the residents of Council Grove feared that he would return with other guerrillas to take vengeance. He never did.

Council Grove was quite a trading center during the early 1860s. The town grew up on both sides of the Santa Fe Trail in a grove of tall trees, and had at least two wagonmakers and more than a dozen businesses to supply freighters moving along the trail. Perhaps the largest business was the Pioneer Store, housed in a long, two-story stone building with oak and black walnut woodwork and several outbuildings nearby. The Pioneer Store was established in 1858 by the firm of Conn, Hill and Munkers. Early in the 1860s, William F. "Billy" Shamleffer moved to Council Grove from Baltimore, Maryland, perhaps to escape from the hardships of the war. He found a job clerking in the Pioneer Store. Many years later he recalled the duties of a Council Grove merchant during the Civil War:

A merchant at this place . . . should be regarded as a good shot, especially with a Colt's revolver, and under no circumstances be guilty of cowardice. He should have a good saddle-horse with a hair lariat, and know how to use it and his spurs successfully. In general, he should be a good mixer, and be at home in the Indian tepees or in the humblest bachelor's dugout or hut on the plains. He should always be ready to do military duty as against the Indians, Quantrill, Bill Anderson, Dick Yeager and [Confederate general] Price. He should be able to eat with relish a bachelor's meal, no matter if he had seen the dog lick the skillet before the bacon was fried; and also, if invited, sit in an Indian's banquet circle, where wombum [?], buffalo tongue, dried spotted corn, dog meat and other delicacies were served. The more languages he could speak the better; and he should have on hand in his store a

WILLIAM F. "BILLY" SHAMLEFFER,
an early storekeeper in Council Grove, Kansas,
as he appeared late in life.

supply of everything from Bibles to whiskey and strychnine, for he had
to deal with all kinds of people . . . With all of the liberality of those
old days, which included two dances a week [held in the Pioneer Store],
entertaining customers on the side with good things to eat and drink
(including "Mum's extra dry") the business netted ten percent in profits.
The merchant had to hustle with business customers all day, and then
entertain them royally at night; for some of them came hundreds of
miles to trade, and the business house had to furnish many of them
with sleeping quarters, place to cook their meals, corrals in which to
keep their stock, and open access to the corn cribs and other feed.

It was the business of the local trader to keep an eye out for sore-footed oxen which usually pulled the great freight wagons, who would buy them for from $25 to $35 apiece, and keep them about thirty or sixty days, have them shod, and sell them back for from $100 to $125 each. He had to deal in all kinds of lumber, from large pieces like saw logs, and also keep all kinds of lumber for sale. In his stock were found every known variety of goods for use on the frontier, from ox yokes and repairs to cambric needles, from small boxes of pills to barrels of whiskey. There was always a larger percent to lose in shipping whiskey "from the river" (the Missouri River), for the freight boys usually carried gimlets, and at convenient watering places on the road tapped the barrels and replaced the liquor used with fresh water from some spring or stream.

The frontier merchant had to take some interest in the local horse races, and have some money in the purse, and set them up all around whether he won or not. It was his duty to prepare and finance the Fourth of July celebration; pay for the music at the Indian dances when he visited their villages near by, and interest himself in the welfare of all of his customers of whatever grade. It was, "How are you, John and Jim?" "How are all the folks getting along?" "Been thinking of you every day, wondering why you didn't come to town"—and he asked them all in a cheerful, wholesouled manner, especially about wife and

SHAMLEFFER'S STORE IN COUNCIL GROVE DURING THE EARLY 1860S.
The street in front is the Santa Fe Trail.

children. If they were with the father, many compliments had to be made, and the wife of the local settler in the valley had to be favored in all things. It would have been an insult to tell a woman that her butter was not good or that she had sold ancient eggs the last time in town; but the merchant had to take her merchandise even if he did lose out on these articles and had to consign them to the rubbish heap in the back yard as soon as she was out of town.[9]

Travel between Council Grove and Santa Fe over the Santa Fe Trail was not affected directly by the Civil War, but the shifting of many Union troops from forts on the plains to fight in the East gave the Plains Indians an advantage. In the absence of soldiers, some Indians raided and burned white settlements. Some white women were kidnapped. This continued until Colonel John Chivington and his Colorado Volunteers attacked a camp of sleeping Arapahoes and Southern Cheyennes on Sand Creek many miles southeast of Denver early on the morning of November 29, 1864. Chivington and his men killed more than two hundred Indians, including women and children. The massacre and mutilation of Indian men, women, and children led other Cheyennes to retaliate in raids on wagon trains and white settlements, and Chivington—a minister—was condemned for his actions by congressional and military committees.

Trade at Santa Fe had also been interrupted for a time early in the Civil War when, in July 1861, Colonel John R. Baylor, CSA, and a force of Texans moved north from Fort Bliss at present-day El Paso, Texas, into the Mesilla Valley of New Mexico. The Confederates forced the evacuation of Fort Fillmore, about five miles south of present-day Mesilla. The fort has the distinction of being the only western post to be surrendered completely without a fight by Union troops during the war. As the Confederates moved north, other Union soldiers abandoned Fort Stanton, located sixty-six miles west of modern Roswell, New Mexico. Still another Confederate force from Texas, headed by General Henry H. Sibley, moved up the Rio Grande Valley early in 1862 toward Albuquerque and Santa Fe. The Confederates wanted to capture all of New Mexico Territory and then take the goldfields of Colorado. Their forces did occupy Albuquerque and Santa Fe, but their push north was stopped in late March of 1862 when Union forces, many from Colorado, defeated the Confederates in the battle of La Glorieta Pass near Santa Fe. The battle has been called "the Gettysburg of the West."

By the summer of 1862 commerce over the trail to Santa Fe was again moving, but the war had caused serious economic problems for the people of New Mexico. The Confederate troops had consumed the surplus agricultural products and mercantile stocks and blotted out the mining and mercantile capital. Although conditions gradually improved once commerce resumed between eastern Kansas and Santa Fe, the war cut trade between New Mexico and Texas, where Confederate forces remained in control. Just prior to the Civil War the road between Mesilla and Port Lavaca, Texas, a distance of eight hundred and fifty miles, had carried millions of dollars in trade goods annually. But the fighting destroyed this commerce. And trade between Mexico and southern portions of New Mexico remained poor. The war with Mexico, beginning in 1846, had first wiped out much of that trade. It had resumed during the 1850s, but paper money was not valued highly and gold was scarce. High rates of duty also helped make profitable trade difficult. According to one account, "sugar which costs from two to six cents a pound in Sonora and Durango, with duties, freighter and profits, make it worth fifty cents a pound in Mesilla Valley. In El Paso, Mexico, it is worth twelve and a half cents; in Mesilla, New Mexico, fifty miles distant, it sells for fifty cents."[10]

THE PATTERN of settlement in the West was unchanged by the Civil War. Oregon, California, and Utah were the primary destination points for most emigrants, and they reached these areas by following the Oregon-California Trail, which was far removed from the battles of the Civil War. Although fifteen thousand emigrants followed the trail along the Platte River in Nebraska Territory in 1860, only five thousand made the journey in 1861, the year the war began. About the same number headed west in 1862, but there were ten thousand emigrants in 1863, twenty thousand in 1864, and twenty-five thousand in 1865, the year the war ended.[11] The increase in 1863 probably resulted from the passage of the Homestead Act by Congress in 1862. It provided that any citizen or intended citizen who was either twenty-one years old or the head of a family could settle a quarter section (160 acres) of unoccupied public land. If the person resided on the land for five years, he could receive patent to it. But the West also had another great attraction—gold and silver. And both were found in new rich deposits just before and during the war.

AS THE RUSH to the goldfields of far western Kansas Territory was underway in the spring of 1859, two prospectors were looking for gold in the mountains

WAGON TRAINS SUCH AS THIS ONE CROSSING THE NEVADA DESERT
supplied the Nevada mining towns during the Civil War.

surrounding the Carson River valley southwest of present-day Reno, Nevada.
Patrick McLaughlin and Peter O'Riley uncovered some heavy, dark soil that
looked rich near a spring located in what was called Six Mile Canyon. Another
man—described in one account as the laziest prospector in the region—
happened on the scene. He was Henry T. P. Comstock. The fast-talking
Comstock soon gained a share of the claim for himself and a couple of
friends. Later the heavy, dark soil assayed out at $3,876 a ton. Comstock
talked so much about "his" discovery and "his" claim that the find became
known as the Comstock Lode. And it started another rush, which created
the town of Virginia City, Nevada, and provided new opportunities for profit
in the West.[12]

The discovery of gold in present-day Nevada on the eve of the Civil
War was only one in a series of discoveries during the dozen years that
followed the California gold rush. Aside from the strikes in Kansas Territory
and what became Nevada, the precious metal was found on the upper Columbia River in 1855, on the Fraser River in British Columbia in 1857,
and along the Clearwater and Salmon rivers in present-day Idaho in 1861
and 1862. But unlike earlier gold rushes—that of 1849, and the push to
the Kansas fields, when gold seekers moved from east to west across the
continent—the gold rushes to the upper Columbia, British Columbia,
the Clearwater and Salmon rivers, and Nevada started from California. The
prospectors already in California were the first to rush to the new fields in
hopes of finding richer claims. When word of the Nevada strike of gold and

silver reached California, hundreds of men came over the mountains and hurriedly staked claims. Many built crude shacks of canvas or sagebrush before the first snow late in 1859. The spring of 1860 found thousands more arriving, most of whom were businessmen, merchants, gamblers, and speculators seeking to take advantage of the opportunity to fulfill the needs of the gold seekers. As they built hotels, saloons, gambling halls, general stores, and houses, the towns of Virginia City and nearby Gold Hill emerged. By the summer of 1860 hundreds of freight wagons and even pack trains of mules were carrying supplies over the mountains from California to the new mining towns. Merchants in Utah also sought to take advantage of the situation, freighting flour and butter to Nevada. Some then sent their trains on to California to pick up merchandise for the Utah market. The *Deseret News* in Salt Lake City, on November 12, 1862, praised the arrival of merchandise from California and added, "This class of enterprise is a decided improvement upon the old style of our merchants," who had relied on goods freighted west from the Missouri River.

One of the best-known observers of early Virginia City, Nevada, was Samuel Langhorne Clemens, better known as Mark Twain. In June 1861, Clemens, twenty-five, ended his voluntary service with a battalion of Confederate irregulars and headed west from Missouri with his brother Orion Clemens, newly appointed secretary of the territory of Nevada. The brothers traveled by stage from St. Joseph, Missouri, to Carson City, the capital of Nevada Territory, a journey that took twenty-two days. Samuel Clemens first tried his hand at prospecting for silver, but succeeded only in running himself into debt. In his spare time he wrote humorous letters for the *Territorial Enterprise,* a newspaper at Virginia City. In August 1863, he joined the newspaper's staff as a reporter and writer. Samuel Clemens wrote the following description of Virginia City's boom days:

Virginia had grown to be the "livest" town, for its age and population, that America had ever produced. The sidewalks swarmed with people— to such an extent, indeed, that it was generally no easy matter to stem the human tide. The streets themselves were just as crowded with quartz wagons, freight teams and other vehicles. The procession was endless. So great was the pack, that buggies frequently had to wait half an hour for an opportunity to cross the principal street. Joy sat on every countenance, and there was a glad, almost fierce, intensity in every eye, that told of the money-getting schemes that were seething in every brain and the high hope that held sway in every heart. Money was as plenty as dust; every individual considered himself wealthy, and a melancholy countenance was nowhere to be seen. There were military companies, fire companies, brass bands, banks, hotels, theatres, "hurdy-gurdy houses," wide-open gambling places, political pow-wows, civic processions, street fights, murders, inquests, riots, a whiskey mill every fifteen steps, a Board of Aldermen, a Mayor, a City Surveyor, a City Engineer, a Chief of the Fire Department, with First, Second and Third Assistants, a Chief of Police, City Marshal and a large police force, two jails and station-houses in full operation, and some talk of building a church. The "flush times" were in magnificent flower! Large fire-proof brick buildings were going up in the principal streets, and the wooden suburbs were spreading out in all directions. Town lots soared up to prices that were amazing.

The great "Comstock lode" stretched its opulent length straight through the town from north to south, and every mine on it was in diligent process of development. One of these mines alone employed six hundred and seventy-five men, and in the matter of elections the adage was, "as the 'Gould and Curry' goes, so goes the city." Laboring men's wages were four and six dollars a day, and they worked in three "shifts" or gangs, and the blasting and picking and shoveling went on without ceasing, night and day.

The "city" of Virginia roosted royally midway up the steep side of Mount Davidson, seven thousand two hundred feet above the level of the sea, and in the clear Nevada atmosphere was visible from a distance of fifty miles! It claimed a population of fifteen thousand to eighteen thousand, and all day long half of this little army swarmed the streets like bees and the other half swarmed among the drifts and tunnels of the "Comstock," hundreds of feet down in the earth directly under those same streets. Often we felt our chairs jar, and heard the faint boom of a blast down in the bowels of the earth under the office. [13]

It was while Samuel Clemens was working on the *Enterprise* that he began signing the name "Mark Twain" to many of his contributions. In May 1864, while filling in as editor of the newspaper, he signed "Mark Twain" to a satiric report of an auction of a sack of flour for the benefit of the Sanitary Fund—the Civil War equivalent of the modern Red Cross—suggesting that the money raised go toward a "Miscegenation society" in the East. Readers became irate. Clemens exchanged insults with James Laird, editor of the Virginia City *Daily Union*, and then challenged Laird to a duel. Laird declined. Clemens then left Virginia City for San Francisco to avoid prosecution under Nevada's anti-dueling law.

Meantime, Nevada boomed, in contrast to many cities and towns in the East that were suffering from the effects of the Civil War. Although Nevada was about two thousand miles west of most major battles, there were heated exchanges between Unionists and secessionists. A group of secessionist recruits even attempted to take over Virginia City by turning three buildings into armed forts. The attempt failed because most citizens supported the North. In 1863, Nevada Territory became the key in a political power play by President Lincoln and his Administration. Many members of Congress favored a constitutional amendment abolishing slavery, but a two-thirds vote in both houses was required. To obtain the three votes needed to swing the decision, Lincoln pushed through an enabling act to make Nevada Territory a state. The next move was for the people of Nevada to draft a constitution. A constitutional convention was quickly assembled late in 1863, and a constitution was written that included taxation of Nevada's mines, which caused it to be defeated. A second constitutional convention was held, and a new constitution was written, eliminating reference to mine taxation. It was submitted to the electorate and passed. Time was by then so important that the entire document was telegraphed to Washington, D.C., at a cost of $3,416.77, and President Lincoln officially proclaimed Nevada a state on October 31, 1864. A governor, state officials, and a representative to Congress were hurriedly selected, and the state legislature chose two U.S. senators. The two senators and the representative rushed to Washington and arrived in time to vote for the Thirteenth Amendment abolishing slavery in the nation. Nevada had paid its debt to the man who made statehood possible only four years after the territory was formed.[14]

To the north and east of Nevada in what is today Montana a man named John Owen found gold early in 1852. He apparently was unimpressed with his find and went on to other things. Later a half-blood named François "Benetsee" Finaly, who seems to have worked for the Hudson's Bay Company, also found gold. When he took it to an official of the Hudson's Bay Company, the official told him not to mention his find to anyone since it would attract gold seekers and ruin the fur trade. But Finaly did tell others. In 1858, James and Granville Stuart, natives of Virginia, heard of Finaly's discovery while passing through Deer Lodge Valley. The Stuarts had gone to California in 1852 to find gold, but they had little success and started back East in 1857. Near Salt Lake City they became alarmed at reports of Mormon hostility and turned north, crossing into what is now western Montana. There, hearing of Finaly's discovery, they prospected for gold using an old spade and a bread pan and found some in a mountain stream. But because there were hostile Indians in the region, they soon moved on. The Stuarts later returned and established a ranch in Deer Lodge Valley where they raised cattle. They also found more gold, and their stories eventually attracted gold seekers to the region. By 1862 there were about forty-five prospectors searching for gold in the vicinity of the Stuart ranch, about seventy-five miles southeast of present-day Missoula.

While searching for gold in Deer Lodge Valley, Granville and James Stuart kept a diary that captures not only the color and flavor of the prospector's life in early Montana but the rapid changes that occurred as merchants and others arrived to meet the needs of the miners. Here are a few selected entries from the Stuarts' diary, written in 1862:

May 20. Working at ditch and sluices. Burr, Powell, and I went to Dixie, found everyone hard at work. Blake and McAdow made ten dollars today. Higgins worked about three hours on bed rock and made three dollars and a half. Doctor Atkinson and Gold Tom are digging tail races to their claims. We sponged on Blake and McAdow for our grub. We had rice, etc., for dinner; beans, etc., for supper. Blake was the cook, enjoyed our visit very much. They are a jovial set of miners and we had much fun at one another's expense in the way of jokes. I like the appearance of the diggings better than I thought I would. There is plenty of hard work, but I think there is good pay doing it. . . .

June 25. Barcier and others arrived from Fort Benton. They say three steamboats have arrived there loaded with emigrants, provisions, and mining tools and supplies. Now everybody talks of going to Fort Benton. . . .

July 4. Five emigrants arrived last night and twelve or fifteen today. All from Benton. Came up the river on those [three] steamboats. . . .

July 12. With the emigrants today is a Mr. B. B. Burchett with his family, consisting of his wife, two very handsome daughters, one a blonde and the other a brunette, and two little tow-headed boys. It looks like home to see little blonde children playing about and to see white women. Miss Sallie Burchett is sixteen years old and a very beautiful girl. Every man in camp has shaved and changed his shirt since this family arrived. We are all trying to appear like civilized men. . . .

July 20. Worden and Higgins's wagon arrived from Fort Benton loaded with merchandise for their store at Hell Gate. Our mining claims at Dixie are not paying expenses. The emigrants are still leaving for Salmon river mines and some are returning to the states. . . .

July 23. Arrived at our town to-day a fine violin player accompanied by his handsome, seventeen years old wife. His name is J. B. Caven. We purchased a good violin sometime ago, so we have the Cavens over often and enjoy the society of an intellectual white woman and good music. Certainly we are approaching civilization or rather civilization is coming to us. All the men are shaving nowadays and most of them indulge in an occasional hair cut. The blue flannel shirt with a black necktie has taken the place of the elaborately beaded buckskin one. The white men wear shoes instead of moccasins and most of us have selected some other day than Sunday for wash day. . . .

July 29. Worden and Higgins concluded to start a branch store in our village and leave a portion of their goods here and to-day I began helping them put up a log store. . . .

August 1. The grocery is doing a flourishing business. Several gambling houses started. . . .

August 4. Many emigrants arriving from Pike's Peak. I bought two wagons and the harness with them for eighty dollars. The grocery is doing a fine business. . . .[15]

As the Stuarts and others were searching for gold during the summer of 1862, a party of prospectors on their way from Colorado to the Salmon River gold strike stopped to pan Grasshopper Creek, many miles south of where the Stuarts were located. The prospecting party, headed by John White, discovered gold and touched off an even greater rush than that started by the Stuarts. Within a year the town of Bannack was born. The Stuarts went to Bannack and opened a butcher shop. In the summer of 1863, not far from Bannack, more gold was discovered in Alder Gulch. Within a few weeks there were perhaps ten thousand gold seekers camped in the area, and modern Virginia City, Montana, was founded. The Stuarts moved to Virginia City and turned to blacksmithing and merchandising.

The new Virginia City was not named after Virginia City, Nevada. It was first named Varina, after the wife of Jefferson Davis, but a Union judge renamed it Virginia. (Virginia City, Nevada, according to tradition, received its name when a prospector named James Finney or James Fennimore, better known as "Old Virginny," fell to the ground and broke his bottle of whiskey. He used the remaining whiskey to christen the settlement "Virginia.")

The arrival of gold seekers in what is now western Montana and Idaho resulted in the formation of Idaho Territory on March 3, 1863. But that territory was so large that effective control of the region that is now western Montana could not be maintained from the Idaho territorial capital at Lewiston. On May 26, 1864, Montana Territory was formed. Bannack became the territorial capital, but after the gold strike in Alder Gulch and the sudden growth of Virginia City, the government moved the capital there. Later, in 1875, Helena was made the capital.

MONTANA TERRITORY enjoyed the advantage of having steamboat transportation to and from points on the lower Missouri River. Although wagon freighters with ox teams brought goods and supplies from Utah, Minnesota, and even Missouri River towns like Atchison, Leavenworth, and Nebraska City, steamboats could deliver goods, supplies, emigrants, and gold seekers faster than wagons and to within about two hundred miles of Virginia City and Bannack. The steamboats would travel thirty-five hundred miles from St. Louis to Fort Benton, which was located on the south bank of the Missouri

THE BOOM TOWN OF VIRGINIA CITY, MONTANA TERRITORY,
soon after gold was discovered in Alder Gulch in the summer of 1863.

River about twelve miles upstream from where the Teton and Marias rivers join the Missouri. The site was selected by the American Fur Company in 1846 because it marked the head of navigation on the Missouri. American Fur began constructing a trading post on the spot and completed it in the fall of 1850. On Christmas Eve that year Alexander Culbertson, the post factor, named it in honor of Senator Thomas H. Benton of Missouri, who had so often rescued the fur company from disaster. The trading post was two hundred and fifty feet square and constructed of adobe bricks. The walls were thirty-two inches thick, and at two corners of the enclosure, diagonally opposite from each other, were two bastions containing cannon that overlooked the nearby rolling prairie.

From the time of its completion until 1860, Fort Benton was important to the Indian trade on the upper Missouri. It is estimated that more than 292,000 buffalo robes plus thousands of salted buffalo tongues and furs were shipped down the Missouri by keelboats and mackinaws from there.[16] The first steamboat to reach the post was the *Chippewa*, arriving in 1859, and soon others came. The steamboats changed the character of Fort Benton from a rather sleepy trading post to a major distribution center for much of

FORT BENTON, LOCATED ON THE MISSOURI RIVER
in present-day Montana, in 1868. The steamer *Success* is tied up at the levee.

the region. Freighting soon became an important business as well, with freighters hauling merchandise and supplies brought by steamboats to settlements in the region. Naturally there was even more growth after the Montana gold rush began in 1861.

According to tradition, the first word of a gold strike to reach Fort Benton came in 1856 when a mountaineer named Silverthorne arrived at the trading post with a buckskin bag filled with gold dust. He said he had struck it rich in the mountains to the southwest of the post. Silverthorne demanded trade articles worth a thousand dollars in exchange for the dust. The American Fur Company people complied and Silverthorne departed. The following spring the gold dust was sent down the Missouri with the American Fur Company's first shipment of furs. When it reached St. Louis, the gold dust was valued at $1,525. Silverthorne's discovery was kept quiet, and no rush to Montana occurred until after James and Granville Stuart spread the word in the early 1860s after finding gold about a hundred and twenty miles

DIAMOND R FREIGHT TRAIN STRUGGLING TO CROSS THE MOUNTAINS.
Painting by Hollin.

TRAIN OF WAGONS CARRYING FREIGHT DELIVERED BY STEAMBOAT
at Fort Benton on the Missouri River through Prickly Pear Canyon on the trail to
Helena, Montana. The wagons belonged to the Overland Freight Line, better
known as the Diamond R because of its trademark, a capital R in a diamond.

southwest of Fort Benton. Next came the gold strike at what became Virginia
City and in Alder Gulch near present-day Bannack, Montana.

During the early years of the Civil War, Fort Benton was a very busy
place during the spring, summer, and early fall. But as winter approached,
it became quiet. Little freighting was attempted during the winter months,
when the Missouri River froze and all steamboat travel ceased. While many
people left Fort Benton to spend the winter in a warmer climate, usually
about a hundred men remained. They were closely confined during the cold
months. There was little entertainment, and the food was plain—aside from
wild game procured by hunters, there was hominy, some rice, sugar, dried
fruit, and occasionally biscuits, depending upon what supplies had been
ordered the previous summer. The person ordering supplies had to anticipate
the needs of those who would remain at the post during the winter. In the
winter of 1861–62, whether that person did not order a sufficient supply of
tobacco or whether there was a scarcity because of the war is not known,
but in March 1862 the trading post's supply of tobacco gave out. Life had

been routinely dull, and without tobacco it was worse for the men, most of whom smoked. They grew sullen. Fights broke out and several men were killed or injured. Occasionally one man would bring forth a small amount of tobacco, which he would sell for ten dollars per ounce in gold. His fellows soon learned that he had obtained it by tearing up the floor and gathering pieces of tobacco that had fallen through the cracks. When word reached Fort Benton that the first steamboat of the year had been held up by low water about twenty miles from the post, several men hurried on foot to meet the boat. They bought all the tobacco they could carry at a dollar and a half a pound and rushed back to Fort Benton, where they sold it for from six to ten dollars per pound in gold dust.[17]

The growth of Fort Benton as a trading center during the Civil War is reflected in the following figures calculated by Joel F. Overholser, Fort Benton writer and historian. They reflect Fort Benton's Missouri River commerce:

TONNAGES

Year	Up	Down	Buffalo robes
1861	175	225	18,000
1862	1,000	200	11,650
1863	800	302	28,890
1864	1,500	212.5	17,000
1865	6,000	362.5	29,000

The tonnage brought up the Missouri River in 1863 was less than in 1862 because the river was at a lower level than usual. This made it impossible for steamboats to pass through the "rocky river" area, a rather straight but boulder-strewn bed stretching from Cow Island to Fort Benton. Steamboats were forced to stop at Cow Island and transfer freight to the shore. Wagons were then used to transport the freight to the post.[18]

Although some state bank notes from eastern states were brought by emigrants to Fort Benton and other settlements in Montana Territory during the Civil War, most were shunned by traders and merchants because of their questionable value. Treasury notes and federal greenbacks, however, were treated as a commodity and bought and sold at market price. The greenbacks were produced beginning in 1862 and were backed solely by the credit of the United States. They were considered legal tender for all debts except the tariff and interest on government bonds. But in Montana Territory and elsewhere in the West, gold remained the principal medium of exchange during the war. Merchants usually made one annual trip East, taking their year's accumulation of gold to pay their bills and to purchase goods and supplies. The gold and silver found in the West helped the Union to recover economically from the depression early in the war, and it continued to attract profit seekers to the West. Of more importance, it helped to lay the foundation for a nation that even before the Civil War was beginning to move from an agrarian to an industrial society that would in turn seek to absorb the West and make it dependent upon the East.

X

THE IRON HORSE ARRIVES

*In the Plains country . . . the railroads preceded the population. There
was nothing, comparatively speaking, in the Plains country to support
them—practically no population to travel on them, few supplies to be
shipped, and, aside from cattle and hides, little produce
to be sent to market.*

—WALTER PRESCOTT WEBB[1]

AFTER the United States acquired California and Oregon in the late
1840s, there were calls to link the Pacific Coast with the Atlantic Coast
by railroad. It was part of the sweeping nationalism, the belief in "manifest
destiny" then infecting the country. By the early 1850s Congress came to
accept the idea, and in 1853 it authorized the Army to survey all feasible
routes between the Mississippi and the Pacific Ocean. When the surveys
were released in 1855, four routes were recommended—two across the South
and two across the North. But the same sectional differences that led to the
Civil War made it impossible for Congress to agree on one of the routes.
Only after Northerners gained control of Congress in 1861 did agreement
come. Congress then ignored the four recommended routes and selected a
fifth one running west from Omaha, Nebraska Territory. It was a central
route.

In 1862 Congress gave the Central Pacific Railroad of California the
task of building its line eastward across California and the Sierra Nevada,
and two years later the Union Pacific Railroad was created to build westward
across the prairies and plains and over the Rockies to meet it. Because much
of the territory to be crossed was unsettled and the cost of construction was
so great, the lawmakers in Washington recognized that the railroads would
need government aid. Since public funds could not be used directly, Congress
passed the Pacific Railroad Act of 1862 authorizing a substantial land grant
to each line similar to land grants given midwestern railroads in the early

1850s. Broad rights-of-way were granted through public lands, and the railroads were given alternate sections of land within a strip from two to ten miles wide on either side of the right-of-way. The alternate sections retained by the government could then be offered for sale at double the minimum price because of their increased value.

The Pacific Railroad Act also provided for a subsidy in the form of United States bonds in the amount of $16,000 per mile of completed track. The railroads, however, were expected to raise construction funds by selling the thirty-year bonds and repaying the government the full face value plus accumulated interest at maturity.

The Central Pacific Railroad began construction first, in 1862, but progress was slow. Manpower and money were scarce because of the Civil War. Manufactured supplies needed for building the line had to be shipped by boat from the East Coast around Cape Horn to California. When the Union Pacific began its construction west of Omaha in 1864, it also had to rely on water transportation for supplies. Until 1867, when the Chicago and Northwestern Railroad reached Council Bluffs, Iowa, most of the materials for the Union Pacific were brought up the Missouri River from Pittsburgh and other eastern cities. By then the Civil War had ended, and many soldiers turned civilians were coming West to seek their fortunes. Often they were Irishmen, and they provided needed labor for the Union Pacific. To the west the Central Pacific had brought in Chinese coolies to help build the line through the Sierra Nevada. After the Central Pacific reached Nevada, Congress gave the railroad the right to lay its tracks across Nevada's deserts until the line linked up with the Union Pacific. Meantime, the Union Pacific had reached South Pass in present-day southwestern Wyoming and continued westward. The two railroads started across Utah from opposite sides, each sought to lay more track than the other—each mile of track laid meant more government bonds and land grants. Because Congress had failed to establish a point where the lines would link up, the grading crews of the Central Pacific and the Union Pacific actually passed each other laying out parallel roads close together. When officials in Washington learned this, they stepped in and ruled that the two lines must join at Promontory near present-day Ogden, Utah.

It was nearly mid-May of 1869 when officials of the two railroads met to link up and drive a final, golden spike, on which was engraved: "May God continue the unity of our country, as this railroad unites the two great oceans of the world." The president of the Central Pacific missed with the first swing of his sledge, and a vice-president of the Union Pacific reportedly hit his own shin. It took a workman in a sweaty undershirt to deal a few well-aimed blows and get the two oceans properly joined.[2]

The men behind the Central Pacific Railroad not only exemplified the successful profit seekers in the American West during the latter half of the nineteenth century, but also had taken advantage of the economic opportunities spurred by the discovery of gold. It was investment capital produced in California that gave them the capability to develop the railroad to expand the market for California products.

First and foremost in the Central Pacific's development was Theodore Dehone Judah, the son of an Episcopal clergyman of Bridgeport, Connecticut. Born in 1826, Judah studied engineering and worked on eastern railroads. He went to California in 1854 to supervise the building of the Sacramento Valley Railroad and became an active supporter of a transcontinental rail-

CHINESE WORKERS ON THE CENTRAL PACIFIC RAILROAD IN CALIFORNIA.
Drawing from *Harper's Weekly*, Dec. 7, 1867.

FREIGHTERS WORKING FOR THE CENTRAL PACIFIC RAILROAD
can be seen hauling supplies to construction crews over the Dutch Flat and
Donner Lake Wagon Road, 1867.

road. Later he lobbied in Washington for the line, and in 1860 he discovered a practical route through the Sierra Nevadas. Judah convinced four other Californians to invest their capital in the railroad, but unfortunately he himself did not live to see the Central Pacific become a reality. In his haste to reach Washington from California, Judah chose to travel by boat to the Isthmus of Panama, cross overland, and continue by boat to New York and on to Washington. He contracted yellow fever and died a week after arriving in New York City.[3]

The four Californians whom Judah got to invest in the Central Pacific were also Easterners who came West to find success. Each of the "Big Four," as they came to be called, became multimillionaires. Leland Stanford, president of the Central Pacific, was born in 1824 at Watervliet, New York. After reading law in nearby Albany, Stanford emigrated with his wife to Port Washington, Wisconsin. But the new town failed to prosper. Learning of the success of his merchant brothers in Sacramento, California, Stanford went West in 1852. He soon entered politics and in 1861 became governor of California. Stanford recognized the importance of a transcontinental railroad to California and the Pacific Coast, and in partnership with Charles Crocker, Mark Hopkins, and Collis P. Huntington, he succeeded in getting several legislative acts passed to smooth the way for the railroad. In 1863, Stanford became president of the Central Pacific. Before his death in 1893, Stanford became not only a wealthy man but also a U.S. senator from California.[4]

Charles Crocker, two years older than Stanford, was the son of an unsuccessful liquor merchant in Troy, New York. He moved with his family to near Marshall, Iowa, where they farmed, but when gold was discovered in California, gold suddenly had more appeal than farming. Crocker led a party of prospectors, including his two younger brothers, to California. After spending two years looking for gold, Crocker realized there was more profit to be found selling goods to the increasing number of residents in San Francisco. Like Stanford, Crocker became wealthy.[5]

The third member of the Big Four was Mark Hopkins, who also was a native of New York State. Born in 1813, he left his home at Henderson, New York, to supply miners with their needs in California. He set up a store, and his business flourished. Soon he became a partner with Collis P. Huntington in a store in Sacramento.[6] Huntington, the son of a Harwinton, Connecticut, tinker, peddled watches until he had enough money to open his own jewelry store in Oneonta, New York. But when the California gold rush began, Huntington went West to find gold, taking with him a trunk full of trading goods. His search for gold in the mines lasted only one day. Finding none, Huntington became a merchant, and like Hopkins and the others, he was soon wealthy.[7]

To protect the western end of the Central Pacific, these four men also built and acquired railroad lines from Sacramento to San Francisco, and they built others south to Los Angeles and San Diego and east to El Paso, Texas. This southern line, incorporated separately, became the Southern Pacific Railroad, and in time it stretched east to New Orleans.

The promoters of the Union Pacific Railroad were not as western in nature as were the Big Four. They were mostly Easterners who remained in the East as capitalists. One was Thomas Clark Durant, born in 1820 in Lee, Massachusetts, who is said to have supplied all of the initial capital needed to form the Union Pacific Railroad. Durant first speculated in grain and stock after he was graduated from medical school. He then became a railroad contractor and built sections of lines east of the Mississippi, including the Rock Island and the Michigan Southern Railroad. He helped to push the Pacific Railway acts through Congress in 1862 and 1864, and when sources of money dried up for the construction of the Union Pacific, Durant organized the Crédit Mobilier, a limited liability finance company chartered by Congress to raise money for the railroad.[8]

Another Massachusetts native, Oakes Ames, became head of Crédit

CHARLES CROCKER.   COLLIS P. HUNTINGTON.

MARK HOPKINS.   LELAND STANFORD.

Mobilier. Born in Easton, Massachusetts, Ames and his brother ran the family business, which manufactured shovels. Ames shovels were then well known throughout much of the world, and their business grew even more after their shovel became a popular digging tool for miners during the California gold rush. In 1867 Ames sold 160 shares of Union Pacific Railroad stock to key congressmen to reduce the possibility that legislation would be introduced to place tight controls on publicly aided railroads. When the stock sale was made public a few years later, a scandal followed, and Ames was censured by Congress.[9]

BUILDING THE RAILROAD

ALTHOUGH the transcontinental railroad crossed what was mostly unsettled territory between Omaha and Sacramento in the summer of 1869, new towns sprang up along the route as the tracks were being laid. Several of these towns began as work camps for the railroad construction gangs, and tents

CHEYENNE IN PRESENT-DAY WYOMING,
about a year after the town was born in late 1867. This view
looks down 16th Street.

and crude shacks constituted the first structures in places like North Platte and Julesburg in present-day Nebraska. Construction workers lived in these "towns" and were taken west by train to the building site. When not working or fighting off Indian attacks—there were few such attacks—most of the workmen enjoyed the offerings of what became known as "Hell on Wheels."

In these large temporary towns there was an oversized tent a hundred feet long and forty feet wide. It held a bar, a dance floor, and fancy gambling equipment. Dotting the area outside the large tent were many smaller tents and crude shacks serving as saloons, dance halls, brothels, and living quarters for the workers. Each morning track trains, as they were called, carried construction workers to the end of the line. When the track was completed to a point about sixty miles beyond the "Hell on Wheels," the word passed quickly that it was time to move. Everyone pitched in. Tents were folded, shacks dismantled, equipment packed and loaded on flatcars, and everything was transported to the western end of the track. There, in a matter of hours, the town reappeared. This temporary town often had three thousand residents.

When the Union Pacific stopped its westward building late in 1867 to await spring, the town of Cheyenne was born. It was built so rapidly that it earned the name "the magic city." After construction resumed in the spring

SALT LAKE CITY IN 1868. OX-DRAWN WAGONS CARRYING FREIGHT
for Walker Brothers are being unloaded.

of 1868 and the railroad reached a point about sixty miles west of Cheyenne at modern Laramie, Wyoming, much of the town moved there. However, Cheyenne lived on because of its location about a hundred miles north of Denver. It became a shipping point for the Colorado goldfields. Freight arrived by rail in Cheyenne and was then shipped by wagon south to Denver and other points. And Laramie also survived when the "Hell on Wheels" pushed another sixty miles westward. Its location in a large valley was ideal for a settlement, and by then more and more people were arriving looking for good opportunities. Laramie bacame permanent, and the residents of Laramie and Cheyenne began calling for the formation of a territory. On July 25, 1868, President Andrew Johnson signed the act creating Wyoming Territory out of portions of Utah, Idaho, and Dakota territories.

Brigham Young had failed to persuade the builders of the Union Pacific to bring the transcontinental route through Salt Lake City. Instead the route passed through Weber Canyon and what had been the sleepy Mormon village of Ogden, about thirty-five miles north of Salt Lake City. Even before the railroad arrived with its "Hell on Wheels," a gold rush occurred to the north of Ogden along the Wyoming and Idaho border. Ogden became a jumping-off point for the new goldfields. Gentiles—anyone who was not a Mormon— rushed to Ogden. New stores were built and stocked, saloons and gambling halls were constructed, and the character of the Mormon settlement changed. It changed even more when the Union Pacific construction crews arrived.

Bernard De Voto, educator, historian, and writer, was born in Ogden less than three decades later, and grew up hearing stories about its early days. In 1925, De Voto wrote of the arrival of gold seekers and the railroad:

Strange sights by day in the streets that had seen nothing more extraordinary than a drove of pigs. Ox teams by the dozen plodding ahead of a freighter's wagon with seven-foot wheels and a bullwhacker snaking his whip above their ears. Mules singly or in tandem packed with the outfits of prospectors, their owners trudging in their dust. Gamblers, settlers, bartenders, Mexicans, Chinks, remittance men. And by night what sounds! In the saloons, the roar of good men singing, the fellowship of males, the debate of a hundred disputants at once, each one an authority. Above them the seduction of fiddles where the women consorted with their prey. In the streets, strayed revelers taking the long way home, the clop-clop of horses as belated ones arrived, the click of dice, sometimes the voice of the Colt. . . . It was a little different from discussions as to the true nature of Satan's fur, or from the hymns with which the Mormon dances had begun. Sin had come to Ogden.

And now descended on Ogden the Hartigans and the McCarthys and the Flahertys. Through the mouth of Weber Canyon, racing against its ten-mile day and the Chinks of the C.P., the Union Pacific burst like a spring flood. Now came Hell on Wheels to Mormonry.

Not long did it pause, this mobile terminal, but never again would righteousness be quite the same. The Irish roared and sang and hammered, like happy devils assaulting the earth, and laid their steel and passed on.[10]

THE UNION PACIFIC'S DEVIL'S GATE BRIDGE THROUGH WEBER CANYON,
Utah Territory (near Ogden), soon after it was constructed.

To the west of Mormon Utah, towns also appeared along the route of the Central Pacific. When the railroad pushed into Nevada late in 1867, Myron C. Lake, who owned a small hotel and a bridge across the Truckee River about thirty-five miles northwest of Virginia City, offered some of his land in the Truckee River valley to the Central Pacific if it would build a station at his river crossing. Since the owners of the line anticipated that much freight for Virginia City and other nearby mining communities would be arriving by rail, they accepted the land and built a station. Thus Reno, Nevada, was founded. Later the towns of Wadsworth, Lovelock, Winnemucca, Argenta, Carlin, and Elko were also established along the Central Pacific route. But the Central Pacific did not have the "Hell on Wheels" reputation of the Union Pacific between Omaha and Ogden. The Central Pacific builders were stricter than those of the Union Pacific, and most of the Central Pacific's workers were Chinese whose lifestyle was considerably different from that of the predominantly Irish construction workers on the Union Pacific.[11]

Most of the new towns established along the route of the transcontinental railroad probably would not have been founded otherwise. The railroad

CORINNE, UTAH TERRITORY, THE LAST "HELL ON WHEELS" TOWN
located on the Union Pacific line. Photograph by William Henry Jackson, 1869.
At one point Corinne had nineteen saloons, several dance halls, and numerous
business houses like those pictured above. It didn't survive.

PROMONTORY SUMMIT, UTAH TERRITORY,
some days after the Central Pacific Railroad joined with the Union Pacific on
May 10, 1869. The American flag (left) marks the parallel spot on the tracks
where the two lines met. Photograph by William Henry Jackson.

established a link to the civilized world for the people who settled in them,
improving communication and enabling residents to obtain with some ease
the good things of civilized life. Even before the transcontinental railroad
was completed, other lines were pushing westward across the prairies and
plains as railroad fever swept into most regions of the West.

One railroad had actually begun construction west from the Missouri
River to meet the Central Pacific before the Union Pacific Railroad started
from Omaha. The Union Pacific Railway, Eastern Division, began laying
track at present-day Kansas City, Kansas, in September 1863. But the line
experienced financial problems, in addition to its chief engineer shooting
and killing the railroad's chief contractor during a dispute in late July 1864.
Construction was delayed, and the line's first forty miles were not completed
until late in 1864. By then the Union Pacific Railroad had begun at Omaha
the race it would win to connect with the Central Pacific.[12]

The Union Pacific Railway, Eastern Division, did, however, continue
to push westward across Kansas. Beyond the settlements established in

eastern Kansas prior to the coming of the railroad, new towns began to appear along its route. Soon the railroad began to carry passengers and freight, but nearly all of the freight carried by the Union Pacific Railway, Eastern Division, was to the frontier towns, since they had little to ship out, and many freight cars returned east empty. Joseph McCoy, however, a native of Illinois, where he and his two brothers were involved in stock raising, had an idea that would change this and make him wealthy as well.

McCoy, twenty-nine years old, knew that Texas cattle raisers were seeking markets for their cattle. Their Texas longhorns, the result of inter-breeding between Spanish and native American cattle, had increased in number during the Civil War. While most of the cattle raisers were off fighting for the Confederacy, old men and boys had been put in charge of watching the animals on the open ranges of Texas, and winter storms in 1863 and '64 had scattered the herds. Few bulls were castrated, and by the end of the war the herds had increased rapidly. The returning Texans began looking for markets where they could sell their longhorns. Some were driven overland to Louisiana. Others were sold to the Morgan Steamship Company, along the Gulf coast. The company in turn shipped the cattle to New Orleans or Cuba, where they were sold for a handsome profit, much to the irritation of the Texas cattle raisers when they learned of it. Other Texans drove herds of longhorns northeast to Missouri, where some markets for them had existed before the Civil War. While they received better prices in Missouri, trailing the lanky longhorns through Indian Territory (now Oklahoma) and into Missouri was not a pleasant journey. Indians demanded tolls to cross their lands, and ex-soldiers turned thieves often stampeded the cattle as the Texans neared the Missouri border. Some of these thieves actually demanded money from the Texans for the return of their cattle. And Texas fever, the splenetic fever carried by ticks on the longhorns, made Texas cattle and their owners unwelcome in Missouri. The longhorns were immune to the fever, but American cattle often died from the disease.

This was the situation early in 1867 when Jospeh McCoy left Kansas City and traveled west on the Union Pacific Railway, Eastern Division. McCoy wanted to establish a shipping point for Texas cattle. After considering several sites along the line, he selected the tiny settlement of Abilene, Kansas, containing perhaps a dozen log huts, about a hundred and forty miles west of Kansas City and Missouri's western border. McCoy found sufficient water and fine grass in the unclaimed area around Abilene, and there he set about building a depot for Texas cattle. He had a shipping yard built next to the railroad tracks that could hold three thousand cattle. He also constructed a barn and a small office building. Later a bank and an elegant three-story hotel were built. In the meantime, McCoy hired a friend from Illinois to ride south on horseback to intercept the Texans driving cattle north and tell them about the new market in Abilene. The first Texas long-horns arrived in Abilene in the summer of 1867.

McCoy later wrote:

The drive of 1867 was about one percent of the supply. Great hardships attended driving that year on account of Osage Indian troubles, exces-sive rain-storms, and flooded rivers. The cholera made sad havoc with many drovers, some of whom died with the malady and many suffered greatly. The heavy rains caused an immense growth of grass, too coarse and washy to be good food for cattle or horses, and but little of the first year's arrivals at Abilene were fit to go to market. However, on the 5th of September, 1867, the first shipment of twenty cars was made to Chicago. Several Illinois stock men and others, joined in an excursion from Springfield, Ill., to Abilene, to celebrate by feast, wine and song, the auspicious event.[13]

The first shipment of cattle east from Abilene marked the beginning of a new era for profit-seeking Texas cattle raisers. But, as McCoy observed, the Texans "could hardly believe that there was not some swindle" in the creation of a depot in Kansas for the selling of Texas cattle. The Texan

beheld more done and doing for him than he had ever seen before in his life. In his own State, great as the wealth of some of its citizens was, no one had manifested public spirit and enterprise sufficient to establish an outlet for her millions of cattle . . . They are all mindful of individual, selfish undertakings, but are stolidly indifferent to public ones. . . . They are, as a class, not liberally educated, and but few of them are extensive readers, but they are possessed of strong natural sense, well skilled in judging human nature, close observers of all events passing before them, thoroughly drilled in the customs of frontier life, more clannish than the Scotch, more suspicious than need be yet often easily gulled by promises of large prices for their stock; very prone to put an erroneous construction upon the acts and words of a Northern man, inclined to sympathize with one from their own State as against another from the North, no matter what the Southern man may have been guilty of.[14]

By the spring of 1868 many Texans had learned that the Abilene market was not a swindle, and about 75,000 longhorns were trailed north that year over what became known as the Chisholm Trail. As the number of cattle increased McCoy began to make money. He not only bought and sold cattle, but he charged the buyers for the use of his shipping pens as the cattle were prepared for shipping east. He worked closely with the railroad in this regard and may have received some payment from the line for his efforts. He also made a profit by buying and selling land, since the value of land had increased in and around Abilene as the town grew in importance as a cattle shipping center. In 1869, more than 350,000 head reached the Abilene area. By then, however, another railroad was pushing west across Kansas to an area north of Abilene. The Central Branch Railroad had completed construction from Atchison to Waterville, a hundred miles west of the Missouri River. Although the line was many miles north of the Union Pacific Railway, Eastern Division, the Central Branch succeeded in attracting several thousand head of Texas cattle to Waterville, where they were sold and shipped east. But Waterville never became the cattle market Abilene did. For one thing, it never had a promoter like Joseph McCoy, an entrepreneur of diverse pursuits. Before McCoy's death in Wichita, Kansas, in 1915, he was at one time or another a stockman, real estate agent, grocer, speculator, wrought-iron fence salesman, author, cattle inspector, proprietor of a flour and feed store, and Treasury Department narcotics agent.

An increasing number of Texas cattle raisers were entrusting their cattle to other men who by 1870 were becoming known as trail drivers, or drovers. The drover would make a contract with a buyer in Kansas to deliver stock. The contract usually specified the number of cattle and their ages, sex, condition, and type. For instance, some buyers wanted young cattle that could be grazed to maturity, or young cows for breeding, or steers and dry cows for Indian agencies to feed Indians. Still other buyers needed cattle for packing houses and other slaughtering places. The drover would then contract with Texas ranchers and take their cattle on consignment. The drover's aim was to "put on the trail what will answer profitably the demands he believes will arise."[15]

More than 350,000 Texas cattle arrived in Kansas in 1870, and more than 700,000 in 1871. It was Abilene's biggest year as a cattle market and McCoy made good money, but it was also the town's last. The railroads that shipped the longhorns east had in the meantime brought settlers west. By 1871, much of the unsettled land around Abilene had been acquired by farmers. These grangers, as they were called by cattlemen and cowboys,

JOSEPH MCCOY,
an Illinois native, who turned Abilene, Kansas, into a cattle town
where Texans could sell their longhorn cattle.

provided year-round business and a stable economy for Abilene's business-men. The cattle business, by contrast, was seasonal, and many of the people associated with it carried off much of the money elsewhere. And it was most especially the farmers' concern about longhorns giving their American cattle Texas fever which led to the collapse of the Abilene cattle market. As the Kansas Pacific Railway Company (the name of the Union Pacific Railway, Eastern Division, was changed on May 31, 1868) pushed west across Kansas, new cattle towns developed. But the same pattern was repeated. As farmers moved into the area where the cattle town was located, state lawmakers restricted the movement of Texas cattle, and new shipping points had to be established farther west along the line. When the Atchison, Topeka and

TEXAS CATTLE IN A KANSAS CORRAL.
Drawing by Frederic Remington, *Harper's Weekly*, 1888. The poor state of the
cows reflected the changes as more and more settlers moved onto the plains.

Santa Fe Railroad started construction across Kansas in 1868, the same thing happened again. Newton, Kansas, was the first cattle town on the Santa Fe in 1871, and the following year Wichita replaced Newton when the railroad reached the Arkansas River and turned west to follow the river into what is now Colorado.

To the north in Nebraska, along the Union Pacific line west of Omaha, few cattle were shipped east until 1869. By then the Union Pacific had realized the potential for profit in shipping cattle. Plans were made to construct cattle depots somewhere along the line. The towns of Schuyler and Columbus competed for the stockyards, and Schuyler, at the northern end of the Blue River trail, won. Stockyards were built, and the following year, 1870, perhaps 50,000 Texas cattle were trailed north from Texas through Kansas to Schuyler, where cattle buyers purchased them and shipped many to the East. By 1871, however, the same pattern that developed in Kansas was repeated in Nebraska: Settlers arriving in the Schuyler area forced the cattle trade farther west to Kearney, Nebraska. Two years later, in 1873, it shifted again to Ogallala, where it remained for more than a decade.

Meantime, however, events in the West had focused attention on the cattle towns. Life in those towns and the long cattle drives to reach them caught the fancy of many Easterners, including those in financial circles. The life of the cowboy seemed different and colorful. Still, however much financiers may have been intrigued by the western way of life, most were more fascinated by the money they saw flowing through western banks. The *National Live Stock Journal* reported in May 1871 that Kansas City banks had handled $3 million in cattle money in 1870, while $500,000 had passed through the banks at Omaha. And by 1871, Kansas City (with seven railroads) had four packing plants in operation. The stockyards there were built that year as well, along with a livestock exchange building. Eastern financiers recognized the obvious: that cattle raising had become a big business—a new industry born in the West.

While the western cattle towns and people in the cattle business prospered during the early 1870s, much of the rest of the nation was beginning to suffer from another economic panic. Events leading up to the panic began in 1871 when, according to tradition, Mrs. O'Leary's cow kicked over a lantern in the O'Leary barn in Chicago, touching off a fire that took perhaps three hundred lives, injured hundreds of people, and caused about $200 million in property damage before it was brought under control two days later. And there was another serious fire in Boston the following year with heavy property damage. These two fires cost insurance companies almost $300 million and bankrupted several major firms. But the actual panic did not occur until the Philadelphia banking house of Jay Cooke collapsed in 1873, after underwriting railroad bonds for the Northern Pacific Railroad, which was pushing westward from Minnesota across North Dakota. Cooke's banking house failed because of poor management, its own and the Northern Pacific's. The railroad had had to pay Cooke heavy bonuses on the sale of bonds, it had given away too many blocks of stock to influential politicians, and it had ended up without sufficient funds for construction. Between 1873 and 1878, more than 18,000 companies failed, and many railroads, including the Northern Pacific, went into receivership.

During this period the cattle towns of Kansas and Nebraska had some of the flavor of the Missouri River jumping-off points during the California and Kansas gold rushes. But there was a greater turnover of profit seekers in the cattle towns thanks to the rapid transportation provided by the railroads. As the summer sun brought warmth to the plains, cattle buyers, gamblers, prostitutes, drummers, land speculators, con artists, and other profit seekers arrived by rail to lie in wait for the cattle drovers and their cowboys. After two or three months on the trail in dust or mud or both, the Texas cowboys delivered their cattle and were paid for their labor, usually in cash. With anywhere from fifty to ninety dollars in accumulated wages, many of them indulged in the offerings of the town. After the last herds arrived in late summer or very early fall and the cowboys started back to Texas, most of the transient profit seekers left.[16]

Certainly not all of the profit seekers in the cattle towns were transient. Although many of the merchants relied on the summer cattle boom for their annual profits, many were year-round residents. And when the cattle trade ceased in a town, some of them followed it to the next railhead. Jacob Karatofsky, a German emigrant, was one such merchant. He owned and operated the Great Western Store in Abilene, selling dry goods, clothing, boots, shoes, hats, caps, and notions. He also carried ladies' fancy-dress goods, which were usually purchased by the transient prostitutes. When Abilene died as a cattle town in late 1871, Karatofsky moved his business to Ellsworth, and later to Wichita. He left Wichita in the fall of 1874, after the cattle trade shifted south from Wichita to Caldwell, along the southern border of Kansas. Instead of moving to Caldwell, Karatofsky traveled through Texas looking for business opportunities, but he found nothing of interest. He later settled in Hot Springs, Arkansas, then a growing resort community, where he resumed business as a merchant.[17]

Still another cattle-town merchant was Robert Wright, a native of Bladensburg, Maryland. Wright, however, had not planned to be a merchant. In fact, he first established a town, which he founded as a market for buffalo hides. The town was Dodge City, Kansas. Wright came West while in his teens. He spent the late 1850s in St. Louis, but left there in 1859 to drive an ox team to Denver for a freighter. After crisscrossing the plains perhaps half a dozen times, working as a mule skinner, Wright went to work for Barlow, Sanderson and Company, a stage line that ran triweekly stages over the Santa Fe Trail between Kansas City and Santa Fe. Wright looked after the company's interests along the trail, including the numerous stage stations. One station was located in the vicinity of Fort Dodge, an Army post constructed in 1864 at a crossing on the Arkansas River to protect travelers from hostile Indians. Wright came to like the area around Fort Dodge, and in 1866 he left the stage company to work as a freighter and a hay and wood contractor for the Army at Fort Dodge. In 1867 Wright was appointed post trader, a position he held until Fort Dodge was closed in 1882.

LEFT: ROBERT M. WRIGHT,
as he appeared a few years after helping to establish Dodge City, Kansas.
RIGHT: Charles Rath, a native of Germany, who became a partner
with Robert M. Wright at Dodge City in 1872.

THE SUTLER'S STORE AT FORT DODGE, KANSAS, IN 1867,
the year Robert M. Wright was appointed post trader or sutler. Drawing by
T. R. Davis, *Harper's Weekly*, May 25, 1867.

Robert Wright took advantage of his position as post trader and entered into other businesses. He began raising a few cattle on the open range west of Fort Dodge. And in 1872 he became partners with Charles Rath, a native of Germany, who had come to Kansas Territory in 1855. Rath worked as a teamster at Fort Riley and later at Bent's Fort, where he learned to speak Cheyenne. Ten years before he was Wright's partner, Rath became a freighter and was operating a trading post, stage stop, lodging house, and restaurant on the north bank of Walnut Creek near present-day Great Bend, Kansas. Because of Wright's position at Fort Dodge, their partnership was called Rath and Company. They built a store five miles west of Fort Dodge, just outside the post's military reservation, and there they outfitted buffalo hunters and purchased buffalo hides. Only months before, tanners along the East Coast and in England and Germany had determined that buffalo hides could be used to make fine leather and had placed orders to buy thousands of buffalo hides. The news spread across the West like a prairie fire. It meant not only a new market for the buffalo runners already killing the shaggies for their robes, but year-round work for those wanting it. No longer did hunters have to wait for the buffalo's winter robe to grow. They could make a profit from the buffalo's hide taken anytime during the year.

The same year Wright and Rath opened their store, Wright formed a town company and arranged for a townsite to be surveyed on the north bank of the Arkansas River. The Santa Fe Trail was the main street. The town

FORT DODGE, KANSAS, IN 1867,
the year Wright was appointed post trader. He held the position until
Fort Dodge was closed in 1882.

FORT DODGE IN 1879.

was first called Buffalo City after the animal that brought it prosperity, but post office officials refused to accept the name. It was too similar to Buffalo, Kansas, and they thought it would cause too much confusion. The name was soon changed to Dodge City, and by the end of 1872 the town claimed a harness shop, a drugstore, two restaurants, a wholesale liquor store, a hardware store, two dry-goods stores, two groceries, a hotel, a blacksmith shop, a dance hall, a barbershop, seven saloons, and four general stores, including the one owned by Robert Wright and Charles Rath.

The Atchison, Topeka and Santa Fe Railroad arrived in Dodge City in September 1872. During the three months that followed, the railroad shipped east 43,029 buffalo hides and 1,436,290 pounds of buffalo meat. One observer concluded that these figures represented about fifty thousand dead buffalo and did not include those animals killed in "wanton cruelty, miscalled sport, and for food for the frontier residents." With the advent of the railroad, Dodge City became the hide capital of the West for the buffalo hunters crisscrossing western Kansas and eastern Colorado.[18]

One of these hunters was Frank H. Mayer. It cost him about two thousand dollars to become a buffalo *runner* (he never called himself a buffalo hunter—that was the mark of a tenderfoot). Mayer recalled:

A buffalo outfit was simple, and I could have made mine simpler but I wanted to do things up brown. All you needed was horses or mules, wagons, camp equipment, and firearms, and you were in business. . . . I bought two wagons in St. Joseph, Missouri. The big one, drawn by twelve mules, we used in hauling hides; the small one, drawn by

TWO WAGONLOADS OF BUFFALO HIDES
on the dusty main street (the Santa Fe Trail) of Dodge City, Kansas, in 1872.
The town was the hide capital of the West until the buffalo on the southern
plains were nearly all slaughtered.

six mules, was our camp wagon. Both were equipped with nine-inch
tread flat iron wheels and steel boxes or bed of ⅛-inch steel. I remember
what I paid for the big wagon—$650. I remember what I paid for the
small one—$400. I already had a couple of good saddle horses, which
I went to much pains to train. I taught them to lie flat while I was
shooting at game, so as to avoid detection by roving Indians. We always
used American horses because they were bigger, stronger, more de-
pendable than the mustangs or Indian ponies which the Indians used
because they didn't have anything better. A good buffalo horse, though,
was worth real money on the range, anywhere from $250 to $500.
. . . When I went into the business, I sat down and figured that I was
indeed one of fortune's children. Just think! There were 20,000,000
buffalo, each worth at least $3—$60,000,000. At the very outside
cartridges cost 25 cents each, so every time I fired one I got my
investment back twelve times over. I could kill a hundred a day, $300
gross, or counting everything, $200 net profit a day. And $200 times
thirty, would be, let me see, $200 times thirty—that would be $6,000
a month—or three times what was paid, it seems to me, the President
of the United States, and a hundred times what a man with a good job
in the '70s could be expected to earn. Was I not lucky that I discovered
this quick and easy way to fortune? I thought I was.[19]

Exactly how many buffalo Mayer and his men killed is not known, but he
made a lot of money. He recalled:

My first two years (1872–1873) I did right well, considering the value of the dollar in those days. My account books show that my share for the two years—that is to say, the net—was right around $6,000. I didn't make as much the first year ($2,900) as the second, when I turned in a profit of $3,100. This was on hides alone. My third year, however (1874), was my big year on the range; after that I slid down to nothingness. By that time I had gone into the smoked tongue, specimen bull heads, and meat business as side issues. I know exactly what I grossed and netted this year (1874), and the account looks as follows:

Hides	$3,020.00
Meat	$1,260.00
Tongues	$ 905.00
Heads	$ 250.00
Total	$5,435.00

ROBERT M. WRIGHT (RIGHT) SITS ATOP A STACK OF BUFFALO HIDES
in the Wright and Rath hide yard in Dodge City about 1873. During the peak of the buffalo slaughter in western Kansas, Wright and Rath handled as many as eighty thousand hides at one time.

This, mind you, was my gross; my net came to $3,125—and that was my big year on the buffalo ranges. . . . And marketing was no problem. Buyers at every frontier [post] offered cash for hides, which were in demand in "the States" for a wide variety of purposes—blankets, sleigh and buggy robes, coats, heavy leather, and God knows what else. I sold mine wherever I happened to be, in Dodge, Denver, Laramie City. Because of the care I gave my hides, I always commanded premium prices. During my years on the range, I had no trouble, because buyers trusted me and I them.[20]

Mayer eventually settled in Colorado, where he died at Fairplay in 1954 at the age of a hundred and four.

The buffalo hunters or runners did their job. By 1873 the wild buffalo population had declined in western Kansas, and many of the hunters moved south into the panhandles of Oklahoma and Texas and into northwestern Texas. While some hides were freighted to Denison in north-central Texas, most appear to have been sold to Dodge City merchants, who followed the hunters south from Dodge City, establishing a trading center at Adobe Walls, about a hundred and sixty miles south-southwest of Dodge City. Ten years earlier, Colonel Kit Carson, commanding U.S. troops, had fought a band of Kiowa and Comanche Indians at the site. Much earlier, before 1840, William Bent had built an adobe trading post called Adobe Fort nearby, but it had been abandoned soon after. Charles Rath and Robert Wright were responsible for the new trading center, which included a saloon, a blacksmith shop, and two stores. They were constructed by the middle of May 1874. Large freight wagons had carried building materials and supplies south from Dodge City. But a little more than a month later, five hundred Indians—Cheyennes, Kiowas, and Arapahoes—attacked the twenty-eight men and one woman at Adobe Walls. They resented the white men's slaughter of their buffalo. The Indians were driven off, but not before three white men and many horses and oxen were killed. The Indians then went on a rampage throughout the southern plains. The merchants and buffalo hunters at Adobe abandoned the site and most returned to Dodge City. But the killing of buffalo soon resumed. By 1876, however, nearly all of the buffalo left on the southern plains were in Texas. Those in the region around Dodge City had been wiped out.[21]

As the hide business began to decline at Dodge City, Robert Wright, Charles Rath, and other merchants sought new business opportunities. They turned to Texas cattle, and 1877 marked Dodge City's first year as a cattle

TWO WHITE MEN TAKING TURNS KILLING BUFFALO.
Whites called this method of buffalo hunting a "stand." Indians called it "still hunting." Regardless, hunters could kill many buffalo by remaining in one position upwind from the animals. Drawing by William Henry Jackson.

SHOOTING BUFFALO FROM THE KANSAS PACIFIC.
As the railroads pushed westward across the plains, hunting buffalo from the train cars became something of a sport. Little sportsmanship was involved. Drawing by Theodore Davis in *Harper's Weekly*, Dec. 14, 1867.

town. A reporter for the Kansas City *Times* visited Dodge City in late May of that year and reported:

> Abilene, Ellsworth, Hays City on the Kansas Pacific railroad, then Newton and Wichita, and now Dodge City on the Atchison, Topeka & Santa Fe road, have all, in their turn, enjoyed the "boil and bubble, toil trouble" of the Texas cattle trade. Three hundred and sixty-seven miles west from Kansas City we step off at Dodge, slumbering as yet (8:30 a.m.) in the tranquil stillness of a May morning. In this respect Dodge is peculiar. She awakes from her slumbers about eleven a.m., takes her sugar and lemon at twelve m., a square meal at one p.m., commences biz at two o'clock, gets lively at four, and at ten it is hip-hip-hurrah! till five in the morning. . . . Dodge City has now about twelve hundred inhabitants—residents we mean, for there is a daily population of twice that many; six or seven large general stores, the largest of which, Rath & Wright, does a quarter of a million retail trade in a year; and the usual complement of drug stores, bakers, butchers, blacksmiths, etc.; and last, but not by any means the least, nineteen saloons—no little ten-by-twelves, but seventy-five to one hundred feet long, glittering with paint and mirrors, and some of them paying one hundred dollars per month rent for the naked room. . . . We had the good luck to interview Judge Beverly of Texas, who is the acknowledged oracle of the cattle trade. He estimates the drive at two hundred and eighty-five thousand, probably amounting to three hundred thousand, including calves. . . . You can hear more about "cutting out," "rounding up," etc., in Dodge, in fifteen minutes, than you can hear in small towns like Chicago and St. Louis in a lifetime.[22]

Six months after these words appeared in the Kansas City paper, Robert Wright and Charles Rath dissolved their partnership. Rath wanted to go south to the staked plains of Texas, where buffalo could still be found, to take charge of a store he had established at Fort Griffin, located on the Clear Fork of the Brazos River in present-day Shackelford County, Texas. He also owned stores on the Palo Duro in the Texas panhandle and one at Sweetwater, Texas. Wright and Rath were good friends, and Wright did not stand in Rath's way.

Robert Wright remained in Dodge City and formed a new partnership with Henry M. Beverley, a former Texas cattle drover who also had worked for a time with a merchant in the cattle town of Ellsworth, Kansas. Being a Texan, Beverley attracted much of the trade from the Texas drovers and cowboys. He even hired another Texan to ride out and solicit trade from the drovers and cowboys approaching Dodge City from the south over the Western Trail. In addition, Beverley and Wright employed several clerks for their store, including Sam Samuels, who spoke fluent Spanish. The Mexican vaqueros working for drovers looked up to Samuels, who was something like their Moses in the foreign land. Wright and Beverley opened a branch store at Fort Griffin, Texas, in 1880 to serve an increased number of ranchers in the region. By then the buffalo on the southern plains were gone, and cattle had replaced them on the open ranges. Wright and Beverley gained much business by permitting ranchers to buy goods in their Fort Griffin store and pay for them at their Dodge City store after the ranchers had driven their cattle north and sold the animals.

In the vicinity of Dodge City there was an increase in the number of farmers settling on cheap government land where cattle were grazing. Perhaps sensing the approach of the end of Dodge City's cattle-trading days, Henry Beverley stepped down from his partnership with Robert Wright. He did stay on briefly as manager of the Dodge City store until he established his own clothing emporium in 1885. That was Dodge City's last year as a cattle-trading center; by then the farmers had settled the outlying areas. Samuel Prouty, editor of the Dodge City *Globe*, examined the reality of the circumstances in August 1885 when he wrote:

> The experience of all cattle towns is that their growth has been held in check during the period when they depended upon the cattle traffic for support. The country surrounding could not be developed while it was being held for stock ranges. Abilene, Wichita, Newton, Ellsworth and Great Bend have all been cattle towns. They all supposed they would be ruined when the cattle trails departed from them. They were mistaken. Those towns all shot ahead with amazing rapidity when the cattle business left them. Dodge City has been for the past ten years an exclusive cattle town. The cattle traffic made money for its citizens but it did not make a town. It was a question whether the country would ever warrant the making of a respectable town here. The rains of the past three years, the assurance that the soil of the country is susceptible of successful cultivation, the recent absorption of the public domain by settlers, the removal of the cattle trail and the rapidly disappearing

cowboy, have now thoroughly convinced our people that a permanent commercial metropolis at this point is demanded by the needs of the country.[23]

The arrival of farmers brought more change to Dodge City. Merchants who had catered to drovers, cowboys, and cattle buyers restocked their shelves with merchandise for farmers and their families. And with the farmers came the institutions of the civilized East—churches, schools, government, and homes—and more dependence upon the East for goods to make life a little easier.

But to the west in Colorado and to the northwest in Wyoming and Montana, these institutions were not yet fully established. Much of the northern plains had been considered unsafe for white settlement until after the "Indian problem," as many ranchers described roaming bands of Indians, was solved in the late 1870s. The Indians were placed on reservations, and ranchers began moving their cattle onto ranges that a decade earlier were covered by countless buffalo. By the early 1880s, however, most of the buffalo had been slaughtered by hide hunters. It was then that many ranchers looked to the East for financial assistance. Without it the growing range cattle industry could not have survived. To obtain capital, many ranchers formed corporations, and businessmen in New York, Boston, Chicago, and elsewhere in the East invested heavily. Some ranchers simply borrowed money, but they borrowed from eastern banks, where interest rates were lower than in western ones. As Gene M. Gressley has observed, in his fine book *Bankers and Cattlemen* (1966): "The significantly higher interest rates in the West cemented this financial bond between East and West long after the period of spectacular growth had passed."[24]

During the period 1880 to 1900, the total number of incorporated cattle companies in Montana reached 181; in Wyoming, 188; in Colorado, 324. And the aggregate capitalization for these states came to more than $27 million for Montana, more than $94 million for Wyoming, and more than $102 million for Colorado. By the late 1880s, however, it was becoming evident that from the standpoint of eastern investors in ranching, the results would be by and large disappointing. Although records are incomplete, it is probably safe to assume that only a small percentage of these investors made any profit, and some lost thousands of dollars. Ranching was a risky business, dependent upon good management; an often fluctuating market; the need for sufficient rain to grow enough grass to feed the cattle; the natural propagation of cattle; and adequate land on which to raise them. And the changing character of the West was also a contributing factor: As more and more settlers followed ranchers into the West in search of homesteads, cattlemen were pushed onto the more arid lands that were too poor to farm. The perception of what, half a century earlier, had been labeled the Great American Desert had changed.

XI

THE SELLING OF THE
GREAT AMERICAN
DESERT

*There is nothing which so generally strikes the imagination and en-
gages the affections of mankind, as the right of property; or that sole
and despotic dominion which one man claims and exercises over the
external things of the world, to the total exclusion of the right of any
other individual in the universe.*

—SIR WILLIAM BLACKSTONE[1]

THE eastern boundary of what many Americans believed was the Great
American Desert had shrunk by 1860. The line of settlement had pushed
westward for more than a hundred miles past the Missouri River. Settlers
had overcome their suspicion of the prairies as being infertile because they
were treeless. They had learned how to break the prairie sod with steel-
tipped plows and were becoming aware of the richness of its soil. And they
found adequate rainfall in the eastern portions of Nebraska and Kansas
territories to raise their crops. But to the west, beyond the prairie region,
were the Great Plains, that tilted plateau formed during many centuries by
streams flowing eastward from the Rocky Mountains. The Great Plains extend
from Texas northward into Canada and eastward from the Rockies for four
hundred miles. The plains were still viewed as a worthless desert by most
Americans. By the end of the Civil War, however, there was more interest
in the West. The Homestead Act of 1862 spurred much of that interest as
war veterans and others sought to rebuild their lives.

Under the Homestead Act of 1862 any person could file for 160 acres
of federal land if he or she was an American citizen, or had filed his or her
intention papers. To file one had to be twenty-one years old or the head of
a family, or to have served fourteen days in the U.S. Army or Navy. And
the person filing could never have fought against the United States. This

excluded some Mexicans, Canadians, and Britons, and many residents of the South; but Congress altered the law in 1866 to make Confederate veterans eligible for homesteads. Once a qualified person filed on a homestead, he or she could secure a fee simple title to the land by residing on or farming the claim for five successive years, and provided, if originally a foreigner, the person had since become a citizen of the United States. If a homesteader did not wish to wait five years, a commutation clause in the filing papers allowed him to purchase 160 acres for $1.25 an acre after six months' residence and rudimentary improvements.

While some people in Kansas and Nebraska filed for homesteads soon after the act became law, the real surge did not begin until after the Civil War. And by 1870 homesteading had greatly increased, especially in central portions of both states on the eastern border of the Great Plains. There was, however, growing confusion over whether settlement there was possible. General John Pope, who had participated in the Pacific railroad surveys before the Civil War, reported in 1866 that the plains were "beyond the reach of agriculture, and must always remain a great uninhabited desert."[2] And General William T. Sherman, writing from Fort Sedgwick in northeastern Colorado in August 1866, observed that it was "impossible to conceive of a more dreary waste."[3] Another military man, General William B. Hazen, provided a slightly less pessimistic report in 1866 after crossing Nebraska. He noted that the soil of the Platte Valley was highly productive for nearly two hundred miles west of Omaha, but once he left the prairie country near Fort Kearny and entered the plains, "the soil was thin and weak and the atmosphere dry and continues so all the way to the Rocky Mountains." Hazen concluded that half of the land between Fort Kearny and the Rockies had no value at all, and the other half was fit only for pasture. Of the pastureland, only about one acre in a thousand could be made productive, and then only by irrigation. Hazen predicted that in time the region would be settled by a "scanty pastoral population," but he added, "No amount of railroad schemes of colonization, or government encouragement can ever make more of it."[4]

Such reports from respected military men who had distinguished themselves for the Union during the war simply reinforced the notion of the plains region as a sterile, barren desert, an idea introduced into the minds of Americans years earlier through the published accounts of explorers Zebulon M. Pike and Stephen H. Long. The idea was perpetuated by the people who produced school geographies and atlases. John Charles Frémont was perhaps the first official explorer to view the Great Plains differently. Frémont, who crossed the plains in 1838 and again in 1843 and 1844, years of abnormally high rainfall, reported that livestock could subsist on the native grasses, and he saw no reason why settlers could not survive on the Great Plains and practice subsistence agriculture.[5] Frémont's optimism, however, did not persuade emigrants to stop and make their homes there during the late 1840s and 1850s. To most emigrants the Great Plains seemed like a desert. The wide horizon and scarcity of trees bothered most, and they hastened to cross the plains to reach Oregon or California.

Another somewhat optimistic report on the area came several years later after Captain William F. Raynolds of the U.S. Army Corps of Topographical Engineers crossed the Great Plains in 1859 and 1860. He led an expedition up the Missouri River to Fort Pierre, then southwest to Fort Laramie by way of the Black Hills, and then north to the Yellowstone River. Raynolds and his party were guided by mountain man Jim Bridger, then in his mid-fifties, as they explored the possibilities of wagon routes, estimated the numbers, culture, and location of Indian tribes, charted the region, and observed the climate and resources of the land. Although Raynolds was not an authority on agriculture, he concluded that perhaps three-fourths of the country crossed possessed "soil that, other conditions being favorable, would render a generous return for the labors of the husbandman." But Raynolds added that "the dryness of the climate must . . . constitute a very serious obstacle to successful agriculture." He correctly observed that reliable information on the amount of rainfall was needed to determine whether the plains could be productive.[6]

Publication of Raynolds's report, however, was delayed by the Civil War until 1868, well after the reports of Hazen, Pope, and Sherman reached the East. Raynolds's observations probably added to the growing confusion in the minds of many Americans over the value of the Great Plains. On one side were those who believed that the plains constituted the Great American Desert, and this belief was reinforced by the reports of the three military men just after the Civil War. But on the other side were optimistic accounts from people praising the agricultural potential of the Great Plains, and they were not calling them a desert. One early booster was Max Greene, a tramp printer from Pennsylvania. Greene spent much time on the plains between 1850 and 1855 and then returned East to write a book entitled *The Kanzas Region*. He observed that the plains were adapted to pasturage, "with enough arable acres to support its probable population." Greene also pointed out why Americans failed to accept the Great Plains for what they were. He wrote:

To the dweller by the Atlantic, where green meadows, abounding har-
vests and babbling brooks are common blessings, it is difficult to picture
aright those scenes of Asian wildness within our national borders. From
childhood, we have so linked descriptions of piles of scoriæ and treeless,
grassless slopes, with dimmest legends of the olden time, and reveries
of the fabulist upon a far-off continent, that we cannot well persuade
ourselves that such things are American realities.[7]

Another early booster of the Great Plains was William Gilpin, a native
of Delaware and the son of wealthy Quaker parents. Gilpin had served as a
soldier in the West, but in 1857 he was practicing law in Independence,
Missouri, where he wrote that while the climate of the Great Plains was
different from that of the humid East and there was a scarcity of timber,
substitute resources were available. Gilpin noted that bituminous coal and
dried buffalo dung were abundant and could serve as fuel, and that buildings
and even fences could be constructed out of sun-dried adobe brick. Gilpin,
who later became the first governor of Colorado Territory, wrote that enough
water could be found in the creek and river valleys to irrigate all kinds of
crops. He added that pastoral husbandry would develop rapidly, followed
by systematic farming with "the culture of cereals, hemp, tobacco, fruits—
and the production of meats, leather, and wool."[8]

Another supporter of the Great Plains, although not as strong a booster
as Gilpin, was Samuel Bowles, editor of the Springfield, Massachusetts,
Republican. He crossed the plains in May 1865 and used the phrase "great
central desert" in his reports sent East. But Bowles hastened to explain that
the plains region was not really a desert and certainly not worthless. He
believed that the Great Plains had a tremendous potential for ranching, and
once the railroads arrived, "it will feed us with beef and mutton, and give
wool and leather immeasurable."[9]

The accounts of Greene, Gilpin, Bowles, and other boosters of the Great
Plains apparently were passed off as inconsequential in the East, as was the
fact that islands of settlement already existed on the plains. Settlements first
appeared along the Santa Fe and then the Oregon and California trails as
trading posts and later as military forts. Traders and some soldiers planted
gardens and raised some of their own food, and such gardens became commonplace just east of the Rockies following the Kansas gold rush in the late
1850s. Gold seekers planted them to have fresh vegetables, and by the early
1860s attractive farms existed on the edge of the plains near Denver, dis-

proving the beliefs of chair-bound authorities in the East, who were convinced that the plains really were part of a Great American Desert.

At the heart of the problem was the fact that the government had not sent agricultural experts onto the Great Plains. Certainly the government had financed many expeditions to map the West and to study its geology, wildlife, and Indians, but no one had been sent West to gather data on rainfall and the soil to determine what crops could be grown on the plains. At the time the science of agriculture was only in its infancy; agricultural chemistry and geology, entomology, and animal husbandry were just beginning to emerge as possible aids to farmers. As historian Paul W. Gates has observed, agricultural authorities were dissatisfied with farming as practiced throughout the United States "and the disinclination of farmers to consider new ideas and improved methods. Belief in the inexhaustibility of the soil and the supply of new land and preoccupation with immediate returns made farmers prodigal of the resources of the land and careless in their practices."[10]

WHEN CONGRESS issued land grants to the railroads, it closed to settlement the alternate sections retained by the government. They were reserved for sale at two dollars and fifty cents per acre, but this was to occur only after the railroads had completed their construction through an area and had received their full grants, something that in most instances took many years. In the meantime, however, the railroads could sell their land at prices ranging from four to ten dollars an acre once it had been surveyed and patented. The Kansas Pacific Railway Company began land sales in eastern Kansas in 1869, a year before its line across the state was completed. But it was 1875 before it could complete a survey of all the land it had acquired. And it did not patent any of its land until 1873, and in Colorado not until 1875. This irritated many early settlers who arrived with money in hand to buy good land near a railroad.

The Atchison, Topeka and Santa Fe Railroad, however, moved much more quickly than the Kansas Pacific to survey, patent, and offer its land for sale in Kansas. Its survey party forwarded reports from along the route to the railroad's land office in Topeka, where maps were prepared showing the location of each section owned by the railroad. The survey party's notes gave officials some idea of the value of the land, and it was priced in Topeka and offered for sale beginning in 1869, the same year the Kansas Pacific began to sell some of its land in eastern Kansas.

In Nebraska the Burlington Railroad appears to have done a better job than the Union Pacific in getting its sections ready for sale, at least at the beginning, but many settlers lured West by the promise of free land rejected the idea of buying railroad land in Nebraska or Kansas. They could not afford it, and they turned instead to homesteading. Since the alternate sections owned by the government along the railroad routes were not yet for sale, the settlers claimed land some distance from the railroad routes. The government appears to have ignored the problem at first, but the railroads realized that there had to be farms and towns along their tracks if they were to earn a profit. The key was the development of railroad land, especially on the plains beyond where settlement was already beginning to occur, and the railroads soon joined promotional efforts already underway in Kansas, Nebraska, and Dakota Territory to attract new settlers.

Although organized campaigns to attract settlers to Kansas began in 1854, when New England abolitionists encouraged free-state supporters to move to the territory, neither Kansas, Nebraska, nor Dakota Territory became actively involved in promotion until late in the Civil War. In 1861 the territorial governor of Nebraska tried unsuccessfully to appropriate funds to hire an emigration agent to live in New York City and steer new settlers West, but it was not until 1865 that a bureau of immigration was formed and funded by the state. A year later the bureau published a small pamphlet titled *Nebraska: Containing a Brief Account of the Soil, Productions, Agricultural and Mineral Resources*. Printed in English and German, it was the first of many such pamphlets, circulars, and other material to be produced by Nebraska.

Officials in Dakota Territory sought to promote emigration as early as 1862, but it was not until 1869 that an official immigration commission was approved. The following year the Illinois Central Railroad reached Sioux City, Iowa, and branch lines were soon linking Yankton and Sioux Falls to the East. But the Dakota immigration commission did not receive any funding until 1870. James S. Foster, hired as commissioner of immigration, wrote a 127-page book called *Outlines of History of the Territory of Dakota, and Emigrant's Guide to the Free Lands of the Northwest*. The book included a map plus descriptions of towns, stage routes, railroads, farming, churches, society, schools, and much more. It was followed by many other promotional publications.

Kansas created its bureau of immigration in 1867, and soon agreed to spend twenty-five hundred dollars on a promotional gazette called *Resources of Kansas*. The author was Clinton C. Hutchinson, a former U.S. Indian agent who had successfully promoted the settlement of Ottawa Indian lands in eastern Kansas a decade earlier. Ten thousand copies of his 287-page illustrated book were printed in July 1871. It painted a rosy picture of life in Kansas, paying considerable attention to the plains region in western Kansas. The railroads, by then becoming heavily involved in promotion, provided Hutchinson with glowing accounts of their routes, the land available, and the towns that were springing up along the lines. Hutchinson quoted letters from settlers who praised life on the plains, and then wrote:

> Travelers who pass through Kansas upon the Kansas Pacific Railway, enter upon the Buffalo grass region after riding about two hundred miles through the fat meadows, the luxuriant corn fields, and the vigorous wild grasses of Eastern Kansas, and as they come in sight of the brown and shriveled buffalo grass, it seems indeed contemptible. It is very true that vast herds of buffalo are seen, extending for miles in either direction, sometimes huddled in distant masses which resemble low islands in the sea, or, at other times, are so numerous and so persistent in keeping to their course, that the engineer is obliged to stop his train and give them the track, until they cross it in their line of march. The traveler also sees the dressed carcasses of buffalo and antelope at every station, which are as fat as stall-fed beef; and yet many people return from the trip and talk about the "Buffalo Grass Desert." . . . Who would suppose that buffalo would return to a "desert" for feed year after year? nay, that they would stay there the year around, as thousands annually do stay in the valleys of the Republican, Solomon, Smokey Hill and Arkansas rivers, and their tributaries? Many an eastern farmer would gladly turn the flocks and herds on to this desert, which crop the low grass in his high priced pastures, or during six months of winter, eat the hay he has so laboriously garnered.[11]

The year Hutchinson's book was published in Topeka, Colorado Territory established its board of immigration and joined Kansas, Nebraska, and Dakota Territory in producing promotional posters, pamphlets, and other printed material designed to attract new settlers.

But it was the railroads, anxious to develop their land, that became the most active boosters of the Great Plains. In most instances the land departments of the railroads coordinated promotional efforts, but in a few instances railroads established their own immigration bureaus or land companies. A seemingly endless supply of maps, pamphlets, circulars, handbills, and other advertising flooded the nation, especially the East, where the railroads advertised extensively in newspapers. And the railroads joined several state immigration bureaus in printing promotional material in foreign languages. Foreign agents were even hired to attract settlers to railroad lands in the West.

Although most of the railroads claimed that they were telling the truth about the Great Plains, their advertising was perhaps the least responsible of all. For instance, in 1876 the Atchison, Topeka and Santa Fe Railroad Company published a forty-six-page pamphlet in Boston titled *How and Where to Get a Living: A Sketch of "The Garden of the West." Presenting Facts Worth Knowing Concerning the Lands of the Atchison, Topeka & Santa Fe Railroad Co., in Southwestern Kansas*. Toward the end of the pamphlet the railroad noted:

> If hard work doesn't agree with you, or you can't get on without luxuries, stay where you are. If you are susceptible to homesickness, if you do not have pluck and perseverance, stay where you are. . . . Wealth here is won only by work. [12]

On its face, this sounded like a warning to those thinking about coming West, but in reality it was a seductive challenge. The railroad's writer knew very well that few people would admit to not having what it took to succeed. After all, the simple agrarian life, hard work, and perseverance were integral to the American way of life. The railroads simply adopted the theme that the Great Plains could be changed only by hard work. They quoted only favorable comments about cheap lands, abundant crops, and the financial independence of the hardworking settlers already in the West. Even the climate was praised, and some promoters claimed that it was so healthy doctors were not needed.

The railroads, however, did not rely solely on their own promotional writers and publications. They provided many western newspaper editors with free passes to ride their lines, and they invited eastern newspaper editors to view firsthand, all expenses paid, the garden in the West and the opportunities awaiting hardworking settlers on the Great Plains. For instance, in June 1875 the Atchison, Topeka and Santa Fe Railroad invited editors from Illinois, Indiana, Ohio, Iowa, Michigan, Missouri, West Virginia, Wisconsin, Kentucky, New Hampshire, New York, and Kansas to join "an editorial excursion through southwestern Kansas to Granada, Colorado." Just how many editors were invited is not known, but two hundred and twenty-seven accepted the invitation and left Atchison, Kansas, at 7 a.m. on June 24, 1875, aboard a special train. When the excursion ended many days later and the editors returned home, the railroad carefully watched the editors' newspapers and clipped stories written about the excursion. Selecting the most positive accounts, the railroad published a twenty-four-page pamphlet titled *Kansas in 1875: Strong and Impartial Testimony to the Wonderful Productiveness of the Cottonwood and Arkansas Valleys. What Over Two Hundred Editors Think of Their Present and Future.* Here are a few examples of what the editors wrote:

Never have we seen such crops as are being garnered along the line of the Atchison, Topeka & Santa Fe road. No grasshoppers are to be seen in this country, except the one common to our section, and in fact this part of Kansas is said to have been credited as being in a worse condition last year than it was by far. *—Nokomis* (Ill.) *Gazette*

The soil of Kansas is certainly one of the best in the world for cereals. For corn growing, the uplands will not compare favorably with Illinois. The valleys of the Neosho, Cottonwood and Arkansas, however, seem to produce everything. *—Cambridge* (Ind.) *Tribune.*

The wheat, corn, oats and potatoes *here* cannot be excelled. *—Charlotte* (Mich.) *Leader.*

No water in Kansas? There is more rain there in a year than in Ohio, and water-courses innumerable. I was amazed at the water privileges. Let me tell you that the corn was as luxuriant and as high there, on the 26th of June, as it will be in this superb valley on the 10th of July. *—Dayton* (O.) *Journal.*

I never saw a finer country in the world than that part of Kansas passed over by the A. T. & Santa Fe road. Corn waist high, wheat in the shock, oats in fine condition, and vegetables in abundance. The people of Kansas are really jubilant over their crop prospects. *—Marion* (Ind.) *Chronicle.*[13]

Around 1870, promoters of the Great Plains introduced another idea into the minds of Americans to help convince potential settlers that conditions on the plains were being changed by man. Clinton C. Hutchinson, in his *Resources of Kansas*, observed that during 1870 a severe drought had occurred in New England. He claimed that it had been caused by the clearing of nearly all the timbered land. Applying this premise in reverse, Hutchinson wrote:

> The effect of railroads and telegrams, is undoubtedly to cause more frequent showers, perhaps by promoting a more even distribution of the magnetic forces. From some cause it is certain that thunder storms are less severe than formerly, in Kansas. A. D. Richardson [a newspaperman], after returning from his last trip across the continent, informed me he was convinced that railroads and telegraphs do have an effect upon the climate and cause an increased and more frequent rainfall. It is quite well understood also that trees and hedges, in various ways tend to increase the fall of rain, and the planting of these objects is the cause usually indicated for our change of seasons.

Hutchinson went on to suggest that the planting of trees and the cultivation of the soil would increase the rainfall on the Great Plains.[14]

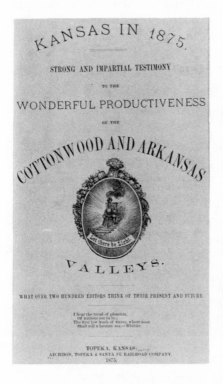

PROMOTIONAL PAMPHLETS BY THE RAILROADS TO ATTRACT IMMIGRANTS.

Exactly who came up with the theory that "rain follows the plow" is not known, but it became a slogan of the promoters, who realized that rain and the plow were the two most treasured symbols of the farmer. The theory was given credibility by Ferdinand V. Hayden, a respected geologist who headed the U.S. Geographical and Geological Survey of the Territories. He said he believed that the use of the plow on the Great Plains was causing increased rainfall. Promoters did not hesitate to quote Hayden in their publications. In retrospect, one wonders how intelligent men could have believed such a theory, which was based on nothing more than wishful thinking, but America had entered the Gilded Age, that post-Civil War period marked by scandals and corruption in business and government when it seemed that anything was possible. The theory was accepted by many people, including lawmakers in Washington. Congress passed the Timber Culture Act in 1873, allowing a homesteader an extra 160 acres if he would plant trees on at least forty acres of the land within four years. The legislation was also designed to solve another problem. While a 160-acre homestead was adequate and could be profitable for a farmer in the more humid areas of eastern Kansas and eastern Nebraska, a farmer on the Great Plains needed as many as 640 acres for a profitable operation. The Timber Culture Act was designed to double the size of a settler's homestead on the Great Plains,

HENRY WORRALL'S "DROUTHY KANSAS."
Done as a joke, but used by railroads and other promoters to attract
settlers to Kansas.

but, as many settlers would learn, 320 acres was still not sufficient to make a profit, especially in dry years.

All of the words written by all the promoters of the Great Plains could not change natural conditions. The plains were dry, and some years they were drier than others. The promoters stressed the "average" rainfall, ignoring the droughts and grasshoppers. In good years the average rainfall was thirty to forty inches, but in 1874 some parts of the plains received half this amount or less. The drought was followed by millions of flying, leaping, plant-eating grasshoppers. They ate what little crops had survived in Kansas, where the temperature reached 110 degrees in late July. One witness to the grasshopper invasion was E. D. Haney, a homesteader in north-central Kansas:

> We were threshing at the Turnby place, and about 10 a.m. the vanguard showed up and in a very short time the air was full of them. They began to drop down and went to work. They damaged grain in the shock soon by shelling it out. Old Mr. Turnby stood leaning on his fork looking at them and finally blurted out, "Wer in 'ell did they hall come from?" He was English. Corn was completely ruined, all garden truck consumed. We had some good sweet corn and I cut it and hauled it, covered with hay, and saved some of it. We had a fine patch of onions. [My] wife told me I had best go and pull them. When I got to the patch there was nothing left but little round holes where the onions had been. They invaded the house and ate holes in the window curtains. They stayed late and laid eggs in all sheltered places. Millions hatched out in the spring.[15]

Conditions were equally bad in parts of Nebraska, where citizens asked for aid. They did the same in Kansas, and in time relief groups were organized. Money and provisions were sent to many settlers, but others were ruined and left the country. The railroads downplayed the conditions and the exodus. Some busted settlers stopped in Topeka to cuss out a man who unknowingly had helped the railroads attract settlers to Kansas. He was Henry Worrall, an Englishman, who came to America and eventually settled in Topeka. Worrall was something of an artist, and when he learned that several friends from Ohio were planning to visit him in Kansas, he remembered that they had been quite outspoken about the dryness of the state. Worrall drew a big charcoal sketch, which he prominently labeled "Drouthy Kansas." It was a humorous drawing showing the state as a "land of plenty" with huge pumpkins, grapes, and other produce plus an abundant supply of water. Worrall had the sketch photographed and ordered a number of prints on postcards to give to his friends when they arrived. Everyone enjoyed the joke. When Worrall's friends left Kansas, they carried a large number of the photos home to Ohio. Worrall was ready to forget his sketch, but others were not. It appeared on the cover of *Kansas Farmer* magazine in late 1869. Clinton C. Hutchinson used it in his promotional gazette, *Resources of Kansas,* and a representative from the Missouri Pacific Railroad took a copy east. Soon the railroads reproduced it on thousands of circulars. The drawing inspired many immigrants to settle in Kansas, and when the drought and grasshopper invasion occurred in 1874 and many were ruined, "the damn sketch of Henry Worrall's" was recalled. One Topeka newspaper reported that some people believed that "had it not been for the diabolical seductiveness of the picture, they never would have come to Kansas to be ruinated and undone by grasshoppers."[16]

ASIDE from buying railroad land or taking a homestead, settlers could acquire government land under the preemption law of 1841, which allowed the purchase of 160 acres of unsurveyed government land for a minimum of $1.25 an acre. But the preemptor, as a settler was called, had to make some improvements and live on the land about fourteen months before he could gain the final title. A settler could file for both a homestead and a preemption claim; thus it was possible to acquire a total of 320 acres directly from the federal government. Under the preemption and homestead laws, the preemptor had to swear that the land was for his own exclusive use and that it was not being acquired for resale or speculation. But land speculators, moving west ahead of surveying crews, often preempted and purchased the best land and held it until it was their property. When settlers came along and offered to buy it, the speculator sold it for hard cash and moved on west to repeat the process. Land speculators were plentiful on the Great Plains, and most came up with devices to circumvent the law. For instance, some rented portable cabins for five dollars and wheeled them onto their "homesteads" so that they could claim there were dwellings on their property. And in some instances a speculator would swear that he had erected a "twelve by fourteen dwelling" on his property, failing to mention that he meant inches rather than feet. The poorly paid and often overworked U.S. Land Office clerks rarely found time to check each homestead because of the vast distances that had to be covered.

Dewain Delp, who settled on the plains in Norton County, Kansas, in 1872, recalled what conditions were like when he arrived. He wrote:

There were only a few people living in Norton County, probably around 200. Ninety-nine percent of these were men—a rough and motley crew they were, not the "noble pioneer" that historians have glorified, but men of the world, adventurers, opportunists, and even thieves—hard, rough and cunning. They were for the most part men who had not been too successful in the home community back east, so had moved on further west with the philosophy that "the early bird gets the worm" and the worms are "easy picking." Some were trappers and hunters, other traders along the line of a huckster, who carried his stock of goods in his wagon—salt pork, flour, salt, whiskey, gun powder, shot, perhaps guns and a few clothes. Then there were the "horse traders" and the "land scalpers"—men who had staked out the best claims along the rivers and streams in the hopes of selling it to the real homesteaders whom they knew would soon be arriving. Most of these men lived alone in hastily constructed dugouts along the creek banks, they needed nor wanted anything better for their stay was to be short. . . .

Few were the luxuries of a housewife in these days, the first real settlers. Their cooking utensils consisted of an iron kettle, two or three pans, and a water bucket—just whatever there was room for in the covered wagon when they had packed to go west. Very few homes had wells and so water was carried from the closest spring. All supplies had to be freighted over-land, a three day journey from Cawker City or WaKeeney—the closest railways. The houses were sod, with native poles, brush, grass and more sod for roofs. Of course, the roof leaked when it rained—worse yet these roofs were favorite haunts of mice and snakes. The furniture was, for the most part, home-made from boxes or any handy material. A few were able to bring some furniture with them. For all the poverty these houses were clean and comfortable. Their usually white-washed interiors were cool in summer and warm in winter. . . .

The majority [of the homesteaders] were honest and sincere in attempting to follow the letter of the law [in taking and proving up their homesteads], but there were others who were artists at evading it. The law made these requirements among others, "there must be a house with glass in the windows, water in a well, growing trees on the farm-

AN UNIDENTIFIED DUGOUT SOMEWHERE ON THE PLAINS IN 1884.
The homesteader, probably the man with a hat, thought highly enough of his
oxen to have them in the photo.

stead, and the owner must use the place for his actual domicile."

Well, when it came time to "prove up" on the homestead the claimant
would take two witnesses with him and they would spend the night in
the sod houses—thus they were able to swear that the claimant slept
in the house on that particular land. The next morning they would see
"water in the well" (which had been placed in the ten foot hole in the
ground a few minutes before, and had been hauled from the river in a
barrel). They could also swear that there was glass in the windows for
in plain sight there hung by a string a swinging beer bottle. For trees,
petite willow branches had been stuck in the ground—green leaves—
sure they were "growing trees."[17]

For the honest homesteaders who stuck it out, life was not easy. Nor
was it easy for those who purchased railroad land. Even without the natural
problems, including droughts and grasshoppers, some homesteaders had
legal problems. Jeff Jenkins, who was sent to Concordia, Kansas, to open
a U.S. Land Office early in 1871, recalled that many litigated cases were
heard in his office in an effort to establish the rights of the parties involved,
especially after the land had been improved and become more valuable. In
one case, a single woman had taken a homestead in company with her
relatives and other settlers. But she was driven off her claim by Indians.

After a short absence the settlers returned, and while her relatives and friends harvested the grain, she cooked for them. In the meantime, she hoed the patch of potatoes on her claim with two navy revolvers in her belt and a good rifle nearby. Jenkins recalled:

"I would have fired my last shot and then fought with my hoe and rifle!" exclaimed the lady, emphatically; and, judging from her physical development, I think she could have given any two Indians a rough hand-to-hand fight. Though modest in her demeanor, at the trial, she exhibited marked evidence of courage and bravery in time of danger. A subsequent Indian raid had driven the settlers from their homestead claims a second time, and she failing to return to her claim within the period limited by law, the contest was brought to cancel her homestead entry. The local officers and the department found, from the evidence, and so held, that being driven from her claim by the Indians was not a voluntary abandonment, and her homestead entry was permitted to remain intact upon the record.[18]

But not all claim problems were settled inside the U.S. Land Office. Jenkins observed that it frequently happened that before a hearing began, the parties involved and their friends would gather outside the Land Office

A DUGOUT IN NORTON COUNTY IN NORTHWEST KANSAS.

and try to settle the matter by "wager of battle." No weapons were used except fists. "The transient character of the residence of many of the settlers, especially those without families, caused many contests, and the excuses given and means resorted to by the parties . . . were as numerous and varied as the adventures of Don Quixote."[19]

During the depression that followed the panic of 1873 and the drought of 1874, many settlers had to borrow capital to continue farming. A settler in need of money would travel to the closest town and seek a loan from a bank. Banks were plentiful, even in the new towns springing up in Nebraska and Kansas. It was not difficult to start a bank, and it was not unusual for merchants to combine banking with their general merchandise business. All that was required was a vault or safe installed in one corner of the store. When a homestead was patented, the owner often mortgaged it for three to five hundred dollars to obtain money to make improvements. But if a settler had not yet received title to the land, the banker nearly always demanded a chattel mortgage on the settler's pigs, chickens, cows, horses, furniture, wagon, or any other items of value. It was not uncommon for a borrower to skip the country with the securities after getting a loan for one or two hundred dollars. In a few cases, even the borrower's house was moved away. Theodore Ackerman of Russell, Kansas, followed one defaulter two hundred miles into Colorado to recover a span of mortgaged mules. When Ackerman caught up with the mules he found that the owner had painted them brown in hopes of disguising them. Another time Ackerman traveled east to Kansas City,

SOD HOUSE

Missouri, to recover a team of horses. He sold the team and made back the value of the loan before returning home.

Ackerman, however, appears to have been more fortunate than many bankers, who frequently lost their loans to borrowers who fled with the securities. Little wonder, then, that bankers charged such high rates of interest, anywhere from 2 to 12 percent per month on notes renewed every sixty or ninety days. By the 1870s, interest rates were lower for homesteaders who had made good on their claims and other settlers who had made partial payment to buy land; they were better risks. But such was not the case for the poor settler who had not yet gained title to his property. Interest above 12 percent was not uncommon for the settlers of the 1870s. In Dakota Territory, for instance, the legal interest rate was 18 percent until 1875, when it was reduced to 12 percent. During the 1880s there was what was called "12–10" borrowing in Dakota Territory. "The borrower got $90 for each $100 on the face of the note and paid twelve percent on the amount named on the note. For example, one approached the banker for a loan of $300. When the note was signed the borrower received not $300 but $270, although he paid interest on the $300. One had to borrow for five years to get that."[20]

For most farmers in the West during the 1870s and 1880s, borrowing money was a way of life. Few had a great deal of money. To be a successful farmer on the plains, improved farm machinery was necessary. The iron plow, first produced by John Deere in 1837, was one essential tool, even though it was still difficult work cutting through the virgin soil. In 1868 John Lane invented what was called "soft center" steel. Layers of the steel were placed on the sides of iron plows, and they worked much better at plowing the virgin land and hard soil. But such plows were more expensive. James Oliver, a blacksmith, patented a method of hardening cast iron in 1868, and by 1870 he was producing a cheaper plow that worked almost as well as the steel-tipped one. Using workhorses, three to a plow, or oxen if the sod was being broken for the first time, a farmer could do about two acres a day with a one-bottom walking plow. By the late 1860s the gang plow—two or more plows in a row—gradually came into use. Farmers could plow more land more quickly with gang plows, and they became very popular, especially on the northern plains in the Red River valley of the Dakotas, where wheat was the primary crop. Other improvements were also made in harrows, seeding equipment, and cultivators, and eastern businessmen soon created new companies and in time a whole industry designed to provide farmers with the equipment they needed.[21]

BUFFALO BONES OFTEN COVERED HOMESTEADS
and served as a reminder of the great slaughter of bison. Before settlers could till
the virgin prairie, they had to pick up the bones. Most did not mind, since the
bones could be sold and used to make fertilizer.

The scarcity of surface water in many areas of the prairie and certainly on the plains created a demand for underground water. Because water was usually located only at considerable depth in these areas, hand-dug wells were not only impractical but too expensive, and wells dug with augers could not go deep enough. The occupation of well driller developed as men acquired mechanical well-drilling equipment and went into business. Such drilling rigs consisted of a "heavy drill bit or other tool fastened to a cable with a suitable apparatus for lifting it and then allowing it to drop, forcing a hole into the ground and pounding rock into fragments small enough to be removed. As the hole was made, water was added so that after the drill had pulverized an amount of the subsurface material, a bailer [a cuplike device] could be let down into the well to remove the earth and water mixture. The process was repeated over and over until the water table was reached. Generally the drilled wells were lined with iron casing to prevent them from caving in."[22]

A well four hundred feet deep might cost six hundred dollars. Well drillers usually charged a flat rate for each foot of the first hundred and fifty feet, a slightly greater charge per foot for the next hundred feet, and then an even greater charge for each foot deeper than two hundred and fifty feet. Cattlemen, who moved into many areas before homesteaders, apparently were the first settlers in the West to drill wells to provide water for their livestock. On the XIT Ranch in the panhandle region of Texas during the middle 1880s, well drillers were paid $1.50 per foot for the first hundred and fifty feet, $2.00 a foot for the next hundred feet, and $2.50 for each subsequent foot until a satisfactory flow of water was obtained. By 1900 the XIT Ranch had three hundred and thirty-three wells, with attached windmills, in operation on the three-million-acre ranch that covered parts of nine Texas counties.[23]

Windmills, needed to draw the water from the wells, became essential for cattlemen and farmers in the West. Although the first commercially successful self-governing windmill in the United States was invented in 1854 by Daniel Halladay, a New England mechanic, the sale of commercially produced windmills on the prairie and plains did not begin until the late 1860s and early 1870s. At first only the wealthy could afford them, but as the competition to sell windmills increased, the prices came down. In 1870 a windmill cost between $140 and $160 depending upon the size and model, but by the early 1880s the average price of a windmill was around $133. It dropped to about $100 by 1890. The demand for windmills opened still

A WATER WELL BEING DRILLED IN NINETEENTH-CENTURY GREELEY COUNTY, KANSAS.

A GREELEY COUNTY HOMESTEADER'S WINDMILL
towers above his dugout home and outbuildings on the plains.

another market for eastern businessmen. A growing number of manufacturers sold them through agents, branch houses, and dealers. By the late 1870s smaller manufacturers on the eastern edges of the prairie and plains were marketing their own windmills directly to customers.[24]

But windmills became commonplace in the West only after the invention of barbed wire, which made it possible to isolate water holes for livestock. The invention of barbed wire in 1873 by Joseph Farwell Glidden, a farmer in De Kalb County, Illinois, was at first viewed with suspicion by cattlemen; many feared that the wire, with sharp metal barbs spaced every few inches, would injure cattle. One of the men who apparently changed cattlemen's minds on the subject was John Warner Gates. In the summer of 1876 he was traveling through Texas representing the barbed-wire manufacturing firm of Glidden and Ellwood. At first, Gates failed to talk ranchers and farmers into buying his product. He decided to give a demonstration and built a barbed-wire corral on one of San Antonio's plazas, probably Military Plaza. He had some Texas longhorns driven into the enclosure as a large crowd gathered. Acting as master of ceremonies, he described the advantages of barbed wire, and then he reportedly had two men with flaming torches frighten the longhorns into pushing against the fence. It held. His demonstration proved convincing for many farmers and ranchers, and the use of barbed wire spread throughout Texas and the West, giving birth to still another new industry.

Barbed-wire salesman Gates took advantage of the opportunities he had helped to create and was soon manufacturing barbed wire on his own. He became chairman of the board of directors of the powerful American Steel & Wire Company, and still later he entered a tiny oil business in southeastern Texas, helped to develop the city of Port Arthur as an oil-shipping center, and built up the Texas Company, better known today as Texaco. John Warner Gates died in 1911 a wealthy man.[25]

Barbed wire enabled farmers to fence their crops, including wheat. But it was a new process of milling that really turned the Great Plains into the breadbasket of the nation well before the turn of the century. The plains, especially in the north, were unsuitable for raising the soft winter wheat raised in the East. Hard-kerneled wheat, known as "Turkey Red," had been brought to the plains by German-speaking Russian Mennonites as early as 1860. It grew well in Kansas and Nebraska, and other varieties of spring wheat from Northern Europe produced excellent yields in Montana, Minnesota, and Dakota Territory. But old methods of milling were not effective with spring wheat. Not until corrugated, chilled-iron rollers produced in the East were substituted for millstones was the problem solved. By 1881 western mills were using the new process and producing fine grades of flour from spring wheat. It was then that grain elevators began to appear on the plains, constructed by railroads near their tracks so that grain could be stored for later shipment. By 1900, agriculture was well established as a major industry of the American West.

The plains farmers of the late nineteenth century had to take greater risks than farmers elsewhere because mechanization was a necessity, and to buy improved equipment the farmer had to borrow money. This brought about a significant change in attitude for the farmer, which reflected changes in the outlook of the entire country. From the nation's beginning until the early 1840s, farmers had very little to do with banks. They did not believe in them. Banks and other corporate bodies were objectionable not only because of what they did but because banks operated on credit. Farmers did not believe in credit. They viewed banks and corporations of all types as sources of instability. Even merchants and businessmen were often thought to be enemies of the farmer, although farmers were usually able to treat them as fellow human beings. It depended upon the individual. But corporations were considered impersonal, privileged, artificial, and soulless. In the eyes of the farmers, they were aggregates of the worst in man.

These attitudes for the most part represented the feelings of the nation, since until the late 1840s the country was mostly agrarian. But as agrarian power began to dwindle around that time, attitudes began to change, and by the early 1850s the easy-money craze of the speculators and entrepreneurs began to supersede and transmute the conservatism of the farmer. By the time the Homestead Act was passed in 1862, America was becoming an industrial and not an agrarian society. The merchant capitalist had become the dominant figure in the American economy, although manufacturing in the key industries was no longer under the control of the merchant. The industrialist rather than the merchant was guiding and controlling manufacturing developments in America even before the end of the Civil War. And the immigrants settling the West were rapidly becoming an important market for the products manufactured in the East.[26]

XII

THE BUSINESS
OF TOWNS

*The twin curses of Kansas, now that the border ruffians have stopped
ravaging her, are land-speculation . . . and one-horse politicians.
. . . It takes three long houses to make a city in Kansas, but they
begin calling it a city so soon as they have staked out the lots.*

—HORACE GREELEY[1]

O N A cold morning early in 1857 a group of businessmen gathered at
the Eldridge House in Lawrence, Kansas Territory, to warm their in-
sides with coffee or tea and perhaps a bite of food. For the dozen or so men
sitting around the large wooden table, it was something of a daily ritual to
come together on working days to talk about business, politics, the weather,
and to exchange news. On this particular morning someone mentioned that
town promoters were making a lot of money. Someone else noted that cer-
tificates for shares in the new towns were circulating as freely as wildcat
currency printed by banks without assets. Another person then suggested,
perhaps jokingly, that the men sitting around the table should lay out their
own town and sell shares. The comment was taken seriously. Before the day
ended, most of the men had organized a town company with Charles Robinson, a future governor of Kansas, as president.

Two or three of the men were surveyors, and one of them soon produced
a fine lithograph certificate from his files showing an illustration of a beautiful
little town. The appropriate words were added to the blank spaces and the
town of Oread, Kansas Territory, was born. But no one knew where their
town would be located. By spring, however, land had been found about
forty-five miles southwest of Lawrence. B. L. Kingsbury, one of the surveyors,
laid out the townsite at the head of Long Creek about twelve miles northeast
of present-day Burlington in Coffey County, Kansas. Shares were put on the

market offering two to ten town lots at prices from ten to fifty dollars. They sold rapidly, and by early summer there were three crude log cabins on the townsite. One of them housed a small general store with a little stock of goods brought to the town by one of the Lawrence men. But the town did not survive. Within a year Kansans had felt the effects of the national economic panic of 1857, and the general store was abandoned, as were the other two cabins. The Lawrence men who had created Oread, however, made a little money before their tiny bubble burst.[2]

Such schemes were commonplace in eastern portions of Kansas and Nebraska territories between 1854 and late 1857. In most instances the town promoters moved into the territories ahead of the immigrants who wanted land to farm. The promoters recognized that towns with businesses would be needed to supply the soon-to-arrive farmers, and that towns located in good farming regions would attract not only farmers but good businesses. Congress realized this as well when it passed the Federal Townsites Act in 1844, making it easy to establish towns, especially in the West. The law-makers provided 320 acres for a townsite when it was occupied, and the land was not subject to the preemption law of 1841, which limited the amount of government land a citizen could buy to 160 acres.

The person or persons starting a town would first organize a town company. That company could then buy the 320 acres for $1.25 an acre, or four hundred dollars. To enlarge the townsite, the company members could also individually preempt adjacent quarter-sections. The town was then cut up into lots, usually a hundred twenty-five by twenty-five feet, and shares were sold, usually on the basis of ten lots per share. The individual town company members would meantime hold the adjacent quarter-sections until the town grew and the nearby land was more valuable. It might then be sold.

Congress gave the state or territory in which the townsite was located the right to regulate the disposal of the lots and the proceeds of the sale. In Kansas and Nebraska territories, the legislatures handled this by encouraging promoters to petition for a special act of incorporation which, with the payment of a small fee, would give them sound title to a townsite. In the first session of the Nebraska territorial legislature, seventeen towns were incorporated, and nearly twenty towns during the first session of the Kansas territorial legislature.[3]

Before the arrival of the railroads, most townsites west of the Missouri were laid out where trails crossed rivers and creeks. During the late 1850s many settlers believed that the Kansas and Platte rivers were navigable and

PARSON'S BRIDGE, SPANNING THE JEFFERSON RIVER
not far from present-day Three Forks, Montana, in 1868. The crossing naturally
attracted stagecoaches traveling between Virginia City and Helena, and a town
sprang up.

that towns along these rivers would become prosperous. But as time and
experience demonstrated, the streams were too shallow for reliable steamboat
travel. Such locations, however, did provide water and usually trees that
could be cut down and used for building materials and fuel. Some enterprising
soul would usually build a ferry or a bridge and collect tolls from travelers
crossing the stream. The same person or a somebody else would then construct a small general store and try to attract not only business from the
travelers but permanent residents, either business or professional men or
farmers, to settle in the surrounding area. If the country nearby offered good
farmland, the community would gradually grow in population and prosper.

Many present-day towns grew in this manner, including North Platte,
Elkhorn, and Milford in Nebraska, and Marysville and Council Grove in
Kansas. Still others grew because they were located near military forts or
gristmills. But many early towns failed because trails were changed or a
nearby town dominated by offering more. In many instances town promoters
had no intention of seeing their towns become realities. Perhaps the worst
example of this in Nebraska was the town of Curlew in Cedar County. A
promoter registered a townsite, laid out and sold ten thousand lots, and

advertised with a fascinating map and illustrations that showed a supposedly prosperous town experiencing tremendous growth. Many of the lots reportedly were sold in the East, especially to investors in New York City. But no house was ever built, and the promoter made off with more than a hundred and fifty thousand dollars without breaking the law.[4]

Another promoter, in Burt County in eastern Nebraska, did not even take the time to incorporate his town company or register his townsite. He mapped out a piece of land and sold twenty thousand dollars' worth of lots. When authorities investigated they learned that the promoter was only a squatter. He had never owned the land that he sold.[5]

In Dakota Territory, the situation was somewhat different. Early town-building efforts were controlled by the Dakota Land Company, chartered by the Minnesota legislature in 1857. The company located nearly every valuable townsite that could be found on the Vermilion and James rivers, and on the Missouri River from the mouth of the Big Sioux River near present-day Sioux City, Iowa, to Fort Lookout, southeast of where Pierre, South Dakota, stands today. The best townsites were almost all gone when settlers, beginning in August 1859, moved into what is now South Dakota.

From Dakota Territory south through Kansas, there was much optimism among those seeking to start a real town. J. Sterling Morton, editor of the Nebraska City *News* and a man who did much to promote the Nebraska City Town Company in the 1850s, recalled years later:

We all felt, as they used to print in large letters on every new town plat, that we were "located adjacent to the very finest groves of timber, surrounded by a very rich agricultural country, in prospective, abundantly supplied with building rock of the finest description, beautifully watered, and possessing very fine indications of lead, iron, coal and salt in great abundance." In my opinion we felt richer, better and more millionairish than any poor deluded mortals ever did on the same amount of moonshine and pluck.[6]

The panic of 1857, however, put most town promoters out of work. They did not resume their activities until after the Civil War, when interest in the West was rekindled and the railroads got into the town-promoting business. As the Union Pacific built across Nebraska and the Union Pacific Railway Company, Eastern Division, pushed westward across Kansas through unsettled country, many towns were planned by the railroads. Settlements were placed six to eight miles apart. Each had a railroad depot, some larger than others, and most had facilities where trains could take on fuel and water. Of course, they were laid out on land owned by the railroads, land platted into townsites and offered for sale to immigrants. Later, as branch lines were established and other railroads came into existence, new towns usually appeared where two or more lines came together. Norfolk, Nebraska, and Minot, North Dakota, are examples of such towns, along with Chanute, Kansas. But the coming of the railroad often meant the death of an existing town if it was bypassed by the railroad. Citizens of towns built before the railroads arrived in their area worked hard to get railroads to serve their communities. Some towns succeeded, but others failed.

When the Union Pacific Railway Company, Eastern Division (later the Kansas Pacific), began building west from present-day Kansas City, Kansas, in 1863, the residents of Lawrence learned that the proposed route on the north side of the Kansas River would miss their town by three miles. Most of the town was south of the river. They asked the railroad to change the route and come through Lawrence. They lobbied hard for the change, but the railroad refused. By early January 1864 the route had been graded past Lawrence to the north and telegraph poles had been set. U.S. Senator James Lane, a resident of Lawrence, then used his political influence to have the route changed so that the line would pass through the portion of Lawrence that lay north of the river. It added two and a half miles to the line's original route, but Lawrence had a railroad.[7]

As the railroad continued construction west from Lawrence, its announced route was through Indianola, a small town on the government road running between Fort Leavenworth and Fort Riley. The road was also used by a stage line, which made Indianola an important point. The town had prospered from its beginning in 1854, even though it was only a few miles northwest of Topeka, founded the same year. But Indianola had been more aggressive. It even had a hotel, built about 1860 by William Clinton, who had married a wealthy older woman. Early in the Civil War, Clinton, who also served as postmaster, was accused of rifling the U.S. mail. Before he could be arraigned, however, he disappeared, taking with him much of his wife's money and an attractive young woman who left her own husband behind. The hotel was sold by Clinton's wife and continued to be the center of the town's life, especially when the railroad announced it would be coming through Indianola. But when Senator James Lane convinced the railroad officials to change its route at Lawrence, he also persuaded them to change from Indianola to nearby Topeka, where Lane had friends. After the railroad arrived in Topeka, most of the residents of Indianola transferred their town to nearby Topeka, except the owner of the hotel, who found his building too large to move. The hotel was soon abandoned to the elements and Indianola died.[8]

The residents of Phelps Center, Nebraska, were luckier than those of Indianola. When the railroad built into Phelps County in south-central Nebraska, it missed Phelps Center, but the residents were offered free lots if they would move their homes or build new ones on a townsite located next to the railroad line. Nearly all of the residents agreed, and Holdrege, Nebraska, was born.[9]

The town boom following the Civil War reached a peak during the late 1870s and early 1880s, especially on the Great Plains. Efforts by the railroads to change the image of the plains to attract settlers were greatly responsible for the boom, and in a few years hundreds of new towns with a variety of names appeared on maps of Kansas, Nebraska, and Dakota Territory. As Everett Dick pointed out in his 1937 classic, *Sod-House Frontier*, town names fell under several classifications. Some represented personal names of national heroes, particularly Presidents and Civil War generals. Others were surnames of early settlers, prominent local figures, and railroad men. Names of railroad men were given especially to towns on the plains planned by the lines. Still other town names were derived from local geog-

THE FIRST OFFICE FOR D. M. DUNN AND E. P. WORCESTER'S
Thomas County Cat in Colby, Kansas, in 1885. The newspaper failed in 1891.

THE "NEOSHO VALLEY REGISTER" AT BURLINGTON, KANSAS TERRITORY.
The upstairs provided quarters for the editor and his family. Extra rooms
probably were rented to boarders.

raphy or natural landmarks such as springs, canyons, rivers, and the like. Some were given names brought from the East or Europe by immigrants, and other names were derived from Indian words. And then there were those coined by the settlers, such as Sodtown in Adams County, Nebraska, and Kanorado, a town located just inside the western border of Kansas on the Colorado line. Still another group of towns were given names from the Bible, including Abilene, Kansas, and Bethany, Nebraska. The residents of one community, not yet named, had gathered to pray for rain. The minister, C. B. French, suggested that the town be called Rain. It was, but Rain, Nebraska, never grew to any size. The town, located in Hayes County, does not even appear on the official state map of Nebraska today.[10]

Between 1854 and 1857, many new towns in Nebraska and Kansas territories had the word "city" appended to their names to make them sound important. Other communities used the word before their town's name, but whether this really helped a town to grow and prosper is doubtful. It may have attracted people, but often when they saw it was not really a city but only a settlement of a few cabins or dugouts, they left. Many towns did survive and prosper without the word "city" attached to their names, and they did so by relying on a formula for success that included several ingredients. First and foremost, a town needed promotion, and to handle that task it had to have a newspaper with a civic-minded editor, one who usually dispensed with objectivity when writing about his town. If a neighboring newspaper tried to attract residents from another town, the editors would often battle each other with their pens. One newspaper, the *Thomas County Cat*, was established at Colby on the plains of northwestern Kansas in 1885 by D. M. Dunn and E. P. Worcester. Its first office was a dugout. As the weekly paper began to increase its circulation, the editor of the *Advisor*, another weekly paper across the county line in neighboring Voltaire, published the following item in the spring of 1886:

> The snooping propensities of the Colby Cat are fully equal to those of the old "yaller" variety, and like the "yaller" cat, is continually in trouble by reason of it. For the past winter the Colby feline has been too much engaged in Sheridan County to smell much in any other direction, but the vigorous kicking it has received from that quarter has driven it out and now the nose of the beast is in this county. We are loaded for bear and don't want to monkey with cats, but if some things continue, there will be an excellent opportunity for someone to start a manufactory of fiddle strings in Thomas County.[11]

It was not unusual for an editor to be given lots in a town if he would start a newspaper there. This motivated the editor to attract more settlers to increase the value of his property as well as the number of potential advertisers. In the meantime, he had to survive on what little advertising and subscriptions he could sell. When money was in short supply, many an editor noted in his columns that he would take corn, potatoes, flour, fruit, and any other foodstuffs produced by his readers in exchange for a year's subscription or for advertising in his paper. Some editors on the plains waited anxiously for homesteaders to prove up their claims, because federal law required each homesteader to run his final proof notice six times in the newspaper nearest to his land. The proof notice told readers to speak now or forever hold their peace regarding the homesteader's claim that he or she had faithfully lived up to the government rules. In some areas of the Great Plains during the boom of the 1880s, newspapers were started to capture the proof-notice business, for each homesteader paid the paper anywhere from five to ten dollars to print the notice six times. In Kansas, for example, the number of newspapers increased from 148 in 1874 to about 400 by 1886. Not all of them were begun to take advantage of the proof-notice business, but many were. Once most homesteaders in an area had proved up on their claims, an editor might discontinue his paper and move it west to another area where homesteaders were about to prove up. In the Dakotas, one editor established thirty printing presses in one region in pursuit of such business.

In addition to a newspaper, a successful town had to have a hotel, which not only provided a place to stay for newcomers and businessmen, especially land speculators, but suggested by its very existence that the community was up and coming. In promoting his town, a newspaper editor usually made frequent reference to the local hotel in his columns, as he did with the stores, the bank, the livery stable, and even the saloons. Some town companies built a hotel and then rented it to someone who agreed to run a respectable establishment. In a few instances, the town helped to raise money to build a hotel. Such was the case at Brownville, Nebraska, where citizens sold lottery tickets for five dollars apiece. First prize was a hundred and forty-seven acres of land adjoining the town, and second prize was eight hundred dollars in town lots. The town raised enough money in this manner to build a decent hotel.[12]

Certainly another element in any successful town was the post office. Whenever a town was started, someone usually asked the federal government to establish a post office. The someone was often a merchant who ran the general store, and if the request was granted, as it usually was, he was the man most likely to be appointed postmaster. It was usually a political appointment, and the merchant who could secure the post office for his store reaped the benefits. The government contract did not provide a large income in the smaller towns, but it did make the merchant's store the focal point of the community. On the plains it was not uncommon for the postmaster to raise the American flag on a high pole when the mail arrived. As people gathered, the mail might be poured out on a counter or placed in a large box and the postmaster would then pick up each piece of mail and read aloud to whom it was addressed. Mail not claimed was held for a reasonable period of time. As a town grew, the postmaster might construct makeshift pigeonholes out of empty crates, one hole for each family. In time regular mailboxes were installed by the government, some with locks for the more important men of the town, including the newspaper editor. A trip to the post office often meant the purchase of goods in the store where it was located. Having the town's post office in your store meant added sales.

During the early years saloons were another important element in the towns of Nebraska, Kansas, and Dakota Territory. Many of the early hotels had bars, and they were usually patronized by the more prominent business people. Some were handsomely furnished, especially in the towns along the Missouri River and perhaps fifty miles to the west. But most of the early saloons in the towns on the prairie and plains were nothing more than long, narrow rooms, dimly lit, with a small and not very fancy bar. There were a few tables and chairs. About the only shiny objects were cuspidors. Everything else was dirty and smelly. Such saloons were unforgettable for their blending odors of tobacco, liquor, straw, horses, kerosene, and the sometimes sizzling spit of tobacco juice on the hot stove during winter months. In the late 1860s whiskey was the principal drink served in most saloons. A few of the better-known "bitters"—the generic term for liquors—were Old Crow, Squirrel, and McBryan, a popular brand. Only saloons located on the Missouri River offered beer on a regular basis. It was shipped up the river by steamboat, but it was too expensive to be had elsewhere to the west because of its bulk and high transportation cost. This began to change when the railroads arrived; soon beer was as plentiful as whiskey in saloons on the prairie and plains.

From the middle 1850s until the early 1870s, most grocery and general merchandise stores also sold whiskey by the bottle. Few if any firms tried to hide the fact. It was not uncommon for such stores to advertise in the local newspaper that they sold whiskey, wines, boots, and stoves, in that order. But businesses other than saloons began to give up selling whiskey during the 1870s. It was then that housewives, not husbands, began to make regular household purchases in person. General merchandise stores and grocery houses found it good for business not to carry whiskey, since most women were opposed to drinking. In Kansas, where the open saloon was outlawed in 1881 by a constitutional amendment, saloons continued to operate in many towns. Some were called "lemonade parlors," and the proprietors paid a monthly fine to the city treasury instead of the tax which had been paid when open saloons were legal. When pressure mounted for the enforcement of the law in such communities, sometimes local druggists undertook the job of dispensing whiskey, in medicine bottles.

Carl Engel (my great-grandfather) may have done this for selected customers in his combination grocery store and drugstore in Manhattan, Kansas. Like so many merchants in the towns on the prairies and plains, Engel had not come West to be a merchant. He was a printer and newspaperman. Born in 1844 in Zorndorf, Neumarkt, Germany, Engel came to America with his parents at the age of ten, arriving in New Orleans in the fall of 1854. The family remained there for several months, but did not like the humid climate and hot summers. They moved to Watertown, Wisconsin, where the climate was more like that of their native Germany, and where many other German immigrants had settled. At the age of twelve, Carl Engel was apprenticed to Carl Schurz, editor and owner of the Watertown *Volkszeitung*, a German-language newspaper. This is the same Carl Schurz who became Secretary of the Interior in the Rutherford B. Hayes Administration. Engel spent at least five years learning the printing trade and then moved from one newspaper to another, seeing much of America in the process.

Late in 1864 Engel arrived in Leavenworth, Kansas, where he became foreman of the Leavenworth *Times* at a salary of thirty dollars a week. He began to save his money, but he soon tired of the printer's trade and looked around for a better opportunity. Early in 1866, he went into partnership with a man named Markwort, who was bookkeeper for the Leavenworth mercantile firm of Rahlfing and Company. Markwort agreed to set Engel up in business as a merchant and selected Manhattan, Kansas, ninety miles west of Leavenworth, as the most likely town for such an enterprise. The Union Pacific Railway Company, Eastern Division, had just reached the town of less than a thousand people, and the community looked promising. Engel went to Manhattan, bought a vacant lot on the town's dusty main street, had a two-story building constructed, stocked it with goods shipped by Markwort from Leavenworth, and opened a general grocery and provision store. During the first year the business grossed $33,000.

In 1867, Engel married Frederika Schaubel, whose father had come from Germany and served as an officer in the Union Army during the Civil War. Two years later, Engel's father-in-law purchased Markwort's interest in the company, but later sold it to Frank Hoyt, another Manhattan businessman. Hoyt remained Engel's working partner for about a year and then sold his interest in 1872 to Phillip Wiest, another German immigrant, who had considerable capital. Wiest gave the business the boost it needed financially, especially following the panic of 1873. But Engel was a patient and prudent man. He saved his money, and by the late 1880s he was able to buy Wiest's interest. Engel than studied to become a pharmacist. With the help of two of his sons—Engel and his wife had seven children—the business prospered as the Engel Mercantile and Drug Company. After Carl Engel died in 1908, one of his sons continued the business well into this century. [13]

During the late 1860s Carl Engel's major competitor in Manhattan was E. B. Purcell, who, unlike Engel, came from a long line of Pennsylvania merchants. Purcell learned the business in his father's store at Newton Hamilton, Pennsylvania, which he ran after his father's death. Like so many

LEFT: CARL ENGEL, A NATIVE OF GERMANY,
worked as a printer and newspaperman before entering the mercantile business
in Manhattan, Kansas, just after the Civil War. He died in 1908.
RIGHT: John O'Loughlin, a pioneer trader, freighter, merchant, rancher,
and banker in southwest Kansas.

A VIEW OF CARL ENGEL'S MERCANTILE AND DRUG COMPANY,
Manhattan, Kansas, in the late nineteenth century.

other people in the East following the Civil War, Purcell was attracted to the West. He went to Manhattan in 1866 and opened a grocery store. His E. B. Purcell Trading Company was located a block and a half west of Engel's store. By the 1870s, however, Purcell sold much more than groceries. He had expanded into five departments or, as he advertised, "five stores under one roof." E. B. Purcell's Trading Company referred to itself as "Dealers in Everything." His stock included:

Dry Goods and Notions, Rugs and Mattings.

Ladies' Ready-to-Wear Goods.

Shoes, Rubbers and Men's Furnishing Goods.

Staple and Fancy Groceries, Crockery, China and Glassware.

Butter, Eggs and Country Produce.

Hardware of all kinds, Ranges, Stoves, etc.

Paints, Oils, Window Glass, etc.

Agricultural Implements.

Ellwood Woven Wire, Barbed Wire.

Wagons, Carriages and Buggies.

Grain, Feed, Hay, etc.

By the 1880s Purcell had erected a stone warehouse, two stories high, behind his store to house implements and vehicles plus carloads of merchandise purchased in the East and shipped in by rail. Purcell had four sons, all of whom were involved in the company's operation at one time or another.[14]

Purcell and Engel were fortunate in that they operated businesses in a town served by a railroad. Merchandise could be delivered with ease and speed from wholesale houses in Kansas City, St. Louis, and points east. But this was not the case for merchants in communities not reached directly by railroads. Merchandise then had to be transported by wagon freighters overland from the nearest railroad station to their stores, and the cost of freighting added to the cost of the goods sold. A merchant in a town without a railroad had to plan carefully to ensure that he would have the items his customers wanted during the winter months. If he did not, he often paid dearly to have goods freighted to his store during cold and often snowy weather. The wise merchant usually had his winter stock on hand by late fall, especially in northern Kansas, Nebraska, and Dakota Territory. In southern Kansas, freighting during the winter months was not as great a problem because the weather was milder.

John O'Loughlin, one of the earliest merchants in southwestern Kansas, came West following the Civil War and hauled freight year-round from Fort Hays southwest to Dodge City over a military trail established in 1867. There the terrain was often more of a problem than the weather. Time and again O'Loughlin found it difficult to get his wagons across Pawnee Creek because of steep banks. In 1868, he quit freighting and settled on Pawnee Creek, about twenty-five miles west of present-day Larned, Kansas, on the military trail. He constructed a bridge of logs cut from trees growing along the stream and charged a dollar for each government team and fifty cents for all others to cross his bridge. Nearby he built a log cabin and enclosed it with a log stockade by setting poles in the ground on end. He also dug a well inside his stockade so that he would not be without water during Indian attacks.

O'Loughlin's trading post, as it was called, did a thriving business with government freighters, soldiers, buffalo hunters, and even Indians. He sold or traded staple groceries and dry goods, feed, rifles, ammunition, saddles, spurs, boots, and other things needed on the frontier. But his business began to fall off when the Atchison, Topeka and Santa Fe Railroad was built into Dodge City in 1872. No longer did the government freight supplies from Fort Hays to Fort Dodge near Dodge City. They were carried instead by the railroad. The arrival of the railroad in southwestern Kansas also reduced the number of travlers by way of O'Loughlin's store. Early in the spring of 1873, O'Loughlin deserted his bridge and store, loaded his merchandise and belongings in some wagons, and started southwest looking for a new opportunity. He found it about sixty-five miles west of Dodge City at a stop on the newly built Santa Fe line around forty miles east of the Colorado border. The country was not yet settled by farmers. The only building at the railroad stop was a small frame structure housing a telegraph office. Nearby O'Loughlin constructed a dugout and a corral and placed his merchandise and belongings inside.

Since the railroad had not yet reached Santa Fe, wagon freighters were still hauling freight between the end of the line and Santa Fe. Freighters, buffalo hunters, and cowboys were his only customers. Because there was little money in the area, O'Loughlin traded provisions in his store for buffalo meat, and later buffalo bones. These he shipped east to wholesalers, who accepted them in trade for provisions, clothing, and ammunition that were then shipped west on the railroad to O'Loughlin. In this manner he built an inventory that included ox shoes. Freighters would trade their worn-out oxen and horses to O'Loughlin for fresh animals. He would then reshoe the oxen, keep and feed them until they were in condition to travel again, and trade them back to freighters for a profit.

By early 1874 O'Loughlin had secured a post office for the train stop. The post office was named Lakin in honor of a director of the Santa Fe line. O'Loughlin was appointed postmaster, and the post office was set up in his dugout store. When the Santa Fe platted the townsite in 1882, the post office's name of Lakin was given to the town. Soon a hotel, a restaurant, and other businesses were established. O'Loughlin prospered, and in 1882 he and I. R. Holmes formed a bank. O'Loughlin was vice-president, Holmes was president. In fifteen years O'Loughlin had moved from wagon freighting to storekeeping to postmaster to banker. He had taken advantage of the opportunities he found.[15] Such was not untypical for other men who found profit and success on the Great Plains as civilization arrived. But life was hard, especially for the women.

When Mrs. B. L. Stotts arrived to live in the newly founded town of Garden City, Kansas, in 1881, life was very difficult. She learned the hard way to love the open country. Late in her life she recalled her days in the new town on the Great Plains:

I never took any credit to myself for being a pioneer, having gone to Colorado in 1870, when the Indians were still making periodical raids on the settlers. There was some spice in that life, but being a pioneer in Western Kansas was different. The spring and summer we came here, 1881, was very dry. For nine consecutive months there was not a single drop of rain. There were no trees. Some cottonwood cuttings had been set out along the streets of Garden City, but as yet furnished no shade, and the soap weeds, the largest thing here, furnished very little.

Each day the sun arose in a blaze of glory, each succeeding day more dazzling than the one before. We kept our eyes turned heavenward looking for clouds, not being so presumptious as to expect rain, but merely seeking a dimmer for the intense sunlight. We saw in the mirage limpid lakes of sparkling water, buildings which might have been churches and theaters, and beautiful groves of stately trees, but it all kept just out of reach and the blazing sun shone on. The certainty that it would be on the job again in the morning took away the pleasure of its setting.

We drank water from driven wells not more than eight or ten feet deep, and rank with alkali. We suffered for ice, though in case of sickness we were sometimes able to get it from the passenger trains.

The awful monotony was killing. There was nothing to do, nothing to see and no where to go, and should we have attempted to go anywhere we would only have become lost, for there were only a few dim trails leading to the claims of a few settlers, so we women crept about from house to house. There was no use to hurry; we had all the time there was. Our conversation each day was a repetition of that of the day before and always concerned the awfulness of living in such a desert, where the wind and the sun had full sweep.

Frequently on wash day, a line of clothes would be seen sailing through the air. On one of those occasions after a woman had rescued and washed her clothes for the second time, she was heard to repeat language similar no doubt to some she had heard her husband use. It was a time to try women's souls. I never heard the men complain, and as a sect, I was sure they did not require much to satisfy them. I am sure the children were sensible of their hardships. One day my little son came into the house, threw himself on the floor in the abandonment of grief, and howled out, "Mamma, will we always have to live here?" and when in my desperation I told him that I thought we would, he, with a more desperate howl, cried out, "And will we have to die here, too?"

We old-timers smile now when we meet, and it's a knowing smile the newer population does not understand, for we are rich in experience.[16]

Two years after she arrived in Garden City, the town's population had grown to four hundred people. The businesses included two hotels, two grocery stores, a general store, a lumber dealer, and a meat market. The town claimed two carpenters, two physicians, and three attorneys, and that year, 1883, a U.S. Land Office was established there. By then many other towns were springing up on the open plains, and in at least one, life was not as difficult as in Garden City.

Perhaps the most unusual town on the Great Plains during the late 1880s and early 1890s was started by an Irishman named Francis J. S. "Ned" Turnly, who came from Drumnasole, County Antrim, Ireland. In late 1885 or early 1886, Turnly arrived in America and came West. He purchased seventeen hundred acres of land at $1.50 an acre a few miles northeast of present-day Harper in south-central Kansas. Much of the land was located in the valley of the Chicaskia River, and he named his combination farm-

and-horse-ranch Chicaskia. Turnly began advertising in English newspapers that he was lord of a western paradise, where golden birds sang in the trees and silver rivers ran tinkling to the sea. For five hundred dollars, Turnly agreed to teach the sons of wealthy English gentlemen "the mysteries of successful farming and stock raising, provide for their physical needs and administer such educational tonics as would enable them to hold the winning hand wherever they might be."[17]

Turnly, in the meantime, laid out a town less than a mile from his ranch house. The town was called Runnymede, the name of the local post office. The name undoubtedly honored the historic spot so dear to Englishmen where the stout barons wrested the charter of British freedom from a reluctant king and the Magna Carta was signed in 1215. Turnly's promotional efforts attracted not only the sons of many Englishmen but several wealthy English-men themselves. Perhaps a hundred Englishmen, a few with their wives, arrived at Runnymede during the months that followed. Many of them stayed at Turnly's ranch until houses were constructed in Runnymede, where Turnly operated the combination general store and post office. The town soon had a meat market, blacksmith shop, restaurant, hardware store, livery stable, and feed store plus a few other businesses. Many of them were established and operated by Englishmen. Trees were planted on the nearly treeless townsite and three large houses were built, along with many small ones. And then came the Runnymede Arms, a large three-story frame hotel that opened in December 1889. It was run by an English couple who brought with them an English cook. Nearby an Episcopal church that could seat a hundred people was constructed.

One of the Englishmen who came to Runnymede was Charles Seton. Many years later he recalled:

> Kansas was known as a prohibition state, and one guileless father thought that Runnymede would be the salvation of his son, who had acquired a big thirst for liquor. The lad kept the trail hot between Runnymede and Harper, and maintained an irrigation plant that would have overwhelmed the children of Israel. He always had some kind of a jag. Kansas prohibition was a failure in Runnymede. The good livers brought whole cargoes of the very best whiskey from Chicago. One youth fell heir to $15,000 a year, and the thermometer in Runnymede went up several degrees. What a time he had!
>
> The men imagined they were in the very heart of the West, where the blood ran wildest and reddest. They wore cowboy outfits, and an

arsenal of guns and knives rattled on them as they walked. They would not go outside the house unless armed to the teeth. They were fond of posing for their portraits in photograph galleries at Harper and Wichita, and I tremble even now at the terrible desperadoes that gaze at me from the faded pictures.[18]

Most of the Englishmen enjoyed life as much as they could. The residents of nearby Harper considered the "Runnymede boys" frivolous and irresponsible since they frequently visited Harper and other nearby towns at night to live it up. This was usually after they had tired of their own activities at Runnymede, which included horse-racing, steeplechasing on their own course, playing polo on their own field, and disporting themselves with a billiard parlor, a bowling alley, and several tennis courts. They hunted coyotes and rabbits in the fox-hunting style of Europe, and on one occasion they invited the boxer Paddy Shea, heavyweight champion of Kansas, to visit. A bout between Shea and one of the Englishmen was arranged, and the Englishman, no match for Shea, was knocked out in less than five minutes. The loser, however, was a good sport. After he had been revived and washed up, he gave Shea his personal pocket watch and the purse, congratulating the champion with the words "You're a bloomin' good lad, don't you know."[19]

Turnly prospered from his English town on the plains, as did a few of the businessmen. A semimonthly newspaper called the Runnymede *Wind Mill* was published for a while, but when Turnly failed to promote a railroad through the town in 1892, the end appeared near. Turnly packed up his belongings and returned to England with his profits. The residents of Runnymede then began to scatter, some returning to England, others settling elsewhere in Kansas and in California. Even the town buildings began to disappear. Some were moved to nearby farms, and much of the hotel was later moved to Alva, Oklahoma, following the opening of the Cherokee Strip in 1893.[20]

XIII

INTO THE SOUTHWEST

*Of the great stretches of rich plains subject to cultivation, no region
was more inviting than that known as the Southwest, embracing the
vast hills and plains of the Indian Territory, Texas, and New Mexico.*

—CARL COKE RISTER[1]

STRETCHING more than four hundred miles from north-central Oklahoma south to central Texas is a belt of woodlands called the Cross
Timbers. This comparatively narrow strip of timber, once five to thirty miles
in width, was broken only by rivers and a few smaller streams. The blackjack,
hickory, and post oak were laced together in many areas with tightly woven
and tangled undergrowth that was, and still is in some areas, difficult to
penetrate. The Cross Timbers served as something of a natural barrier for
early travelers and as a landmark. It marked the division between the prairies
to the east and the plains to the west. Indians used the wooded belt to mark
the dividing line between their hunting grounds. In Texas, where the woodlands run south from the Red River near present-day Denton to the Brazos
River near modern Waco, it served as the western boundary of settlement
in the early 1870s. To the west ranged the warlike Comanche and Pawnee
Indians.

North of the Red River was also Indian Territory, land set aside by the
federal government early in the nineteenth century for the five civilized
tribes—the Cherokee, Choctaw, Creek, Chickasaw, and Seminole—removed
from their lands in the East. These five Indian nations organized their own
governments, farmed, and raised livestock, and their children went to mission
schools established by white church groups from the East. There were a few
government forts in Indian Territory, ostensibly to keep white settlers out
and to protect the Indians. When the Civil War began, most though not all
of the Indians sided with the Confederacy. Many Indians on both sides were
killed in the fighting, and all Indians suffered as their governments were

torn by dissension, their livestock stolen, and their homes burned by troops or Indians supporting the opposite side. Many died of starvation. When the Civil War ended, the federal government imposed harsh punishment on the Indians regardless of whether they fought against the Union or not, and made them sign new treaties. They were pressured to cede land in present-day western Oklahoma to the government for reservations for tribes being removed from other sections of the Great Plains. By the end of the war railroads, banks, and large businesses saw potential profit for themselves if they could somehow open Indian Territory to white settlement. A few bills were introduced in Congress to do just that, but each failed, and the businessmen began to seek other ways to open up the Territory. The railroads led the way by seeking routes through it.

The Indians, trying to recover from the effects of the Civil War and Reconstruction, knew what would happen if the white man's railroad entered Indian Territory. The trains would bring more whites and the evils of the white man's world. They had already suffered from those evils. They fought as best they could to keep the railroads out, but under pressure from the federal government they reluctantly agreed to grant railroads planning to build across Indian Territory a right-of-way only two hundred feet wide. The railroads, of course, wanted large land grants but did not receive them when Congress, in July 1866, passed legislation authorizing three lines to extend their tracks in Kansas to the northern border of Indian Territory. The first line to reach the border would have the privilege of extending its line south through Indian Territory to Preston, Texas, just across the Red River from Indian Territory. Three railroads—the Leavenworth, Lawrence and Fort Gibson; the Neosho Valley; and the Union Pacific Railway Company, Southern Branch, reorganized as the Missouri, Kansas and Texas Railroad in 1870—raced to lay their tracks to the southern border of Kansas. The Missouri, Kansas and Texas Railroad won. By late June 1870 it had laid track into Indian Territory, and by February 1871 its trains were running south from Kansas to Muskogee in Indian Territory.[2]

To the north and east, meantime, the Atlantic and Pacific Railroad Company (later known as the "Frisco" line) built from St. Louis across Missouri to the state's southwestern border. The line entered Indian Territory in May 1871 and by the end of the year had reached the Missouri, Kansas and Texas Railroad. The point where the Atlantic and Pacific hoped to link up with the M.K.&T. was on Cherokee land. The Cherokee council had passed an act reserving for their people an area of one square mile around each railroad station. The law provided that each of these reserves was to

RAILROAD OFFICIALS INSPECT ROCK CUT
on the Missouri, Kansas and Texas Railroad line in 1872
near present-day McAlister, Oklahoma.

A MISSOURI, KANSAS AND TEXAS TRAIN PAUSES ON THE BRIDGE
crossing the North Boggy in present-day southern Oklahoma in 1872.
The train may have stopped on the bridge to accommodate the photographer.

be surveyed and the town lots sold only to Cherokee citizens. But before the official Cherokee survey of the land around the junction could be made, Elias C. Boudinot, a prominent Cherokee of mixed blood and an attorney, made his own survey, opened city lots for sale, and named the proposed town Vinita for his friend Vinnie Ream, a noted sculptress. Cherokee officials refused to recognize Boudinot's action and called the town Dowingville. Boudinot, however, eventually succeeded in having the town's name changed back to Vinita, as it is known today. Meantime, as the Atlantic and Pacific Railroad's track laying approached present-day Vinita, it apparently built on land claimed by the Missouri, Kansas and Texas Railroad. M.K.&T. crews tore up the Atlantic and Pacific's track in what has been described as the "Battle of Vinita." It was a bloody fight, with men on both sides using ax handles as weapons. The Atlantic and Pacific lost the battle.[3]

The Missouri, Kansas and Texas Railroad continued to lay tracks south toward Texas. As stations were established along the line, the railroad began to ship Texas cattle north from their railheads. Texans drove their cattle north into Indian Territory until they reached the railroad. There cattle buyers purchased the animals and either shipped them north through Kansas to eastern markets or transferred the cattle to the Atlantic and Pacific line at Vinita and transported them northeast to Missouri and points east. The presence of the railroad shortened the time it took for Texas cattle to reach the marketplace, and the cattle were generally in better condition, since they had not been driven overland all the way to Kansas or Missouri.

After the M.K.&T. crossed the Red River and entered Texas, the line's southern terminal of Denison became a major shipping point. The town was laid out in early September 1872 five miles south of the Red River and near the early settlement of Preston. It was named for George Denison, vice-president of the Missouri, Kansas and Texas Railroad. The first through train from Kansas arrived in Denison on Christmas night in 1872, and passengers on that train, including cattle buyers and speculators, found a new town that was a strange blend of the North and the South. The town was laid out like most northern towns without a square or plaza. Unlike most southern towns, its streets were broad, but the houses reflected southern architecture, as did many of the business buildings. Razorback hogs and scrawny cattle were seen wallowing in mudholes. And the fare offered in cafés was more southern than northern. All of the town's streets were laid out north and south, except for a wide main street running east and west. The Denison Town Company wanted their town to appear respectable, so all saloons, pool halls, dance halls, and houses of prostitution had to be

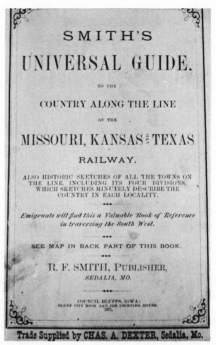

LEFT: THIS 1875 POSTER WAS USED BY THE MISSOURI, KANSAS AND TEXAS
Railroad to sell land along its route. RIGHT: The front cover of an 1871
pamphlet, printed by the Missouri, Kansas and Texas a year before it reached
Denison, Texas, to encourage travel along the line.

built on a side street to the south. To visitors walking the town's main street
Denison appeared to be a clean and upright community, but south of the
main street it was one of the toughest towns along the border with Indian
Territory.

The arrival of the railroad and the establishment of Denison gave business in northern Texas new life. Until then, Houston, Galveston, Austin,
and San Antonio had been the cultural, social, political, and economic
centers of Texas where money could be borrowed, raw materials traded and
purchased, and manufactured goods bought. These cities had grown in part
because of their closeness to the Gulf of Mexico. Between 1836 and the end
of the Civil War, most goods produced outside of Texas had been transported
by ship to Houston and Galveston and then freighted inland, but the coming
of the railroad from the north brought sudden change.

Denison grew rapidly. Many Texans arrived seeking opportunities for

profit, and some of the men associated with the railroad's construction—
most of them Northerners—also took advantage of the circumstances and
settled in Denison. For instance, the commissary firm of Hanna and Owens,
which had carried groceries by wagon to railroad workers ahead of where
track was being laid as the line crossed Indian Territory, established its
headquarters in Denison. The firm then used its wagons to haul freight to
points throughout northern Texas after it arrived in Denison by rail. In time
the firm became the leading grocery house in the region. Other men who
had helped to construct the railroad invested heavily in real estate and made
money selling property to the people arriving daily from the north by rail.
Denison became the northern gateway to Texas.

One young man who settled in Texas was W. S. Adair, a nineteen-
year-old farm boy from Missouri. He had gone to Kansas in the fall of 1872
but found little opportunity to make money. At Fort Scott, he jumped a
Missouri, Kansas and Texas freight train and rode south to Denison, arriving
only a few days after the first through train. Adair's description of Denison
in its early days is one of the best, because it not only captures the color
and flavor of the new town but also pictures the profit seekers at work. Adair
wrote:

Denison was the trade center of an immense region and was on a wild
boom. To all appearances there were plenty of easy ways of making
money, but they were not open to farmer boys unhackneyed in the ways
of the world. I got a job carrying a hod. Horsemen, stages and freight
wagons came from and went in every direction. Big wagons, sometimes
lashed two or three together and carrying several tons, were in some
instances pulled by as many as twenty-four mules. Some of these outfits
came from as far as Brown County [in central Texas].

The cotton produced within a radius of 100 miles of the freak town
was wagoned in and sold for 17¢ a pound in gold, gold being worth
10¢ more on the dollar than greenbacks. Practically all of the prairie
lands of Texas were open range.

Up to that time the only way of getting Texas cattle to market had
been to drive them to Kansas. The Katy [Missouri, Kansas and Texas
Railroad] offered railroad transportation direct to the packing houses.
So many cattle were offered for shipment that the railroad was obliged
to build stock pens covering more than 100 acres, and still it was unable
to handle the cattle promptly. . . .

I have never seen elsewhere any such an aggregation of saloons and dance and gambling halls. Nor was the supply a whit in advance of the demand. Fighting and killings occurred almost nightly. It was there I viewed for the first time the body of a man who had died with his boots on. He had been killed the night before in a dance hall. The testimony at the Coroner's inquest developed the fact that when the shooting began the lights went out, and for that reason no one could say with any certainty who fired the fatal shot. . . .

Indians, drifting in from the Territory, got drunk and now and then figured in the fighting and killing. The gamblers made it a business to rob farmers of the proceeds of their cotton and grain, and when the fleeced farmer made complaint, the court usually clapped a fine to him for gambling and to that added the cost of the trial.

Texas was all out-of-doors in those days. The population was sparse and the towns few and small. It was not supposed that the land could be depended upon to produce anything but grass and cotton. Land was no object.[4]

When Adair visited Denison late in 1872, the town was near the western edge of settlement in northern Texas. About twenty miles to the west was the Cross Timbers, and beyond it were hostile Indians. The region beyond the Cross Timbers was not deemed safe for settlement, but some people had moved into the region from the south. West into New Mexico Territory and from the panhandle of Texas south to the Pecos River, the land offered good grazing for cattle. It was part of the Great Plains. Many Texans called a large portion of the region by its Spanish name, Llano Estacado, meaning Staked Plain. Early travelers, according to tradition, gave the region the name because there were no trees and they had to stake their horses to the ground. The Staked Plain is a high plateau with little surface water, extending from the central western part of Texas northward over most of the panhandle. The region had been shunned both by buffalo and by Indians because of the lack of water, but as settlers began to move north from the Pecos River, the buffalo and Indians moved onto the Staked Plain. Most of the Indians became hostile.

To protect the settlers from the Indians, the federal government established a line of military posts stretching from El Paso to the northeastern border of Texas. Near the center of this line was Camp Hatch, established in 1867, soon renamed Camp Kelly and then Fort Concho in 1868. It was located near present-day San Angelo. About one hundred thirty miles to the northeast of Fort Concho was another post, Fort Griffin, also established in

1867. From these and other posts in the chain, troops escorted the government mail, surveying parties, and cattlemen driving herds of longhorn cattle overland.

As elsewhere in the West, the military posts offered security and naturally attracted settlers, who built their homes and ranches nearby. When the Republic of Texas became a state, it retained its public lands, and by the late 1860s land was cheap. Settlement was encouraged. The forts became social and trading centers where the new settlers could sell milk, butter, eggs, and fresh beef and buy needed supplies, including canned tomatoes, oysters, fruits, sperm candles, and Borden's Eagle Brand canned milk from the post sutlers. At Fort Concho, there were five trading houses in the nearby village of St. Angela (later San Angelo) by 1869. They provided supplies to soldiers and settlers alike.[5]

The soldiers from the forts also tracked down marauding Indians. The federal government and the Comanche Indians had signed a treaty in 1867 at Medicine Lodge, Kansas, in which the Comanches ceded away all of their territory except for about five thousand acres in southwestern Oklahoma. But many of the Indians did not stay on their land and continued to roam much of the region west of the Cross Timbers in Texas and in the Texas and Oklahoma panhandles in search of buffalo. After a general uprising in 1874 in which Comanches, Cheyennes, and Kiowas attacked whites, the military began a campaign to rid Texas of the marauding Indians. By the fall of 1875 the Indians were gone from Texas, and the region west of the Cross Timbers was safe for white settlement. To encourage settlement, the Texas legislature set the price of land in the region ridiculously low and in some instances even gave it away. Settlers came, but the rush was not of the magnitude then underway in Kansas and Nebraska. The railroad had not yet arrived in that portion of Texas; in 1876 the closest line was the Texas and Pacific Railroad, which ran from Marshall in the eastern part of the state to Fort Worth. West of Fort Worth were a few small towns and military posts. The region could be reached only by overland travel. Wagon freighters kept the small-town merchants and forts supplied, but the merchants first had to order their goods. By the 1870s traveling salesmen, or drummers, as they were called, were becoming commonplace in the West.

Little has been written about the drummer, a vocation that can be traced to England nearly four centuries ago. The first traveling salesman was called a rider or bagman, and he carried only samples of his stock. During the colonial period in America, riders were commonplace, taking orders for firms in London, Manchester, and Liverpool. After the American Revolution, a averaged about thirty-five miles apart. On this occasion I was riding horse-back alone from Coleman to Eastland, when I discovered after going thirty miles that I was lost completely. Presently a blue norther made its appearance on the distant horizon and with it a misty rain and darkness. I was tired and revenously [sic] hungry. Plodding along I discerned in the distance a light, a hopeful beacon that shone from the window of a lonely ranch house on that November night! I spurred up my jaded steed and soon arrived at the front door. With the accustomed "Hello," the head of the house came out and bade me get down and come in. Seeing that my horse was properly cared for, I returned to the house, and after performing my ablutions was invited in to supper.

And, O boy! what a feast! A goat had been killed that day and the housewife had broiled it over mesquite coals to the queen's taste. Fresh buttermilk and hot biscuits in abundance, with bee-made honey, completed the menu. No banquet that I ever attended since could hold a candle to that simple but abundant feast of goat meat, at that ranch in West Texas. That night, ensconced in the billows of an old-time feather bed, I dreamed of goats galore.[6]

Peak recalled that early settlers in Texas regarded their spoken word scrupulously. "Their ways were rough, due to their environment, but they were free from duplicity. In all their dealings, they were open and above board. Their word could always be taken literally for their bond," he wrote. Peak noted that the business foundation of a country merchant depended upon the confidence he had in his wholesale house and the drummer from whom he purchased supplies. "It seemed to be not so much a matter of a 'little better price' offered by another salesman, as faith in the one with which relationships had been already established. The drummer, therefore, knew that once an order had been given there would be no countermanding. . . No brother traveler following in his footsteps would dream of working to have that order cancelled. The very suggestion of such a thing branded the interfering drummer as a sneaking and contemptible highwayman. It marked his merchant conspirator, too, for boycott by the traveling fraternity," wrote Peak.

Howard Peak described the approach used by drummers as "straightforward." Everything was on a plain and unpretentious basis. "If the salesman approached his prospect in a dignified manner, he was given a hearing. But

firm in Philadelphia sent out men on horseback to drum up
label "drummer" was born. One of the few recollections of
the American West was left by Howard W. Peak, the son of a
who was born in Fort Worth, Texas. After his schooling, Pe.
Fort Worth store, and in 1876 became a drummer representin
hardware firm of J. N. Manuel and Company of Fort Worth. Pe
with four other traveling salesmen representing other Fort Wor
obtained two two-horse Concord buggies, and set out on a
trip to sell goods to merchants in perhaps a dozen towns west
of Fort Worth. They tried to visit a town a day. Peak recalle

We were always welcome at the towns visited and, alon;
sized orders, we were almost always complimented with ar
dance. City chaps were few and far between, and a new ci
add to the repertoire of the interior's program was always
appreciation.

The most unpleasant part of traveling those days was the e
of bothersome pests that infested some of the hotel beds. At
invaders would become so annoying that we would have to
and go out of doors and spread it on the grass in order to s

The most miserable night I ever spent on the road was at
[about fifty-five miles west of Fort Worth], soon after I begai
I arrived at the little mountain village one evening during d
and had to hustle around for lodging. My customer, who was
invited me to share his bed which was located in the store.
the invitation. When we turned in, I drew the "fur" side, ad
green groceries department, and soon discerned a hideous
anating I thought from that part of the store nearest where
but delicacy forbade my mentioning it. But after an hour o
the room got warmed up, the stench became so foul that I t
in bed which placed my face in close proximity to my host's
hair was greased with rancid bear's oil! So there I was, be
smells, both terrible. When I could not bear the scent from
oil longer, I'd turn over and the odor from whatever it was or
side would knock me out. Surviving that sleepless night, I
the grocery odor came from a hunk of Limburger cheese!

The most enjoyable meal that I ever partook of in my fifty
on the road was one eaten soon after I began traveling. W
was yet a wilderness. Towns I made were mostly county sea

let him display unusual airs, or bemean his surroundings, criticizing people and customs of the frontier, and he might as well pack his grips and leave town. In fact, a committee might escort him out," observed Peak, who recalled the day when a drummer for Sanger Brothers of Dallas arrived in Graham, Texas, about eighty miles west of Fort Worth, in a wagon drawn by two mules and driven by a black man.

The drummer was dressed in a fashionable suit, shining derby and sharply pointed shoes. Soon after he stepped down from the wagon he began to criticize the Graham hotel. Other things failed to suit his fancy. News of his actions spread quickly through the small town. When he visited the local saloon after supper, he found most of the men in town waiting. He was invited to drink but declined. That did not help matters. Without a word, a tall, lanky cowboy stepped up, jerked the derby from the drummer's head, threw it up into the air and before it fell to the floor, shot two holes through it with his six-gun. The drummer quickly changed his attitude, and before leaving the saloon he had finished several drinks and accepted a new Stetson hat.[7]

The country merchant of the late nineteenth century did not conduct business with a great deal of alertness to customer interest. He was more relaxed, and his duty as a merchant seems to be reflected in his daily routine. He would usually open his store early, put out his samples, and then sit down and wait for his customers. During hot summer days it was not unusual for a merchant to move a chair out in front of his store under an overhang to catch the breeze and to play checkers with someone. In the winter he could usually be found near a wood stove in the center of the store, also playing checkers. When a customer arrived, the merchant would slide from his seat, asking his checkers partner to wait a moment, and after serving the customer return to the game. The country merchant did little advertising. Even his newspaper advertising during the 1870s and 1880s usually contained only his firm's name and perhaps a list of supplies offered for sale. The same was true in many larger towns. Such advertising was not meant to be appealing, and there was nothing in the ads to arouse the imagination of the buyer. One Texas firm, Sanger Brothers, was the exception. It sought to attract buyers with its newspaper ads and handbills.

One Sanger Brothers handbill, printed on sheets of paper eleven by seventeen inches in 1873, reads:

A WOMAN'S DREAM

SHE SAT ALONE

In the moonlight, her beautiful cheek resting upon her hand, so soft and white and dimpled. You could tell as you looked at her that her thoughts were far away and that she was thinking of something beautiful. Her eyes were wistful, the dimples in her cheeks had died out, and only the dimple in her chin remained, that little rosy cleft, the impress of Love's finger. She was less glowing at times, but nonetheless lovely. I thought to myself as I looked at her that she was nearer heaven than we coarser mortals, and I longed to know whither her pure heart turned itself. I approached her; she did not see me. I spoke; she did not answer. I touched her softly on the arm; she looked up and smiled, a far-away smile, such as an angel might have given. "You are thinking very intently," I said. She answered, "Yes, I am thinking of SANGER BROS. who, owing to the Removal of their Stock and the LACK OF ROOM to exhibit their great quantity of Goods, are determined to reduce their stock at great sacrifice."

All goods reduced from former prices, Special bargains in Dress Goods and Silks. WHITE GOODS at greatly reduced figures. Notions, Ribbons, Embroideries, Corsets, Laces, Hosiery for less than can be had elsewhere.

CLOTHING, GENTS FURNISHING [sic] GOODS
From 10 to 25 per cent less than ever

GREAT BARGAINS IN HATS

GREAT INDUCEMENTS
to wholesale trade

We are determined to sell goods at astonishing low rates. Call and examine our stock and prices, with the assurance that it will be to your advantage in making your purchases at the store of

SANGER BROS.'

DALLAS, TEXAS[8]

Sanger Brothers was not your typical western business even in Texas. It was run by five immigrant brothers who came to America from Germany with the determination to succeed. Isaac Sanger arrived in Texas from New York City in 1858. He and a man named Baum opened a store at McKinney, north of what was then the tiny village of Dallas. Soon Lehman Sanger, a brother, arrived and went to work in the store. The Sangers and Baum operated the McKinney store for about two years and then moved it to Weatherford, about twelve miles west of present-day Fort Worth, near the line of western settlement in Texas. Fort Worth, like Dallas, was then only a village serving as a supply point for cattlemen.

Sanger and Baum bought a lot on the town square in Weatherford for fifty-five dollars, constructed a stone building, and opened their store. They purchased goods in the East that were shipped to the Texas Gulf Coast and then transported by freight wagons to Weatherford, a trip of a few weeks. Soon after establishing their store in Weatherford, the Sangers and Baum started another one at Decatur, Texas, about forty-five miles northwest of Fort Worth. Lehman Sanger was sent to run the Decatur store. There was little paper money then in circulation in Texas. The state constitution prohibited banks from issuing their own paper money, so what little actual money there was in circulation was gold and silver. Merchants, including the Sangers and Baum, conducted much of their business on the basis of barter. According to one source: "The ladies brought in jeans, socks, eggs, butter, or whatever else they had to offer for trade, and exchanged those articles for such merchandise as they desired to purchase. In payment of purchases of goods, the men would tender hides, wool, or the products of their farms."[9]

The firm of Sanger and Baum made money even under the barter system, but soon after the Civil War began the two Sanger brothers and Baum closed down their business and fought for the Confederacy. The partnership of Sanger and Baum was dissolved. When the war ended, Isaac and Lehman Sanger were joined by another brother, Philip, and together they formed the firm of Sanger Brothers. At the time, the Houston and Texas Central Railroad was building north across Texas from the Gulf, and the Sangers began to establish stores along the railroad's route, beginning at Millican, eighty-five miles northwest of Houston. As the railroad slowly built northward, the Sangers followed, starting stores in Bryan, Hearne, Calvert, Bremond, Kosse, Groesbeck, Corsicana, and Dallas, where Alexander Sanger, the fourth brother to join the firm, opened and ran a store. Dallas was a town of fewer than three thousand people in 1872. The following year Sanger Brothers opened stores in Sherman and Waco. Samuel Sanger, the fifth brother, ran the Waco store.

As Texas grew, so did the empire of the Sangers, who encouraged competition, knowing well that they could effectively compete. Isaac Sanger, however, left Texas in 1868 and moved to New York, where he purchased merchandise for the Texas stores until his death in 1918. Lehman Sanger retired because of poor health in 1882, though he lived on until 1912. The firm survived periods of economic difficulties, adjusted to population shifts, and by early in this century placed a great deal of emphasis on its operations in Dallas. But gradually the Sanger brothers died—Philip on a trip to California in 1902 at the age of sixty-one; Isaac in 1918, at eighty-one, in New York City; Samuel, also in 1918, at seventy-five, in Texas; and Alexander in 1925, at seventy-eight, in Dallas. In 1926, Sanger Brothers mercantile was sold for several million dollars to Stifel, Nicholaus and Company, who operated the firm as Sanger Brothers, Inc. In 1951, it changed hands again. Federated Department Stores purchased Sanger Brothers, Inc., and Sangers' longtime competitor, A. Harris and Company. Today there are about a dozen Sanger-Harris stores in the Dallas–Fort Worth area, continuing the traditions established by the five brothers, traditions that today reflect the fashionable and prestigious merchandise that became the mark of Sanger Brothers.[10]

Another early Texas firm still very much in existence was established at Kerrville on the upper Guadalupe River northwest of present-day San Antonio. It was started by Charles Schreiner, who was born in France in 1838, the fourth of five children. In 1852, at the age of fourteen, Charles Schreiner came to America with his parents and settled in San Antonio, but his father died soon after the family arrived. At the age of sixteen Schreiner joined the Texas Rangers and served with them until 1857, when at the age of nineteen he entered the cattle business along Turtle Creek near Kerrville. When the Civil War began, Schreiner, like many other Texans, left his herd to fight for the Confederacy, and when the war ended he returned to his ranch near Kerrville and struggled to scrape together a living during the Reconstruction period. Deciding that the small settlement of Kerrville needed a general store, he traveled seventeen miles southeast of Kerrville to the town of Comfort to consult its leading merchant, August Faltin. Schreiner told him of his desire to start a store at Kerrville, and Faltin backed him, promising to teach him merchandising. On Christmas Eve 1869, Charles Schreiner opened his general store in Kerrville.

By modern standards the store was small. Constructed of cypress slabs with three-inch battens covering the seams, the thirty-by-sixty-foot building looked more like a ranch house, especially with the picket fence surrounding the building to keep stray stock and even the customers' teams and mounts at a safe distance. But inside it was a country store. Along the back wall was a stock of groceries. To the right of the double front doors was a rough board counter in the shape of an L. Toward the back it created a small office area. Nearby were barrels of lard, rice, coffee, sugar, and dried fruit. To the left of the front doors was another counter in front of bolts of cloth, including calico, which hung from the wall. On the opposite wall were saddles and harness, and wooden ware, including kegs, buckets, and tubs, hung nearby. There was an assortment of patent medicines, tobacco, snuff, rock candy, and the typical fare one would find in a western general store of the period. On the back side of the building was a lean-to shed used as a storehouse, and toward the back of the shed was a cellar that held barrels of coal oil, whiskey, beer, and molasses. For the people living in the vicinity, Charlie Schreiner's store meant they were one step closer to civilization.

From what is known, August Faltin provided Schreiner with ten thousand dollars to start the store. Their partnership was to run for ten years, during which time Schreiner was to draw his living expenses from the venture and Faltin an equal amount of cash. But times were lean. People in that part of Texas had little money, and the men used trade and barter. What money there was in circulation was gold coin. Schreiner's customers usually settled their accounts once a year, paying him after they sold their cattle, sheep, and wool. J. Evetts Haley, who went over the early records of the company many years ago, wrote that Schreiner

> was ready to buy whatever his customers brought in to sell. . . . In 1872 John S. Lowrance was credited with eighty-six pounds of bear oil—that stay-comb of the frontiersman's hair—at nine and a half cents a pound, and a bundle of deer hides besides. These hides were staple articles of trade, as were the hams when the season was right. For some reason—perhaps the absence of bacteria and blow-flies that follow the civilized trail of man—meat was more easily cured and kept in an early day, and the season was often "right." . . . Cow hides, goat hides, wolf hides—apparently hides of all kinds—were taken in trade and piled into one of the little warehouses that sprang up, in keeping with expanding resources and needs, to the back of the general store. In an odoriferous and unpleasant way they advertised the growing influence of Schreiner's business, and attracted hosts of flies and bugs besides.[11]

During the years that followed, Charles Schreiner's business grew. So did his service to his community. As cattlemen from the surrounding region began driving their longhorn cattle up the trails to Kansas, where they were sold for good hard cash, they paid for goods in Schreiner's store with cash.

His business prospered. Some cattlemen turned over their excess money to Schreiner for safekeeping, and he soon established a banking department within the store. In 1893 he opened a separate private bank, called the Charles Schreiner Bank, in Kerrville, an institution that still exists today. During the 1870s he began buying raw wool from sheep raisers and selling it, and then he began raising his own sheep. Kerrville soon became the sheep center of Texas. Schreiner worked to get railroad service for Kerrville, and in 1887 the San Antonio and Aransas Pass Railroad arrived. It eliminated the need for freight wagons to supply his store and to transport hides, wool, and other products to markets elsewhere. Schreiner also operated a gristmill, a sawmill, and a cotton gin, and he had a large elevated tank of cypress timber constructed to supply water to homes and businesses in Kerrville. This led to the formation of the Kerrville Water Works Company, and it was Schreiner who established the town's first electric light and power plant. Charles Schreiner left his mark on Kerrville and the surrounding portion of Texas, and his descendants continue to operate the businesses in the traditions of their founder.[12]

There were other men like Charles Schreiner in the West, and the business empires of several continue to prosper today, but such men seem to have been the exception to the rule. The businesses of many failed for one reason or another, and Doan's Store, located on the Texas side of the Red River, is a good example. The Doan story began in 1872 when Jonathan Doan, a widower; his older brother, Calvin W. Doan; a cousin, R. E. Doan; and Corwin F. Doan, Jonathan's nephew, arrived at Fort Sill in the southwestern part of present-day Oklahoma. Jonathan and Calvin Doan went to work for a man named Smith, the Indian agent at the fort. Soon Smith let the two Doans start a small fur-trading post and store. According to family tradition, Calvin Doan put up the money for the partnership. They purchased merchandise and traded it for buffalo hides and other pelts, which were freighted to Gainesville or Denison, Texas, and sold.

In the spring of 1874, Jonathan and Cal Doan decided to find greener pastures. At about the same time R. E. Doan and Corwin F. Doan returned to Ohio, having had their fill of the West. Jonathan and Cal Doan soon established a trading post for buffalo hunters northeast of where Memphis, Texas, stands now, and later they moved their post to near present-day Chillicothe, Texas. But as the killing of buffalo continued on the Texas plains, they realized that the business from buffalo hunters would not last. The buffalo were nearly gone. In the spring of 1875 they moved their trading post to a crossing on the Red River in present-day Wilbarger County, Texas.

JONATHAN DOAN, WHO WITH HIS OLDER BROTHER CALVIN W. DOAN
established Doan's Store on the Red River near Vernon, Texas, in 1875.

A few Texas cattlemen had used the crossing as they drove their longhorns
north to the Kansas cattle towns.

Jonathan and Cal Doan, along with two other men—Tim Pete and Ed
Miller—built a picket house twenty-four by thirty feet. According to the
Doan family recollections, the house was constructed of hackberry and china-
berry trees. The limbs were cut off and the trunks of the trees were put into
good shape with axes. The trunks were then cut off to the same length and
placed upright in a ditch that was filled in with dirt. The spaces between
the tree trunks were chinked in as well as possible with mud. A roof with
a long ridgepole was constructed in about the same manner as the sides.

DOAN'S STORE IN 1899.

The picket house had a dirt floor with a buffalo hide over the door, and it was divided into two sections—one for the store, the other for living quarters. Nearby along the river there were plenty of trees for a wood supply, and water was plentiful. Doan's Store, as it was called, was opened for business. Supplies were freighted in from northern Texas, and the store did fairly well as word spread that there was a general merchandise store at the crossing.

By 1878, Jonathan Doan wanted two of his daughters to join him in Texas. Cal Doan went to Ohio to bring them back. While he was there, Corwin F. Doan decided to move to Texas with his wife and baby daughter. When the party reached the crossing on the Red River, they found that the store was low on supplies. One of the employees had taken two wagons loaded with buffalo hides to Henrietta, Texas. He was supposed to sell the hides and bring the wagons back loaded with goods, but after the sale he fled to parts unknown with the money. Jonathan Doan was out searching for the employee when Cal and Corwin Doan and the others arrived at the store. They found a jar of stale mustard, a keg of powder, a large quantity of strychnine, and many cans of sardines and crackers on the almost bare shelves. They lived on the sardines and crackers until new supplies arrived.

The spot where Doan's Store had been built was located on what became known as the Western Cattle Trail, which led to Dodge City, Kansas. In 1879, for example, a hundred thousand longhorns passed the store during the spring and summer months, and the trail drivers stopped to do business at Doan's. Soon the Texas Cattle Raisers' Association, founded in 1877, stationed inspectors at what became known as Doan's Crossing to check the herds for strays or cattle belonging to Texas ranchmen other than the owners of the trail herds. Doan's Store prospered. Corwin F. Doan worked for Jonathan and Cal Doan and in 1880 helped to build an adobe store and two log cabins to replace the picket house. About a year later a wooden store was constructed.

In 1922, Corwin F. Doan, then seventy-four years old, recalled his early days working in the store on the Red River:

This store did a thriving business and thought nothing of selling bacon and flour in car-load lots, though getting our supplies from Denison, Sherman, Gainesville, and later, Wichita Falls. The postoffice was established here in 1879 and I was the first postmaster. It was at this office all mail for the trail herds was directed as, like canned goods and other commodities, this was the last chance. One night while a crowd sat around the little adobe store someone struck up a lively air on a French harp and the door opened and in sailed a hat followed closely by a big black fellow who commenced to dance. It was one of Ab Blocker's men who had been sent up for the mail, giving first notice of the herd's arrival. Many a sweetheart down the trail received her letter bearing the postmark of Doan's and many a cowboy asked self-consciously if there was any mail for him while his face turned a beet red when a dainty missive was handed him.[13]

About 1880, Jonathan and Cal Doan opened another store at Eagle Flats, a new settlement several miles to the south. When Corwin F. Doan offered to buy their first store, they agreed, and the name over the door soon read "C. F. Doan and Company." Nearby was a sign reading "Good Cigars and Bad Whiskey." By 1885, a small settlement of nearly three hundred people had grown up around the store. There was even a hotel of sorts. Cowboys called it "the Bat's Cave," an uncomplimentary reference to the gamy women in residence. When word reached the settlement that the Fort Worth and Denver Railroad was laying track across northwestern Texas toward their area, the people dreamed that their little community, called Doans, would become a city. But the railroad passed several miles to the south, and many people in the vicinity moved down to what had been called Eagle Flats (the town had been renamed Vernon after Washington's home, Mount Vernon). Jonathan and Cal Doan had made the correct decision in starting a store there, and Jonathan Doan later became a judge. But for

C. F. Doan, it was the beginning of the end. After trail drives shifted farther west in 1888, business in the store declined. Doan continued to operate it, but devoted more attention to farming. He no longer sold carloads of staples to passing trail drivers, and Doan's became simply another country store located at a rural crossroads. Early in this century it was a gas station. Today, where Ranch Road 924 dead-ends near the Red River in northwestern Wilbarger County, there is a granite monument, erected in 1931, marking the site of Doan's Crossing. The monument also bears scores of cattle brands that were well known during the years when the Doans provided a service to countless Texas cattlemen and cowboys and made money in the process.[14]

OF ALL THE ENTREPRENEURS who made a name for themselves in Texas, Charles William Post, a native of Illinois, may have been the most unusual. Post went to Texas in 1886 for his health. In Fort Worth, he found that people were making a good deal of money in real estate. Unlike many profit-seekers, Post had already made his mark in the business world. In 1871, at the age of seventeen, he had borrowed a thousand dollars from his mother, and with a partner, Charles Moody, had opened a hardware store in Independence, Kansas. Two years later, after doubling his investment, he returned to Illinois, where he worked for a farm machinery company, first as a salesman and then as a manager. At the age of twenty he married. As farmers moved onto the western plains to buy railroad land or to homestead, the demand for farm machinery grew. Post sought to improve farm equipment, and he and a friend, A. L. Ide, perfected a seed planter and were granted a patent for it in 1878. Post soon opened a small factory to manufacture farm machinery. During the eight years that followed, Post applied for and received patents on three different cultivators, a sulky plow, a harrow, and a hay-stacker. In 1885, he organized a corporation called the Illinois Agricultural Works, with a capital stock of $300,000. His future looked bright, but Post had worked too hard. He suffered a severe nervous breakdown in August 1886 and went to Texas to recover his health.

When Post realized the potential of Fort Worth real estate, he organized his own real estate company with a brother and a cousin. But in the fall of 1888, he suffered another nervous breakdown from overwork, and went east for several months. He was back in Forth Worth about a year later and built a woolen mill on the Houston and Texas Central Railway nearby. He also made plans to build another mill where Texas cottonseed hulls could be made into paper. But again his health declined. Post took his family and moved to Battle

Creek, Michigan, early in 1891. As he recuperated, Post remembered how farmers' wives in Texas had mixed chicory with roasted wheat and other ground grains to produce a makeshift coffee, and he experimented to produce a beverage that tasted like coffee but did not have the ill effects of caffeine. Within a year he had developed a mixture of wheat, bran, and molasses that he considered superior to the Texas substitute for coffee, which used chicory. Post gave his invention the name "Postum Food Coffee."

A grocer friend in Grand Rapids, Michigan, told Post no one would buy the new beverage, but Post thought otherwise. Post visited the editor of the Grand Rapids *Evening Press* and brewed some Postum in the editor's office. The editor liked it, and he had his entire staff try it. When the newspaper carried a story about Postum, Post realized that he could sell his drink through advertising. He had saved much of his profit from earlier investments, and was able to advertise heavily both Postum and Grape-Nuts, a breakfast cereal developed in 1893. His sales grew from about $5,000 in 1895 to $840,000 by 1898. Still interested in real estate, Post decided to build and sell houses to his workers in Grand Rapids. Workers who had been with the company at least a year could pay eight to ten dollars a month and own their own homes.

By 1900, C. W. Post had retired from the day-to-day management of the Postum Cereal Company in Michigan. He traveled to Europe and opened an English branch of his company, and frequently visited Texas, where he enjoyed the climate and the people. By 1907, Post had purchased 213,324 acres in Garza and Lynn counties southeast of Lubbock in west Texas, where he planned to found a town and farm colony. He staked out the new town and soon ran an advertisement titled "Making Money in Texas" in major daily newspapers in Kansas, Missouri, and elsewhere. Meantime, he chartered a corporation in Texas called the Double U Company with a capital stock of $50,000, of which he owned $49,600 worth. He hired a Texas manager and made arrangements to have lumber and other building supplies transported west on the Texas and Pacific Railroad to Big Spring, Texas, located about seventy miles south of his townsite. Post ordered seventy-two of the best Missouri mules available, and twenty-four wagons and harness from South Bend, Indiana, to carry the lumber and building materials overland to the townsite. Mule skinners were hired to drive the wagons, and carpenters, stonemasons, and other workers to build the buildings. Soon the town of Post City, Texas, was born.

The workmen first lived in tents, but by the end of 1907 about fifty houses had been constructed. Most were occupied. There were eight stores in one large stone building, and a stone hotel called the Algerita was opened in the summer of 1908. Post gave instructions on food preparation in the hotel, where Postum was served along with Grape-Nuts. Post even gave directions on how to cook steaks and what the daily menu should be. When Post was away from Texas, as he frequently was, he had the hotel menu sent to him daily. His concern for detail extended to all aspects of the town. He selected the colors that buildings were to be painted, and directed the planting of trees, shrubs, and flowers.

But Post City, Texas, was isolated. Post worked to get a railroad, and in late 1910 the Santa Fe arrived—Post had induced the line to lay track from Lubbock to Post City. In that year the community claimed seven to eight hundred residents. By the end of 1911, however, the population had grown to nearly fifteen hundred. Post promoted dry farming, and many farmsteads were sold at twenty to thirty dollars an acre. In 1911, he bought a hundred and fifty head of Aberdeen Angus cattle and established a ranching operation on 150,000 acres of pasture land.

By 1913, Post was fifty-nine, and gradually turning over his responsibility for the community to others, encouraging the residents to take over the town. Although a multimillionaire with a large business in Michigan and homes in Connecticut and California, Post directed that a bungalow be built for him in Post City. But he never had an opportunity to enjoy the small one-story house. Post's health declined, and on the morning of May 9, 1914, C. W. Post died in Santa Barbara, California.

His town, however, survived. Located at the intersection of U.S. highways 380 and 84, Post, Texas, as it is now called, claims a population of nearly four thousand people and serves as the county seat of Garza County.[15]

DURING the mid-1880s all of what is now Oklahoma remained off limits to settlement except by Indians. The Missouri, Kansas and Texas Railroad and the Atlantic and Pacific (Frisco) line had penetrated the sparsely populated Indian lands and linked Kansas and Missouri to Texas by 1880, and in 1887 the Atchison, Topeka and Santa Fe built south from Wichita, Kansas, crossing the western part of Indian Territory to Fort Worth. But the Indians made little use of these railroads except in what is now southeastern Oklahoma, where, with the help of some whites, they began to ship timber and coal. Even many Texas cattlemen refused to ship their longhorns north by rail. It was cheaper to drive them overland across Indian Territory to the Kansas markets.

The railroads' hope that their move into Indian Territory would open the region to settlement had not materialized. But the fact that their lines were in place only whetted the appetites of the railroad companies and the people who rode the trains across the Indian lands. The rolling country was ideal for farms, and the railroad stations already in existence provided a nucleus around which towns could grow and prosper. The railroads dreamed of the day when farmers could settle the land and ship their produce to markets in Kansas, Missouri, Texas, and elsewhere. Even bankers, merchants, and farm equipment manufacturers had visions of new markets and investment opportunities in Indian Territory. The leaders of the five civilized tribes, however, fought every move to organize the territory for statehood. Only the cattlemen's lobby sided with the Indians: the cattlemen, who leased grazing land from the Indians, did not want farmers moving onto the land, tilling it and fencing it.

To bring about the change they desired, railroad companies, banks, wholesale distributors, and farm equipment manufacturers now quietly turned to lawyers, among them T. C. Sears, an attorney for the Missouri, Kansas and Texas Railroad, and Elias C. Boudinot, the Cherokee attorney, who had laid out present-day Vinita, Oklahoma. Like Sears, Boudinot probably was paid by the railroad. Sears announced early in 1879 that he and Boudinot had carefully examined the laws relating to Indian treaties and land titles and had found fourteen million acres of land in Indian Territory that had not been given to the Indians. Sears and Boudinot claimed the land belonged in the public domain of the United States and was therefore subject to settlement by qualified people. Boudinot then began to make speeches seeking public support for their position, and they distributed literature describing the wonderful opportunities awaiting settlers in Indian Territory.

Sears and Boudinot became known as "boomers." They were really the late-nineteenth-century version of modern-day public relations men. With the support of some newspapers, including the Wichita *Eagle* in Kansas and the Kansas City *Times* in Missouri, the promoters organized three groups of purported settlers, people who claimed they wanted to make their homes in Indian Territory. One group was assembled in northern Texas, another at Topeka, Kansas, and still another in Kansas City, Missouri. The Kansas City group, headed by Charles C. Carpenter, established offices in several towns along the southern border of Kansas. Settlers gathered in them in anticipation of crossing into Indian land and establishing homes. The U.S. government and courts, however, had rejected Sears and Boudinot's contentions; and when the leaders of the Cherokee Nation learned of the threatened invasion, they protested to the federal authorities, which stationed troops at strategic points along the border to keep the squatters out. Several attempts to settle on Indian lands failed, and soon most of the would-be settlers gave up.[16]

By 1880 another campaign was launched, this time by David L. Payne, William L. Couch, and Samuel Crocker. Payne, a native of Indiana, was the leader. He had come to Kansas Territory in 1858 and served as a frontier scout and then as a member of the Kansas legislature. He later went to Washington, D.C., where he became assistant doorkeeper of the House of Representatives. There he made many political contacts, among them Elias C. Boudinot. When he returned West in 1879, he launched his boomer campaign, apparently with the blessing of, and perhaps some assistance from, Boudinot and others. As the campaign developed, Payne began quoting from the Bible. His favorite quote seems to have been ". . . and the Lord commanded unto Moses, 'Go forth and possess the Promised Land.' " As he attracted followers, he charged each home seeker two dollars for a certificate guaranteeing a quarter-section of land in present-day Oklahoma or twenty-five dollars for a town lot in a future town in the territory. Payne tried several times to lead expeditions onto Indian lands, but each time the expedition was turned back by federal officials. When he was taken to court at Fort Smith, Arkansas, and Topeka and Wichita, Payne used the court appearances as a forum to claim that people had the right to settle in Indian Territory. At one point after he had been arrested on a charge of conspiracy against the United States, Payne was tried in the U.S. District Court in Topeka. To his surprise the charge was dismissed on the grounds that title to the Indian lands was vested in the United States and they were thus in the public domain. The court ruled that settlement by U.S. citizens on the land was therefore not a crime. The court's decision was a victory not only for Payne and his followers but for the railroads and other business interests who wanted to open Indian Territory to settlement for their own benefit. David Payne, however, died suddenly in a Wellington, Kansas, hotel on November 29, 1884, just after eating breakfast. William L. Couch, one of Payne's lieutenants, took over the leadership role.[17]

Government attorneys, in the meantime, had undertaken a review of Indian Territory lands. They soon pointed out that the Creek and Seminole Indians had a "residual interest" in some of the unassigned lands that the court had declared to be in the public domain. The lands were located in present-day west-central Oklahoma and had been taken by the government from the Indians for the purpose of resettling other tribes, but no other

DAVID L. PAYNE,
a native of Indiana, who led a boomer campaign to open
part of present-day Oklahoma to settlement.

Indians had been placed there. The attorneys said the land would not be public domain until the matter was resolved.

Exactly who moved next is unclear, but the report of the government attorneys, the success of the boomers in gaining public support for the settlement of Indian lands, and some political maneuvering by sympathetic lawmakers resulted in Congress giving the Creek and Seminole Indians cash payments in return for agreements relinquishing their rights to the land in west-central Oklahoma. Business interests in Kansas undoubtedly exerted their influence in Washington, and just before Congress adjourned in early March 1889, lawmakers approved a measure opening the unassigned lands to settlement. A few weeks later President Benjamin Harrison issued a proclamation declaring that the land would be opened to settlement at noon

A BOOMERS CAMP NEAR ARKANSAS CITY,
close to the southern border of Kansas, about 1880.

on Monday, April 22, 1889. And to give all potential settlers an equal chance, government officials decided to stage a land run. Three days before the land was to be opened, the government lifted its ban against trespassing on Indian lands and permitted the prospective settlers the opportunity of gathering on all four sides of the approximately two million acres up for grabs.

By late morning on April 22, about fifty thousand home seekers had assembled at the borders of the land to be opened. A detachment of U.S. cavalry had been dispersed to supervise the land run, and at noon sharp a cavalry signal officer raised a bugle to his lips with one hand and dropped a flag at the same moment that he gave the blast. Other military men gave similar signals at other points along the four sides. The race was on. It was as though people were running for their lives, as home seekers on horseback, in buggies and wagons, and even a few on foot entered the unsettled region to stake their claims. Others arrived by special trains jammed to overflowing with settlers who thought they would reach their promised land faster than those on horseback. Unfortunately, the trains traveled slowly, stopping every few miles to let passengers off. A few home seekers, frustrated by the speed of the train, jumped off and ran ahead. It was a day the participants would never forget, and by dusk, seven hours later, nearly every town lot in what became Norman, Oklahoma City, Guthrie, and Kingfisher had been staked. Settlers erected tents, built crude cabins, constructed dugouts, and even

THE SCENE, MOMENTS AFTER NOON ON MONDAY, APRIL 22, 1889,
when perhaps fifty thousand home seekers raced to make their claim on parts of
two million acres of land in present-day Oklahoma just opened for settlement.

THE SCENE, SOUTH OF CALDWELL, KANSAS,
shortly before noon on September 16, 1893, when the Cherokee Strip
was thrown open to settlement. At noon the Rock Island train overflowing
with land seekers raced south.

used wagon boxes for housing on their town lots. The same was true outside the new towns, where every homestead claim was staked by dusk. The settlers claimed quarter-section farms as provided by the homestead laws. This meant there was an average of about a half mile of prairie separating one farmhouse from another.

Many of the people claiming townsites were, of course, businessmen. Some brought merchandise with them to sell and made arrangements for lumber and other building materials to be transported to the new town within a few days. Some had ties to firms in Kansas and Missouri that had been waiting for the opportunity to open new markets in Indian Territory. About fifteen thousand people made Guthrie their home that day, and its future seemed bright, since it was the site of the projected capital of the new territory and it already had two land offices. About thirty-five miles to the south, perhaps ten thousand people were on the site of Oklahoma City by dusk. Lesser numbers of people chose Norman, several miles south of Oklahoma City, and Kingfisher, a former stage station about thirty miles west of Guthrie.

On that day in 1889 present-day Oklahoma gained the reputation of being perhaps the only area of the American West where cities were built before farmers in the surrounding areas had planted their first crops. Oklahoma Territory also differed from most other territories in the West in that it had no government at its start. In its haste to open the unassigned Indian lands to settlement, Congress failed to provide for a territorial government. For more than a year the settlers in the new towns and rural areas relied on their own grass-roots democracy, providing the essential rudiments of law and order through town marshals and mayors. Boards of citizens were elected to arbitrate land disputes and to organize schools, which were supported on a subscription basis. But Congress remedied the situation by passing the Oklahoma Organic Act on May 2, 1890, providing for a territorial governor, a supreme court, a territorial legislature, and a delegate to Congress from what was called the Territory of Oklahoma. The name "Oklahoma" is derived from two Choctaw words: *okla*, meaning "people," and *humma*, meaning "red."

The Oklahoma Organic Act of 1890 attached No Man's Land—the present Oklahoma panhandle—to the Territory of Oklahoma, and the act stipulated that as other Indian land was opened to settlement, the land would automatically become part of the Territory of Oklahoma. More Indian land was opened in 1891 and 1892, when much of present-day western Oklahoma was settled. And perhaps the most publicized land opening occurred in

A TENT CITY IN THE CHEROKEE STRIP
a day or so after the region was opened to settlement. The site may be
present-day Perry, Oklahoma.

FIVE MEN POSE FOR THE PHOTOGRAPHER IN FRONT OF A CABIN
located in the Cherokee Strip just across the southern border of Kansas.

1893, when the Cherokee Strip was thrown open to settlement at noon on
September 16. About a hundred thousand people participated in that land
run to settle six million acres just across the southern border of Kansas.[18]

Again, in the Cherokee Strip new towns appeared within hours. One
of them was Woodward, located in present-day northwestern Oklahoma. And

like so many other western towns, Woodward soon had the false-front buildings and board sidewalks that were common to such communities. At the
center of Woodward's business district was the Cattle King Hotel. The town's
other businesses were located along the main street. They included a few
eating houses, dry-goods and general merchandise stores, a Chinese laundry,
two banks, and twenty-three saloons, some with mahogany and walnut bars.
During Woodward's early years it was primarily a cattle town, and businesses
catered to ranchers and cattle buyers. During those years water was scarce.
Nearly all businesses and homes had water barrels just outside their doors.
These barrels were filled daily by an enterprising young businessman who
operated a horse-drawn tank wagon and charged twenty-five cents a day to
fill each barrel. In time wells were dug and water became more plentiful in
Woodward. But water was still scarce in many areas of western Oklahoma
and the panhandle when, in 1907, the Territory of Oklahoma and Indian
Territory joined together and were admitted to the Union as the forty-sixth
state, called Oklahoma. The lack of rainfall and the scarcity of water in
western Oklahoma restricted the growth of settlement as it had done elsewhere
on the Great Plains. In turn it has limited the extension of business. The
lack of water was also one of the factors that restricted the growth and
development of the last two western states to be admitted to the Union—
New Mexico and Arizona.

XIV

THE DESERT
SOUTHWEST

*The most sensible people to be met with in society are men of business
and of the world, who argue from what they see and know, instead of
spinning cobweb distinctions of what things ought to be.*

—WILLIAM HAZLITT[1]

IT SEEMS ironic that New Mexico, where Anglo-Americans first established regular trade in the nineteenth-century American West, was one
of the last two territories in the continental United States to join the Union.
One would think that the vast amount of trade between Missouri and Santa
Fe would have set the stage for New Mexico's early entry into the Union
after it became a territory of the United States following the MexicanWar.
But such was not the case. The sparse, predominantly Spanish-speaking
population and the growing Anglo-American ethnocentrism created an unstable political situation. The Catholic clergy had much influence over the
people and exerted much pressure on territorial politics. Territorial delegates
in Congress usually came from old families, and rivalries between political
parties created bitter partisan feuds that added to the turmoil. At the same
time there were the holders of large land grants who wished to maintain the
status quo, as did many politically strong merchants who feared that statehood
might damage their business interests. Statehood was delayed. New Mexico
Territory, which included much of present-day Arizona until the Territory
of Arizona was established in 1863, did not become a state until 1912, the
same year Arizona was admitted to the Union.

When the Civil War ended in 1865, the territories of New Mexico and
Arizona had a combined population of fewer than ninety thousand people.
Most of them were Hispanics and Indians. There were fewer than two thou-
sand Anglo-Americans in Arizona Territory and fewer than twelve thousand

in New Mexico Territory. Many of the Anglos were engaged in business, and their numbers increased during the years immediately following the Civil War as more immigrants pushed westward in search of opportunities. But few of the Anglo-Americans arriving just after the war were traditional settlers. The mountains and deserts of New Mexico and Arizona had little appeal. Farmland was limited to the river valleys, and much of it was taken by Hispanics, especially after Congress abolished peonage in the United States and its territories on March 2, 1867. This enabled many Hispanics to spread out across New Mexico and southern Arizona and establish settlements and sheep camps. Homesteaders like those on the Great Plains were conspicuously absent.

Most of the Anglo-Americans who came to New Mexico immediately following the Civil War were mining and railroad promoters and merchants, and their hustle and bustle set off something of an economic boom. The establishment of daily mail deliveries from the East to Santa Fe in 1868 and the completion of the military telegraph line from Fort Leavenworth, Kansas, in the summer of 1869 added to the belief that the region was on the verge of economic prosperity. Many Hispanics caught the spirit and joined the Anglo-Americans in seeking material wealth, some through sheep-raising. At the same time the influx of new merchants caused the older merchants who had been in business well before the Civil War to change their approach. Instead of seeking to make as much money as possible in order to retire

LEFT: SOLOMON JACOB SPIEGELBERG,
who arrived in Santa Fe, New Mexico, in 1884.
RIGHT: The Spiegelberg Brothers building in Santa Fe, about 1902.

SPIEGELBERG BROTHERS
across the street from the plaza in Santa Fe, 1889.

early, merchants sought to build more permanent enterprises. Leaders of this change were German immigrants, especially German Jews. Although Jews were already well established in eastern states, where many had begun as peddlers and become prosperous merchants, they did not begin to move into the West until after the Mexican War. Many arrived along the coast of Texas during the 1840s. Others went to California following the gold rush, and some settled in Salt Lake City. By the 1850s many Jews had settled in the larger towns along the Santa Fe Trail, especially from Trinidad in present-day southeastern Colorado south into New Mexico.[2]

One of the early merchants was Solomon Jacob Spiegelberg. He arrived in Santa Fe as a young man in 1844 and went to work in a general merchandise store. He worked hard and learned Spanish and the commercial needs of the inhabitants. In the fall of 1847, he reportedly quit his job, took three hundred and sixty-five dollars in savings, and invested in merchandise. He then followed Colonel W. A. Doniphan and his army south as they marched to Chihuahua during the Mexican War. Spiegelberg made a good profit on his investment and returned to Santa Fe in the summer of 1848. With his profits he traveled East, purchased more goods, and returned to Santa Fe, where he opened his own mercantile business late in 1848.

In the meantime, a younger brother, Levi Spiegelberg, came to Santa Fe to help Solomon run the store. And between 1848 and 1861 four other younger brothers arrived from Germany to join the firm. But before all of them had arrived, Solomon Jacob Spiegelberg left New Mexico because of poor health and a doctor's prognosis that he had only six months to live. He returned to his native Germany to die but surprised everyone by living until 1898. Back in Santa Fe, his younger brothers continued to operate the family business with much success.

From a store on the south side of the plaza across from the Palace of the Governors, the Spiegelbergs dealt in groceries and dry goods. They used the Anglo-owned Spanish-language newspapers to advertise their merchandise, and attracted many Spanish-speaking customers in addition to Anglos. Because many Hispanics were laborers earning only about fifteen dollars a month (compared with thirty dollars for Anglo-Americans doing similar work), cash was scarce among them. The Spiegelbergs therefore allowed them to use a barter system, accepting fresh produce in exchange for Spiegelberg script. The Hispanics then used the script to purchase clothing, household goods, and groceries as needed. Many Anglos did the same, but the Spiegelbergs would sell much of the fresh produce and other merchandise to Anglo-Americans for cash, U.S. coins, and bills.

As the Spiegelbergs' assets increased, they became wholesalers and made other investments, including real estate. They also helped to organize a bank, and became government contractors, providing goods for military posts and for the Indians under government care. In 1873, for example, the Spiegelbergs signed one contract with the government to provide fifty thousand pounds of Best Taos Flour for $2,135, three thousand pounds of Rio Coffee for $840, and six thousand pounds of light brown sugar costing $953.40. These supplies were delivered to the Superintendent of Indian Affairs for distribution among Indians in New Mexico Territory. But the Spiegelbergs often found it difficult to collect from the government. The problem was a combination of government paperwork and the Spiegelbergs' difficulties in keeping up with changing government procedures.[3]

The Spiegelbergs and other merchants in New Mexico and Arizona, and everyone else in the two terrritories, relied heavily on wagon freighting for food, supplies, machinery, and other items not produced in the region. Until the 1870s most such goods were brought into the territory of New Mexico in wagons that traversed the Santa Fe Trail from Missouri or wherever the nearest railroad was located in Kansas. But after the Kansas Pacific Railroad reached Denver, and the Denver and Rio Grande Western Railroad built south from Denver to El Moro near present-day Trinidad, Colorado, freight destined for New Mexico and Arizona was shipped by rail from the East to Denver and then south to El Moro. There wagon freighters loaded it on their wagons and drove their teams south into New Mexico to Las Vegas, Santa Fe, or some other trading center. If the freight was bound for Arizona the wagons followed a route south along the Rio Grande from Colorado to Mesilla in southern New Mexico and then west to Tucson. Mesilla at one time was to have been the capital of a vast new state that would have combined what is now southern New Mexico and all of Arizona. It was about six hundred and fifty miles from the railroad terminal at El Moro to Tucson. After the Atchison, Topeka and Santa Fe Railroad linked up with the Denver and Rio Grande at Pueblo, Colorado, in 1876, even more freight reached New Mexico and Arizona over this route.

But this route from Colorado south through New Mexico and then west was not the only one used to carry freight to Tucson and other points in Arizona Territory. Freight was shipped from New York and other points in the East over the transcontinental railroad to San Francisco. There it was loaded aboard steamers and transported by sea around Lower California to where the Colorado River empties into the Gulf of California. The freight would then be transferred to steamboats and taken up the Colorado River as far as Hardyville, a town founded about 1864 by Captain William H. Hardy, nine miles up the Colorado River from Fort Mohave. From Hardyville or any other point along the river, freighters could then carry the cargo overland to its destination. Hardyville was the head of steamboat navigation on the Colorado. But this lengthy route around Lower California was shortened considerably in the middle 1870s after the Southern Pacific Railroad

MULES ON THE DESERT

CAPTAIN WILLIAM H. HARDY,
who founded the town of Hardyville nine miles up the
Colorado River from Fort Mohave.

THE STEAMBOAT "COCOPAH" ON THE COLORADO RIVER IN ARIZONA,
late in the nineteenth century.

pushed into southern California. Using the California towns of Banning, Indio, Dos Palmas, or wherever the railhead happened to be located reduced the distance and the cost of shipping freight to Arizona. Freighters could pick up goods at the railhead and haul it east into Arizona or stop at Fort Yuma on the Colorado River and transfer the freight to steamboats for the journey up the river.

Another German Jew who made extensive use of freighting was Charles Ilfeld. He came to New Mexico Territory just after the Civil War to take advantage of the mercantile opportunities there. He was eighteen years old when he sailed from Hamburg in late April 1865. He arrived in Santa Fe in August of that year and soon found work with the mercantile firm of Adolph Letcher and Company at Taos, about ninety-five miles northeast of Santa Fe. There young Ilfeld served as clerk and bookkeeper for Letcher, but it soon became evident that Taos was dying as a commercial center. The region around Taos had been trapped out by the late 1820s. Although the Santa Fe Trail and Bent's Fort to the northeast on the Arkansas River had revived business in Taos for a time, trade had been reduced to serving only local residents by the early 1860s. The number of traders moving over the Taos branch of the Santa Fe Trail had dwindled during the Civil War.

In the spring of 1867, Adolph Letcher decided to move his company to Las Vegas, about forty miles east of Santa Fe. Las Vegas had a population of about two thousand people and was becoming a trading center for a wide area of eastern New Mexico Territory. Letcher took over an empty store on the north side of the plaza in Las Vegas. Soon townspeople, ranchers, and others made the store their headquarters. Letcher made Ilfeld a partner as the business prospered. At the end of their first year Letcher and Ilfeld had grossed forty thousand dollars. Eighteen thousand was profit. They captured some trade from Fort Union, about twenty-five miles north of Las Vegas. The sutler at the post also provided a service to Letcher and Ilfeld. When they needed a draft to pay an eastern bill, they only had to send the currency to the sutler and they would receive a draft in exchange. This was very helpful in paying bills and paying freighters for their services. As long as such drafts were transferred between merchants, there was no service change.[4]

Letcher began traveling a great deal, going from one military post to another soliciting business. Ilfeld ran the store. By 1869, however, it became evident that the firm needed a representative in the East to select merchandise personally, "since eastern wholesalers had little 'feel' of the southwestern markets, and the time element in replacing poorly selected merchandise was

CHARLES ILFELD AS HE APPEARED IN HIS MID-TWENTIES, ABOUT 1870.

INTERIOR OF THE CHARLES ILFELD STORE, ABOUT 1915.

long, and involved heavy cost."[5] In December 1869, Letcher headed East, not only to select merchandise but to establish connections with eastern wholesale houses, including Samuel Rosenthal and Company of Baltimore. Letcher returned to Las Vegas in May 1870, left again in January 1871 for six months in the East, and took another trip East in October 1871. He returned in December 1871 with his wife, but she apparently did not like Las Vegas and New Mexico. In June 1872, Letcher and his wife took a stage from Las Vegas to Kit Carson, Colorado, where they climbed aboard a Kansas Pacific train and headed East again. Letcher was gone for nearly a year.

While Letcher was away but apparently with his approval, Ilfeld expanded the firm's operation by establishing a store and corral about nine miles south of Las Vegas on a branch of the Santa Fe Trail leading to Anton Chico, Puerto de Luna, and Roswell. Ilfeld was also about to purchase property the firm had been renting several miles north of Las Vegas. In addition, he succeeded in attracting new business. But even before Letcher and his wife returned to Las Vegas in April 1873, Ilfeld was making plans not only to go East but to visit his native Germany. He apparently felt he had proved himself as a businessman. Soon after the Letchers' return, Ilfeld traveled to Germany, where he renewed acquaintance with a rabbi's daughter whom he had first met when she was eight years old. But the girl was now a beautiful young woman of nineteen, and Ilfeld fell in love and proposed marriage. She accepted and promised to follow Ilfeld to America after a proper waiting period. Ilfeld returned to the United States, bringing with him his fifteen-year-old brother, Louis. Before returning to New Mexico, Charles Ilfeld visited merchants in New York City and the firm of Samuel Rosenthal and Company, among others, in Baltimore. On the way across the country, Ilfeld also visited the wholesale firm of McCartney and Company in St. Louis to cement business relations.

Ilfeld returned to Las Vegas with his younger brother, who began working with the firm. In the spring of 1874, Charles Ilfeld again traveled to New York City, where he met his bride-to-be. They were married there and then moved on to New Mexico. About two months after Ilfeld's return to Las Vegas, Letcher sold his interest in the company to him for twelve thousand dollars in cash and six notes of four thousand dollars each. Letcher took his wife East, where she presumably thought she would be happier. From all indications, Ilfeld's wife liked New Mexico, and she undoubtedly inspired her husband in his work. He soon established new stores in present-day Los Alamos, Watrous, and Tecolote and used them as assembling points in buying raw materials, including wool, produce, lumber, and grain. Ilfeld concentrated on retailing until the arrival of the railroad. When the Texas and Pacific completed its line westward from San Antonio to El Paso in January 1883, connecting with the Southern Pacific, the position of Las Vegas as a gathering center was jeopardized. Ilfeld rather reluctantly moved to establish wholesaling as part of his firm's operation. At the same time he opened other stores in New Mexico. In time Charles Ilfeld and Company had branch warehouses throughout the territory, and his company dominated much trade, especially in groceries. When Ilfeld died in January 1929 at the age of eighty-one, he had built a mercantile empire that stretched the width and breadth of New Mexico.[6]

Another prominent Jewish name in the early mercantile business of New Mexico Territory was Zeckendorf. There were three brothers—Aaron, Louis, and William. Aaron and Louis owned a mercantile store in Santa Fe during the 1850s. In 1856, their younger brother William, fourteen, came to Santa Fe from Germany to work in the store. He soon acquired fluency in English and Spanish, and he learned how to purchase local produce,

WILLIAM ZECKENDORF AND FAMILY IN 1889,
about two years before Zeckendorf sold out his Tucson business.

including eggs, peppers, vegetables, and livestock, and how to haul freight and supply the Army on contract. During the Civil War, William served as a lieutenant and quartermaster in the Union Army. After the war he traveled to Arizona to see what business opportunities existed, and he found Tucson much to his liking. It was the largest town in Arizona Territory, with a population of about fifteen hundred. The town had grown up around the Spanish presidio, or fort, called San Agustín de Tuguison, on the east bank of the Santa Cruz River. First under Spanish and then under Mexican rule, Tucson had been a northern terminal for trade with Mexico. After the Mexican War it became a trading center for ranchers, miners, and soldiers stationed at several military forts in the territory. And it grew in importance in March 1867, when the military headquarters of Arizona Territory was moved there from Prescott, and soon afterward it became the territorial capital. Perhaps of more importance, there were only four merchants in Tucson immediately following the Civil War.

William Zeckendorf returned to New Mexico, where in the meantime

AN EARLY VIEW OF THE MAIN STREET IN TUCSON,
Arizona Territory. Zeckendorf's store is on the left next to the horse and wagon.

his brother Aaron had established a store in Albuquerque. Louis Zeckendorf was in New York City serving as the firm's resident buyer. William told Aaron what he had found in Arizona. The decision was made, and in February 1869, William Zeckendorf led a wagon train loaded with merchandise from Albuquerque to Tucson and opened a branch of A. & L. Zeckendorf Company. By then William was a partner in the firm. The Tucson store thrived. When Aaron died in 1873, Louis and William reorganized and changed the firm's name to Zeckendorf Brothers and operated as such until April 1878. It was then that William Zeckendorf became a partner with Zadoc Staab, another Arizona merchant, and formed Zeckendorf and Staab. Their mercantile business was located at the corner of Main and Congress in Tucson, and it prospered until a fire destroyed the store a few years later. Staab then withdrew from the business, and Zeckendorf rebuilt the firm. Unfortunately, it failed early in 1883 because Mexican currency, which was accepted by Zeckendorf from Mexican customers, was unstable, quantities of inexpensive goods were arriving by train, and he had overextended credit to customers. But William Zeckendorf again rebuilt his business. In 1891, after thirty-

LEFT: ESTEBAN OCHOA, A PIONEER MERCHANT IN TUCSON, ARIZONA.
RIGHT: Charles Trumbull Hayden, a Connecticut native, who established a large freighting business in early Arizona.

THE OFFICES OF THE "DAILY & WEEKLY ARIZONA STAR,"
a newspaper founded by Pinckney Randolph Tully, Esteban Ochoa's partner.

two years in Tucson, he sold out and retired, moving to New York City, where he lived until his death in 1906.[7]

An early competitor of William Zeckendorf in Tucson was Esteban Ochoa. Born in Chihuahua, Mexico, in 1831, he was sent to Kansas City, Missouri, by his parents as a young man to study English and to learn mercantile practices. He became a naturalized American citizen and moved to Mesilla, New Mexico. There he operated a mercantile business until the 1850s, when he moved west to Arizona and entered a partnership with Pinckney Randolph Tully. The two men opened a store in Tucson and soon added stores in other Arizona communities. Tucson, however, was the firm's headquarters, and both men became wealthy. Ochoa and Tully also established a freighting business to supply their stores and to carry freight for other businesses. And they founded a stage line that ran between Yuma, Tucson, and Santa Fe. Although Ochoa was expelled from the region during the Civil War because he refused to take an oath of allegiance to the Confederacy, he returned after Union forces arrived and recovered his property. Ochoa became a strong link between Hispanics and Anglo-Americans, and he helped to found the first public schools in Arizona Territory. His partner, Pinckney Randolph Tully, became a banker, territorial treasurer, mayor of Tucson, and founder of the newspaper *Weekly Star*.[8]

Still another early Arizona merchant was Charles Trumbull Hayden. Born in Connecticut in 1825, Hayden arrived in Tucson on the first overland stage to reach the town in 1857. He soon headed a large freighting business that carried government cargo to military posts and supplied stores he had started at Tubac and Hayden's Ferry, a settlement he established on the Salt River, where he built the first ferry. That settlement is today Tempe, Arizona. He also operated a cattle ranch near Prescott and for a time served as a probate judge in Tucson. His son Carl Hayden later became a U.S. senator from Arizona.[9]

Perhaps the best-known mercantile name in Arizona today is Goldwater, but this is due in part to the prominence of one family member, the five-term U.S. senator Barry Goldwater, who was the Republican presidential nominee in 1964. Around 1850, Barry Goldwater's Polish-Jewish grandfather, Michel "Big Mike" Goldwater, came from Europe to California with a younger brother, Joseph, to search for gold. Michel's wife, Sarah, and their two children soon joined them. The Goldwater brothers started two business ventures in the Sonora, California, area, but they failed, as did a third venture in Los Angeles. Then a business friend asked them to open and run a store in La Paz, a new mining town in present-day western Arizona on the east bank of the Colorado River. They opened the store in 1862. Although La Paz was hot and dry, they succeeded, and four years later Michel and Joseph Goldwater owned the business, which included retailing, wholesaling, freighting, and the forwarding of merchandise. They became wealthy and were known as J. Goldwater and Brother, but Michel's wife reportedly never joined her husband in La Paz. She remained in California

LEFT: MICHEL "BIG MIKE" GOLDWATER,
Barry Goldwater's Polish-Jewish grandfather. RIGHT: Morris Goldwater,
Barry Goldwater's uncle.

THE GOLDWATERS' FIRST STORE IN PRESCOTT, ARIZONA,
built in 1876 and used until 1879. It was located at the intersection of Cortez
and Goodwin.

with the children, eventually making San Francisco her permanent home. Michel made frequent visits to see his wife and through the years they had eight children. He retired in 1885 and joined Sarah in San Francisco, where he acted as buyer for the growing family enterprises in Arizona Territory.

Back in Arizona the Goldwater businesses were run by Joseph. Michel's son Morris joined the firm in Arizona in 1867, and another brother, Baron, who had been born in Los Angeles in 1865, came into the business in 1885, the year his father retired to California. Both Morris and Baron married outside their faith. After the death of his mother, Morris married a non-Jewish widow, Sarah Shivers Fisher, and Baron married Episcopalian Josephine Williams in 1907. Baron and Josephine Goldwater had three children, their first being Barry, who was born in 1909. In time he headed the Goldwater enterprises in Arizona until entering public office.

The Goldwater family founded a store in Prescott, Arizona Territory, about 1876, four years after opening their first store in Phoenix, a town that came into existence to supply nearby Fort McDowell. The Goldwaters sold out in Phoenix to an eastern firm a few years later but returned to open another store in 1888, about a year before Phoenix became the territorial capital. Today Goldwater's is a major department store in Phoenix.[10]

Perhaps it was only natural that the pioneer merchants who worked the hardest and relied on sound business practices were the ones who survived. Many pioneer families like the Goldwaters laid the foundations of family fortunes that still endure. One such family in northern Arizona is the Babbitts. Their trading dynasty began in the early 1880s when the five Babbitt brothers from Ohio started a general store in Flagstaff, about seven thousand feet above sea level some sixty miles northeast of Prescott. The town was only about ten years old when the Babbitts arrived. It had grown up around a saloon built on the future townsite by Edward Whipple in 1871. Another early settler was F. F. McMillan, who built a corral just north of Flagstaff in 1876. Lumbering became the prime source of revenue in the area, and after the Atlantic and Pacific Railroad reached Flagstaff in the early 1880s, the Babbitts parlayed their general store into an empire of stores, trading posts, lumber mills, lumberyards, banks, and cattle ranches, and in modern times supermarkets throughout northern Arizona and on the Navajo reservation that covers much of northwestern New Mexico and northeastern Arizona.[11]

Although the Babbitts were involved in Indian trading, they did not gain the reputation of John Lorenzo Hubbell, perhaps the best-known Indian trader in the nineteenth-century Southwest. Born in 1853 at Pajarito, New

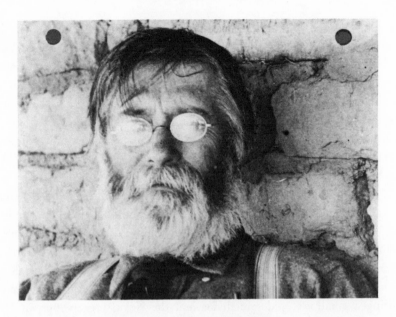

JOHN LORENZO HUBBELL,
the son of a Connecticut Yankee, who became the best-known
Indian trader in the nineteenth-century Southwest.

AN INTERIOR VIEW OF HUBBELL'S RESIDENCE
at the Hubbell Trading Post, Ganado, Arizona, about 1890.

Mexico, Hubbell was the son of a Connecticut Yankee who had gone to New Mexico as a soldier and married into a family of Spanish descent. Young Hubbell attended school in New Mexico, but he learned the life, ways, and language of the Navajo Indians while traveling about the region and working as a clerk and Spanish interpreter at a trading post. In 1876, he began working for William Leonard, an Indian trader who operated a trading post at Ganado, Arizona Territory, about a hundred and fifteen miles northeast of Flagstaff. The trading post was located on the Navajo reservation. About two years later Hubbell bought out the business from Leonard.

Navajo Indians flocked to the trading post, where they called Hubbell "Old Mexican" or "Double Glasses." They relied on Hubbell not only for supplies but for guidance. He became something of a teacher, helping the Indians understand the ways of the white man. He was also a trusted friend, translating and writing letters for the Indians, settling family quarrels, explaining government policy, and even helping them when they became ill. During a smallpox epidemic that swept the Navajo reservation in 1886, Hubbell worked night and day caring for the sick and dying, and used his own home as a hospital. Hubbell was immune to smallpox because he had had the disease as a boy, but the Indians ascribed this immunity to a higher power.

Hubbell built a trading empire that included several trading posts, stage lines, and freight lines to supply the trading posts. He and his two sons, separately or together, owned at various times twenty-four trading posts, a wholesale house in Winslow, Arizona, and other business and ranch properties. And his influence on Navajo silversmithing and rug weaving was unsurpassed. He demanded excellence in craftsmanship and quality. He is recognized today as the foremost Navajo trader. But in Arizona he is also remembered for other things. He was active in politics. His career inspired novels and other literature, including a short story by Hamlin Garland about his service as sheriff of Apache County in the 1880s. He also served in the territorial council, helped to guide Arizona to statehood, and was a state senator. He ran unsuccessfully for the U.S. Senate.

Early in this century, Hubbell described his business philosophy with these words:

> The first job of an Indian trader, in my belief, is to look after the material welfare of his neighbors; to advise them to produce that which their natural inclinations and talent best adapts them; to treat them honestly and insist upon getting the same treatment from them . . . to

find a market for their products and vigilantly watch that they keep
improving in the production of same, and advise them which commands
the best price. This does not mean that the trader should forget that
he is to see that he makes a fair profit for himself, for whatever would
injure him would naturally injure those with whom he comes in contact.[12]

Hubbell's trading post at Ganado was typical of the many Hubbell
posts. The long one-story stone building had a rectangular iron stove in the
center of what was called the "bull pen." During the cold winter months
there was always plenty of pinyon and juniper wood stacked nearby to keep
a fire going. And around the fire the Indians would gather to talk and laugh
and to soak up the warmth. Closer to the stone walls were massive counters
at least eight inches to a foot higher and wider than store counters found
elsewhere in western towns and cities during the nineteenth century. These
counters not only provided surface space for the packaging of merchandise
but served as barriers should any Indians become hostile. Behind the counters
were shelves filled with coffee, flour, sugar, candy, Pendleton blankets,
tobacco, calico, pocketknives, and canned goods. Hardware and harnesses
hung from the ceiling.

Hubbell's trading post at Ganado included a blacksmith shop, a bakery, a farm, and at one point a one-room school staffed by a teacher Hubbell hired. Books and paintings provided the family with its own library
and art gallery, and the opportunity to celebrate birthdays and holidays
was never overlooked. For the Indians, the trading post was a place of
social life as well as business. It was the center for news, gossip, and
endless talk. Trading, like the Indians' lifestyle, was slow and no effort was
made to hurry it.

John Lorenzo Hubbell died on November 12, 1930, and he was buried
on Hubbell Hill, overlooking the trading post, next to his wife, Lina Rubi,
and his closest Navajo friend, Many Horses. When another old Navajo heard
of Hubbell's death, he said:

> *You wear out your shoes, you buy another pair;*
> *When the food is all gone, you buy more;*
> *You gather melons, and more will grow on the vine;*
> *You grind your corn and make bread which you eat;*
> *And next year you have plenty more corn.*
> *But my friend Don Lorenzo is gone, and none to take his place.*

THE HUBBELL TRADING POST ON THE NAVAJO INDIAN RESERVATION.
Hubbell is seated in the center. Photograph by Ben Wittick.

A VIEW OF THE INTERIOR OF THE WAREHOUSE
at the Hubbell Trading Post. Photograph by Ben Wittick.

Hubbell's trading post at Ganado is no longer in operation as such. Today it is a National Historic Site preserved for all to see, a mirror of the past when Indian traders provided an invaluable service while earning a comfortable living.[13]

While many of the successful pioneers in nineteenth-century Arizona and New Mexico were traders or merchants, others found profit in land rather than merchandise. Perhaps best known for this was Lucien Bonaparte Maxwell, a native of Kaskaskia, Illinois. He was of French and Irish ancestry. As a young man Maxwell worked with the American Fur Company. In 1842, while employed by John C. Frémont, Maxwell became friends with Kit Carson, and perhaps at Carson's suggestion, Maxwell settled in Taos, New Mexico. There he married María de la Luz Beaubien in 1844. From his father-in-law, Carlos Beaubien, Maxwell acquired an interest in the huge Beaubien-Miranda land grant east of Taos. After Beaubien's death, Maxwell bought up the rights of other heirs and became sole owner about 1865. The land grant extended from present-day Springer, New Mexico, northward into Colorado and covered ninety-seven thousand acres. Maxwell was the largest individual landowner in the United States.

Cimarron, a small settlement about eighty miles northeast of Santa Fe, became Maxwell's headquarters. There he constructed what became known as Maxwell's House, a building covering about the equivalent of today's city block. It had not only living quarters and an office area but a gambling room, billiard room, and dance hall. Women were not permitted in the public areas, where each evening sums of money changed hands as the gambling ranchers, cowboys, gunmen, and others gathered to play faro, roulette, monte, poker, and dice. Maxwell's soon became the principal stopping place for travelers on the Santa Fe Trail and the starting point for prospectors, hunters, and trappers, as well as the "cowboy capital" of northern New Mexico. Its guests, according to tradition, are said to have included Kit Carson, gunfighter Clay Allison, W. F. "Buffalo Bill" Cody, Tom Boggs, grandson of Daniel Boone, and many other prominent figures in the nineteenth-century American West.

Maxwell was a large and powerful man, an expert horseman who loved gambling, drinking, and furniture. Buying furniture was a hobby. At one point he had five hundred Mexican peons working on the grant and looking after several thousand acres of land under cultivation. Thousands of cattle and sheep grazed on its fertile plains. Maxwell started many small ranchers in the stock business, giving each a herd of cattle, sheep, or horses and a small parcel of land to be run on shares. The agreements were always verbal,

LEFT: LUCIEN BONAPARTE MAXWELL,
a native of Illinois, who acquired a 97,000-acre land grant about 1865, becoming
the largest individual landowner in the United States. Maxwell died in 1875.
RIGHT: John Simpson Chisum, a native of Tennessee, who became known as the
Cattle King of New Mexico. Born in 1824, Chisum died in 1884 in
Eureka Springs, Arkansas.

and sometimes two or three years would pass without a division. When
Maxwell needed stock, hay, or grain to fill a government contract, he would
call in his shareholders, ask for an accounting—always verbal—and direct
them to bring in the surplus to him. According to tradition, this was done
without question.

In 1867, Maxwell entered the mercantile business after gold was discovered in the western part of the land grant. He not only sold goods to gold
seekers but made money through the sale of real estate in the boom mining
camp of Elizabethtown near present-day Eagle Nest, a resort area in northeastern New Mexico. But Maxwell soon found it more and more difficult to
administer his huge empire and decided to offer it for sale. When word of
the offer spread East, four groups of investors—two American and two
European—expressed an interest. In 1870, Maxwell sold his grant for
$1,350,000, but he made poor investments with much of the money and
was forced to return to ranching. He had enough money to purchase old Fort
Sumner and much nearby land. There he lived and ranched until 1875,
when he died at the age of fifty-six.[14]

Maxwell did not live to see the arrival of the railroad in New Mexico. The Southern Pacific did not push eastward into New Mexico until 1880, reaching Deming in December 1880. And it was not until March 8, 1881, that the Santa Fe and the Southern Pacific linked up at Deming, completing the nation's second transcontinental railroad. The railroad brought a new boom with fresh opportunities for profit seekers, some of whom were already in the territories of New Mexico and Arizona.

Until the arrival of the railroad, much of the wealth of both territories had flowed out to pay for merchandise, equipment, and other finished goods. But the railroad changed that. Long-haul wagon freighting was reduced dramatically as the railroad not only delivered goods from the east and west but provided a means of shipping raw materials, including lumber and minerals, to outside markets. While silver and gold were important in both territories, copper became king, especially in Arizona. But because the extracting and smelting of copper ore is profitable only after a considerable investment, copper quickly became a corporate business in Arizona. James Douglas, a Scotch Canadian, had much to do with making copper supreme

LUCIEN B. MAXWELL'S HOME AT CIMARRON, NEW MEXICO,
during the late 1880s. The structure, made of adobe, was partly destroyed
by fire in 1886.

in Arizona. Douglas, a scientist, was sent to Arizona Territory by a New York company of metal dealers called Phelps Dodge. Douglas was to report on a copper claim at Bisbee. He did, and in time he was greatly responsible for developing copper mining and smelting and the industrial organization necessary to make it profitable. For a time copper was the most important mineral in New Mexico, but by the late nineteenth century other minerals, including lead, iron, molybdenum, manganese, and zinc, became more important.

The coming of the railroad to Arizona and New Mexico also set off an explosion in cattle raising. Long trail drives to railheads in Colorado or elsewhere were no longer necessary. Ranchers could drive their cattle to shipping points reasonably close to their ranches, and the cattle could be sped to market by rail. And just as the opening of the northern plains spurred the range cattle industry there beginning about 1880, so did the coming of the railroad in New Mexico and parts of Arizona. Again, the need for eastern capital resulted in the formation of incorporated cattle companies. Between 1880 and 1900 a hundred and eighty-six such corporations were formed in New Mexico with an aggregate capitalization of more than sixty-one million dollars. Slightly more than a hundred of these companies were formed between 1882 and 1886. But as was the case to the north, not many investors made a killing in cattle.

One New Mexico rancher who became wealthy from cattle was John Simpson Chisum, but he did so before the Southern Pacific and Santa Fe linked up in the spring of 1881. Born in Madison County, Tennessee, on August 15, 1824, Chisum moved as a boy with his family to northeastern Texas near present-day Paris during the late 1830s. He grew to manhood and became a farmer and was later elected county clerk, but the inside work apparently was too confining. In 1857, Chisum moved to Denton County, Texas, and established a cattle ranch. He soon gained the reputation of being a shrewd cattle buyer, but when settlers wanting to farm began moving into the county, Chisum felt crowded. It was the same feeling countless other men in the West had felt. Chisum left and moved to southwestern Texas, establishing a ranch on the Concho River, near where San Angelo now stands.

Most of the cattle that Chisum took to the Concho River region belonged to other men. He was handling them on shares for a part of the calf crop. Indians and Mexican bandits caused Chisum much trouble, often stealing or driving off his cattle. In one instance, Mexican bandits came north from below the Rio Grande and drove off a large herd. Chisum gathered his cowboys and gave chase, killing three of the outlaws and recovering the cattle.

When the government brought troublesome Navajos and Apaches to Fort Sumner, New Mexico, it had to feed them and the soldiers guarding them. Chisum and some of his cowboys drove six hundred head of cattle to Fort Sumner and sold them, and Chisum contracted with the government to furnish the military post with ten thousand beef cattle a year to distribute to Indians over a wide area. Most of these cattle were bought cheap in Texas, driven to New Mexico, and sold for a profit. Chisum began to accumulate wealth. He formed a partnership with Charles Goodnight, a pioneer rancher in the Texas panhandle. For two years they were very successful in driving and marketing cattle, and Chisum's profit enabled him to establish a ranch on the Pecos River in New Mexico in the early 1870s. His first ranch headquarters was constructed in a large cottonwood grove thirty miles south of Fort Sumner. It was called Bosque Grande. There was not another ranch in the valley or for a distance of two hundred miles in any direction. The Indians had kept the Mexicans out of the fertile valley lying between Fort Sumner and the western border of Texas. Chisum had seized the opportunity to be close to his market at Fort Sumner and at the same time acquire very desirable cattle range.

With the move to New Mexico, Chisum began to build a huge ranch on the Pecos. His cattle ranged over a million acres, his holdings being more than two hundred miles long and thirty miles wide. He soon became known as the Cattle King of New Mexico. His herd increased to ninety thousand head—some accounts say a hundred thousand—and tradition has it that he could fill an order for fifty thousand beef cattle in ten days. John Chisum eventually became the largest cattle raiser in the United States. He employed at least a hundred cowboys to look after the stock, and the ranch covered an area equal to three or four New England states. It was so large that it extended, according to the Las Vegas *Gazette*, "as far as a man can travel, on a good horse, during a summer."[15] Its size demanded that Chisum establish two outposts, or large cow camps, to provide supplies for his cowboys. One was located on South Springs, where Roswell, New Mexico, stands today, while the other was established at Carlsbad Caverns, about seventy-five miles from the Roswell camp. Like Maxwell's House, Chisum's headquarters ranch house was always open to friends and travelers. His dining table, according to tradition, was ready for unexpected guests at all hours of the day or night, and it could seat forty persons.

By 1873, when the government and the Indians in the region had made peace and the Indians had been moved to reservations, other cattlemen began to eye the rich Pecos Valley where Chisum's cattle grazed on the open range. L. G. Murphy moved his herds into the region, sparking a range war which finally had to be stopped by Governor Lew Wallace of New Mexico, but not before many lives were lost. It was during that war that Billy the Kid killed several people before he was shot down by Sheriff Pat Garrett.

John Chisum disposed of most of his property in 1879 for a third of a million dollars. He died at Eureka Springs, Arkansas, in 1884, leaving an estate of a half million dollars. His Bosque Grande property passed into the hands of George W. and W. P. Littlefield, of Gonzales, Texas.[16]

John Simpson Chisum took advantage of opportunities as he found them, like Lucien Bonaparte Maxwell, John Lorenzo Hubbell, Michel "Big Mike" Goldwater, Solomon Jacob Spiegelberg, and countless others. It is doubtful that they felt like members of an army as each went independently about his own business. But collectively they constituted a silent army of human beings seeking their personal benefit within the free enterprise system, and in turn they laid the foundation for the belief that America is the land of opportunity.

AFTERWORD

You will find him [the American] a close calculator, and yet susceptible to enthusiasm—passionately fond of money, and yet far from being avaricious—nay often very prodigal.

—MICHAEL CHEVALIER[1]

THUS the story of the silent army is the story of individuals from all walks of life. Some were book-educated, but many were not. Some came west with financial wealth to invest, but most did not. Some came west in search of fulfilling their dreams, but others were simply seeking better opportunities. Individually their stories are interesting pages of history, but together they form a mosaic that shows an American West often ignored by historians, writers, and those who portray the West in motion pictures and television programs. Members of the silent army were not seeking a wild and free outdoor life as many early pioneers appear to be doing in romantic historical myths. They were seeking profit, and in so doing were linking the East with the West.

By the time the territories of Arizona and New Mexico joined the Union in 1912, the link was reasonably complete. Communication and transportation problems had been largely eliminated. There was little good land left for homesteaders. Towns were established and businesses, schools, churches, and other eastern institutions were fully entrenched in the West. In short, the West appeared to be conquered and settled, and the glory days of the silent army were fading into memory. But the contributions, and in turn the beliefs and values, forged by three generations of that army were still very much in evidence, not only in the West but in the character of Americans everywhere.

The Santa Fe merchants, mountain men, and fur traders who first headed west early in the nineteenth century formed the unwitting vanguard of the wagon freighters, homesteaders, cattlemen, stageline operators, town builders, land speculators, merchants, railroad men, and other entrepreneurs who arrived later. The dreams and aspirations of this vanguard were probably similar to those of people elsewhere in the world, but as they crossed the unsettled prairies and plains a unique spirit that was less trammeled by tradition began to emerge. It was rooted in the American Revolution, when our nation was born. Our Constitution, ratified by thirteen states in 1787, recognizes the *people* as the ultimate source of power. And the first ten amendments to that Constitution—the Bill of Rights—emphasized the "natural rights of man."

The Constitution and the Bill of Rights gave citizens not only faith in democratic institutions but faith in the individual's right to advance and make progress. And Americans believed, moreover, that the progress of the nation as a whole depended not on government but upon the individual. This belief was quite different from that of people in other countries. Faith in progress became the basic creed of most American pioneers who cherished their freedom of self-advancement.

As the second wave of the silent army began moving west and crossed the unsettled regions, respect for the individual was intensified, in part because people had to rely on one another—people from other walks of life, people from different ethnic and cultural backgrounds. The motif of equality was accentuated, especially in the face of the many obstacles and hardships of pioneer life. These qualities of independence, self-reliance, and a sense of equality came to characterize "Westerners," who were considered, and considered themselves, something of a new breed.

In the new world, physical wants had to be taken care of before the intellectual. John L. McConnel observed this in 1835, when his book *Western Characters or Types of Border Life in the Western States* was published in New York City. McConnel wrote: "Men appreciate the necessity of covering their backs and lining their stomachs before storing their minds."[2] The old letters, diaries, narratives, recollections, and other forms of documentation leave no doubt about this, but it caused people to measure accomplishment by material standards. As areas of the West were settled, a person would think of a neighbor in terms of how much he was worth in dollars, and in the growing towns the homes and buildings were judged by their size and cost rather than beauty. The belief that physical well-being and worldly possessions constitute the greatest good and highest value in life became firmly entrenched in the minds of the silent army.

Daniel Webster wrote early in the nineteenth century of the "growing propensity" of Americans to seek wealth even as they were pushing westward.

And it was Washington Irving who coined the term "Almighty Dollar" in 1837, in his book *The Adventures of Captain Bonneville*, which told of fur traders in the West and their search for beaver pelts and wealth. Charles Dickens borrowed the term and used it with some frequency in his writings during the early 1840s to denote the American obsession with wealth. And even later, in 1889, Rudyard Kipling visited the American West and observed that "the first thing I have been taught to believe is that money was everything in America."[3]

Most members of the silent army believed that they could accumulate wealth through hard work. This passion for work eventually created intense competition, which served as a further stimulus for their money-making efforts, and leisure became a luxury as spare time was sacrificed to this pursuit. As they accumulated money, they began acquiring the cultural amenities that were believed to be the key to elevated social status. The immediate result, however, was the creation of a way of thinking that stressed the importance of individual success through individual initiative and enterprise.

The heritage of the silent army appears today in the American notion that wealth and material possessions are essential for happiness, in the intense competition of Americans in business and other endeavors, in the mobility of Americans forever seeking better opportunities elsewhere, and in the conviction that money is indispensable to the enjoyment of the comforts of culture and, in turn, elevated social status. All of these combined have created what we call the free enterprise system, the system we have generally held to be the surest route to achieving the American dream of wealth, success, and happiness. The dream still exists, but the optimism that happiness can be attained by material success is not as strong as it once was.

NOTES

Chapter I: To Where There Was Little Water

1. Ralph Waldo Emerson, *Nature: Addresses and Lectures* (Boston and New York: Houghton Mifflin Company, 1903), p. 378. The quote is from "The Young American," an essay read before the Mercantile Library Association, Boston, Feb. 7, 1844.

2. Seymour Dunbar, *A History of Travel in America* (Indianapolis: Bobbs-Merrill Co., 1915), Vol. I, pp. 268–287. See also Archer Butler Hulbert, *Waterways of Westward Expansion: The Ohio River and Its Tributaries* (Cleveland: Arthur H. Clark Co., 1903), pp. 100–135. Vol. IX in the publisher's "Historic Highways of America" series.

3. Isaac Lippincott, *Economic Development of the United States* (New York and London: D. Appleton and Co., 1927), pp. 141–142. Although the Articles of Confederation adopted the Spanish dollar as the basic monetary unit of the United States, the right of coinage was retained by the states. Until 1792 the money medium in the United States contained a great variety of foreign coins, including those of English, French, and Spanish mintage. There was no uniform standard of value for the nation; different values were given to similar coins in different parts of the country. In 1792, however, Congress passed the Mint Act, which established a bimetallic currency based on gold and silver. The gold dollar was fixed at 24.7 grains of gold and the silver dollar contained 371.21 grains of silver. The ratio was approximately fifteen to one and corresponded to the market value of the two metals at the time. By 1799, however, the value of silver had declined relative to gold, and the market rate was almost sixteen to one. This made the sale of gold as a metal more profitable than coinage, and gold coins practically disappeared from circulation.

4. Hulbert, *Waterways of Westward Expansion*, pp. 107–108, 133.

5. The term "bushwhacking," originated by boatmen on the Ohio River, also came to mean "ambushing." The term "bushwhacker" was used in Missouri during the nineteenth century to denote someone who made a surprise attack from a concealed position, usually behind a tree or large bush.

6. Emory R. Johnson et al., *History of Domestic and Foreign Commerce of the United States* (Washington, D.C.: Carnegie Institution, 1915), Vol. I, pp. 206–208. See also Howard R. Lamar, *The Reader's Encyclopedia of the American West* (New York: Thomas Y. Crowell Co., 1977), pp. 1194–1195.

7. Duane Meyer, *The Heritage of Missouri—A History* (St. Louis: State Publishing Co., 1965), p. 103. See also John Bakeless, *Daniel Boone: Master of the Wilderness* (New York: W. Morrow & Co., 1939), one of the better biographies of Boone.

8. Albert Watkins, ed., *Publications of the Nebraska State Historical Society*, Vol. XX (Lincoln: Nebraska State Historical Society, 1922), pp. 19, 22.

9. *Ibid.*, pp. 20–22.

10. Donald Jackson, ed., *The Journals*

of Zebulon Montgomery Pike (Norman: University of Oklahoma Press, 1966), Vol. II, pp. 27–28.

11. Edwin James, *Account of an Expedition from Pittsburgh to the Rocky Mountains* . . . (Cleveland: Arthur H. Clark Co., 1905), p. 183. Vol. XV in the publisher's "Early Western Travels" series.

12. Walter Prescott Webb, *The Great Plains* (Boston: Ginn and Co., 1931), pp. 507–508.

13. Louise Barry, compiler, *The Beginning of the West: Annals of the Kansas Gateway to the American West, 1540–1854* (Topeka: Kansas State Historical Society, 1972), pp. 21, 22. See also Herbert Eugene Bolton, *Texas in the Middle Eighteenth Century* (Berkeley: University of California Press, 1915), pp. 66–68. Vol. III of the university's "Publications in History" series.

14. Bolton, *Texas in the Middle Eighteenth Century*, pp. 66–68.

15. *Ibid.*, pp. 126–133, citing Vial's diary as a source.

16. Jackson, ed., *The Journals of Zebulon Montgomery Pike*, Vol. II, pp. 133–136.

17. See a biographical sketch of Clamorgan in LeRoy R. Hafen, ed., *The Mountain Men and the Fur Trade of the Far West* (Glendale: Arthur H. Clark Co., 1965), Vol. II, pp. 81–94.

18. Jackson, ed., *The Journals of Zebulon Montgomery Pike*, Vol. II, pp. 50–51.

19. F. A. Sampson, ed., "The Journals of Capt. Thomas [sic] Becknell From Boone's Lick to Santa Fe, and From Santa Cruz to Green River," *Missouri Historical Review*, Vol. IV (1910), pp. 65–84. The article contains William Becknell's accounts as published in the *Missouri Intelligencer* at Franklin, Mo.

20. *Ibid.*, pp. 78–80.

21. Cleve Hallenbeck and Juanita H. Williams, *Legends of the Spanish Southwest* (Glendale: Arthur H. Clark Co., 1938), pp. 315–316.

Chapter II: Over the Road to Santa Fe

1. Jack D. Rittenhouse, *The Santa Fe Trail: A Historical Bibliography* (Albuquerque: University of New Mexico Press, 1971), p. 4.

2. Elliott Coues, ed., *The Journal of Jacob Fowler* (New York, 1898), p. 167.

3. Sampson, ed., "The Journals of Capt. Thomas [sic] Becknell From Boone's Lick to Santa Fe, and From Santa Cruz to Green River," pp. 80–81.

4. *Missouri Intelligencer*, June 25, 1821, as quoted in full by F. F. Stephens, "Missouri and the Santa Fe Trade," *Missouri Historical Review*, Vol. XI (1910), pp. 292–293.

5. Larry M. Beachum, *William Becknell: Father of the Santa Fe Trade* (El Paso: Texas Western Press, 1982), pp. 54–70. Beachum provides the most complete biography of Becknell yet written.

6. Josiah Gregg, *Commerce of the Prairies* (New York: Henry G. Langley, 1844), Vol. I, p. 22.

7. F. A. Sampson, ed., "M. M. Marmaduke Journal," *Missouri Historical Review*, Vol. VI (1911), p. 3.

8. *Ibid.*, pp. 3–8.

9. J. Evarts Greene, *The Santa Fe Trade: Its Route and Character* (St. Louis: North Point, 1970), pp. 16–17. A reprint of Greene's report to the American Antiquarian Society meeting, April 26, 1893, in Boston.

10. *Ibid.*, p. 17.

11. *Missouri Intelligencer*, April 22, 1823.

12. Barry, compiler, *The Beginning of the West*, pp. 122–123. See also Dunbar, *A History of Travel in America*, Vol. II, pp. 444–445.

13. St. Louis *Beacon*, July 4, 1829.

14. Jonas Viles, "Old Franklin: A Frontier Town of the Twenties," *Mississippi Valley Historical Review*, Vol. IX 1923), pp. 269–282. See also Lewis E. Atherton, "Business Techniques in the Santa Fe Trade," *Missouri Historical Review*, Vol. XXXIV (1940), p. 339.

15. Hattie M. Anderson, "Frontier Economic Problems in Missouri," *Missouri Historical Review*, Vol. XXXIV (1940), p. 184.

16. Lewis E. Atherton, "James and Robert Aull—a Frontier Missouri Mercantile Firm," *Missouri Historical Review*, Vol. XXX (1935), pp. 3–27.

17. Gregg, *Commerce of the Prairies*, Vol. II, p. 161. See also Max L. Moorhead, *New Mexico's Royal Road* (Norman: University of Oklahoma Press, 1958), pp. 80–81.

18. Greene, *The Santa Fe Trade*, p. 17.

19. Gregg, *Commerce of the Prairies*, Vol. II, pp. 165–166.

20. The story of Milton Bryan's adventures on the road to Santa Fe is told in detail in my *True Tales of the Old-Time Plains* (New York: Crown, 1979), pp. 2–10. The island where the specie was buried was known as Chouteau's Island in 1828. Bryan and the other traders apparently did not know it had been the site of a battle between Auguste P. Chouteau and perhaps twenty other trappers and two hundred Indians several years earlier. Chouteau and the trappers successfully fought off the Indians. Bryan's account says he and the other traders buried about ten thousand dollars in silver specie on the island. Apparently all of it was recovered in 1829.

21. Barry, compiler, *The Beginning of the West*, pp. 157–165.

22. John Ashton, "History of Jack Stock and Mules in Missouri," *Monthly Bulletin*, Missouri State Board of Agriculture, Vol. XXII (August 1940). See also David P. Willoughby, *The Empire of Equus: The Horse, Past, Present and Future* (South Brunswick and New York: A. S. Barnes and Co., 1974), pp. 390–395.

23. George Shumway and Howard C. Frey, *Conestoga Wagon 1750–1850* (York, Pa.: George Shumway, Publisher, 1964), pp. 14–22. See also Jerome H. Wood, Jr., *Conestoga Crossroads, Lancaster, Pennsylvania, 1730–1790* (Harrisburg: Pennsylvania Historical and Museum Commission, 1979), p. 109.

24. Emily A. O. Bott, "Joseph Murphy's Contributions to the Developments of the West," *Missouri Historical Review*, Vol. XLVII (1952), pp. 22–23.

Chapter III: Along the Upper Missouri and Beyond

1. Unless otherwise cited, the sources consulted for this chapter were Hiram Martin Chittenden's two-volume classic, *The American Fur Trade of the Far West* (New York: Barnes & Noble, 1935), first published at New York City in 1902 and reprinted in 1954; the ten-volume *The Mountain Men and the Fur Trade of the Far West*, edited by LeRoy R. Hafen, perhaps the most comprehensive work to date on the participants of the fur trade; Richard M. Clokey's *William H. Ashley: Enterprise and Politics in the Trans-Mississippi West* (Norman: University of Oklahoma Press, 1980); C. P. Russell's *Firearms, Traps and Tools of the Mountain Men* (New York: Alfred A. Knopf, 1967); Paul Chrisler Phillips's *The Fur Trade* (Norman: University of Oklahoma Press, 1961), a comprehensive two-volume work; and the files of the *Missouri Gazette*, a newspaper that continued publication from 1808 to 1861 under various names, including the *Louisiana Gazette, Missouri Gazette and Illinois Advertiser, Missouri Gazette and Public Advertiser*, and *Missouri Republican*. These newspaper files, preserved by the State Historical Society of Missouri at Columbia, provide excellent contemporary accounts of the fur trade.

2. Chittenden, *The American Fur Trade of the Far West*, Vol. I, pp. ix–x.

3. For the complete history of the "factory system," see Ora Brooks Peake, *A History of the United States Indian Factory System, 1795–1822* (Denver: Sage Books, 1954).

4. Frances F. Victor, ed., *The River of the West* (Hartford: Bliss and Co., 1870), pp. 64–65. Additional material on beaver traps may be found in A. W. Schorger's "A Brief History of the Steel Trap and Its Use

in North America," *Transactions of the Wisconsin Academy of Sciences, Arts, and Letters*, Vol. XL (1951), pp. 171–179.

5. C. E. Hanson, Jr., "Castoreum," *Museum of the Fur Trade Quarterly*, Vol. VIII (1972), pp. 1–4.

6. Much of the background on Manuel Lisa was found in Richard E. Oglesby's fine biography, *Manuel Lisa and the Opening of the Missouri Fur Trade* (Norman: University of Oklahoma Press, 1963), and in Oglesby's biographical sketch of Lisa's life in Hafen, ed., *The Mountain Men and the Fur Trade of the Far West*, Vol. V (1968), pp. 179–201.

7. Gilbert C. Fite and Jim E. Reese, *An Economic History of the United States* (Boston: Houghton Mifflin Company, 1959), pp. 120–137. See also Bray Hammond, *Banks and Politics in America from the Revolution to the Civil War* (Princeton: Princeton University Press, 1957), pp. 114–285.

8. Lippincott, *Economic Development of the United States*, pp. 235–237.

9. *Missouri Gazette and Public Advertiser* (St. Louis), Feb. 13, 1822.

10. No book-length biography of Andrew Henry is known to have been published. Perhaps the most complete biographical sketch of his life was written by Louis J. Clements of Rexburg, Idaho, a Henry scholar. The sketch appears in Hafen, ed., *The Mountain Men and the Fur Trade of the Far West*, Vol. VI (1968), pp. 173–184. Additional bits and pieces were found in Clokey's *William H. Ashley*; Dale L. Morgan's *The West of William H. Ashley* (Denver: Old West Publishing Co., 1964); Donald M. Frost's *Notes on General Ashley: The Overland Trail, and South Pass* (Barre, Mass.: Barre Gazette, 1960); and Ashley's "Diary . . . March 25–June 27, 1825," *Missouri Historical Society Bulletin*, Vol. XI (1954–1955).

11. Morgan, *The West of William Ashley*, pp. 118–119.

12. Potts's letter 1826, cited by Gerald C. Bagley in "Daniel T. Potts," in Hafen, ed., *The Mountain Men and the Fur Trade of the Far West*, Vol. II (1966), p. 257.

13. *Missouri Herald and St. Louis Advertiser*, Nov. 8, 1826. Keemle, a native of Philadelphia, moved to St. Louis in 1817 and worked as a newspaperman. He joined the Missouri Fur Company as a clerk in the fall of 1820 and spent much time with company expeditions on the upper Missouri. In 1825, he returned to newspaper work in St. Louis.

14. Victor, ed. *The River of the West*, p. 264.

15. *Ibid.*, pp. 110–112.

16. Several accounts of the battle of Pierre's Hole are reproduced in Appendix A of Fred R. Gowan's fine book *Rocky Mountain Rendezvous* (Provo: Brigham Young University Press, 1975).

17. Victor, ed., *The River of the West*, pp. 264–265.

18. Richard J. Fehrman, "The Mountain Men—A Statistical View," in Hafen, ed., *The Mountain Men and the Fur Trade of the Far West*, Vol. X (1972), pp. 9–15.

Chapter IV: Traders and Indians

1. Howard R. Lamar, *The Trader on the American Frontier: Myth's Victim* (College Station, Tex., and London: Texas A. & M. University Press, 1977), p. 39.

2. Letter from Pratte, Chouteau and Company to Ramsey Crooks, March 28, 1835, in *American Fur Company Letterbooks*, New-York Historical Society, New York City. See also J. E. Sunday, *The Fur Trade on the Upper Missouri, 1840–65* (Norman: University of Oklahoma Press, 1968), p. 117.

3. Chittenden, *The American Fur Trade of the Far West*, Vol. I, pp. 337–338; Vol. II, p. 933.

4. *Ibid.*, Vol. I, p. 338.

5. *Ibid.*, Vol. I, p. 340.

6. *Ibid.*, Vol. II, pp. 933–934.

7. George Catlin, *Letters and Notes on the Manners, Customs, and Condition of the North American Indians* (London, 1842), Vol. II, p. 34.

8. John C. Frémont, *The Exploring Expedition of the Rocky Mountains, Oregon and*

California (Buffalo: Geo. H. Derby and Co., 1850), p. 189.

9. Rev. Joab Spencer, "The Kaw or Kansas Indians: Their Customs, Manners, and Folk-lore," *Kansas State Historical Society Collections*, Vol. X (Topeka: State Printing Office, 1908), pp. 379–380.

10. John E. Sunder, *The Fur Trade on the Upper Missouri, 1840–1865* (Norman: University of Oklahoma Press, 1965), pp. 37–82.

11. David Lavender tells this story in his fine book *Bent's Fort* (Garden City, N.Y.: Doubleday & Co., 1954), pp. 120–122. Samuel P. Arnold repeats it in "William W. Bent," a biographical sketch in Hafen, ed., *The Mountain Men and the Fur Trade of the Far West*, Vol. VI (1968), pp. 66–67.

12. George Bird Grinnell, "Bent's Old Fort and Its Builders," *Kansas State Historical Society Collections*, Vol. XV (Topeka: State Printing Plant, 1923), pp. 38–42.

13. Lavender, *Bent's Fort*, p. 181. For a more detailed description of the inventory at Fort Jackson, see Philip W. Whiteley's article "Trade Beads Among the American Indians," in *Original Contributions to Western History, Brand Book VII*, edited by Nolie Mumey (Denver: The Westerners, 1952), pp. 284–285.

14. Grinnell, "Bent's Old Fort and Its Builders," pp. 51–55.

15. *Ibid.*, pp. 54–56.

16. Frederick Merk, *History of the Westward Movement* (New York: Alfred A. Knopf, 1980), p. 263. For a scholarly discussion of manifest destiny, see Norman A. Graebner's *Empire on the Pacific: A Study in American Continental Expansion* (1955) and *Manifest Destiny* (1968); Frederick Merk's *Manifest Destiny and Mission in American History* (1963); and Albert K. Weinberg's *Manifest Destiny: A Study of Nationalist Expansionism in American History* (1935). The phrase "manifest destiny" was first used by the Irish-American newspaper editor John L. O'Sullivan in July 1845 with regard to the crisis caused by the proposed annexation of Texas. It immediately gained wide popularity.

17. Frederick Jackson Turner, *The Frontier in American History* (New York: Henry Holt and Co., 1948), p. 37.

Chapter V: When the Emigrants Started West

1. Ray Allen Billington, *Westward Expansion: A History of the American Frontier* (New York: Macmillan Co., 1967), p. 9.

2. *The Christian Advocate and Journal* (New York), March 1, 1833. Bernard De Voto, in his classic *Across the Wide Missouri* (Boston: Houghton Mifflin Company, 1947), suggests that someone invented the oration, perhaps an editor with the Methodist publication (pp. 6–10).

3. Grenville M. Dodge, "Biographical Sketch of James Bridger," reprinted as appendix in J. Cecil Alter's *James Bridger: Trapper, Frontiersman, Scout and Guide* (Salt Lake City, 1925), p. 513.

4. Gregory M. Franzwa, *Maps of the Oregon Trail* (Gerald, Mo.: Patrice Press, 1982), is an invaluable reference work containing 133 full-page maps of the areas through which the old trail passed.

5. Dodge, "Biographical Sketch of James Bridger," pp. 512–513. Dodge does not cite his source for the letter.

6. John D. Unruh, Jr., in his definitive *The Plains Across: The Overland Emigrants and the Trans-Mississippi West, 1840–60* (Urbana: University of Illinois Press, 1979), p. 119, provides the following total numbers of emigrants who traveled to Oregon and California: 1843: 1,109; 1844: 2,637; 1845: 5,397; and 1846: 8,097. Many of these emigrants probably stopped at Fort Bridger.

7. Joel Palmer, *Journal of Travels over the Rocky Mountains, to the Mouth of the Columbia River; Made During the Years 1845 and 1846 . . .* (Cincinnati: J. A. and U. P. James, 1850), p. 35. Palmer's journal was first published in 1847.

8. Lansford W. Hastings and Fort Bridger are closely linked to the Donner party tragedy in 1846. Hastings's guidebook was used by the party, and Hastings reportedly prom-

ised to lead the party to California over the Hastings Cutoff from Fort Bridger. Hastings, however, was not at Fort Bridger when the party arrived. His agent informed the party that Hastings had gone ahead as pilot of a large emigrant train. Hastings supposedly left instructions for all later arrivals to follow his trail. The Donner party did just that. Unfortunately, the party took a full month to go from Fort Bridger to Salt Lake Valley. They were eventually marooned by an early snowstorm in the high Sierras. Forty-five of the eighty-one members in the party survived only by eating the bodies of those who did not.

9. William G. Johnston, *Experiences of a Forty-Niner* (New York: Coward-McCann, 1931), June 10 entry. A later reprint of Johnston's journal first published in 1892.

10. *Ibid.*, June 17 entry.

11. Fred R. Gowans and Eugene E. Campbell, *Fort Bridger: Island in the Wilderness* (Provo: Brigham Young University Press, 1975).

12. Merrill J. Mattes, *The Great Platte River Road* (Lincoln: Nebraska State Historical Society, 1969), pp. 438–447. The author provides what is undoubtedly the most complete sketch of Joseph E. Robidoux's trading post yet researched and written.

13. Palmer, *Journal of Travels over the Rocky Mountains*, p. 42. See also Aubrey L. Haines, *Historic Sites Along the Oregon Trail* (Gerald, Mo.: Patrice Press, 1981), pp. 293–305.

14. Frémont, *The Exploring Expedition of the Rocky Mountains, Oregon and California*, pp. 233–234.

15. Osborne Russell, *Journal of a Trapper* (Boise, Idaho: Syms-York Co., 1914), p. 63.

16. Wilbur R. Jacobs, ed. *Letters of Francis Parkman* (Norman: University of Oklahoma Press, 1960), Vol. I, p. 44.

17. Mason Wade, ed., *The Journals of Francis Parkman* (New York and London: Harper & Brothers, 1947), p. 440.

18. *Ibid.*, pp. 617–618.

19. June 23 and July 17, 1846, entries

in Edwin Bryant's *What I Saw in California* (1849), pp. 107, 143, as cited by Unruh, *The Plains Across*, p. 252.

20. Kimball Webster, *The Gold Seekers of '49: A Personal Narrative of Overland Trail and Adventures in California and Oregon from 1849 to 1854* . . . (Manchester, N.H.: Standard Book Co., 1917), pp. 34–35.

21. St. Joseph (Missouri) *Gazette*, May 19, 1847.

22. *Ibid.*, Dec. 25, 1846; Dec. 8, 1848; March 2, 1853. There are other references to Corby in the files of the newspaper.

23. Palmer, *Journal of Travels over the Rocky Mountains*, p. 144. Material on Isaac Miller may be found in Thomas W. Carneal, "Trade in Northwest Missouri, 1843–1873," *The Trail Guide* (Kansas City, Mo.: Kansas City Posse, The Westerners, March 1972), pp. 5–6.

24. Kanesville's *Frontier Guardian* newspaper provides much detail on the town's emigrant and forty-niner trade, especially in the May–June issues of 1849, 1850, and 1851. See also D. C. Bloomer's "Notes on the History of Pottawatomie County," *Annals of Iowa*, 1st Series, Vol. IX (1871), pp. 526–527, 666–683; and Watkins, ed. *Publications of the Nebraska State Historical Society*, Vol. XX, pp. 218–220.

25. Frederick H. Piercy, *Route from Liverpool to Great Salt Lake Valley* . . . (Liverpool: published by Franklin D. Richards, 1855), pp. 75–76.

26. C. C. Spalding, *Annals of the City of Kansas: Embracing Full Details of the Trade and Commerce of the Great Western Plains* . . . (Kansas City, Mo.: Frank Glenn Publishing Co., 1950), pp. 19–20. This is a facsimile reprint of the original 1858 edition published in Kansas City by Van Horn and Abeel's Printing House.

Chapter VI: Along the Pacific Slope

1. Reuben L. Underhill, *From Cowhides to Golden Fleece* (Stanford: Stanford University Press, 1939), p. 2.

2. John S. McGroarty, *California: Its*

History and Romance (Los Angeles: Grafton Publishing Co., 1911), pp. 163–164.

3. Richard H. Dana, *Two Years Before the Mast* (New York: P. F. Collier & Son, 1909), pp. 81–82.

4. Howard R. Lamar, "Persistent Frontier: The West in the 20th Century," *Western Historical Quarterly*, January 1973, p. 16.

5. Underhill, *From Cowhides to Golden Fleece*, pp. 19–28.

6. William Heath Davis, *Seventy-five Years in California* (San Francisco: John Howell Books, 1967), p. 190. A reprint of the 1889 first edition.

7. David Dary, *Cowboy Culture* (New York: Alfred A. Knopf, 1981), pp. 44–66.

8. Josiah Belden, *Josiah Belden, 1841 California Overland Pioneer: His Memoir and Early Letters* (Georgetown, Calif.: Talisman Press, 1962), pp. 76–78. Edited by Doyce B. Nunis, Jr.

9. Davis, *Seventy-five Years in California*, p. 239.

10. Samuel Bowles, *Across the Continent: A Summer's Journey to the Rocky Mountains, the Mormons, and the Pacific States* (Springfield, Mass.: Samuel Bowles & Co., 1865), pp. 294–295.

11. *Ibid.*, pp. 292–293.

12. W. H. Hutchinson, "California's Economic Imperialism," in John Alexander Carroll, ed., *Reflections of Western Historians* (Tucson: University of Arizona Press, 1969), p. 80.

13. *Ibid.*

Chapter VII:
Military Posts and Freighters

1. John J. and Barbara Gregg, *Best Loved Poems of the American West* (Garden City, N.Y.: Doubleday & Co., 1980), p. 43.

2. New York *Tribune*, Dec. 4, 1847, quoting the St. Louis *Era*.

3. Henry Pickering Walker, *The Wagonmasters: High Plains Freighting from the Earliest Days of the Santa Fe Trail to 1880* (Norman: University of Oklahoma Press, 1966), pp. 230–231.

4. 31st Cong., 1st Sess., Sen. Ex. Doc. No. 26 (Serial 554), p. 22.

5. *Ibid.*, p. 24.

6. *Weekly Tribune* (Liberty, Mo.), Oct. 5, 1849, and New York *Weekly Tribune*, Oct. 6, 13, 1849, as cited by Barry, compiler, *The Beginning of the West*, p. 889.

7. St. Louis *Reveille*, Jan. 26, 1850, as cited by Barry, compiler, *The Beginning of the West*, p. 890.

8. Barry, compiler, *The Beginning of the West*, p. 965.

9. Records of Army freighting contracts cited may be found in the following government documents: 31st Cong., 1st Sess., Sen. Ex. Doc. No. 26 (Serial 554), pp. 12, 19, 24; 31st Cong., 2d Sess., House Ex. Doc. No. 23 (serial 599), pp. 15, 17, 18, 22; 32d Cong., 1st Sess., Sen. Ex. Doc. No. 12 (Serial 614), pp. 20, 22, 23; 32d Cong., 1st Sess., Sen. Ex. Doc. No. 1 (Serial 611), p. 295; 32d Cong., 2d Sess., Sen. Ex. Doc. No. 18 (serial 660), pp. 4, 7.

10. 32d Cong., 1st Sess., Sen. Ex. Doc. (Serial 611), p. 295.

11. Alexander Majors, *Seventy Years on the Frontier* (Columbus, Ohio: Long's College Book Co., 1950), p. 140. This is a reprint of the 1893 first edition.

12. Dary, *Cowboy Culture*, pp. 117–118.

13. Majors, *Seventy Years on the Frontier*, p. 72.

14. 32d Cong., 1st Sess., Sen. Ex. Doc. (Serial 611), p. 252.

15. Walker D. Wyman, "The Military Phase of Santa Fe Freighting, 1846–1865," *Kansas State Historical Quarterly*, Vol. I (Topeka: Kansas State Historical Society, 1931–1932), pp. 425–426.

16. Until 1858 the firm of Russell and Majors is listed on quartermaster contracts. William B. Waddell, however, was a partner in the firm and is identified as such in the firm's title used in the text. Beginning in 1858, Waddell's name appears with Russell and Majors on government contracts. Perhaps the most comprehensive history of Russell, Majors and Waddell is Raymond W. and Mary Lund Settle's fine work titled *War*

Drums and Wagon Wheels (Lincoln: University of Nebraska Press, 1966).

17. A. G. Hawes, *A Historical Sketch and Review of the Business of the City of Leavenworth, Kansas Territory* . . . (Leavenworth City: Journal Book and Job Office, 1857). This work contains good information on the freighting firm, as do contemporary issues of the Leavenworth *Times, Herald of Freedom* (Lawrence, K.T.), and the *Journal of Commerce* (Kansas City, Mo.).

18. Majors, *Seventy Years on the Frontier*, p. 141.

19. *Ibid.*

20. Percival G. Lowe, *Five Years a Dragoon ('49 to '54) and Other Adventures on the Great Plains* (Kansas City, Mo.: Franklin Hudson Publishing Co., 1906), pp. 187–201. Lowe was at Fort Riley when cholera struck. His narrative is most interesting.

21. Settle and Settle, *War Drums and Wagon Wheels*, p. 50.

22. Many works contain reliable information on the Mormon War. One of the better works is Norman F. Furniss, *The Mormon Conflict, 1850–1859* (New Haven: Yale University Press, 1960). Orson F. Whitney's four-volume *History of Utah* (Salt Lake City: George Q. Cannon and Sons, 1892) also contains some good information.

23. Majors, *Seventy Years on the Frontier*, p. 142.

24. Settle and Settle, *War Drums and Wagon Wheels*, pp. 85–86.

25. *Nebraska News* (Nebraska City, N.T.), March 22, 1858.

Chapter VIII: Rush to the Rockies

1. Samuel Johnson, *Irene*, Act I, scene 1, as cited by George Seldes, compiler, *The Great Quotations* (New York: Pocket Books, 1967), p. 431.

2. LeRoy R. Hafen, ed., *Pike's Peak Gold Rush Guidebooks of 1859* (Glendale: Arthur H. Clark Co., 1941), p. 21–46.

3. Perhaps the best account of William G. Russell's gold party may be found in Luke Tierney's *History of the Gold Discoveries on the South Platte River* . . . (Pacific City, Iowa: Herald Office, 1859), pp. 5–12. Tierney was one of twelve men with Russell who found gold near present-day Englewood, Colorado, in early July 1858. Tierney lists the party members as W. G. Russell, J. O. Russell, L. J. Russell, J. H. Pierce, R. J. Pierce, Samuel Bates, Solomon Roe, all from Georgia; V. W. Young, of Iowa; Theodore Herring, of Manhattan, Kansas Territory; William A. McFadding, of North Carolina; William W. Remnins, of Pennsylvania; and J. T. Masterson and Luke Tierney, of the vicinity of Leavenworth, Kansas Territory. Tierney's work was reprinted by Nolie Mumey at Denver, Colorado, in 1949. Perhaps the best material on Fall Leaf is contained in an account of the Lecompton party's expedition as told by Ely Moore, a participant, in *Transactions of the Kansas State Historical Society, 1901–1902*, Vol. VII (Topeka: W. Y. Morgan, State Printer, 1902), pp. 446–451. The article also includes material on the Lawrence and Russell parties. See also Hafen, ed., *Pike's Peak Gold Rush Guidebooks of 1859*, pp. 21–80.

4. Leavenworth (K.T.) *Weekly Journal*, Sept. 14, 1858.

5. *Freedom's Champion* (Atchison, K.T.), Feb. 19, 1859.

6. *Journal of Commerce* (Kansas City, Mo.), Aug. 26, 1858.

7. *Ibid.*, Feb. 20, 1859.

8. *Ibid.*, Jan. 21, 1859, quoting the Palmero (K.T.) *Leader*.

9. Wyoming (K.T.) *Telescope*, April 9, 1859, quoting a letter mailed at St. Joseph, Mo., March 12, 1859.

10. *Nebraska Advertiser* (Brownville, N.T.), March 31, 1859.

11. A. T. Andreas, *History of the State of Nebraska* (Chicago: Western Historical Co., 1882), Vol. I, p. 700.

12. Richard Dunlop, *Wheels West, 1590–1900* (Chicago: Rand McNally, 1977), pp. 103–135. See also Wilbur Hoffman, *Saga of Old Western Travel & Transport* (San Diego: Howell-North Books, 1980), pp. 81–87, 99–102.

13. Settle and Settle, *War Drums and Wagon Wheels*, p. 97.

14. George A. Root and Russell K. Hickman, "Pike's Peak Express Companies," *Kansas Historical Quarterly*, Vol. XIII (Topeka: Kansas State Historical Society, 1945), pp. 167–174.

15. Albert D. Richardson, *Beyond the Mississippi: From the Great River to the Great Ocean . . .* (Hartford: American Publishing Co., 1867), p. 159.

16. Horace Greeley, *An Overland Journey, From New York to San Francisco, in the Summer of 1859* (New York: C. M. Saxton, Barker & Co., 1860), pp. 78–79.

17. Richardson, *Beyond the Mississippi*, p. 159.

18. Libeus Barney, *Letters of the Pike's Peak Gold Rush . . . Early-Day Letters by Libeus Barney, Reprinted from the Bennington Banner, Vermont, 1859–1860* (San Jose, Calif.: Talisman Press, 1959), p. 40.

19. Gerry's Account Book 4, State Historical Society of Colorado, Denver. For a biographical sketch of John Smith, see Ann W. Hafen's "John Simpson Smith," in Hafen, ed., *The Mountain Men and the Fur Trade of the Far West*, Vol. V (1968), pp. 325–345. For a biographical sketch of Elbridge Gerry, see Ann W. Hafen's "Elbridge Gerry," in Hafen, ed., *The Mountain Men and the Fur Trade of the Far West*, Vol. VI (1968), pp. 153–160.

20. Walker, *The Wagonmasters*, p. 180.

21. *Ibid.*, p. 181, citing LeRoy R. Hafen's *Colorado Gold Rush: Contemporary Letters and Reports, 1858–1859* (Glendale: Arthur H. Clark Co., 1941), p. 35.

22. Barney, *Letters of the Pike's Peak Gold Rush*, p. 41.

23. Settle and Settle, *War Drums and Wagon Wheels*, p. 100.

24. *Missouri Republican* (St. Louis), Aug. 31, 1859.

25. Frank A. Root and William Elsey Connelley, *The Overland Stage to California* (Topeka: published by the authors, 1901), p. 303.

26. *Ibid.*, pp. 303–304.

27. Settle and Settle, *War Drums and Wagon Wheels*, pp. 111–114.

Chapter IX: The Civil War

1. Introduction by Allan Nevins to Paul W. Gates, *Agriculture and the Civil War* (New York: Alfred A. Knopf, 1965), p. v.

2. Ray C. Colton, *The Civil War in the Western Territories: Arizona, Colorado, New Mexico and Utah* (Norman: University of Oklahoma Press, 1959), pp. 171–206.

3. Lowe, *Five Years a Dragoon*, pp. 360–361.

4. R. M. Rolfe, "The Overland Freighting Business in the Early Sixties," undated article in clipping scrapbook on wagon freighting, pp. 392–394, Kansas State Historical Society Library, Topeka.

5. *Ibid.*

6. Daniel Geary, "War Incidents at Kansas City," *Kansas State Historical Society Collections*, Vol. XI (Topeka: State Printing Office, 1910), pp. 282–291. Geary was born in Geneva, New York, in 1835. At the age of twenty-one he moved to Kansas City, Missouri, where he witnessed the border troubles and the Civil War firsthand. He supported the Union and served as a captain and adjutant in the Missouri militia. He also served as provost marshal of Kansas City, Missouri, during the war.

7. Hiram Martin Chittenden, *History of Early Steamboat Navigation on the Missouri River: Life and Adventures of Joseph La Barge, Pioneer Navigator and Indian Trader for Fifty Years Identified with the Commerce of the Missouri Valley* (New York: Francis P. Harper, 1903), Vol. II, pp. 249–250.

8. George F. Ruxton, *Adventures in Mexico and the Rocky Mountains* (New York: Harper & Brothers, 1848), p. 292.

9. William F. Shamleffer, "Merchandising Sixty Years Ago," *Kansas State Historical Society Collections*, Vol. XVI (Topeka: Kansas State Printing Plant, 1925), pp. 567–569.

10. Floyd S. Fierman, *Merchant-Bankers of Early Santa Fe, 1844–1893* (El Paso:

Texas Western College Press, 1964), pp. 4–7. This work is monograph No. 4 in the publisher's "Southwestern Studies" series.

11. Mattes, *The Great Platte River Road*, p. 23.

12. James W. Hulse, *The Nevada Adventure: A History* (Reno: University of Nevada Press, 1981), pp. 78–82. Hulse describes Henry Comstock as "a lazy, loud-mouthed wanderer."

13. James E. Camp and X. J. Kennedy, *Mark Twain's Frontier* (New York: Holt, Rinehart and Winston, 1963),pp. 44–46, quoting from "Virginia City and the *Enterprise*" in Mark Twain's *Roughing It*.

14. Nevada's first governor was H. G. Blasdel. H. G. Worthington was elected the first representative to Congress, and the Nevada legislature elected James Nye and William Stewart as the first U.S. senators. Worthington, Nye, and Stewart cast the deciding votes for the Thirteenth Amendment abolishing slavery in the United States. See also Hulse, *The Nevada Adventure*, and Robert Laxalt, *Nevada: A Bicentennial History* (New York: W. W. Norton & Co., 1977).

15. Granville Stuart, *Forty Years on the Frontier* (Cleveland: Arthur H. Clark Co., 1925), Vol. I, pp. 209–216.

16. Letter from Joel F. Overholser, Fort Benton, Mont., to Montana State Historical Society, Helena, Aug. 5, 1979.

17. *Missoulian* (Missoula, Mont.), Oct. 8, 1922. Article titled "Fort Benton Great 'Port.' "

18. Letter from Overholser to Montana State Historical Society, Aug. 5, 1979.

Chapter X: The Iron Horse Arrives

1. Webb, *The Great Plains*, p. 274.

2. An excellent work containing the financial and economic history of the railroad is Robert W. Fogel's *The Union Pacific Railroad: A Case in Premature Enterprise* (Baltimore: Johns Hopkins University Press, 1960).

3. Oscar Lewis, *The Big Four: The Story of Huntington, Stanford, Hopkins, and Crocker, and of the Building of the Central Pacific* (New York and London: Alfred A. Knopf, 1938), pp. 20–27, 32–47.

4. Norman E. Tutorow, *Leland Stanford: Man of Many Careers* (Menlo Park, Calif.: Pacific Coast Publishers, 1971), pp. 3–41, 66–144, 244–295.

5. Lewis, *The Big Four*, pp. 49–94.

6. *Ibid.*, pp. 124–129, 139–140.

7. *Ibid.*, pp. 86–87, 211–212, 221–223. See also David Lavender, *The Great Persuader* (Garden City, N.Y.: Doubleday & Co., 1970), a fine biography of Huntington.

8. Arthur M. Johnson and Barry E. Supple, *Boston Capitalists and Western Railroads: A Study in the Nineteenth-Century Railroad Investment Process* (Cambridge: Harvard University Press, 1967), pp. 198–204, 207–211, 220, 263.

9. *Ibid.*, pp. 201–203, 213–215, 241–243, 246–266. See also Charles E. Ames, *Pioneering the Union Pacific* (New York: Appleton-Century-Crofts, 1969).

10. Duncan Aikman, ed., *The Taming of the Frontier* (New York: Minton, Balch & Co., 1925), pp. 42–43. A collection of essays by different writers on western cities. De Voto's essay is titled "The Underwriters of Salvation."

11. Hulse, *The Nevada Adventure*, pp. 122–126.

12. Joseph W. Snell and Robert W. Richmond, "When the Union and Kansas Pacific Built Through Kansas," *Kansas Historical Quarterly*, Vol. XXXII (Summer 1966), pp. 161–186, 334–352.

13. Joseph McCoy, *Historic Sketches of the Cattle Trade of the West and Southwest* (Kansas City, Mo.: Ramsey, Millett & Hudson, 1874), p. 52. See also Dary, *Cowboy Culture.*

14. McCoy, *Historic Sketches*, p. 54.

15. Dary, *Cowboy Culture*, p. 190.

16. *Ibid.*, pp. 190–193.

17. Robert R. Dykstra, *The Cattle Towns: A Social History of the Kansas Cattle Trading Centers* (New York: Alfred A. Knopf, 1968), pp. 89–90, 93.

18. *Forest and Stream*, February 1873.

19. Frank H. Mayer and Charles B. Roth, *The Buffalo Harvest* (Denver: Sage Books, 1958), pp. 49–62.

20. *Ibid.*, pp. 48, 63–64.

21. Ida Ellen Rath, *The Rath Trail* (Wichita: McCormick-Armstrong Co., 1961), pp. 101–117. See also Robert M. Wright, *Dodge City, The Cowboy Capital and The Great Southwest* (Wichita: published by the author, 1913), pp. 186–205.

22. Kansas City *Times*, undated newspaper clipping cited by Wright, *Dodge City*, pp. 258–260.

23. Dodge City (Kan.) *Globe*, Aug. 18, 1885.

24. Gene M. Gressley, *Bankers and Cattlemen* (New York: Alfred A. Knopf, 1966), p. 295.

Chapter XI: The Selling of the Great American Desert

1. Quote cited by Vernon Carstensen in *The Public Lands: Studies in the History of the Public Domain* (Madison: University of Wisconsin Press, 1963), p. xiii.

2. General John Pope, "Report on the Department of the Missouri, February 25, 1866." 39th Cong., 1st Sess., House Ex. Doc. No. 76 (Serial No. 1263), 1866, p. 2.

3. General William T. Sherman to General J. A. Rawlins, Aug. 24 and 31, 1866. 39th Cong., 2d Sess., House Ex. Doc. No. 23 (Serial No. 1288), 1866–1867, pp. 7, 9.

4. General William B. Hazen to Major H. G. Litchfield, Oct. 16, 1866. 40th Cong., 2d Sess., House Ex. Document No. 45 (Serial No. 1289), 1867, p. 2.

5. Frémont, *The Exploring Expedition to the Rocky Mountains, Oregon and California*, pp. 34–72.

6. "Report of Brevet Colonel W. F. Raynolds, . . . On the Exploration of the Yellowstone and Missouri Rivers, in 1859–'60." 40th Cong., 2d Sess., Sen. Ex. Doc. No. 77, pp. 15, 16, 115, 153.

7. Max Greene, *The Kanzas Region: Forest, Prairie, Desert, Mountain, Vale, and River* (New York: Fowler and Wells, 1856), p. 47.

8. *Report of the Commissioner of Patents, 1856, Agriculture* (Washington, D.C.: Cornelius Wendell, Printer, 1857).

9. Bowles, *Across the Continent*, pp. 18–19.

10. Gates, *Agriculture and the Civil War*, pp. 254–255.

11. Clinton C. Hutchinson, *Resources of Kansas: Fifteen Years Experience* (Topeka: published by the author, 1871), pp. 97–98.

12. Atchison, Topeka and Santa Fe Railroad Company, *How and Where to Get a Living: A Sketch of "The Garden of the West." Presenting Facts Worth Knowing Concerning the Lands of the Atchison, Topeka & Santa Fe Railroad Co., in Southwestern Kansas* (Boston: published by the Company, 1876), pp. 45–46.

13. Atchison, Topeka and Santa Fe Railroad Company, *Kansas in 1875. Strong and Impartial Testimony to the Wonderful Productiveness of the Cottonwood and Arkansas Valleys . . .* (Topeka: published by the Company, 1875), pp. 2–23.

14. Hutchinson, *Resources of Kansas*, pp. 38–39.

15. E. D. Haney, "Experience of a Homesteader in Kansas," *Kansas State Historical Society Collections*, Vol. XVII (Topeka: State Printer, 1928), pp. 316–318.

16. David Dary, *True Tales of Old-Time Kansas* (Lawrence: University Press of Kansas, 1984), pp. 292–296.

17. Darius N. Bowers, *Seventy Years in Norton County, Kansas, 1872–1942* (Norton, Kan.: Norton County Champion, 1942), pp. 138–143.

18. Jeff Jenkins, *The Northern Tier: Or, Life Among the Homestead Settlers* (Topeka: Geo. W. Martin, Kansas Publishing House, 1880), pp. 143–145.

19. *Ibid.*, p. 142.

20. John W. Scott, "The Pioneer Farmer," *Quarterly Journal*, University of North Dakota, Vol. XIII, p. 292, as cited by Everett Dick, *Sod-House Frontier* (New York: D. Appleton Century Co., 1937), p. 96.

21. John T. Schlebecker, *Whereby We Thrive: A History of American Farming, 1607–1972* (Ames: Iowa State University Press, 1975), pp. 174–180, 264–266.

22. T. Lindsay Baker, *A Field Guide to American Windmills* (Norman: University of Oklahoma Press, 1985), p. 90.

23. *Ibid.*, p. 91. See also J. Evetts Haley, *The XIT Ranch of Texas* (Chicago: Lakeside Press, 1929), p. 97.

24. For a comprehensive history of windmills in the United States, see Baker's *A Field Guide to American Windmills*. Additional information may be found in Webb's *The Great Plains*, pp. 333–348.

25. Dary, *Cowboy Culture*, pp. 311–314.

26. For detailed information relating to the early history of banking in the United States, see William M. Gouge, *A Short History of Paper Money and Banking in the United States* (New York: Augustus M. Kelley, Publishers, 1968), a reprint of the 1833 first edition, and Hammond, *Banks and Politics in America from the Revolution to the Civil War*.

Chapter XII: The Business of Towns

1. Greeley, *An Overland Journey*, pp. 36, 39.

2. George W. Martin, "Some of the Lost Towns of Kansas," *Kansas State Historical Society Collections*, Vol. XII (Topeka: State Printing Office, 1912), pp. 432–433, reprinting the letters of James G. Sands and Orson Kent regarding the history of Oread.

3. United States Public Statutes at Large, 28th Cong., 1st Sess., Vol. V, p. 657.

4. William Huse, *History of Dixon County* [Nebraska], pp. 26–27, as cited by Dick, *Sod-House Frontier*, pp. 48–49.

5. A. L. Child, *Centennial History of Plattsmouth and Cass County, Nebraska*, p. 78, as cited by Dick, *Sod-House Frontier*, p. 50.

6. James C. Olson, *J. Sterling Morton* (Lincoln: University of Nebraska Press, 1942), pp. 52–53.

7. David Dary, *Lawrence Douglas County*

Kansas: An Informal History (Lawrence: Allen Books, 1982), pp. 127–128.

8. Martin, "Some of the Lost Towns of Kansas," pp. 427–428.

9. Dick, *Sod-House Frontier*, p. 387.

10. *Ibid.*, pp. 388–389. See also Elton A. Perkey, *Perkey's Nebraska Place Names* (Lincoln: Nebraska State Historical Society, 1982), p. 97.

11. David Dary, "Editors Carried Guns, Tossed Pointed Words," Topeka *Capital-Journal*, March 14, 1971.

12. *Nebraska Advertiser*, Sept. 3, 1857, as cited by Dick, *Sod-House Frontier*, p. 44.

13. Family records, including the papers of Carl Engel in the possession of the author.

14. *Ibid.* plus *Log Cabin Days* (Manhattan, Kan.: Riley County Historical Society, 1929), pp. 70–71.

15. Leola H. Blanchard, *Conquest of Southwest Kansas* (Wichita: published by the author, 1931), pp. 215–220.

16. *Ibid.*, pp. 66–68.

17. T. A. McNeal, *When Kansas Was Young* (New York: Macmillan Co., 1922), pp. 57–61. See also Nyle H. Miller, "An English Runnymede in Kansas," *Kansas Historical Quarterly* (Topeka: Kansas State Historical Society, 1975), Vol. XLI, pp. 22–62, 183–224.

18. Charles Seton, "Reminiscences of Runnymede," *Kansas State Historical Society Collections*, Vol. XII (Topeka: State Printing Office, 1912), pp. 467–469.

19. *Ibid.*, p. 468.

20. Miller, "An English Runnymede in Kansas," p. 222.

Chapter XIII: Into the Southwest

1. Carl Coke Rister, *The Southwestern Frontier—1865–1881* (Cleveland: Arthur H. Clark Co., 1928), p. 19.

2. V. V. Masterson, *The Katy Railroad and the Last Frontier* (Norman: University of Oklahoma Press, 1952), pp. 46–47. See also Donald V. Fraser, *"Katy" Pioneer Railroad of the Southwest! 1865* (New York: Newco-

men Society in North America, 1953), pp. 9–12.

3. Masterson, *The Katy Railroad and the Last Frontier*, pp. 126–130, citing the railroad's Letter Book No. 6 and the General Manager's Reports as principal sources.

4. W. S. Adair, "Denison, Texas, 1872," *Frontier Times*, Vol. VII, No. 5 (February 1930).

5. J. Evetts Haley, *Fort Concho and the Texas Frontier* (San Angelo, Texas: San Angelo Standard Times, 1952), pp. 301–303. See also Carl Coke Rister, *Fort Griffin on the Texas Frontier* (Norman: University of Oklahoma Press, 1956), pp. 67–73.

6. Howard W. Peak, *A Ranger of Commerce* (San Antonio: Naylor Printing Co., 1929), pp. 14–15.

7. *Ibid.*, pp. 31–37.

8. Leon Joseph Rosenberg, *Sangers' Pioneer Texas Merchants* (Austin: Texas State Historical Association, 1978), pp. 21–22.

9. *Ibid.*, p. 19.

10. *Ibid.*, pp. 100–115.

11. J. Evetts Haley, *Charles Schreiner General Merchandise: The Story of a Country Store* (Austin: Texas State Historical Association, 1944), p. 22–23.

12. The best sources for material on Charles Schreiner are Haley's *Charles Schreiner General Merchandise* and Neal Barrett's *Long Days and Short Nights: A Century of Texas Ranching on the YO 1880–1980* (Mountain Home, Texas: Y-O Press, 1980).

13. C. F. Doan, "Reminiscences of the Old Trails," in J. Marvin Hunter, ed., *The Trail Drivers of Texas* (Nashville: Cokesbury Press, 1925), pp. 778–779.

14. C. F. Doan file in possession of Robert R. Wheatley, Albuquerque, N.M., a descendant. See also J. E. Collins, "Doan Family Among County's Earliest Pioneers," in *Early-Day History of Wilbarger County* (Vernon, Texas: Vernon Times, 1933), pp. 16–20. The clipping file on the Doan family in the library, University of Texas, Austin, was also consulted.

15. Charles D. Eaves and C. A. Hutchinson, *Post City, Texas* (Austin: Texas State Historical Association, 1952), pp. 3–162.

16. Although the Kansas City (Mo.) *Times* was the most active of the western newspapers to back the opening of Oklahoma to settlement, the Wichita *Beacon* also championed the cause. Issues of these newspapers published between the spring of 1879 and late 1884 contain a vast amount of information relating to the boomers, as does the migratory *Oklahoma War Chief*, the official newspaper of the boomers, published at various points along the southern border of Kansas between early 1883 and late 1884. Newspapers opposing the opening of Oklahoma to settlement include the Caldwell (Kan.) *Commercial* and *Sumner County Press*, also published in Caldwell, and Indian Territory newspapers including the *Cherokee Advocate*, *Indian Champion*, and *Cheyenne Transporter*.

17. The best and most complete account of David L. Payne's efforts to open Oklahoma is Carl Coke Rister's *Land Hunger: David L. Payne and the Oklahoma Boomers* (Norman: University of Oklahoma Press, 1942).

18. See Arrell Morgan Gibson, *Oklahoma: A History of Five Centuries* (2d ed.; Norman: University of Oklahoma Press, 1981), for a careful examination of the state's early history.

Chapter XIV: The Desert Southwest

1. William Hazlitt, "On the Ignorance of the Learned" (1821), as cited by Leonard and Thelma Spinrad, *Speaker's Lifetime Library* (West Nyack, N.Y.: Parker Publishing Co., 1979), pp. 43–44.

2. William J. Parish, *The Charles Ilfeld Company: A Study of the Rise and Decline of Mercantile Capitalism in New Mexico* (Cambridge: Harvard University Press, 1961), pp. 6–7.

3. Floyd S. Fierman, *The Spiegelbergs of New Mexico: Merchants and Bankers, 1844–*

1893 (El Paso: Texas Western College Press, 1964), pp. 3–48.

4. Parish, *The Charles Ilfeld Company*, pp. 20–32.

5. *Ibid.*, p. 27.

6. *Ibid.*, pp. 35 ff. This work is perhaps the most comprehensive examination of any early New Mexico merchant yet produced. It recounts Ilfeld's business dealings and how he prospered as a general merchant and dominated the smaller businessmen of the area through his drive for monetary exchange and the gathering of merchant credit. Parish made use of Ilfeld's business records. The material on Ilfeld included in this chapter is intended as only a sketch of his business career in New Mexico. The serious reader should consult Parish's work.

7. Harriet Rochlin and Fred Rochlin, *Pioneer Jews: A New Life in the Far West* (Boston: Houghton Mifflin Company, 1984), pp. 57–58. An exceedingly interesting work.

8. Elizabeth Albrecht, "Esteban Ochoa: Mexican-American Businessman," *Arizoniana* (Summer 1963), pp. 34–40.

9. Frank C. Lockwood, *Pioneer Days in Arizona* (New York: Macmillan Co., 1932), p. 143.

10. Rochlin and Rochlin, *Pioneer Jews*, pp. 127, 129, 138–139, 153, 157, 224. See also Raymond Carlson, "Goldwaters: Merchants Since 1862," *Arizona Highways*, May 1939, pp. 6–7, 26–27.

11. Frank McNitt, *The Indian Traders* (Norman: University of Oklahoma Press, 1962), pp. 263–273.

12. National Park Service, *Hubbell Trading Post National Historic Site* (Washington, D.C.: Department of the Interior, n.d.). Brochure.

13. *Ibid.* See also McNitt, *The Indian Traders*, pp. 72–85, 200–211, 282–284.

14. Lawrence R. Murphy, *Lucien Bonaparte Maxwell: Napoleon of the Southwest* (Norman: University of Oklahoma Press, 1983). The first biography of Maxwell. See also Jim Berry Pearson's *The Maxwell Land Grant* (Norman: University of Oklahoma Press, 1961) and William A. Keleher's *Maxwell Land Grant: A New Mexico Item* (Santa Fe: Rydal Press, 1942).

15. Las Vegas (N.M.T.) *Gazette*, Nov. 25, 1875.

16. James Cox, *Historical and Biographical Record of the Cattle Industry and the Cattlemen of Texas and Adjacent Territory* (St. Louis: Woodward & Tiernan Printing Co., 1895), pp. 299–301. See also John A. Lomax, *Cow Camps & Cattle Herds* (Austin: Encino Press, 1967), p. 48; Work Projects Administration, *New Mexico: A Guide to the Colorful State* (New York: Hastings House, 1940), p. 348; and Minnie Timms Harper and George Dewey Harper, *Old Ranches* (Dallas: Dealey and Lowe, 1936), pp. 61–65.

Afterword

1. Michael Chevalier, "The Western Steamboats," *Western Monthly Magazine*, Dec. 1835, p. 414.

2. John L. McConnel, *Western Characters or Types of Border Life in the Western States* (New York: Redfield, 1853), p. 288.

3. See Ray Allen Billington, *America's Frontier Heritage* (New York: Holt, Rinehart and Winston, 1966), pp. 163–166, for a comprehensive examination of our frontier heritage.

BIBLIOGRAPHY

Unpublished Materials

Doan, C. F. Family records and documents in the possession of Robert R. Wheatley, Albuquerque, N.M., a descendant, plus related material in the Doan family file, Library, University of Texas, Austin.

Engel, Carl F. Family records and documents in the possession of the author, a great-grandson.

Gerry, Elbridge. Account Book 4, Library, State Historical Society of Colorado, Denver.

Marshall, Audrey. Manuscript material titled "Southwest Jewish Traders," Special Collections, University of Arizona Library, Tucson.

Overholser, Joel F., Fort Benton, Mont. Letter to Montana State Historical Society, Helena, Aug. 5, 1979, in Society files.

Pratte, Chouteau and Company, St. Louis. Letter to Ramsey Crooks, March 28, 1835, in the letterbooks, American Fur Company, New-York Historical Society, New York City.

Wyman, Walker D. "The Missouri River Towns in the Westward Movement." Thesis, Department of History, Iowa State University, June 1935.

Government Documents

Report of the Commissioner of Patents, 1856, Agriculture. Washington, D.C.: Cornelius Wendell, Printer, 1857.

United States Public Statutes at Large:
28th Cong., 1st Sess., Vol. V.
31st Cong., 1st Sess., Sen. Ex. Doc. No. 26.
31st Cong., 2d Sess., House Ex. Doc. No. 23.
32d Cong., 1st Sess., Sen. Ex. Doc. No. 1.
32d Cong., 1st Sess., Sen. Ex. Doc. No. 12.
32d Cong., 2d Sess., Sen. Ex. Doc. No. 18.
39th Cong., 2d Sess., House Ex. Doc. No. 23.
39th Cong., 1st Sess., House Ex. Doc. No. 76.
40th Cong., 2d Sess., Sen. Ex. Doc. No. 77.
40th Cong., 2d Sess., House Ex. Doc. No. 45.

Newspapers

Caldwell (Kan.) *Commercial*, 1880–1883.
The Christian Advocate and Journal (New York), 1833.
Dodge City (Kan.) *Globe*, 1885.
Freedom's Champion (Atchison, K.T.), 1859.
Frontier Guardian (Kanesville, Iowa), 1859.
Gazette (St. Joseph, Mo.), 1846–1847, 1853.
Herald of Freedom (Lawrence, K.T.), 1855–1859.
Journal of Commerce (Kansas City, Mo.), 1858–1861.
Kansas City *Times*, 1879–1884.

Las Vegas (N.M.T.) *Gazette*, 1875.

Leavenworth (K.T.) *Times*, 1856–1860.

Leavenworth (K.T.) *Weekly Journal*, 1858.

Missouri Gazette and Public Advertiser (St. Louis), 1822.

Missouri Herald and St. Louis Advertiser (St. Louis), 1826.

Missouri Intelligencer (St. Louis), 1821, 1823.

Missouri Republican (St. Louis), 1840, 1858.

Nebraska Advertiser (Brownville, N.T.), 1857, 1859.

Nebraska News (Nebraska City, N.T.), 1858.

New York *Tribune*, 1847.

New York *Weekly Tribune*, 1849.

Oklahoma War Chief (published at various points in southern Kansas), 1883–1884.

Reveille (St. Louis), 1850.

St. Louis *Beacon*, 1829.

Sumner County Press (Wellington, Kan.), 1879–1884.

Telescope (Wyoming, K.T.), 1859.

Weekly Tribune (Liberty, Mo.), 1849.

Wichita (Kan.) *Beacon*, 1879–1844.

Books

Aikman, Duncan, ed. *The Taming of the Frontier*. New York: Minton, Balch & Co., 1925. Stories of western towns by well-known authors.

Alter, J. Cecil. *James Bridger: Trapper, Frontiersman, Scout and Guide*. Salt Lake City, 1925.

Ames, Charles E. *Pioneering the Union Pacific*. New York: Appleton-Century-Crofts, 1969.

Andreas, A. T. *History of the State of Nebraska*. Chicago: Western Historical Co., 1882.

Atherton, Lewis E. *The Frontier Merchant in Mid-America*. Columbia: University of Missouri Press, 1971. An examination of frontier merchants, especially in Missouri, during the early nineteenth century.

Bakeless, John E. *Daniel Boone: Master of the Wilderness*. New York: W. Morrow & Co., 1939.

Baker, T. Lindsay. *A Field Guide to American Windmills*. Norman: University of Oklahoma Press, 1985. A valuable reference work.

Barney, Libeus. *Letters of the Pike's Peak Gold Rush . . . Early-Day Letters by Libeus Barney, Reprinted from the Bennington Banner, Vermont, 1859–1860*. San Jose, Calif.: Talisman Press, 1959.

Barrett, Neal. *Long Days and Short Nights: A Century of Texas Ranching on the YO 1880–1980*. Mountain Home, Texas: Y-O Press, 1980.

Barry, Louise, compiler. *The Beginning of the West: Annals of the Kansas Gateway to the American West, 1540–1854*. Topeka: Kansas State Historical Society, 1972. An extremely valuable reference not limited to Kansas.

Beachum, Larry M. *William Becknell: Father of the Santa Fe Trade*. El Paso: Texas Western Press, 1982. A fine contribution toward a biography.

Belden, Josiah. *Josiah Belden, 1841 California Overland Pioneer: His Memoir and Early Letters*. Georgetown, Calif.: Talisman Press, 1962. Edited by Doyce B. Nunis, Jr.

Billington, Ray Allen. *America's Frontier Heritage*. New York: Holt, Rinehart and Winston, 1966. A scholarly review of what our frontier heritage means.

———. *Westward Expansion: A History of the American Frontier*. New York: Macmillan Co., 1967. Perhaps the most comprehensive history to date.

Blanchard, Leola H. *Conquest of Southwest Kansas*. Wichita: published by the author, 1931. An interesting narrative.

Bolton, Herbert Eugene. *Texas in the Middle Eighteenth Century*. Berkeley: University of California Press, 1915. Vol. III in the university's "Publications in History" series.

Bowers, Darius N. *Seventy Years in North County, Kansas, 1872–1942*. Norton, Kan.: Norton County Champion, 1942. A better-than-average county history.

Bowles, Samuel. *Across the Continent: A Summer's Journey to the Rocky Moun-*

tains, the Mormons, and the Pacific States. Springfield, Mass.: Samuel Bowles & Co., 1865. Interesting observations by an eastern newspaper editor.

Bratt, John. *Trails of Yesterday.* Lincoln: University Publications Co., 1921. Well-written recollections.

Camp, James E., and X. J. Kennedy. *Mark Twain's Frontier.* New York: Holt, Rinehart and Winston, 1963.

Carroll, John Alexander, ed. *Reflections of Western Historians.* Tucson: University of Arizona Press, 1969.

Carstensen, Vernon. *The Public Lands: Studies in the History of the Public Domain.* Madison: University of Wisconsin Press, 1963.

Catlin, George. *Letters and Notes on the Manners, Customs, and Condition of the North American Indians.* London, 1842. Two volumes.

Chittenden, Hiram Martin. *The American Fur Trade of the Far West.* New York: Barnes & Noble, 1935. Two volumes. This work was first published in 1902 and is a standard reference on the fur trade.

———. *History of Early Steamboat Navigation on the Missouri River: Life and Adventures of Joseph La Barge, Pioneer Navigator and Indian Trader for Fifty Years Identified with the Commerce of the Missouri Valley.* New York: Francis P. Harper, 1903. Two volumes.

Clokey, Richard M. *William H. Ashley: Enterprise and Politics in the Trans-Mississippi West.* Norman: University of Oklahoma Press, 1980.

Colton, Ray C. *The Civil War in the Western Territories: Arizona, Colorado, New Mexico and Utah.* Norman: University of Oklahoma Press, 1959.

Comeaux, Malcolm L. *Arizona: A Geography.* Boulder: Westview Press, 1981.

Cox, James. *Historical and Biographical Record of the Cattle Industry and the Cattlemen of Texas and Adjacent Territory.* St. Louis: Woodward & Tiernan Printing Co., 1895. A classic.

Dana, Richard H. *Two Years Before the Mast.*

New York: P. F. Collier & Son, 1909. This work was first published in 1840.

Dary, David A. *Cowboy Culture.* New York: Alfred A. Knopf, 1981.

———. *Lawrence Douglas County Kansas: An Informal History.* Lawrence: Allen Books, 1982.

———. *True Tales of Old-Time Kansas.* Lawrence: University Press of Kansas, 1984.

Davis, Stephen C. *California Gold Rush Merchant: The Journal of Stephen Chapin Davis.* San Marino: The Huntington Library, 1956.

Davis, William Heath. *Seventy-five Years in California.* San Francisco: John Howell Books, 1967. A reprint of the 1889 first edition.

Debo, Angie. *Prairie City: The Story of an American Community.* New York: Alfred A. Knopf, 1940.

De Voto, Bernard. *Across the Wide Missouri.* Boston: Houghton Mifflin Company, 1947.

Dick, Everett. *Sod-House Frontier, 1854–1890.* New York: D. Appleton Century Co., 1937.

Dunbar, Seymour. *A History of Travel in America.* Indianapolis: Bobbs-Merrill, 1915. Four volumes.

Dunlop, Richard. *Wheels West, 1590–1900.* Chicago: Rand McNally, 1977.

Dykstra, Robert R. *The Cattle Towns: A Social History of the Kansas Cattle Trading Centers.* New York: Alfred A. Knopf, 1968.

Emerson, Ralph Waldo. *Nature: Addresses and Lectures.* Boston and New York: Houghton Mifflin Company, 1903.

Emmons, David M. *Garden in the Grasslands: Boomer Literature of the Central Great Plains.* Lincoln: University of Nebraska Press, 1971.

Fite, Gilbert C. *The Farmers' Frontier, 1865–1900.* New York: Holt, Rinehart and Winston, 1966.

———, and Jim E. Reese. *An Economic History of the United States.* Boston: Houghton Mifflin Company, 1959.

Fogel, Robert W. *The Union Pacific Railroad: A Case in Premature Enterprise.* Baltimore: Johns Hopkins University Press, 1960.

Franzwa, Gregory M. *Maps of the Oregon Trail*. Gerald, Mo: Patrice Press, 1982. A valuable reference work on the Oregon Trail.

Frémont, John C. *The Exploring Expedition to the Rocky Mountains, Oregon and California*. Buffalo: Geo. H. Derby and Co., 1850.

Furniss, Norman F. *The Mormon Conflict, 1850–1859*. New Haven: Yale University Press, 1960.

Gates, Paul W. *Agriculture and the Civil War*. New York: Alfred A. Knopf, 1965.

Gibson, Arrell Morgan. *Oklahoma: A History of Five Centuries*. 2d ed.; Norman: University of Oklahoma Press, 1981.

Gouge, William M. *A Short History of Paper Money and Banking in the United States*. New York: Augustus M. Kelley, Publishers, 1968. A reprint of the 1833 first edition.

Gowan, Fred R. *Rocky Mountain Rendezvous*. Provo: Brigham Young University Press, 1975.

———, and Eugene E. Campbell. *Fort Bridger: Island in the Wilderness*. Provo: Brigham Young University Press, 1975. The most comprehensive history of Fort Bridger to date.

Graebner, Norman A. *Empire on the Pacific: A Study in American Continental Expansion*. New York: Ronald Press Co., 1955.

———. *Manifest Destiny*. Indianapolis: Bobbs-Merrill, 1968.

Greeley, Horace. *An Overland Journey, From New York to San Francisco, in the Summer of 1859*. New York: C. M. Saxton, Barker & Co., 1860.

Greene, J. Evarts. *The Santa Fe Trade: Its Route and Character*. St. Louis: North Point, 1970. A reprint of Greene's 1893 paper.

Greene, Max. *The Kanzas Region: Forest, Prairie, Desert, Mountain, Vale, and River*. New York: Fowler and Wells, 1856.

Gregg, John J., and Barbara Gregg. *Best*

Loved Poems of the American West. Garden City, N.Y.: Doubleday & Co., 1980.

Gregg, Josiah. *Commerce of the Prairies*. New York: Henry G. Langley, 1844. Two volumes. A classic.

Gressley, Gene M. *Bankers and Cattlemen*. New York: Alfred A. Knopf, 1966. The often ignored side of ranching.

Hafen, LeRoy R. *Colorado Gold Rush: Contemporary Letters and Reports, 1858–1859*. Glendale: Arthur H. Clark Co., 1941.

———, ed. *Pike's Peak Gold Rush Guidebooks of 1859*. Glendale: Arthur H. Clark Co., 1941.

———, ed. *The Mountain Men and the Fur Trade of the Far West*. Glendale: Arthur H. Clark Co., 1965–1972. Ten volumes. Perhaps the most comprehensive work to date on the participants of the fur trade.

Haines, Aubrey L. *Historic Sites Along the Oregon Trail*. Gerald, Mo.: Patrice Press, 1981. A worthwhile reference.

Haley, J. Evetts. *The XIT Ranch of Texas*. Chicago: Lakeside Press, 1929.

———. *Charles Schreiner General Merchandise: The Story of a Country Store*. Austin: Texas State Historical Association, 1944.

———. *Fort Concho and the Texas Frontier*. San Angelo, Texas: San Angelo Standard Times, 1952.

Hallenbeck, Cleve, and Juanita H. Williams. *Legends of the Spanish Southwest*. Glendale: Arthur H. Clark Co., 1938.

Hammond, Bray, *Banks and Politics in America from the Revolution to the Civil War*. Princeton: Princeton University Press, 1957.

Harper, Minnie Timms, and George Dewey Harper. *Old Ranches*. Dallas: Dealey and Lowe, 1936.

Hartley, Cecil B. *The Life of Daniel Boone*. New York and Chicago: A. L. Burt Co., n.d.

Hawes, A. G. *A Historical Sketch and Review of the Business of the City of Leavenworth, Kansas Territory . . .* Leavenworth City: Journal Book and Job Office, 1857.

Hoffman, Wilbur. *Saga of Old Western Travel*

& *Transport*. San Diego: Howell-North Books, 1980.

Hollon, W. Eugene. *The Great American Desert Then and Now*. New York: Oxford University Press, 1966.

Hulbert, Archer Butler. *Waterways of Westward Expansion: The Ohio River and Its Tributaries*. Cleveland: Arthur H. Clark Co., 1903. Vol. IX in the publisher's "Historic Highways of America" series.

Hulse, James W. *The Nevada Adventure: A History*. Reno: University of Nevada Press, 1981.

Hunter, J. Marvin, ed. *The Trail Drivers of Texas*. Nashville: Cokesbury Press, 1925. Recollections of nineteenth-century trail drivers.

Hutchinson, Clinton C. *Resources of Kansas: Fifteen Years Experience*. Topeka: published by the author, 1871.

Jackson, Clarence S. *Picture Maker of the Old West: William Henry Jackson*. New York and London: Charles Scribner's Sons, 1947.

Jackson, Donald, ed. *The Journals of Zebulon Montgomery Pike*. Norman: University of Oklahoma Press, 1966.

Jacobs, Wilbur R., ed. *Letters of Francis Parkman*. Norman: University of Oklahoma Press, 1960.

James, Edwin. *Account of an Expedition from Pittsburgh to the Rocky Mountains . . .* Cleveland: Arthur H. Clark Co., 1905. Vol. XV in the publisher's "Early Western Travels" series, edited by Reuben G. Thwaites; thirty-two volumes.

Jenkins, Jeff. *The Northern Tier: Or, Life Among the Homestead Settlers*. Topeka: Geo. W. Martin, Kansas Publishing House, 1880.

Johnson, Arthur M., and Barry E. Supple. *Boston Capitalists and Western Railroads: A Study in the Nineteenth-Century Railroad Investment Process*. Cambridge: Harvard University Press, 1967.

Johnson, Emory R., et al. *History of Domestic and Foreign Commerce of the United States*. Washington, D.C.: Carnegie Institution, 1915.

Johnston, William G. *Experiences of a Forty-Niner*. New York: Coward-McCann, 1931.

Keleher, William A. *Maxwell Land Grant: A New Mexico Item*. Santa Fe: Rydal Press, 1942.

Lamar, Howard P. *The Reader's Encyclopedia of the American West*. New York: Thomas Y. Crowell Co., 1977. A valuable reference.

Lass, William E. *From the Missouri to the Great Salt Lake*. Lincoln: Nebraska State Historical Society, 1972. Vol. XXVI in the Society's *Publications*.

Lavender, David. *Bent's Fort*. Garden City, N.Y.: Doubleday & Co., 1954.

———. *The Great Persuader*. Garden City, N.Y.: Doubleday & Co., 1970.

Laxalt, Robert. *Nevada: A Bicentennial History*. New York: W. W. Norton & Co., 1977.

Lewis, Oscar. *The Big Four: The Story of Huntington, Stanford, Hopkins, and Crocker, and of the Building of the Central Pacific*. New York and London: Alfred A. Knopf, 1938.

———. *The Autobiography of the West: Personal Narratives of the Discovery and Settlement of the American West*. New York: Henry Holt & Co., 1958.

Lippincott, Isaac. *Economic Development of the United States*. New York and London: D. Appleton and Co., 1927.

Lockwood, Frank C. *Pioneer Days in Arizona*. New York: Macmillan Co., 1932.

Lomax, John A. *Cow Camps & Cattle Herds*. Austin: Encino Press, 1967.

Lowe, Percival G. *Five Years a Dragoon ('49 to '54) and Other Adventures on the Great Plains*. Kansas City, Mo.: Franklin Hudson Publishing Co., 1906.

Majors, Alexander. *Seventy Years on the Frontier*. Columbus, Ohio: Long's College Book Co., 1950. A reprint of the 1893 first edition.

Masterson, V. V. *The Katy Railroad and the*

Last Frontier. Norman: University of Oklahoma Press, 1952.

Mattes, Merrill J. *The Great Platte River Road*. Lincoln: Nebraska State Historical Society, 1969.

Mayer, Frank H., and Charles B. Roth. *The Buffalo Harvest*. Denver: Sage Books, 1958.

McConnel, John L. *Western Characters or Types of Border Life in the Western States*. New York: Redfield, 1853.

McCoy, Joseph. *Historic Sketches of the Cattle Trade of the West and Southwest*. Kansas City, Mo.: Ramsey, Millett & Hudson, 1874. A classic on the early western cattle trade by the man who made Abilene a cattle town.

McGroarty, John S. *California: Its History and Romance*. Los Angeles: Grafton Publishing Co., 1911.

McIlhany, Edward. *Recollections of a Forty-Niner*. Kansas City, Mo.: Hailman Printing Co., 1908. The author traveled overland to California, arriving in the fall of 1849.

McNeal, T. A. *When Kansas Was Young*. New York: Macmillan Co., 1922.

McNitt, Frank. *The Indian Traders*. Norman: University of Oklahoma Press, 1962. A delightful work.

Merk, Frederick. *Manifest Destiny and Mission in American History*. New York: Alfred A. Knopf, 1963.

———. *History of the Westward Movement*. New York: Alfred A. Knopf, 1980.

Meyer, Duane. *The Heritage of Missouri— A History*. St. Louis: State Publishing Co., 1965.

Moorhead, Max L. *New Mexico's Royal Road*. Norman: University of Oklahoma Press, 1958. Informative.

Morgan, Dale L. *The West of William H. Ashley*. Denver: Old West Publishing Co., 1964. Good reading.

Murphy, Lawrence R. *Lucien Bonaparte Maxwell: Napoleon of the Southwest*. Norman: University of Oklahoma Press, 1983. A good biography.

Nash, Roderick. *Wilderness and the Amer-*

ican Mind. New Haven and London: Yale University Press, 1967.

Oglesby, Richard E. *Manuel Lisa and the Opening of the Missouri Fur Trade*. Norman: University of Oklahoma Press, 1963.

Olson, James C. *J. Sterling Morton*. Lincoln: University of Nebraska Press, 1942. An interesting biography.

Palmer, Joel. *Journal of Travels over the Rocky Mountains, to the Mouth of the Columbia River; Made During the Years 1845 and 1846* . . . Cincinnati: J. A. and U. P. James, 1850. A later printing of the 1847 first edition.

Parish, William J. *The Charles Ilfeld Company: A Study of the Rise and Decline of Mercantile Capitalism in New Mexico*. Cambridge: Harvard University Press, 1961.

Peak, Howard W. *A Ranger of Commerce*. San Antonio: Naylor Printing Co., 1929. One of the few recollections of a drummer in print.

Peake, Ora Brooks. *A History of the United States Indian Factory System, 1795–1822*. Denver: Sage Books, 1954.

Pearson, Jim Berry. *The Maxwell Land Grant*. Norman: University of Oklahoma Press, 1961.

Perkey, Elton A. *Perkey's Nebraska Place Names*. Lincoln: Nebraska State Historical Society, 1982.

Phillips, Paul Chrisler. *The Fur Trade*. Norman: University of Oklahoma Press, 1961. Two volumes. Very comprehensive.

Piercy, Frederick H. *Route from Liverpool to Great Salt Lake Valley* . . . Liverpool: published by Franklin D. Richards, 1855.

Pomeroy, Earl S. *The Pacific Slope: A History of California, Oregon, Washington, Idaho, Utah, and Nevada*. New York: Alfred A. Knopf, 1968.

Powell, Lawrence Clark. *Arizona: A Bicentennial History*. New York: W. W. Norton & Co., 1976.

Powell, Lyman P. *Historic Towns of the Western States*. New York and London: G. P. Putnam's Sons, 1901.

Rath, Ida Ellen. *The Rath Trail*. Wichita: McCormick-Armstrong Co., 1961.

Riegel, Robert E. *America Moves West*. New York: Henry Holt and Co., 1947.

Richardson, Albert D. *Beyond the Mississippi: From the Great River to the Great Ocean* . . . Hartford: American Publishing Co., 1867. Observations of an eastern newspaperman.

Richardson, Rupert Norval. *Texas: The Lone Star State*. New York: Prentice-Hall, 1943.

———, and Carl Coke Rister. *The Greater Southwest*. Glendale: Arthur H. Clark Co., 1935.

Rister, Carl Coke. *The Southwestern Frontier—1865–1881*. Cleveland: Arthur H. Clark Co., 1928.

———. *Land Hunger: David L. Payne and the Oklahoma Boomers*. Norman: University of Oklahoma Press, 1942.

———. *Fort Griffin on the Texas Frontier*. Norman: University of Oklahoma Press, 1956.

Rittenhouse, Jack D. *The Santa Fe Trail: A Historical Bibliography*. Albuquerque: University of New Mexico Press, 1971. Excellent.

Rochlin, Harriet, and Fred Rochlin. *Pioneer Jews: A New Life in the Far West*. Boston: Houghton Mifflin Company, 1984.

Root, Frank A., and William E. Connelley. *The Overland Stage to California*. Topeka: published by the authors, 1901.

Rosenberg, Leon Joseph. *Sangers' Pioneer Texas Merchants*. Austin: Texas State Historical Association, 1978.

Russell, C. P. *Firearms, Traps and Tools of the Mountain Men*. New York: Alfred A. Knopf, 1967.

Russell, Osborne. *Journal of a Trapper*. Boise, Idaho: Syms-York Co., 1914.

Ruxton, George F. *Adventures in Mexico and the Rocky Mountains*. New York: Harper & Brothers, 1848.

Salisbury, Albert, and Jane Salisbury. *Here Rolled the Covered Wagons*. Seattle: Superior Publishing Co., 1948.

Santleben, August. *A Texas Pioneer*. New York and Washington: Neale Publishing Co., 1910.

Schlebecker, John T. *Whereby We Thrive: A History of American Farming, 1607–1972*. Ames: Iowa State University Press, 1975.

Schweikart, Larry. *A History of Banking in Arizona*. Tucson: University of Arizona Press, 1982.

Seldes, George, compiler. *The Great Quotations*. New York: Pocket Books, 1967.

Settle, Raymond W., and Mary Lund Settle. *War Drums and Wagon Wheels: The Story of Russell, Majors and Waddell*. Lincoln: University of Nebraska Press, 1966.

Shumway, George, and Howard C. Frey. *Conestoga Wagon 1750–1850*. York, Pa.: George Shumway, Publisher, 1964.

Simmons, Marc. *New Mexico: A Bicentennial History*. New York: W. W. Norton & Co., 1977.

Sonnichsen, C. L. *Tucson: The Life and Times of an American City*. Norman: University of Oklahoma Press, 1982.

Spalding, C. C. *Annals of the City of Kansas: Embracing Full Details of the Trade and Commerce of the Great Western Plains* . . . Kansas City, Mo.: Frank Glenn Publishing Co., 1950. A facsimile reprint of the 1858 first edition.

Spence, Clark C. *Montana: A Bicentennial History*. New York: W. W. Norton & Co., 1978.

———. *The Sinews of American Capitalism*. New York: Hill and Wang, 1964.

Stewart, Edgar I. *Penny-an-Acre Empire in the West*. Norman: University of Oklahoma Press, 1968.

Stuart, Granville. *Forty Years on the Frontier*. Cleveland: Arthur H. Clark Co., 1925. Two volumes.

Sunder, John E. *The Fur Trade on the Upper Missouri, 1840–1865*. Norman: University of Oklahoma Press, 1965.

Tierney, Luke. *History of the Gold Discoveries on the South Platte River* . . . Pacific City, Iowa: Herald Office, 1859.

Trachtenberg, Alan. *The Incorporation of America: Culture & Society in the Gilded Age*. New York: Hill and Wang, 1982.

Turner, Frederick Jackson. *The Frontier in American History*. New York: Henry Holt and Co., 1948.

Tutorow, Norman E. *Leland Stanford: Man of Many Careers*. Menlo Park, Calif.: Pacific Coast Publishers, 1971.

Vernon Times. *Early-Day History of Wilbarger County*. Vernon, Texas: Vernon Times, 1933.

Wade, Mason, ed. *The Journals of Francis Parkman*. New York and London: Harper & Brothers, 1947. Two volumes.

Wagoner, Jay J. *Arizona Territory 1863–1912: A Political History*. Tucson: University of Arizona Press, 1970.

Walker, Henry Pickering. *The Wagonmasters: High Plains Freighting from the Earliest Days of the Santa Fe Trail to 1880*. Norman: University of Oklahoma Press, 1966.

Watkins, Albert, ed. *Publications of the Nebraska State Historical Society*, Vol. XX. Lincoln: Nebraska State Historical Society, 1922. Containing accounts of the adventures of the fur-trade founders of St. Louis on the Great Plains of the Missouri Valley and in the Rocky Mountains.

Webb, Walter Prescott. *The Great Plains*. Boston: Ginn and Co., 1931.

———, ed. *The Handbook of Texas*. Austin: Texas State Historical Association, 1952. Two volumes. A valuable reference work.

Webster, Kimball. *The Gold Seekers of '49: A Personal Narrative of Overland Trail and Adventures in California and Oregon from 1849 to 1854* . . . Manchester, N.H.: Standard Book Co., 1917.

Weinberg, Albert K. *Manifest Destiny: A Study of Nationalist Expansionism in American History*. Chicago: Quadrangle Books, 1963. First published in 1935.

Whitney, Orson F. *History of Utah*. Salt Lake City: George Q. Cannon and Sons, 1892. Four volumes.

Willoughby, David P. *The Empire of Equus: The Horse, Past, Present and Future*. South Brunswick and New York: A. S. Barnes and Co., 1974.

Winther, Oscar Osburn. *Express and Stagecoach Days in California from the Gold Rush to the Civil War*. Stanford: Stanford University Press, 1936.

Wood, Jerome H. *Conestoga Crossroads, Lancaster, Pennsylvania, 1730–1790*. Harrisburg: Pennsylvania Historical and Museum Commission, 1979.

Work Projects Administration. *New Mexico: A Guide to the Colorful State*. New York: Hastings House, 1940.

Wright, Robert M. *Dodge City, The Cowboy Capital and The Great Southwest*. Wichita: published by the author, 1913.

Underhill, Reuben L. *From Cowhides to Golden Fleece*. Stanford: Stanford University Press, 1939.

Unruh, John D., Jr. *The Plains Across: The Overland Emigrants and the Trans-Mississippi West, 1840–60*. Urbana: University of Illinois Press, 1979.

Victor, Frances F., ed. *The River of the West*. Hartford: Bliss and Co., 1870. The story of mountainman Joe Meek.

Monographs and Pamphlets

Atchison, Topeka and Santa Fe Railroad Co. *Kansas in 1875. Strong and Impartial Testimony to the Wonderful Productiveness of the Cottonwood and Arkansas Valleys* . . . Topeka: published by the Company, 1875. Promotional pamphlet.

———. *How and Where to Get a Living: A Sketch of "The Garden of the West." Presenting Facts Worth Knowing Concerning the Lands of the Atchison, Topeka & Santa Fe Railroad Co., in Southwestern Kansas*. Boston: published by the Company, 1876. Promotional pamphlet.

Fierman, Floyd S. *Some Early Jewish Settlers on the Southwestern Frontier*. El Paso: Texas Western College Press, 1960. An informative monograph.

———. *The Spiegelbergs of New Mexico: Merchants and Bankers, 1844–1893*. El Paso: Texas Western College Press, 1964. Vol. I, No. 4, in the publisher's "Southwestern Studies" series.

Fraser, Donald V. *"Katy" Pioneer Railroad*

of the Southwest! 1865. New York: Newcomen Society in North America, 1953.

Freudenthal, Samuel J. *El Paso Merchant and Civic Leader from the 1880's through the Mexican Revolution*. El Paso: Texas Western College Press, 1965. Vol. III, No. 3, in the publisher's "Southwestern Studies" series. Edited by Floyd S. Fierman.

Frost, Donald M. *Notes on General Ashley: The Overland Trail, and South Pass*. Barre, Mass.: Barre Gazette, 1960. Contains the letters of Daniel T. Potts, who was in the Rocky Mountains with Ashley's men from 1822 to 1827.

Hopkins, Ernest J. *Financing the Frontier: A Fifty Year History of the Valley National Bank, 1899–1949*. Phoenix: Arizona Printers, 1950.

Lamar, Howard R. *The Trader on the American Frontier: Myth's Victim*. College Station and London: Texas A. & M. University Press, 1977. An interesting monograph.

Muir, Ross L., and Carl J. White. *Over the Long Term . . . : The Story of J. and W. Seligman and Company*. New York: J. & W. Seligman & Co., 1964.

National Park Service. *Hubbell Trading Post National Historic Site*. Washington, D.C.: Department of the Interior, n.d. Brochure.

Riley County Historical Society. *Log Cabin Days*. Manhattan, Kan.: Riley County Historical Society, 1929.

Articles

Adair, W. S. "Denison, Texas, 1872," *Frontier Times*, February 1930.

Albrecht, Elizabeth. "Esteban Ochoa: Mexican-American Businessman," *Arizoniana*, Summer 1963.

Anderson, Hattie M. "Frontier Economic Problems in Missouri," *Missouri Historical Review*, Vol. XXXIV (1940).

Ashley, William H. "Diary . . . March 25–June 27, 1825," *Missouri Historical Society Bulletin*, Vol. XI (1954–1955).

Ashton, John. "History of Jack Stock and Mules in Missouri," *Monthly Bulletin* (Missouri State Board of Agriculture), Vol. XXII (1940).

Atherton, Lewis E. "James and Robert Aull—a Frontier Missouri Mercantile Firm," *Missouri Historical Review*, Vol. XXX (1935).

———. "Business Techniques in the Santa Fe Trade," *Missouri Historical Review*, Vol. XXXIV (1940).

Bloomer, D.C. "Notes on the History of Pottawatomie County," *Annals of Iowa*, Vol. IX (1871).

Bott, Emily A. O. "Joseph Murphy's Contributions to the Developments of the West," *Missouri Historical Review*, Vol. XLII (1952).

Carlson, Raymond. "Goldwaters: Merchants Since 1862," *Arizona Highways*, May 1939.

Carneal, Thomas W. "Trade in Northwest Missouri, 1843–1873," *The Trail Guide*, March 1972.

Chevalier, Michael. "The Western Steamboats," *Western Monthly Magazine*, Dec. 1835.

Dary, David. "Editors Carried Guns, Tossed Pointed Words," *Topeka Capital-Journal*, March 14, 1971.

Fierman, Floyd S. "The Drachmans of Arizona," *American Jewish Archives*, Nov. 1964.

———. "The Goldwater Brothers: Arizona Pioneers," *American Jewish Archives*, April 1966.

Geary, Daniel. "War Incidents at Kansas City," *Kansas State Historical Society Collections*, Vol. XI (1910).

Goldwater, Barry M. "Three Generations of Pants and Politics in Arizona," *Journal of Arizona History*, Autumn 1972.

Grinnell, George Bird. "Bent's Old Fort and Its Builders," *Kansas State Historical Society Collections*, Vol. XV (1923).

Haney, E. D. "Experiences of a Homesteader in Kansas," *Kansas State Historical Society Collections*, Vol. XVII (1928).

Hanson, C. E., Jr. "Castoreum," *Museum of the Fur Trade Quarterly*. Vol. VIII (1972).

Lamar, Howard R. "Persistent Frontier: The West in the 20th Century," *Western Historical Quarterly*, Jan. 1973.

Lummis, Charles F. "Pioneer Transportation in America," *McClure's Magazine*, Oct. 1905 and Nov. 1905. Two-part series.

Martin, George W. "Some of the Lost Towns of Kansas," *Kansas State Historical Society Collections*, Vol. XII (1912).

Miller, Nyle H. "An English Runnymede in Kansas," *Kansas Historical Quarterly*, Vol. XLI (1975).

Moore, Ely. "The Lecompton Party Which Located Denver," *Transactions of the Kansas State Historical Society*, Vol. VII (1902).

Parish, William J. "The German Jew and the Commercial Revolution in Territorial New Mexico, 1850–1900," *New Mexico Quarterly*, Autumn 1959, Winter 1960, Spring 1960.

Rolfe, R. M. "The Overland Freighting Business in the Early Sixties," undated article in clipping scrapbook on wagon freighting, Kansas State Historical Society Library, Topeka.

Root, George A., and Russell K. Hickman. "Pike's Peak Express Companies," *Kansas Historical Quarterly*, Vol. XIII (1945).

Sampson, F. A., ed. "The Journals of Capt. Thomas [sic] Becknell From Boone's Lick to Santa Fe, and From Santa Cruz to Green River," *Missouri Historical Review*, Vol. IV (1910).

——, ed. "M. M. Marmaduke Journal,"

Missouri Historical Review, Vol. VI (1911).

Schorger, A. W. "A Brief History of the Steel Trap and Its Use in North America," *Transactions of the Wisconsin Academy of Sciences, Arts, and Letters*, Vol. XL (1951).

Seton, Charles. "Reminiscences of Runnymede," *Kansas State Historical Society Collections*, Vol. XII (1912).

Shamleffer, William F. "Merchandising Sixty Years Ago," *Kansas State Historical Society Collections*, Vol. XVI (1925).

Snell, Joseph W., and Robert W. Richmond. "When the Union and Kansas Pacific Built Through Kansas," *Kansas Historical Quarterly*, Vol. XXXII (Summer 1966).

Spencer, Rev. Joab. "The Kaw or Kansas Indians: Their Customs, Manners, and Folk-lore," *Kansas State Historical Society Collections*, Vol. X (1908).

Viles, Jonas. "Old Franklin: A Frontier Town of the Twenties," *Mississippi Valley Historical Review*, Vol. IX (1923).

Walter, Paul A. F. "New Mexico's Pioneer Bank and Bankers," *New Mexico Historical Review*, Vol. XXI (1946).

Whiteley, Philip W. "Trade Beads Among the American Indians," *Original Contributions to Western History, Brand Book VII*. Denver: The Westerners, 1952. Edited by Nolie Mumey.

Wyman, Walker D. "The Military Phase of Santa Fe Freighting, 1846–1865," *Kansas State Historical Quarterly*, Vol. I (1931–1932).

INDEX

Grateful acknowledgment is made to the following for permission to reprint previously published material:

Alfred A. Knopf, Inc.: Excerpt from *Agriculture and the Civil War*, by Paul W. Gates. Copyright © 1965 by Paul W. Gates. Reprinted by permission of Alfred A. Knopf, Inc.

The Arthur H. Clark Company: Excerpt from *Forty Years on the Frontier* by Granville Stuart (1925). Reprinted by permission of The Arthur H. Clark Company.

Curtis Brown, Ltd: Excerpt from *Mark Twain's Frontier*, by James F. Camp and X. J. Kennedy. Copyright © 1963 by James F. Camp and X. J. Kennedy. Reprinted by permission of Curtis Brown, Ltd.

The Talisman Press: Excerpts from *Josiah Belden; 1841 California Overland Pioneer: His Memoir and Early Letters*, by Josiah Belden (1962), edited by Doyce B. Nunis, Jr. Reprinted by permission of The Talisman Press.

Drawings on pages 4, 6, 9, 19, 21, 45, 49, 65, 70, 71, 73, 74, 133, 202, 242, and 301 are by Al Napoletano.

Grateful acknowledgment is made to the following for permission to use illustrations from their collections:

Arizona Historical Society: Illustrations on pages 302, 306, 307, 308, 309, 311. California Historical Society/Ticor Title Insurance (Los Angeles): Illustrations on pages 113, 114, 115, 117, 118.

California State Library: Illustration on page 111.

Colorado Historical Society: Illustration on page 164.
David Dary: Illustrations on pages 37, 260 (above left and below).
The Edison Institute, Henry Ford Museum & Greenfield Village: Illustration on page 122.

Kansas State Historical Society: Illustrations on pages 17, 36, 39 (above), 55, 56, 69, 79, 84, 92, 102, 103, 105, 130, 131, 142, 158, 169, 180, 181, 190, 191, 198, 203 (below), 211, 212, 215, 216, 217, 218, 219, 221 (below), 235, 236, 240, 241, 244, 245, 246, 251, 254, 255, 260 (above right), 269, 271, 284, 291, 292, 293, 295.

Montana Historical Society: Illustration on page 193.
The National Museum of American History, Smithsonian Institution: Illustration on page 39 (below).
Museum of New Mexico: Illustrations on pages 298, 299, 304, 313, 316, 318, 319.

Nebraska State Historical Society: Illustrations on pages 145, 168.

Mr. & Mrs. James Nottage: Illustration on page 166.

Union Pacific Railroad Museum: Illustrations on pages 106, 205.

United States Department of the Interior:
  Geological Survey: Illustrations on pages 206, 207.
  Scotts Bluff National Monument, National Park Service: Illustrations on pages 120, 139, 221 (above).

Robert R. Wheatley: Illustration on page 283.

University of Wyoming, American Heritage Center: Illustrations on pages 184, 192, 199, 203 (above).

A NOTE ABOUT THE AUTHOR

DAVID DARY is a professor at the William Allen White School of Journalism and Mass Communications at the University of Kansas. He is a native of Manhattan, Kansas, where his great-grandfather settled in the 1860s. Before returning to Kansas to teach in 1969, he lived in both Texas and Washington, D.C., where he worked with CBS News and NBC News. He is the author of other books on the West including—*The Buffalo Book* (1974), *True Tales of the Old-Time Plains* (1979), and *Cowboy Culture* (1981)—and is a leading reviewer of books on western subjects.

A NOTE ON THE TYPE

THIS BOOK was set in a digitized version of Bodoni Book, so called after Giambattista Bodoni (1740–1813), son of a printer of Piedmont. After gaining experience and fame as superintendent of the Press of the Propaganda in Rome, Bodoni became in 1766 the head of the ducal printing house at Parma, which he soon made the foremost of its kind in Europe. In type designing he was an innovator, making his new faces rounder, wider, and lighter, with greater openness and delicacy. His types were rather too rigidly perfect in detail, the thick lines contrasting sharply with the thin wiry lines. It was doubtless this feature that caused William Morris to condemn the Bodoni types as "swelteringly hideous." Bodoni Book, as reproduced by the Linotype Company, is a modern version based not upon any one of Bodoni's fonts, but upon a composite conception of the Bodoni manner, designed to avoid the details stigmatized as bad by typographical experts and to secure the pleasing and effective results of which the Bodoni types are capable.

Composed by Maryland Linotype, Inc., Baltimore, Maryland.
Printed and bound by The Murray Printing Company,
Westford, Massachusetts.
Typography and binding design by Virginia Tan.
Endpaper maps by Al M. Napoletano
and David Lindroth.

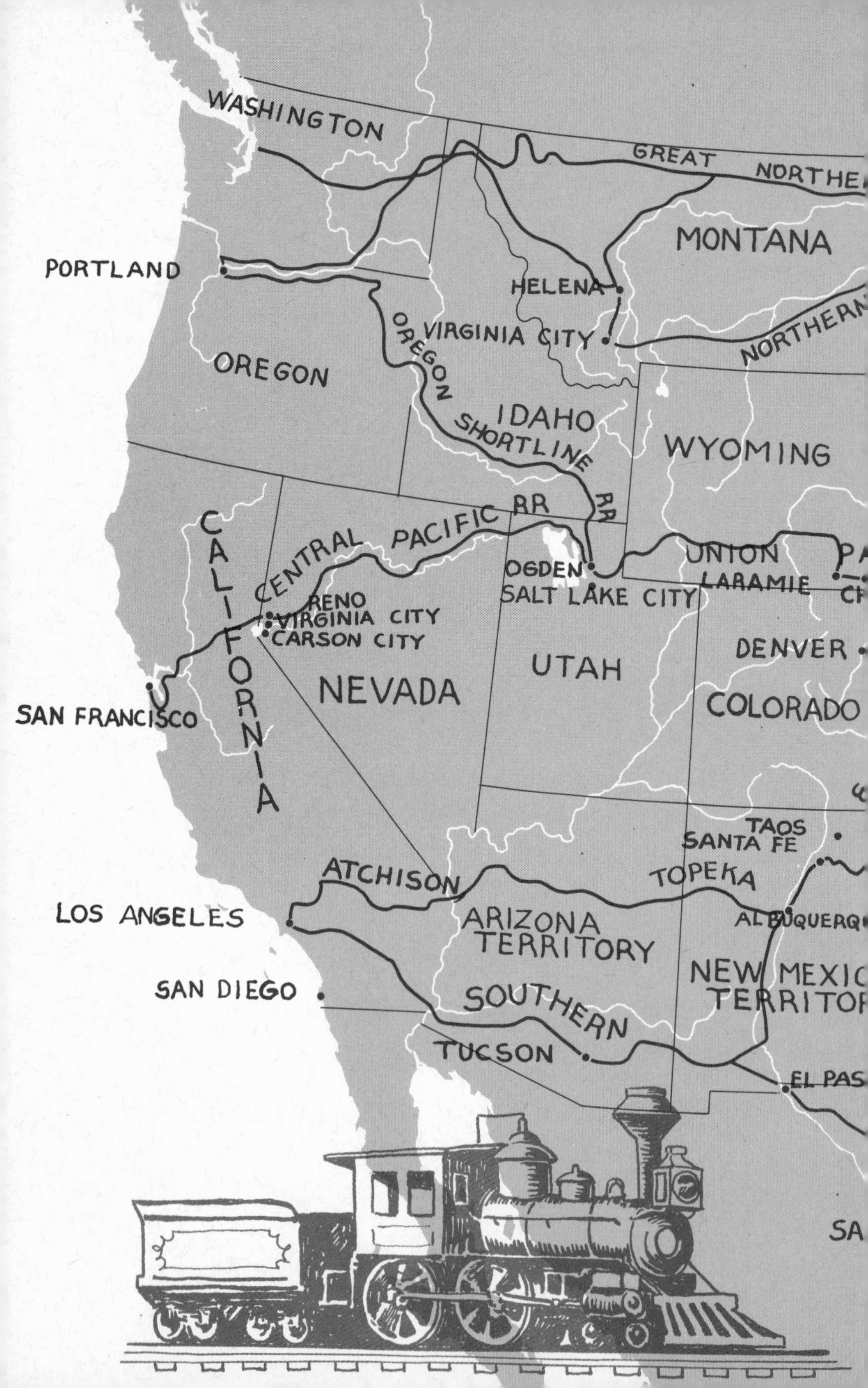

WASHINGTON

GREAT NORTHE

MONTANA

PORTLAND

HELENA

NORTHERN

VIRGINIA CITY

OREGON

IDAHO

WYOMING

OREGON SHORTLINE RR

CALIFORNIA

CENTRAL PACIFIC RR

OGDEN

UNION

PA

RENO

SALT LAKE CITY

LARAMIE

CH

VIRGINIA CITY

CARSON CITY

DENVER

SAN FRANCISCO

NEVADA

UTAH

COLORADO

TAOS

SANTA FE

ATCHISON

TOPEKA

LOS ANGELES

ARIZONA
TERRITORY

ALBUQUERQ

SAN DIEGO

SOUTHERN

NEW MEXIC
TERRITOR

TUCSON

EL PAS

SA